Non-Traditional Security in Asia

The **Institute of Southeast Asian Studies (ISEAS)** was established as an autonomous organization in 1968. It is a regional centre dedicated to the study of socio-political, security and economic trends and developments in Southeast Asia and its wider geostrategic and economic environment. The Institute's research programmes are the Regional Economic Studies (RES, including ASEAN and APEC), Regional Strategic and Political Studies (RSPS), and Regional Social and Cultural Studies (RSCS).

ISEAS Publishing, an established academic press, has issued more than 2,000 books and journals. It is the largest scholarly publisher of research about Southeast Asia from within the region. ISEAS Publishing works with many other academic and trade publishers and distributors to disseminate important research and analyses from and about Southeast Asia to the rest of the world.

CONTENTS

ACKNOWLEDGEMENTS

This book has been a collaborative effort from the very beginning and draws on the research conducted by a dedicated, young and dynamic team. The mission of the Centre for Non-Traditional Security (NTS) Studies in the S. Rajaratnam School of International Studies (RSIS) is to conduct research and produce policy-relevant analyses aimed at furthering awareness and building capacity to address NTS issues and challenges in the Asia-Pacific region and beyond. Indeed to fulfil its mission, this collection is an important contribution to the dissemination of knowledge and understanding of the salient policy challenges Asia faces today. Through this book, we aim to inform scholars, students and policy-makers about the range of prevalent NTS issues and how to approach them in a systematic and informed fashion. We recognize that the policy areas covered are not an exhaustive list of NTS challenges. Rather, we see this book as the starting point of a much larger conversation about Asian human security and the multiple policy dilemmas faced across this region. It is through this contribution that we and the contributors hope to advance the understanding of NTS issues and challenges in Asia by highlighting gaps in knowledge and policy, and identifying best practices among state and non-state actors in responding to these challenges. We also hope to contribute to building the institutional capacity of governments, and regional and international organizations to respond to NTS challenges through this conversation.

We are grateful to the Ford Foundation for providing the funding to establish a regional network of scholars and institutions from which this collection has benefited greatly. Known as NTS-Asia, with its secretariat housed at the RSIS Centre for NTS Studies, network members include nineteen members apart from the RSIS Centre for NTS Studies. These are the Asia Human Community (AHC), Japan; Asia-Pacific Centre for the Responsibility to Protect (APR2P); Bangladesh Institute of International and Strategic Studies (BIISS); Bangladesh Institute of Peace and Security Studies (BIPSS); Centre of Asian Studies (CAS), University of Hong Kong; Centre

x

Acknowledgements

for International Security Studies (CISS), University of Sydney; Centre for the Study of Developing Societies (CSDS), India; Centre for Strategic and International Studies (CSIS), Indonesia; Centre for Peace and Conflict Studies, Chulalongkorn University; Institute of Asia-Pacific Studies (IAPS), Chinese Academy of Social Sciences (CASS), China; La Trobe University Institute for Human Security; Ilmin International Relations Institute (IIRI), Korea University; Institute for Strategic and Development Studies (ISDS), Philippines; Institute of World Economics and Politics (IWEP), China; Institute for World Economics and Politics (IWEP), Vietnam; Refugee and Migratory Movements Research Unity (RMMRU), Bangladesh; Regional Centre for Strategic Studies (RCSS), Sri Lanka; Women In Security, Conflict Management and Peace (WISCOMP), Foundation for His Holiness the Dalai Lama, India; and The WorldFish Center, Malaysia. These organizations have provided key perspectives at regional meetings and conferences addressing the various NTS challenges Asia faces today.

Indeed, our thanks also go to the John D. and Catherine T. MacArthur Foundation for providing a multi-year grant that enabled us to bring together many of those from the regional network and contributed to the sustainability of our global research team at the centre and their ability to experience NTS challenges first hand. Furthermore our internal and cross-border conflict programme benefited from a two-year grant from the Australian Responsibility to Protect Fund to assess the traction of the Responsibility to Protect norm in Asia. Without our funders and networks, the depth and breadth of issues and challenges covered would not have been possible.

We would like to extend our appreciation to the whole NTS research team who have worked hard in getting this publication out. A special thanks goes to Ong Suet Yen, Cheryl Lim, Steven Poh, and the late Jaspal Singh of the publication team and to Regina Arokiasamy, Belinda Chng, and Josephine Ng for their administrative support. Finally, we would like to express our deep thanks to those that have engaged with us and the contributors on our various fieldwork trips, telephone interviews and meetings. Without listening to those affected by various policy responses, it is impossible to contribute meaningfully to policy development. It is with this in mind that we hope we have listened and understood, and have added in a meaningful way to these political and policy debates. All errors remain the authors' own.

Mely Caballero-Anthony (Ph.D.) and Alistair D.B. Cook (Ph.D.)
Singapore
1 December 2012

LIST OF CONTRIBUTORS

Mely Caballero-Anthony is an Associate Professor and Head of the RSIS Centre for Non-Traditional Security (NTS) Studies at the S. Rajaratnam School of International Studies (RSIS), Nanyang Technological University, Singapore. Until May 2012, she served as Director of External Relations at the ASEAN Secretariat. She is also a member of the World Economic Forum (WEF) Global Agenda Council on Conflict Prevention and Secretary-General of the Consortium of Non-Traditional Security Studies in Asia (NTS-Asia). Dr Anthony's research interests include regionalism and regional security in the Asia Pacific, multilateral security cooperation, politics and international relations in ASEAN, conflict prevention and management, as well as human security. She has published extensively in peer-reviewed journals on a broad range of security issues in the Asia Pacific. Her latest publications, both single-authored and co-edited, include: "The Responsibility to Protect in Southeast Asia: Opening Up Spaces for Advancing Human Security", *Pacific Review*, vol. 25, no. 1 (2012); "ASEAN and Climate Change: Building Resilience through Regional Initiative", in *Human Security and Climate Change in Southeast Asia: Managing Risk and Resilience* (2012); *Energy and Non-Traditional Security (NTS) in Asia* and *Rethinking Energy Security in Asia: A Non-Traditional View of Human Security* (both 2012). Dr Anthony is a member of the Council for Security Cooperation in the Asia Pacific (CSCAP) Study Group on the Responsibility to Protect, and also a member of the International Advisory Board of the Asia Pacific Centre for the Responsibility to Protect (APCR2P), and the Global Consortium on Security Transformation (GCST). Her current research focus takes on the broad theme of Governance and Non-traditional Security issues. She is also working on a project on Revisiting Regionalism in Asia.

Julie Balen is a health systems and policy researcher at Imperial College London, based at the Centre for Health Policy and supported by Imperial's Junior Research Fellowship. Her research includes exploratory, descriptive and comparative studies of selected health systems, with a focus on human resource management, capacity building and health service delivery, using a trans-disciplinary approach. Julie is a former Overseas Research Fellow at the London School of Hygiene and Tropical Medicine, based in Thailand, and a former Post-doctoral Fellow at the RSIS Centre for Non-Traditional Security (NTS) Studies in Singapore, where she conducted policy-relevant research on health systems integration, global health security and governance, and pandemic preparedness across Southeast Asia. Julie has substantial fieldwork experience within numerous ASEAN member states and across West Africa. She obtained her Ph.D. in Public Health and Epidemiology from the University of Queensland, Australia and her B.Sc in Biology from Imperial College, London.

Priyanka Bhalla is currently pursuing her Ph.D. in the Lee Kuan Yew School of Public Policy at the National University of Singapore. Prior to this she was an Associate Research Fellow at the RSIS Centre for Non-Traditional Security (NTS) Studies in Singapore and a Project Manager with the United Nations Population Fund and the Department of Peacekeeping Operations, both in Nepal and New York. Her research interests include property rights transitions during forest tenure reform, disaster preparedness and response in the Asia region, and issues related to migration, including internal displacement and statelessness.

Belinda Chng is Programme Development Manager and Researcher for the Health Security and the Irregular Migration Programmes at the RSIS Centre for Non-Traditional Security (NTS) Studies in Singapore. Previously, as Programme Manager, she oversaw coordination of five research programmes and managed a range of projects funded by government and private foundations. She was formerly Associate Research Fellow for NTS and Research Analyst at the International Center for Political Violence and Terrorism Research. Prior to her current role, she was Policy Advisor at the APEC Policy Support Unit, where she advised the Unit on strategic planning, mandate extension, outreach and engagement of APEC stakeholders, development of research capacity, and conducted research on emergency preparedness and food security. Her interests are in the areas of crisis preparedness, conflict prevention and management, human security in ASEAN, state-society relations, governance, organizational analysis and communications.

Alistair D. B. Cook is a Visiting Research Fellow at the East Asian Institute at the National University of Singapore. He is a former research fellow and programme lead for the internal and cross-border conflict and NTS-Plus programmes at the RSIS Centre for Non-Traditional Security (NTS) Studies in Singapore and a former honorary fellow at the School of Social and Political Sciences, Melbourne University, Australia. His current research projects include non-traditional security issues in East and Southeast Asia with a focus on China-ASEAN relations and Asia-Pacific regionalism. His most recent publications, both single and co-authored, include: "Myanmar's China Policy: Agendas, Strategies and Challenges", *China Report* 48, no. 3 (2012), and "Unpacking the Scarborough Shoal Dispute", *East Asian Policy*, vol. 4, issue 3 (2012).

Pau Khan Khup Hangzo is an Associate Research Fellow at the RSIS Centre for Non-Traditional Security (NTS) Studies in Singapore. He currently researches on the geopolitics of Transboundary Rivers in South and Southeast Asia and the practice of water diplomacy by small, resource-scarce states such as Singapore and Israel. His other research interest includes transnational crime and irregular movement of people whose research he lead under the Centre's NTS-Plus programme. He also has a special interest in analysing identity-based ethnic conflicts including those in India and Myanmar. He has a Bachelor's degree in Geography from the University of Delhi, India and a Masters degree in Strategic Studies from the S. Rajaratnam School of International Studies.

Lina Gong is a Ph.D. candidate at the S. Rajaratnam School of International Studies (RSIS) and Research Associate with the RSIS Centre for Non-Traditional Security (NTS) Studies. She holds a BA and MA in English Language and Literature from Sichuan University, China, and a MSc. in International Relations from Nanyang Technological University, Singapore. Lina's research interests include conflict-induced NTS issues in Southeast Asia, the diffusion of the responsibility to protect in East Asia, and Chinese foreign policy. Her master's thesis examines the evolution of the Responsibility to Protect between 2001 and 2009. Her Ph.D. dissertation explores the reasons behind China's increasing receptiveness for UN peacekeeping operations.

Sofiah Jamil is an Adjunct Research Associate at the RSIS Centre for Non-Traditional Security (NTS) Studies in Singapore. She holds a masters degree in international relations from NTU and is currently pursuing her doctorate in international, political and strategic studies at The Australian National University. Prior to pursuing her doctorate, Sofiah was an Associate Research Fellow at the RSIS Centre for NTS Studies. Her published works include "Development as a double-edged sword: Managing environmental movement in Singapore's urban environment", in *Environmental Movements around the world: Shades of Green in Politics and Culture* (2013); two co-authored chapters in an edited volume on *Energy and Non-Traditional Security in East Asia* (2012); and "Islam & Environmentalism: Greening Our Youth", in *Igniting Thought, Unleashing Youth: Perspectives on Muslim Youth and Activism in Singapore* (2009).

Manpavan Kaur is lecturer-in-law with the University of London (UOL), International Programmes at ITC School of Laws, Singapore. Prior to this position, Manpavan was research analyst at the RSIS Centre for Non-Traditional Security (NTS) Studies. In this position, Manpavan undertook research in her interest areas, particularly internal conflict and international criminal law. In addition, Manpavan has keen research interests in the areas of human security and international development, human rights, and transnational crimes such as human trafficking. Manpavan graduated with a second upper class LLB (Hons) from Brunel University, London and possesses an LLM (Merit) in International Development Law and Human Rights from the University of Warwick, United Kingdom obtained in 2009. Manpavan has previously worked as a case manager with revenue and customs on criminal border detections and with immigration authorities in the United Kingdom.

Koh Swee Lean Collin is an Associate Research Fellow in the Military Studies Programme at the Institute of Defense and Strategic Studies (IDSS), S. Rajaratnam School of International Studies, Nanyang Technological University. Prior to this, he was a research analyst at the RSIS Centre for Non-Traditional Security (NTS) Studies in Singapore. His research interests are vested in both non-traditional and traditional security studies, in particular energy security issues and military developments in the Asia Pacific. He received his B.Sc in materials science and engineering from Nanyang Technological University and his M.Sc in strategic studies from the S. Rajaratnam School of International Studies. His most recent publications include two co-authored chapters "Rethinking Energy Security:

A Non-Traditional View of Human Security" (2012) and "Rethinking Market Governance and Energy Security" (2012).

Irene A. Kuntjoro is a Senior Researcher for political, security and foreign affairs at the Embassy of the Republic of Korea in Jakarta, Indonesia. Previously she was an analyst at a British risk consultancy firm based in Singapore. She is a former Associate Research Fellow and Centre Event Manager at the RSIS Centre for Non-Traditional Security (NTS) Studies in Singapore. Prior to Singapore, Irene worked for a number of NGOs in Jakarta as a junior consultant and in other capacities. Her most recent published work is "Climate Security and Development in Southeast Asia: The Limits of UNESCAP's Green Growth Approach", in *Human Security and Climate Change in Southeast Asia: Managing Risk and Resilience* (2012). She holds a BA in International Relations from the University of Indonesia and masters in International Security and Terrorism from the University of Nottingham, UK where she was a Chevening scholar.

Arpita Mathur is a Singapore-based scholar and is a former visiting research fellow, S. Rajaratnam School of International Studies (RSIS) and at the RSIS Centre for Non-Traditional Security (NTS) Studies. Prior to her engagement with the RSIS, she was an associate fellow at the Institute for Defence Studies and Analyses, New Delhi, India. She completed her doctorate in International Politics from Jawaharlal Nehru University, New Delhi, India. Her areas of interest include East Asian politics and relations with South Asia, Japan's domestic politics, foreign and security policies. She has also been working on gender and food security issues and has written an Asia Security Initiative Policy Series working paper entitled "Women and Food Security: A Comparison of South Asia and Southeast Asia" (March 2011). Besides, she has authored a monograph, several papers in peer-reviewed journals, book chapters, policy brief and commentaries on these issues. She had also been involved in teaching post-graduate masters students while at the RSIS.

Kevin Punzalan is a Lecturer in the Consular & Diplomatic Affairs Program at De La Salle-College of St. Benilde in Manila, the Philippines. He also lectured at the International Studies Department of De La Salle University. Previously, he was a research analyst for the RSIS Centre for Non-Traditional Security (NTS) Studies in Singapore. He published several single and co-authored papers for the Centre. He maintains an interest in both history and security studies. Current research interests include the evolution of renewable energy policy in Southeast Asia, particularly the Philippines. He has also studied the history of nuclear energy policy in the Philippines and the role of civil society organizations in shaping energy policy. Aside from these fields, he also comments on domestic Philippine politics. He holds a Master's Degree in Strategic Studies from the S. Rajaratnam School of International Studies, Nanyang Technological University, Singapore.

Nur Azha Putra is Research Associate at the Energy Security Division of the Energy Studies Institute (ESI), National University of Singapore. His research interests include geopolitics, hydro politics, and cyber security. He is a former Associate Research Fellow at the RSIS Centre for Non-Traditional Security (NTS) Studies in Singapore and a former journalist with the national Malay newspaper, *Berita Harian* (BH), where he received the "Special Award for Excellence". Azha frequently writes on community and nation building, and geopolitics. His most recent publications include: *Energy and Non-Traditional Security (NTS) in Asia* and *Rethinking Energy Security: A Non-Traditional View of Human Security* (both 2012). He obtained his masters from Nanyang Technological University and his Bachelor of Information Technology from Central Queensland University, Australia. He was recently awarded a Professional Diploma in Risk Planning from NUS-Asia Institute of Risk Management and is also a certified Enterprise Risk Manager (2012).

Sadhavi Sharma is currently pursuing her Ph.D. in International Political Economy at the S. Rajaratnam School of International Studies, Nanyang Technological University, Singapore. She is a former visiting researcher with the RSIS Centre for Non-Traditional Security (NTS) Studies. She is currently researching the politics of palm oil — how the sustainability norm is advocated by the interplay between state, civil society and industry. She is also interested in examining the current international development agenda and the culture of limits. She has previously worked with news organizations such as *Hindustan Times* and *Bloomberg*, as well as in the non-profit sector, and has published in *Spiked-online*, *Indian Express*, and *Bengal Post* among others.

1

NTS FRAMEWORK[1]

Mely Caballero-Anthony and Alistair D.B. Cook

Over the last two decades, the global security environment has changed dramatically. While the risks of major armed conflict and interstate wars are now on the decline (Human Security Centre 2005), the global community is increasingly confronted with security challenges emerging from a host of local as well as transnational threats which are primarily non-military in nature but also include the threat of state sponsored violence on its own population and the emergence of non-state armed actors. These security challenges, now referred to as non-traditional security (NTS) are proving to be more severe and more likely to inflict more harm to a greater number of people than conventional threats of interstate wars and conflicts. As a consequence, policy-makers around the world have had to re-think their security agendas and find new and creative ways to address these security challenges. This has occurred with a necessary reimagining of what constitutes security threats to the state through conceptualizing the state through its population rather than traditional notions of sovereignty.

Within Asia, the shift in understanding what constitutes a security threat has changed the way states interact as they face common threats and longer term consequences that face their societies. Examples of non-military security challenges to Asia include the spread of infectious diseases like Dengue Fever, H5N1 (the "bird flu") or Severe Acute Respiratory Syndrome ("SARS"), managing the aftermath of natural disasters like the 2004 and 2011 tsunamis, trans-border pollution which has caused "the haze" over Southeast Asia, as well as problems of irregular migration and transnational crime. These NTS challenges pose dangers to the region irrespective of national boundaries and in return, they demand trans-national solutions and the building of states capacities to respond to these security threats.

Since many of these security challenges are transnational, states tend to draw closer and establish institutional and procedural arrangements to respond to what are often complex security challenges. As a consequence, there is a noticeable trend among state and non-state actors to turn to regional and multilevel relationships as a preferred framework to respond to trans-border and non-traditional security problems. These, in turn, have had profound implications for regional security cooperation among states in Asia.

The implications for Asian security are that the nature of security cooperation in Asia continues to evolve and respond to challenges and the other is the very nature of what constitutes security. The trend in Asia is for increased engagement between state and non-state actors across the various local and transnational challenges states and societies face in the region.

When considering increased interaction between state and non-state actors in Asia, the tendency has been to engage more and build consensus rather than foster tit-for-tat exchanges when responding to non-traditional security challenges. In international relations theory, liberal and neoliberal institutionalists posit that states will engage in cooperation where and when there are actual or potential mutual interests and gains to be derived. This is most obviously present in transnational challenges and within regions with a shared history. Institutions are one mechanism with which cooperative security can occur. Indeed, institutions occur at the formalization of interaction between states or even between state and non-state actors. It is important to note that formal bricks and mortar are the signs of an established relationship but many forums for dialogue have emerged in response to non-traditional security challenges. With the rising interdependence of states regarding security issues, multiple stakeholders can assist in defining states' interests. Indeed, in Asia this is most prevalent where responses need to be framed within states interests to ensure continued interaction and cooperation. Further, cooperative security as a "security system" among states has been developed into the building of "security communities" wherein states through a sustained process of close interaction and learning, forge and consolidate shared norms and values.[2] These communities are more likely in Asia to take on multiple issue-dependent forms than other regions where the cooperation system is more rigid, such as in the case of the European Union — a much more formalized continent-wide and systematic institutional arrangement.

More importantly, the trend toward closer security cooperation has been largely defined by the changing nature of security challenges which are no longer confined to threats to the territoriality and sovereignty of states. Events have shown that contemporary security challenges such as environmental degradation, infectious diseases, poverty and extremism cannot be addressed by military means alone, and require a multi-stakeholder response. The capacity of a state to respond to a number of security challenges has also been rendered inadequate and a greater focus on developing robust response mechanisms is required. Rather, the nature of transnational challenges highlight the need for cooperation among states in order to find effective policies through participation by stakeholders in the decision-making process, such as those focused on cyber security, health, energy the environment, food and water, migration, natural disasters and transnational crime.

In seeking responses to these evolving NTS challenges, researchers have therefore gone beyond traditional understandings and frameworks of security threats to look beyond the nation state to address these issues that do not respect national borders and directly affect the livelihoods of those within them. Analysts focusing on NTS have instead called for the replacement of state-centrism with a framework that encompasses the security of individuals, societies and groups.

Within the Southeast Asian sub-region of Asia,[3] comprehensive security has, for a long time, been considered as the dominant concept and had structured the understanding among the political elites about what security means for the region. As noted by an Asian security scholar, Muthiah Alagappa, regardless of the labels and the varied interpretations that came with the term, comprehensive security implied that security "goes beyond (but does not exclude) the military to embrace the political, economic and socio-cultural dimensions".[4] However, as the state remained the security referent the concept of comprehensive security came under strong criticism particularly in the aftermath of the Asian financial crisis that hit the region in 1997–98. Vulnerable groups in societies that suffered as a direct consequence of the economic crisis highlighted deeper rooted and structural inequalities that threatened the viability of the systems in place and reconceptualized security in ways that better accounted for the challenges that faced the region.

The debates on the reconceptualization of security have therefore gone beyond the general expansion of security to include non-military threats towards promoting "human security" as a possible framework in order to replace the conventional state-centric approach with an approach that accounts for the multiple challenges faced by individuals and societies.

Essentially, advocates of human security call for a re-thinking of security by expanding the security referent beyond the state to include the chronic and complex insecurities commonly faced by these individuals and societies.[5] Human security, at least in the Southeast Asian context, has provided an important avenue to address the developing world's experience with non-traditional security challenges, which has in turn broadened and deepened the discourse on security and international relations more generally.

However, while the concept of human security reconceptualized security to account for individuals and societies, it has been criticized by various scholars. The 1994 United Nations Development Programme's Human Development Report on human security is more commonly referred to as the seven-part response including economic, food, health, environmental, personal, political and community security and highlights not only the policy relevance of the concept but also the challenges to its value as an analytical concept. Roland Paris has pointed out that its definition of human security is too broad and covers "'virtually any kind of unexpected or irregular discomfort' which could constitute a threat to a person's security". The list of seven specific elements comprising human security in the report was also considered too broad and "difficult to determine what, if anything, might be excluded".[6] After examining various statements and assertions from proponents of human security, Paris concludes that "if human security means almost anything, then it effectively means nothing" (Paris 2001, p. 93). However, in the same way other theories have different schools of thought, human security is no different. Within human security there are three broad schools that have formed to understand the challenges faced by individuals and societies.

Notably these schools of thought have proponents characterized by regional governments illustrating the policy relevance of the debate but the academic silence to more robustly engage with the concept. The first school follows the 1994 UNDP Report and keeps its understanding of the concept comprehensive and tied to the seven-part approach. The second school envisions human security as more dependent on social safety nets, championed by Japan, which largely grew in popularity in the aftermath of the 1997 Asian Financial Crisis as a response to the exposed vulnerabilities of individuals and societies across Asia. The third school once part of Canadian foreign policy and championed by Norway reigns in the concept of human security to focus on reducing the human consequences of violent conflict. This understanding of human security seeks to address the challenges that face the international system with ensuring that states do not inflict harm on their populations through human rights abuses. The most notable policy document to evolve from this conception of human security is from the International Commission on Intervention and State Sovereignty (ICISS) which produced the landmark report *The Responsibility to Protect.*

Overall, "human security" may be labelled as a broad category of research in the field of security studies, one that is "primarily concerned with nonmilitary threats to the safety of societies, groups and individuals", and that security studies have benefitted from both a "broadening" and "deepening" of the field due to the addition of non-conventional or "non-traditional" security studies.[7] It is this conception of human security that has gained the most traction throughout Asia as it largely avoids condemnatory approaches and seeks to generate preventive measures to avoid the escalation of violence and ensure an equitable system to individuals and societies.

Against this background, where would one then fit in the concept of NTS? One could suggest that if comprehensive security (CS) is the expanded notion of security beyond military security, then NTS can be viewed as a subset of comprehensive security that characteristically and primarily requires non-military responses to address a number of emerging security threats through the humanitarian use of the military. NTS could also be considered as the broader umbrella that brings in issues of human security since its security referent extends beyond the state to include individuals and societies.

The second point has to do with the question of the kinds of issues/threats that would fall under NTS. One would note that despite the emerging trend towards security framing, there is yet to be a consensus definition on what it really means since the issues that would fall under NTS are often contextually defined. For example, what may be NTS issues in one country like economic security, food security or energy security could already be part of the traditional concept of security in the other. As one scholar had previously argued, energy security which is now included in the rubric of NTS in Asia had long been a part of a country's (i.e. Japan) traditional security concerns and on its policy agenda.[8] These two points are highlighted to emphasize the fact that NTS issues are not only contested but also complex.

To help in the conceptualization of NTS, the Consortium on Non-Traditional Security Studies in Asia (NTS-Asia) has defined NTS issues as those challenges that affect the survival and well-being of peoples and states that arise primarily out of non-military sources, such as climate change, resource scarcity, infectious diseases, natural disasters, irregular migration, famine, people smuggling, drug trafficking and transnational crime. Aside from these issues being non-military in nature, they also share common characteristics, namely: transnational in scope (neither purely domestic, nor purely interstate); come at very short notice and are transmitted rapidly due to globalization, communication revolution, etc.; cannot entirely be prevented but coping mechanisms can be devised; national solutions are often inadequate and would thus essentially require regional and multilateral cooperation; and finally, the object of security is no longer just the state (state sovereignty or territorial integrity), but also the peoples (survival, well-being, dignity), both at individual and societal levels.[9]

In brief, while efforts are being made to bring more attention to non-traditional security issues, the main argument here is to examine not just the emerging threats or risks to peoples' lives and security; but more importantly also, to identify/explore approaches that can allow for a concept of security that addresses the security concerns of both states and societies and tackles both traditional and non-traditional security threats.[10] In fact, a study undertaken for the SIPRI Yearbook 2007 had similarly argued that, "[i]f the ultimate objective of security is to save human beings from preventable premature death and disability, then the appropriate security policy [should] focus on prevention instruments and risk reduction strategies for their causes".[11]

SECURITIZATION ANALYSIS

To analyse the growing list of non-traditional security challenges in Asia, a methodology for investigating acts of securitization and desecuritization has been constructed by scholars at the S. Rajaratnam School of International Studies.[12] Taking off from the Copenhagen School and its securitization model, the modified framework combines theoretical and empirical analysis. It involves asking the *why* and *how* questions of securitization and desecuritization, and identifies the catalysts and motivations that drive such processes. One of the objectives of this approach was to move away from the Euro-centric orientation of the Copenhagen School and examine its application in Asia. The revised model of the securitization theory therefore identifies the following steps to evaluate the securitization process:

1. *Issue Area:* Beyond identifying what the security threat is, an examination of whether there is a consensus among various actors is the first step, such as governments and civil society groups, on the nature of the threat. By doing so, the dynamics are explored in the process of securitization and

highlight the problems encountered by securitizing actors in convincing a specific audience that a referent object is existentially threatened.

2. *Securitizing Actors:*   The second step is to identify who the securitizing actors are and whose interests they represent: government and its bureaucracy, civil society, epistemic communities, or international institutions. This involves addressing the following questions: is the state the main actor in the act of securitization? What about the other sectors of society? Are the voices of the marginalized represented in the act of securitization? What are the motivations for securitizing the issue?

3. *Security Concept:*   The third step is to identify whose security is under threat. States usually securitize by invoking national security. Non-governmental organizations (NGOs) may securitize by invoking human security, while international institutions may securitize by invoking international or global security as opposed to national security. Depending on the security concept invoked, the referent objects of security can vary among states, individuals, ethnic groups, women, communities, multinational corporations, or the international community. Relevant questions to be addressed include: What is the interaction between these actors? Does contestation take place between and among these actors?

4. *Process:*   The fourth issue to address is how speech acts are utilized which is critical to an act of securitization. Speech acts of international and non-state actors may be as important as those of domestic elites. An examination of the politics of threat identification is needed to determine whether the speech act creates the threat or whether the threat creates the speech act. A further investigation into whether there are cases of "grafting" present, i.e. an attempt to define a threat by linking it with a prior recognized threat. This allows for acts of persuasion to be accounted for and evaluated with a particular speech act.

5. *Intervening Variables:*   Throughout the securitization or desecuritization process several factors have been identified that will, to a greater or lesser degree, influence the process. These are:

   • *Interplay of different concepts of security:*   This involves examining the concepts of national or state security, comprehensive security, human security, the imperatives of global security and their linkages to the securization and desecuritization process.

   • *Issue inkage:*   This requires analysing how securitizing actors may have the ability to link an emerging problem that has not yet been securitized with an issue that has already been recognized as a security threat.

- *Role of stakeholders*: This important factor highlights the role of state and non-state actors in advancing or hindering the cause of non-traditional security. It is important to examine whether pressure from powerful actors (be it domestically or internationally) is more likely to lead to an act of securitization. In essence this intervening variable seeks to identify the degree of persuasion by particular stakeholders to advance a particular security policy framework.

- *Domestic political systems*: The role of domestic politics in securitizing NTS threats and the extent to which differing political systems influence the success or failure of securitization is another important consideration. A pertinent question here is whether securitization will more likely succeed in authoritarian states where the military traditionally plays an important role in domestic politics?

POLICY EVALUATION AND ANALYSING GOVERNANCE

The first analytical framework sought to track the rise and fall, or indeed the fall and rise of policies which have been securitized and thus have been given access to a more prominent place in the national or international consciousness as an issue of central importance to the well-being of a given population or state. In this second section it provides an analytical framework that evaluates the success or failure of a given policy. In sum, the first section provides an analytical framework to assess how and why a particular policy is securitized; this second section provides an analytical framework to assess whether a policy response to a non-traditional security threat has been a success or failure.

This analytical framework draws on the notions of governance and utilizes it to evaluate the success or failure of a given non-traditional security policy response. The concept of governance has always existed but has become increasingly salient in political science literature more broadly, and the security, development and international relations literatures in particular. It is of greatest importance to provide a definition of the concept at hand. In this framework, governance is defined as *the process of decision-making and the process through which decisions are (or are not) implemented.*

Through the identification of eight characteristics this conceptual framework provides a method to evaluate the decision-making process of a given non-traditional security policy. It is important to include in the analytical framework an analysis on both the formal and informal structures and actors that are in place to arrive at, and implement, a policy decision. Through the analysis it is imperative to note that while governments are of fundamental importance they are not necessarily the only actor involved in making decisions. In rural areas other actors may include influential land lords, farmers associations, trades unions, the military, religious leaders, business groups, NGOs, political parties and so on. Many of these actors are often times grouped together to form civil society and their formal and informal role in the decision-making process is key to better understanding the process. While these actors do not necessarily play a formal role in decision-making, their influence and impact on policy decisions need to be accounted for in our study of the decision-making process. Indeed, the informal actors do not only fall outside of the government structure, they also fall within them, with influential informal actors such as "kitchen cabinets" or policy advisors or even powerful families or individuals.

As a result of the increasing interaction between states and societies in the international system, more multifaceted governance structures have appeared and continue to appear, some with competing or joint mandates, depending on your perspective. These can appear in various forms such as regional groupings of states, like the Association of Southeast Asian Nations (ASEAN) or groups based on themes such as the Bali Democracy Forum. Finally, without a shadow-of-doubt is the global level associated with the United Nations system, which is based on worldwide and universal membership of states, various international efforts at the global level to tackle worldwide policy issues.

Alongside these layers of governance is the inevitable interaction across and between these layers of governance, in various forms and depending on a particular issue. These may take the form of the United Nations Global Compact — a strategic policy for businesses to adhere to ten universally accepted principles in the areas of human rights, labour, environment and anti-corruption; the U.K. government and the U.S. State of California government's agreement on climate change and clean energy collaboration in 2006; or the World Cities Summit that brings together countries like Singapore together with New York to bring together decision-makers facing similar issues. Through recognizing the complex nature of the decision-making process, it is now possible to evaluate the potential bids and influences on decision-making in the international system.

There are eight characteristics that have been identified to evaluate the decision-making process to provide the basis for understanding how a particular non-traditional security policy was reached. They are: participation; the rule of law; transparency; responsiveness; consensus-oriented decisions; equity and inclusiveness; effectiveness and efficiency; and accountability. This normative framework provides the means to a comprehensive understanding of the decision-making process. The eight characteristics identified by the United Nations are elaborated below.

1. *Participation* by both men and women is essential in the decision-making process. This participation can be through direct participation or legitimate representatives or institutions. When evaluating participation the level of information available needs to be accounted for; in other words whether those in the decision-making process are informed and organized. In this sense decision-makers can also be informed by civil society and informal actors, all of which need to be accounted for.

2. *A fair and accessible legal framework* that is enforced impartially is needed. It also requires the protection of minorities to avoid "mob rule".

3. *Transparency* is where it is easy to trace the decision-making process so that those affected by the decisions can trace and understand a particular policy process and who made the decision.

4. *Responsiveness* is the ability of institutions to respond in a timely manner to issues of concern.

5. *Consensus orientated decision-making process* ensures that multiple stakeholders' opinions are taken into consideration when reaching a decision. This ensures that as much information as is reasonably possible is utilized to inform the decision-makers.

6. *Equity and inclusiveness* allows all people to have ownership of the decision-making process and have equal access to it.

7. *Effectiveness and efficiency* refers to the ability of decision-makers to utilize available resources in the best way possible.

8. Finally *accountability* is the means to hold decision-makers to their word and deed. Accountability goes hand-in-hand with transparency and the rule of law.

With these eight variables researchers are able to identify the conceptual underpinnings of good governance and begin to evaluate situations on their strengths and weaknesses, and arguing for policy successes or failures. See Figure 1.1.

Through this book, there is an investigation into nine key Non-Traditional Security threats to states and societies to introduce the reader to practical examples of current and evolving areas of Non-Traditional Security. In the second chapter an investigation into issues of health security and the current system of global health governance and how states and societies in the region respond to health challenges such as pandemic preparedness is undertaken.

The third and fourth chapters address food and water security and investigate the responses to the challenges of access, poverty and displacement

Figure 1.1
NTS Analysis

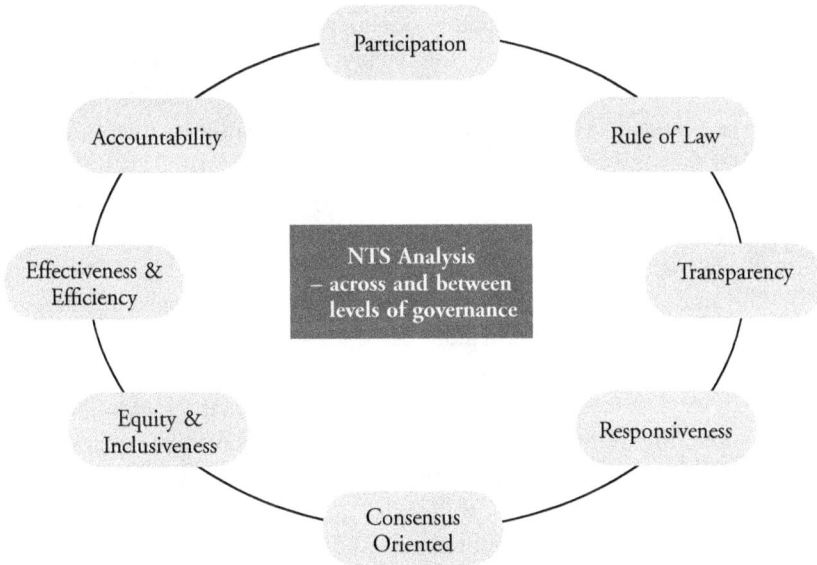

of people in the region when considering food and water security. Through providing seven case studies of non-traditional security challenges this book aims not only to provide an introduction to the study of non-traditional security but also include the various challenges that face states and societies in Asia, how and why they respond in particular ways to provide the reader with case studies.

The fifth chapter undertakes an analysis of current government responses to natural disasters, and provides an assessment of the levels of preparedness in dealing with natural disasters in the region. The second half of the chapter investigates the trend towards increasing adaptability into development policy as one policy response to the current challenges that exposure to natural disasters gives states and societies in the region. The sixth chapter focuses on internal conflicts in Asia and examines the role and impact of small arms and light weapons in continuing the internal conflicts across the region. In the second half of the chapter there is a focus on Myanmar and Early Warning Systems to evaluate the predictability of conflict escalation and the prospect for mass atrocities to occur. This is an effort to test the water on the current surge in interest in the utility of systematic prediction efforts. The seventh chapter focuses on the issue of forced migration and in particular investigates the issue of statelessness and how it affects states and societies in the region, which is of particular concern as the recent and ongoing treatment of particular social groups in the region.

The eighth chapter covers energy security which continues to play a significant part in the sustainable development of economies particularly in Asia. In order to respond to the energy needs states and societies have there is a focus on not only who has access to energy but in what form energy is provided. The first half of this chapter focuses on the emergence of nuclear fuel and what threats and challenges are associated with this. The second half of the chapter evaluates the energy policies that governments in Asia have adopted to ensure that they continue developing in a secure and sustainable way.

The ninth chapter looks at the challenges that transnational crime presents to states and societies in the region, provides an overview of the evolution of the phenomena since it was coined as a phrase in 1974 and how states and societies approach and understand it. The tenth chapter addresses cyber security and how states and societies respond to the threats of cyber-attacks, for example those in Georgia in 2008 and Estonia in 2007. These attacks demonstrated an area of vulnerability that affects states and societies which needs an appropriate policy response. In the second half of the chapter the issues and responses to the governance deficit come under close examination to better understand the ways and means to manage, mitigate and adapt to a realm that currently falls far short of responding to the threats and challenges in cyberspace. The final chapter reviews the collection and provides some areas for future research and identifies some of the challenges faced both in studying and identifying NTS challenges.

Notes

1   Some of the initial section of this chapter was adapted from an earlier version in Mely Caballero-Anthony, "The New World of Security", in *Issues in 21st Century World Politics*, edited by Mark Beeson and Nick Bisley (Palgrave Macmillan, 2010).

2   On discussions of security communities, see for example, Emanuel Adler and Michael Barnett, *Security Communities* (Cambridge: Cambridge University Press, 1998); Amitav Acharya, *Constructing A Security Community in Southeast Asia: ASEAN and the Problem of Regional Order* (London and New York: Routledge, 2001).

3   In this chapter, Southeast Asia is used interchangeably with ASEAN. ASEAN groups the ten states of Brunei, Cambodia, Laos, Indonesia, Malaysia, Myanmar, Philippines, Thailand, Singapore and Vietnam.

4   Muthiah Alagappa, *Asian Security Practices: Material and Ideational Influences* (Stanford: Stanford University Press, 1998), and "Comprehensive Security: Interpretations in ASEAN Countries", in *Asian Security Issues: Regional and Global*, edited by Robert Scalapino et al. Berkeley: Institute of East Asian Studies, University of California, 1988.

5   For Asian debates on human security see, for example, Mely Caballero-Anthony, "Re-visioning Human Security in Southeast Asia", *Asian Perspectives*, vol. 28, no. 3 (2004): 155–89; William Tow, Ramesh Thakur and In-Taek Hyun, eds., *Asia's Emerging Regional Order* (Tokyo: United Nations University Press, 2000); Japan Institute of International Affairs, *In Quest of Human Security* (Tokyo: Japan Institute of International Affairs, 2001); Pranee Thiparat, ed., *The Quest for Human Security: The Next Phase of ASEAN?* (Bangkok: Institute of Security and International Studies, 2001). For works on the general topic on human security, see also Fen Osler Hampson et al., *Madness in the Multitude: Human Security and World Disorder* (Oxford: Oxford University Press, 2002); Jennifer Leaning and Sam Arie, "Human Security: A Framework for Assessment in Conflict and Transition", Harvard Center for Population and Development Studies Working Paper, vol. 11, no. 3 (2001); Sverre Lodgaard, "Human Security: Concept and Operationalisation", available at <www.cpdsindia.org/globalhumansecurity/security/operationalisation.htm>.

6   Roland Paris, "Human Security: Paradigm Shift or Hot Air?", *International Security* 26, no. 2 (Fall 2001): 80–90.

7   Roland Paris, "Human Security: Paradigm Shift or Hot Air?", *International Security* 26, no. 2 (Fall 2001): 96–97.

8   Akaha Tsuneo, "Non-traditional Security Cooperation in Northeast Asia", in *Broadening Asia's Security Discourse and Agenda: Political, Social and Environmental Perspectives*, edited by Ramesh Thakur and Edward Newman (Tokyo: United Nations University Press, 2004), pp. 306–39.

9   Mely Caballero-Anthony, *Studying Non-Traditional Security in Asia: Trends and Issues* (Singapore: Marshall Cavendish, 2006*b*).

10   For more on this type of argument, see Oxford Research Group, "Global Response to Global Threats: Security for the 21ˢᵗ Century", Briefing Paper, June 2006.

11   Elizabeth Skons, "Analysing Risks to Human Lives", in *SIPRI Yearbook 2007: Armaments, Disarmament and International Security* (2007), p. 243.

12   An earlier version of this framework was prepared by Amitav Acharya, Project Director, IDSS-Ford Project on Non-Traditional Security in Asia in 2007. It was subsequently modified in Mely Caballero-Anthony, Ralf Emmers and Amitav Acharya, eds., *Non-Traditional Security in Asia: Dilemmas in Securitisation*, and *Studying Non-Traditional Security in Asia: Trends and Issues* (Singapore: Marshall Cavendish, 2006). Further amendments have been made here by Alistair D.B. Cook and Mely Caballero-Anthony in 2010.

References

Acharya, Amitav. *Constructing A Security Community in Southeast Asia: ASEAN and the Problem of Regional Order*. London and New York: Routledge, 2001.

Adler, Emanuel and Michael Barnett. *Security Communities*. Cambridge: Cambridge University Press, 1998.

Alagappa, Muthiah. *Asian Security Practices: Material and Ideational Influences*. Stanford: Stanford University Press, 1998.

————. "Comprehensive Security: Interpretations in ASEAN Countries". In *Asian Security Issues: Regional and Global*, edited by Robert Scalapino et al. Berkeley: Institute of East Asian Studies, University of California, 1988.

Caballero-Anthony, Mely. "The New World of Security". In *Issues in 21ˢᵗ Century World Politics*, edited by Mark Beeson and Nick Bisley. Palgrave Macmillan, 2010.

————. "Re-visioning Human Security in Southeast Asia". *Asian Perspectives*, vol. 28, no. 3 (2004): 155–89.

Caballero-Anthony, Mely, Ralf Emmers and Amitav Acharya, eds. *Non-Traditional Security in Asia: Dilemmas in Securitisation*. London: Ashgate, 2006*a*.

————. *Studying Non-Traditional Security in Asia: Trends and Issues*. Singapore: Marshall Cavendish, 2006*b*.

Hampson, Fen Osler, et al. *Madness in the Multitude: Human Security and World Disorder*. Oxford: Oxford University Press, 2002.

Japan Institute of International Affairs. *In Quest of Human Security*. Tokyo: Japan Institute of International Affairs, 2001.

Leaning, Jennifer and Sam Arie. "Human Security: A Framework for Assessment in Conflict and Transition". Harvard Center for Population and Development Studies Working Paper, vol. 11, no. 3 (2001).

Lodgaard, Sverre. "Human Security: Concept and Operationalisation". Available at <ww.cpdsindia.org/globalhumansecurity/security/operationalisation.htm>.

Oxford Research Group. "Global Response to Global Threats: Security for the 21ˢᵗ Century". Briefing Paper, June 2006.

Paris, Roland. "Human Security: Paradigm Shift or Hot Air?". *International Security* 26, no. 2 (Fall 2001).

Skons, Elizabeth. "Analysing Risks to Human Lives". In *SIPRI Yearbook 2007: Armaments, Disarmament and International Security* (2007).

Thiparat, Pranee, ed. *The Quest for Human Security: The Next Phase of ASEAN?* Bangkok: Institute of Security and International Studies, 2001.

Tow, William, Ramesh Thakur and In-Taek Hyun, eds. *Asia's Emerging Regional Order*. Tokyo: United Nations University Press, 2000.

Tsuneo, Akaha. "Non-traditional Security Cooperation in Northeast Asia". In *Broadening Asia's Security Discourse and Agenda: Political, Social and Environmental Perspectives*, edited by Ramesh Thakur and Edward Newman. Tokyo: United Nations University Press, 2004.

2

HEALTH

Mely Caballero-Anthony, Alistair D.B. Cook, Belinda Chng and Julie Balen

Health is one of the seven threat areas identified by Dr Mahbub ul Haq in the 1994 Human Development Report's definition of human security, and restated by the 2003 UN Commission on Human Security. In the 1994 report, health security recognizes that in developing countries "the major causes of death are infectious and parasitic diseases" and most of these are linked with poor nutrition and an unsafe environment — particularly polluted water. It identifies that in the developed world the major killers are diseases of the circulatory system, often linked with lifestyle and diet, followed by cancer.[1] One common characteristic identified by the report is the need to address the disparities between rich and poor, urban-rural and both in the developed and the developing world.[2] However, most infectious diseases do not gain exceptional traction in politics "because their effects are mild, they are familiar to physicians, or their geographic occurrence is limited".[3] Indeed, the contested nature of health security ensures that there is an ongoing tension between the different political actors framing the debate.

Alongside the 1994 UNDP Human Development Report, health security has evolved and is defined by the actors securitizing health matters. As a result, as with other areas of human security, the definition of what constitutes health security is contested. This contestation is not limited to the definition of health security but also over the utility of securitizing health in the first place. In Asia, health security came to prominence in 2003 with the emergence of Severe Acute Respiratory Syndrome (SARS) and avian influenza (commonly referred to as "bird flu"). With the spread of emerging and re-emerging infectious diseases, there has also been an increasing awareness of the significance of global health governance in an interconnected world. However, the 2003 SARS outbreak highlighted that international health governance was only as strong as its weakest link. By 2005 the International Health Regulations were reformed with a greater emphasis on national surveillance and verification systems.[4] Indeed, these reforms saw the function of the World Health Organisation (WHO) change from a focus on "health work" to "global health security".

As a result of this change in focus the WHO became one of the securitizing actors, cooperating with both state and non-state actors to develop national strategies and build capacity. While there are a plethora of actors involved including governments, charities, corporations, and non-governmental organizations who have committed funding to capacity building initiatives, there remains one dimension neglected in adopting a truly global approach, which is the absence of citizens.[5] Without the involvement of those people the policies affect and their input into the democratic decision-making process that drafts and frames global health governance, then it is difficult to critically examine whether or not the policies implemented are appropriate, effective or even directed at the right "threat". Indeed, the current movement towards greater technocratic and lesser accountability severely undermines the very process established to better govern health matters affecting people in their communities. Concurrently, however, the IHR 2005 has established a global health security framework, which alters the earlier state-centric priorities towards "one of an international framework of standardized core capacities to prevent, or at the very least, minimize the severity of an infectious disease epidemic".[6] While these debates flourish there is a need to identify the evolution of the concept in order to be able to assess the internal and external bids and influences on the use of the term by governments, international agencies and civil society organizations in Asia and what current threats face the region's people today.

INTERNATIONAL HEALTH GOVERNANCE

International health governance emerged with the 1851 International Sanitary Conference in response to infectious diseases. The international sanitary conventions adopted between 1851 and the Second World War and the World Health Organisation (WHO)'s International Sanitary Regulations (1951) (later renamed the International Health Regulations) represent the emergence of international health governance.[7] The IHR established international norms that required states to notify other states about specific disease outbreaks and maintain adequate public health capabilities at points of entry and exit. In addition these norms also required disease-prevention measures that restricted international trade and travel be based upon scientific evidence and public health principles.[8] These legal obligations overlapped with the emergence of global health institutions and the international trade system.

The establishment of the WHO was to facilitate cooperation between states rather than act as an arbiter of international laws concerning health. Indeed, the international laws covering global health did not impose specific duties regarding infectious disease control.[9] Alongside the emergence of international laws on global health and the WHO, the signing of the General Agreement on Tariffs and Trade (GATT) in 1947 liberalized trade but also established the principle that states may restrict trade to protect health.[10] It is through the development of these international mechanisms that states and, more recently, civil society organizations interact when concerned with international health security.

Asian Health Security

In Asia, people suffer a disproportionate burden of communicable diseases compared to the rest of the world. Of the 14 million deaths that occur annually in the region, 40 per cent are due to communicable diseases compared with the global average of 28 per cent. For instance, the region bears 80 per cent of the global leprosy burden, 34 per cent of tuberculosis (TB), and has the highest rate of drug-resistant malaria cases. Each year, 250,000 children die of measles and 750,000 adults die of TB. More than 5 million people in the region are living with HIV/AIDS, with India, Thailand, Myanmar, Indonesia and Nepal accounting for the majority of cases. In the case of malaria approximately 250 million people in the region are at risk, while age-old neglected diseases such as leprosy continue to tax large numbers of poor and socially marginalized populations.

Alongside the adoption in the 1994 Human Development Report of Human Security, the essence of the concept was already in use in many parts of Asia such as Japan, who was first to coin the phrase "comprehensive security" as well as Indonesia, Malaysia and Singapore. Since the Soeharto era, Indonesia has expressed its security in the idea of Ketahanan Nasional (National Resilience) including political, economic, socio-cultural, and military aspects covering both domestic and the international environment. Resilience was to be achieved through economic development as the driving force behind this multifaceted approach to security.[11] Indeed, neighbouring

Malaysia also promoted a similar concept of security as enunciated by the then Prime Minister Mahathir Mohamad that "national security is inseparable from political stability, economic success and social harmony". Similar themes can be found across East Asia in the security policies of Brunei Darussalam, the Philippines, Singapore and Thailand.[12]

By the mid-1990s, the concept of "comprehensive security" was being articulated in forums such as the Council for Security Cooperation in the Asia-Pacific (CSCAP), a track-two level organization involving several research institutes across the region.[13] Indeed, the body came to define "comprehensive security as the pursuit of sustainable security in all fields (personal, political, economic, social, cultural, military, and environmental) in both domestic as well as external spheres, essentially through cooperative means". The definition operationalized several principles, including mutual interdependence, cooperative and shared security, and good citizenship.[14] The absence of health security per se is noticeable in this definition. However, the 2003 SARS outbreak in Asia illustrated the close nexus between health and security and placed it on the policy agenda.[15]

As a result of the changing dynamics and causes of global human insecurity,[16] the United Nations Security Council in 2000 passed Resolution 1308, highlighting the threat HIV/AIDS has on global security, particularly in conflict and peacekeeping scenarios. In response to this, the UNAIDS Secretariat established the office on AIDS, Security and the Humanitarian Response with a global strategy focused on (1) international security and in particular peacekeeping operations; (2) national security including defense and personnel; and (3) humanitarian response including humanitarian workers and vulnerable populations affected by conflict. Since then, and over the past decade, there has been some noteworthy progress, which is illustrated through the prevention rates of HIV transmission from mother-to-child with Thailand having 90 per cent coverage and Malaysia 80 per cent coverage but with the comparison of India, which has the largest unmet need with about 90 per cent of mothers with HIV needing services for preventing new infections amongst their children.[17] However, since the initial focus of HIV/AIDS as a security issue from 2000–05, the debate has become more complex and high profile. Indeed, UNAIDS have been criticized for making bold claims about the link between militaries and HIV/AIDS. The agency admitted in 2005 that there was little reliable information on this, and, that a focus on the state of the armed forces in general would illustrate a state's capacity to respond to such a threat.[18]

It is clear that as a result of the securitization of HIV/AIDS there has been increased awareness, and efforts across and between different actors to address the epidemic in the 2000s than before. The next section will map out what the current status of HIV/AIDS is in Asia to illustrate that through the non-traditional security lens, we are able to critically evaluate the situation and provide a way to conceptualize what is now recognized as a complex phenomenon. This chapter proceeds to then focus on the regional experience with Influenza pandemics. It seeks to evaluate the emergence of these two cases as security issues, map the traction that these two cases have had in the region, and what current challenges and potential threats the region faces when focusing on health security.

HIV/AIDS in Asia

In regions of the world where HIV/AIDS is an epidemic, it threatens the very nature of a state — its people and it affects all levels of society, individuals and communities, as well as those who make up the formal state institutions such as the police, security and military forces. HIV/AIDS is both a cause and an effect of human, and indeed, global insecurity. In the current century, the world experiences more deaths as a result of HIV/AIDS than it does through the human consequences of armed conflict, leaving not only populations devastated by the deaths of individuals but also those formal institutions that uphold the human security of others.

In other words, it poses longer-term insecurities as a threat multiplier to states and societies. Through the non-traditional security lens, HIV/AIDS threatens human security in a variety of ways, some of which are contested. Once the epidemic reaches between 5 and 20 per cent of a population then any gains in life expectancy and health more generally are lost, which threatens national resilience as those most likely affected are those people of working age.[19] It is important to note that the link between HIV/AIDS and security is multifaceted with its impact on the state both in terms of the nature of the epidemic and in terms of its social conseqences.[20]

> There is a world of difference between the root causes of terrorism and the impact of AIDS on security. But at some deep level, we should be reminded that in many parts of the world, AIDS has caused a normal way of life to be called into question. As a global issue, therefore we must pay attention to AIDS as a threat to our human security, and redouble our efforts against the epidemic and its impact.
>
> — Dr Peter Piot,
> UNAIDS Executive Director (1995–2008)

The diversity of the HIV/AIDS epidemic in Asia is significant, particularly because of over half the world's population lives in Asia, which makes even small differences in the infection rates account for huge increases in the absolute number of people infected. The total number of people infected with HIV/AIDS in Asia is estimated around 4.9 million people. Around half (2.4 million) of these were in India followed by China (740,000), Thailand (530,000) and Myanmar (240,000).[21] See Table 2.1. Indeed, the highest prevalence rates within Asia are found in Southeast Asia. As a result of some Asian countries having large geographical areas, national averages oftentimes overlook the significant sub-national variations in infection rates. It is therefore of importance to utilize the NTS framework to identify these variations and the internal and cross-border implications.

In most Asian countries the epidemic is centred among particular high-risk groups, particularly injecting drug users, men who have sex with men, and sex workers and their partners. Indeed the epidemic has potentially destabilizing effects facilitated by the sex and drugs trade, and the associated movement of people within and across borders. If HIV/AIDS in Asia is not adequately addressed, then serious epidemics could also emerge, most notably

Table 2.1
Countries with Highest Burden of HIV in the Asia Pacific

Country	Number Living with HIV	Low Estimate	High Estimate	Number of New Infections	Low Estimate	High Estimate
India	2,400,000	2,100,000	2,800,000	140,000	110,000	160,000
China	740,000	540,000	1,000,000	–	47,000	140,000
Thailand	530,000	420,000	660,000	12,000	9,800	15,000
Indonesia	310,000	200,000	460,000	–	29,000	87,000
Vietnam	280,000	220,000	350,000	–	16,000	38,000
Myanmar	240,000	200,000	350,000	–	16,000	38,000
Malaysia	100,000	83,000	120,000	10,000	8,400	13,000
Pakistan	98,000	79,000	120,000	–	7,300	15,000
Nepal	64,000	51,000	80,000	4,800	2,700	7,800
Cambodia	63,000	42,000	90,000	1,700	<1,000	4,200
PNG	34,000	30,000	39,000	3,200	2,400	4,800

Note: New infection point estimates were not published for countries where there was a lack of agreement between the UNAIDS and country estimate.
Source: Report on the Global AIDS Epidemic (Geneva: Joint United Nations Programme on HIV/AIDS, 2010).

in China and India. As the effects of HIV/AIDS are felt across states and societies, there have been several key policy developments.

At the Ninth International Congress on AIDS in Asia and the Pacific in Bali 2009, Indonesian President Dr H. Susilo Bambang Yudhoyono identified four key policy responses needed to combat the spread of HIV/AIDS. The first area is leadership in effective and sustained multi-sectoral policies. He noted the establishment in 2006 of the National AIDS Commission in Indonesia (Komisi Nasional Penanggulangan AIDS) which reports directly to the President. The second area is the importance of community involvement. As HIV/AIDS spreads across states and societies, the communities it affects provide the network and agency to raise awareness, promote prevention strategies, and work with the government. The third area is the necessity of regional and international cooperation and recognizing the important role that UN has in the global policy response. Finally, the fourth area that was identified was the increased investment in the efforts to find a vaccine or a cure. This will necessarily include partnerships with both state and non-state actors from private businesses to government departments and civil society organizations.[22]

Across Asia and the Pacific region, there has been a 20 per cent reduction in new HIV infections since 2001 — from an estimated 450,000 to 360,000. However, there are almost two new HIV infections for every person who starts treatment, with expenditure on AIDS inadequate at an estimated one third of needed funds and international funding is falling, according to UNAIDS. At present 47 per cent of funds comes from international sources with 53 per cent coming from domestic sources. Notably, however, China, Malaysia, Pakistan, Samoa and Thailand fund the bulk of their HIV/AIDS policies from domestic resources.[23]

Policy Challenges

In Asia, an estimated 90 per cent of HIV resources for young people are focused on people with low risks of HIV infection, and as a result there are fewer resources for those most at risk. However, a significant issue is obtaining reliable data on those who are most at risk, as many in these categories face numerous challenges from discrimination to reluctance to engage with the surveys. Indeed, many in these groups do not identify themselves as a high risk category and so the programmes established to reach these communities often fail. Peer outreach programmes have offered a way to interact with these high risk groups but they remain small in number and size.[24] Across the Asian region, there are also notable social and cultural challenges to the HIV/AIDS epidemic. There are different religions from Roman Catholicism in the Philippines to Islam in Pakistan, both of which object to the use of condoms. It also varies by government type and department with the tensions in communist Vietnam approaching the HIV/AIDS epidemic through a "societal evil" lens but still promoting HIV/AIDS prevention programmes.[25]

Pandemic Preparedness

Over a decade ago, the first human cases of a disease caused by Avian Influenza A (H5N1) virus appeared in the Hong Kong Special Administrative Region, People's Republic of China, and six years ago it re-emerged to cause a highly lethal human disease in the Southeast Asian region. To date however, the H5N1 virus remains primarily a threat to poultry, having already caused tremendous losses to those involved in the poultry industry. Some years later, in 2002, the epidemic outbreak of SARS spread rapidly from China to several other countries and demonstrated that even infectious diseases with very low incidence but high mortality rates can generate significant economic, political and diplomatic fallout. Dengue Haemorrhagic Fever (DHF), first recognized in the Philippines in 1953, has recently been seen in India, Malaysia, Singapore, Indonesia, Vietnam, Cambodia and Sri Lanka. Additionally, food-borne parasitic infections are significant emerging public health problems in East Asia.

A combination of underlying eco-social determinants of disease provide prime hot-spots for emerging and re-emerging infectious diseases (ERIDs), whilst human migration patterns disperse vectors and viruses into non-endemic areas. Outbreaks of infectious diseases, including zoonoses, vector-borne diseases and drug-resistant pathogens, have been occurring more frequently and in new areas, with the potential of causing enormous socioeconomic hardship that extends beyond national borders. Indeed, with its large and dense population, Asia is at a high risk for ERIDs and has been a breeding ground for many new diseases over the past decade.

In November 2002, there was an outbreak of Severe Acute Respiratory Syndrome (SARS) in Foshan city, Guangdong province in Southern China, and within three months it had spread to Hong Kong. From then on it spread across Southeast Asia and was identified as creating human insecurity because it was a threat to the health and well-being of people. However, some warned against the consequences of framing health issues within the security discourse because it represented risks for national security or economic growth rather than global public health.[26] Indeed, this was an acknowledgment of how health security is understood or can be misappropriated. Rather human security and health security as a subset of it ensures that people's welling is at the centre of the response effort. From February to June 2003, SARS had infected about 8,300 people, causing 783 reported deaths in 28 countries by the time it was contained. The rapid spread of the disease highlighted to Asian states their populations' vulnerability to pandemics, illustrated the limitations to state pandemic response systems, and the need for cooperation across and between all stakeholders. These three tenets form the basis of defining a human security threat. Indeed, as the WHO Weekly Epidemiological Report in 2006 notes, there are four assessment criteria: will the event have a serious public health impact? Is the event unusual or unexpected? Does the event have the potential to spread internationally? Will the event result in the risk of restrictions to travel or trade?[27]

The most significant policy impact of the SARS pandemic was to highlight to policy-makers and the medical community writ large that the pandemic threat required a coordinated multisectoral approach, which was

Table 2.2

SARS Infections in Asia from 1 November 2002 to 31 July 2003

	Total Number of SARS Cases	Total Number of SARS Fatalities
China	5,327	349
China [SAR Hong Kong]	1,755	299
China [SAR Macao]	1	0
China [Taiwan]	346	37
India	3	0
Indonesia	2	0
Malaysia	5	2
Mongolia	9	0
Philippines	14	2
Republic of Korea	3	0
Singapore	238	33
Thailand	9	2
Vietnam	63	5
Total	7,775	729

Source: Adapted from WHO (2003).[28]

seen in Singapore with its establishment of a ministerial-rank task force to respond to the SARS outbreak. The power distributed to the ministerial task force cut across individual departments to decide policies to stem the SARS outbreak.[29] Indeed, the emerging trend continues to be through dialogue between the health, security and foreign policy communities,[30] leading to what is commonly referred to as a "whole-of-government" approach. In its essence this approach draws on the relevant stakeholders and institutional support to combat the threat, which oftentimes requires a complex network of interactions to adequately respond to the pandemic.

In recent years, considerable mounting pressure to develop early warning systems for ERIDs has indeed prompted noteworthy efforts among many nations. Accordingly, many industrialized and developing countries have mounted extensive pandemic preparedness efforts, which have evolved further with the introduction of the revised International Health Regulations (IHR) mentioned earlier and the Global Outbreak Alert and Response Network. Broadly speaking, the goals of national pandemic preparedness plans are to prevent and minimize the public health consequences of a pandemic, ensure that the economic consequences are limited, and maintain social stability for a speedy recovery.

Table 2.3
Pandemic Preparedness in Southeast Asia

	Description
Phase 1	No infections in humans are being caused by viruses circulating in animals.
Phase 2	Animal flu virus causes infection in humans, and is a potential pandemic threat.
Phase 3	Flu causes sporadic cases in people, but no significant human-to-human transmission.
Phase 4	Human-to-human transmission and community-level outbreaks.
Phase 5	Human-to-human transmission in at least two countries. Strong signal pandemic imminent.
Phase 6	Virus spreads to another country in a different region; global pandemic underway.
Post-peak	Pandemic activity appears to be decreasing though second wave possible.
Post-pandemic	Activity returns to normal, seasonal flu levels.

However, in the subsequent period of 2004–10, local, national, international and non-state actors have been engaged in a policy debate over how to best respond to future pandemics. In Asia, the Association of Southeast Asian Nations (ASEAN), the ASEAN Regional Forum and the ASEAN+3 countries are among the important actors in the health security agenda. There have been several regional initiatives for combating ERIDs, such as the ASEAN Task Force on H5N1, the Regional Framework for Control and Eradication of Highly Pathogenic Avian Influenza, ASEAN Agreement on Disaster Management and Emergency Response, and a regional working group known as the ASEAN Technical Working Group on Pandemic Preparedness and Response. Beyond ASEAN, there have also been collaborations with other non-ASEAN countries and international organizations such as the WHO. Health ministers from ASEAN member states signalled their commitment to (1) improving inter-sectoral communication between relevant authorities; (2) strengthening core capacities of surveillance and response systems; (3) allowing the transfer of technology for the production of antiviral medicines and influenza vaccines; (4) conducting logistical exercises to ensure effective and timely deployment of medicines and supplies in the event of a pandemic.

The Joint Ministerial statement also called upon international agencies such as the WHO to, when necessary, provide technical and financial help to deal with the crisis. In general, the regional mechanisms proposed and developed since the SARS outbreak have greatly facilitated information sharing among experts, helped address existing gaps in expertise, capacity and information, strengthened disease surveillance systems, and built hospital isolation units. It is clear that the achievements have been substantial, although gaps still remain. Importantly, while regional cooperation continues to grow, situational analyses suggest that profound governance, capacity and operational hurdles remain widespread and must now urgently be addressed.

HEALTH SECURITY AND POLICY: CHALLENGES AND OPPORTUNITIES

The Importance of Health Systems

Moving beyond the existing frameworks and mechanisms, health systems are at the heart of how individual countries, and the international community as a whole, respond to disease outbreaks. Local health systems often become rapidly overwhelmed, however, and too often fail to deliver care to those in greatest need in a comprehensive way and on an adequate scale. In order for the IHR and the global outbreak response system to be effective, every country must strengthen and maintain their respective health systems, since the effectiveness of international collaborations, partnerships and networks whose role it is to identify and respond to pandemic outbreaks depends on the alert and response capacities of the weaker health systems. If one looks at the key issues that affect the health security of states and societies in the region, the agenda for strengthening health systems in Asia is therefore critical.

Strong health care systems are created through continuous, long-term processes of economic change and political negotiation, and by the implementation of effective policies and management within the health sector. While the majority of the now developed countries had built up universal services from a patchwork of public, private profit-making and charitable providers, this challenge now exists for many developing countries. It requires technical information, political knowledge and sustained action.

Going Back to Basics: Six Building Blocks of Health Systems

Health systems are highly context-specific, and hence there is no single set of best practices that can be put forward as a model for improved perfor-mance. However, there are certain characteristics that define a strong and robust health system. These include service delivery; health workforce; information; medical products, vaccines, technologies and tools; health financing; and leadership and governance.

Enhancing these building blocks and managing their interactions is essential for effective targeting of the underlying barriers to health security. In seeking to attain global health security, states and other actors must grapple with challenges such as the inequitable distribution of resources that largely lead to widening gaps in health outcomes of developed and developing countries. In the developing world in particular, in addition to financial limitations, health systems also suffer from a shortage of human resources and weak supply chain management, poor information, an inability to scale-up interventions, crumbling infrastructures and poor access to health care for the most vulnerable. For example, at present there is an estimated shortage of 4.3 million doctors, midwives, nurses and support staff worldwide.

Increased efficiency and effectiveness can be achieved by ensuring standards and norms, enabling accountability and transparency through inter-national health law, facilitating rapid public-private responses and sharing available knowledge. Additionally, future agendas towards strengthening health systems should focus on socio-cultural aspects and the role of civil society organizations. Just as importantly, while pandemic preparedness frameworks and programmes have proliferated, metrics to test their effectiveness remain mostly based on subjective indicators. Continued monitoring and evaluation of the performance, from policy and strategy development to implementation are essential, and approaches must be adapted accordingly. Indeed, it is in the interests of stakeholders to find novel ways of testing operational readiness and strengthening successful systems, using research that is grounded in local realities.

Other resource gaps include capacity limitations for the surveillance, case investigations and treatments that are necessary in order to prevent the spread of diseases within the community. However, while externally funded capacity building efforts often reflect donor priorities, domestically supported programmes may be vulnerable to economic and political cycles; therefore capacity building efforts have often focused on near-term investments in physical infrastructure and equipment, but have somewhat failed to anticipate ongoing demands for quality control, quality assurance and continual workforce training. Hence there is an urgent need to focus on the human element of capacity building.

Surge and Surge Capacity

The concepts of surge and surge capacity form the cornerstone of pandemic preparedness and response. Surge capacity could be defined as the elasticity of a health system that enables it to expand quickly and cope with a surge in demand of services beyond usual levels. A disease outbreak will trigger the surge, leading to a rise in demand for both medical and non-medical services. It is important to control the surge (demand side), whilst maximizing the surge capacity of the system (supply side). Whilst globalization has increased the surge by enabling faster and easier spread of diseases, it has also increased the world's interdependence in terms of the goods and services that are indispensible for sustaining and maximizing surge capacity.

Optimizing the ability to control the surge and maximize the surge capacity may thus be possible through a proactive approach with an increased focus on prevention, strengthening government effectiveness and empowering local communities and civil society groups, who may play an important role in complementing an already stretched public health system. Effective civil society engagement can best be achieved by empowering health-promoting non-governmental, community-based and faith-based organizations via a free media. Furthermore, the ability of civil society to hold governments and other actors accountable should therefore be improved to enable sustained activism. Crucially, while capacity building in the health sector is vital, it must be matched by a strong capacity in education and other sectors, as well as in terms of overall governance.

Health Information

Research is a critical part of any effort to improve the world's health. In many developing countries, however, the benefits of health research are not optimized due to low investments, an absence of a culture of evidence-based decision-making and/or a lack of capacity. Moreover, inadequate resources for data collection and analyses mean that within Asia, several countries have a weak health information system that lacks vital registration data on births, deaths and other demographic information. Research for health can therefore make a major contribution, both to health and more generally to social development. International aid effectiveness could be amplified by ensuring that health research forms part of the total package in a manner that enhances national health information systems.

There is an urgent need for increased problem-based and evidence-based health policy planning, including spatio-temporal approaches that focus on disease dynamics and improved ways of setting priorities that direct resources toward the most critical challenges. Increased training for local scientists and public health practitioners in field epidemiology and laboratory methods is vital. Indeed, local research capacity strengthening is an important tool for developing local ownership and improving long-term sustainability of any health project. On a more cautious note, it is important to be aware that while translating evidence into policy is clearly vital, pandemic preparedness plans often assume that people will act rationally in a crisis, which cannot be counted upon in the event of a severe global pandemic.

A MULTI-SECTORAL APPROACH TO PANDEMIC PREPAREDNESS

Multi-sectoral pandemic preparedness is based upon the need to maintain optimum readiness for the government and the health sectors which, as a result of widespread interdependence between different parts of society, is impossible if other sectors remain unprepared. However, most so-called "multi-sectoral pandemic preparedness plans" are actually just health sector preparedness and national response plans, with little guidance on how to ensure the operational continuity of other sectors. Prolonged absenteeism in the agricultural sector, for example, could lead to a decrease in food production as a result of reduced manpower in harvesting and affect a nation's food security. Absenteeism may also result in an increase in demand for particular resources in the telecommunications, health protection and military sectors. Furthermore, the key to interrupting emerging pathogens is early detection of the disease as close to the source as possible. Approximately 60 per cent of recently-identified ERIDs affecting humans have been diseases of animal origins. Because these have affected humans as a result of close interactions between humans and livestock, veterinary expertise is essential. Strengthening capacity to detect and respond to zoonotic diseases hence requires enhanced partnerships and coordination between the ministries of agriculture and ministries of health within every host country — an added challenge for nascent surveillance systems.

Multi-Level Preparedness

All countries recognized the importance of a potential influenza pandemic and the government of each country has shown political will and support towards planning for a pandemic. To a certain extent, each has followed the general guidelines set out by the WHO, proposing measures for early containment on the basis that an original outbreak within their country is a likely scenario. This is true even for the Philippines (see Figure 2.1) which has, thus far, remained "bird-flu free". Within the countries, specific targets, such as strengthening influenza surveillance systems, have been set and work is currently being conducted to ensure that these targets are met in a timely fashion. Figure 2.1 shows a diagrammatic representation of the pandemic preparedness system in the Philippines.

As illustrated by the figure, the Philippine approach includes a system that is heavily reliant on community-based responses, via a reporting chain structure, of which the highest echelon is the National Avian Influenza Task Force while the lowest are local community members, for example poultry owners. Similarly, Thailand has developed a sustainable and integrated management system, termed an "incident command system", at various levels of government, the aim of which is to empower provincial and local authorities and to include the civil society as the primary force for early warning and monitoring.

Figure 2.1

**Task Forces and their Communications, Response and
Reporting Chain of Command**

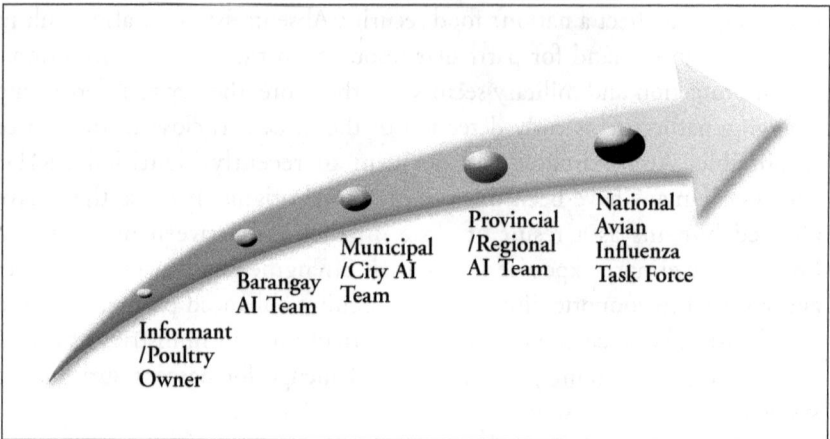

Source: Wiput Phoolcharoen, "Thailand's Pandemic Preparedness: Operations, Systems and Frameworks", in *Pandemic Preparedness in Asia*, edited by Mely Caballero-Anthony, RSIS Monograph No. 16 (Singapore: S. Rajaratnam School of International Studies, 2009).

Partnerships at Global, Regional and Local Levels

Most ASEAN countries such as Indonesia, Thailand, Vietnam, Cambodia, Malaysia and the Philippines are conscious of the need to engage civil society actors who maintain a strong presence at the grassroots level to improve education and awareness among the population. The involvement of civil societies and inclusion of local inputs are seen as vital. For example, Indonesia has a strong campaign from the faith-based organization, Muhammadiyah, in raising awareness with regards to improved hygiene practices, while in Thailand, non-governmental organizations (NGOs) and the Thai Red Cross Society are working towards empowering and training the community. Public relations and educational materials have also been developed in Thailand. Mercy Malaysia has conducted simulation exercises in partnership with the Malaysian government, the World Food Program and the National Security Council. The exercises simulated logistics situations involving quarantines and airport, port and ground security and transport. These examples demonstrate government-to-government partnerships under the ASEAN framework at the regional level, and also government partnerships with the WHO at the global level, showing both horizontal as well as top-down and bottom-up vertical approaches, respectively.

Improvement of Surveillance and Laboratory Capacity

All countries are aware of the need to strengthen surveillance and reinforce laboratory capacity in the region. Indonesia, Thailand, and particularly Singapore have made significant steps towards combining short-term and long-term actions. Indonesia, for instance, has developed the Integrated Epidemiological Surveillance Managing Virus System to control outbreaks in animals through means of bio-security, vaccination, compensation for culling of birds and long-term capacity building of health services. Thailand has systematically linked the animal and human health surveillance system and included the community, hospital, laboratory, and medical networks within the framework.

Attempts at Multi-Sectoral Planning

Some ASEAN member states have also made efforts to incorporate multi-sectoral pandemic preparedness planning. Indonesia has brought together a committee with members from seventeen ministries, the National Planning Agency, the army and the police. Thailand has adopted a broader disaster management framework that clearly prioritized pandemic influenza together with the management of other types of disaster such as floods, landslides and dangerous chemicals, by developing a sustainable and integrated system. These efforts are notable attempts at broadening the scope of pandemic preparedness as multi-sectoral planning requires the involvement of major stakeholders from health, agriculture, business and civil society sectors. It also requires substantial collaboration, communication and cooperation between the various actors in order to make it truly multi-sectoral, multi-disciplinary and holistic. In sharp contrast to this, Vietnam's strategy is focused more on preventive measures such as surveillance, improved hygiene, dissemination of information, vaccination, border quarantine and early containment, rather than on holistic preparedness. It boasts a two-pronged strategy with speed, transparency and high-level government commitment.

Simulation Exercises and Legal Frameworks

In addition to adopting these vital strategies, Indonesia, Malaysia and Singapore have also held preparedness simulation exercises in order to test out their plans. Indonesia issued the Presidential Instruction 1/2007 to relevant national institutions, including the army, for coordination of national and local pandemic preparedness plans. It has established a number of guidelines and protocols that were followed by local and national-level pandemic preparedness simulations exercises. This is important since collective behaviour may not be very rational during a crisis, and simulation exercises may help to evaluate and improve current plans. Similarly, the Philippines has issued legal mandates and local ordinances to ensure that the national and local preparedness plans are executed. However, the laws may be open to legal challenge if there is inadequate compensation given for the culling of birds.

Indeed, achievements have been substantial and, overall in the region, there has been a dramatic shift in attitudes towards pandemic preparedness. However, when one takes a closer and more analytical look, it becomes clear that the extent to which this applies at national, sub-national or local levels varies. Many challenges remain on the road ahead.

COMMON POLICY CHALLENGES

Variations in approaches to economic development and in the governing styles and structures of each country have resulted in several core distinctions among members of ASEAN regarding health and human security. Furthermore, systemic challenges include a profound lack of economic, technical and human resources, of inequitable allocations of such resources as well as of relevant grassroots level demographic and health data. In fact, perhaps it is for these reasons that several national plans did not provide adequate operational procedures for key stakeholders during each phase of the pandemic, resulting in a lack of clarity and coherence.

The Thai plan, for example, retained the format of a strategic framework rather than an operational guide and although the organizations responsible for achieving a specific goal were identified, precise operational tasks remained unclear and unaccountable, especially at the local level. Vietnam has recently experienced numerous shifts in pandemic preparedness approaches which may destabilize the system. Furthermore, the current framework appears to be reactionary rather than future-oriented, partly because pandemics are seen to be of socioeconomic and medical concern, but not a matter of national security.

Wide Geographical Area and Decentralized Authority

Indonesia is challenged both by its vast geographical disconnectedness and its decentralized geopolitical organization. There are a total of 440 districts with elected local governments, hence causing major challenges for administration, coordination and continuity of health care provision in crises. While the human population is approximately 220 million, it is unclear what the vast poultry population amounts to, particularly within the more at risk poultry sectors 3 and 4, or the small scale farms and backyard farms, respectively. Of the 33 provinces, 23 are endemic for avian influenza (AI) in poultry while 13 have had outbreaks within the human population. In the Philippines, 50 per cent of poultry comes from backyard raisers and problems arise amidst fragmented financing and compensation. In Cambodia, for example, there are accessibility barriers in reaching remote villages and little incentive for residents to report disease outbreak because of travel costs and lack of compensation for culled animals.

Stockpiling and Accessibility to Vaccines

Since stockpiling of antivirals at a level currently feasible would only provide coverage for a very small proportion of the population, tough questions remain about logistics for provision of antiviral drugs and regarding which groups within the population should or would receive these drugs as a priority. There is an inadequate vaccine manufacturing capacity in the region and to address the shortage, there is some possibility of setting up local production even though it is estimated that developing an antigenically matching vaccine could take six months, or longer. Few countries have defined priority groups for vaccination, such as health practitioners, the army and so on in their national plans.

Lack of Interconnectedness and Cross-Border Collaboration

Integrating pandemic preparedness and response into general emergency preparedness is also important, and the focus of all but Singapore was on situations involving outbreaks of H5N1 that originated within their borders, without thoroughly discussing measures to address an imported epidemic. This should include the possibility of AI being carried across borders by illegal migration of birds and/or humans. Lastly, there is still a lack of interconnectedness and cross-border collaboration within the region even with the international frameworks currently in place.

Larger Threat of Emerging Infectious Diseases (EIDs)

Faced with these challenges, it is sobering to hear the facts that more than 300 diseases have emerged in the past 70 years, a majority of which are the result of jumps from wild animal to human. Experts claim that outbreaks will increase as humans delve into ever-closer contact with wildlife and disease multipliers, such as environmental degradation and climate change, alter the life cycles of disease vectors. Meanwhile, older diseases are rapidly crisscrossing the planet as humans travel to more exotic and distant corners of the world.

Equitable Sharing of Virus Samples and Open Information

Indonesia raised the important issue of more equitable sharing of virus samples and open information. The WHO system of sharing influenza virus samples, Global Influenza Surveillance Network, has limited effectiveness as it obtains resources from developing countries but leaves them vulnerable to an influenza pandemic, thus placing emphasis on risk assessment at the expense of pandemic response. Furthermore, limited global production capacity for influenza vaccine is a serious challenge for developing countries, as they are likely to face an acute shortage of H5N1 vaccines — a challenge compounded by advanced vaccine orders placed by developed countries. With a maximum production capacity of 500 million dosages for a global population of 6.7 billion, an immense gap exists between demand and supply.

To address these limitations, the WHO has adopted Resolution 60.28 which requires WHO to "identify and propose ... frameworks and mechanisms that aim to ensure fair and equitable sharing of benefits ... taking strongly into consideration the specific needs of developing countries". At the Inter-Governmental Meeting (IGM) convened in December 2008 to implement the terms of the resolution, Member States committed to sharing influenza viruses and the benefits on an equal footing. The elements of the benefit sharing system are as follows: provision of diagnostic tests and materials; laboratory capacity building; regulatory capacity building; WHO antiviral stockpile; WHO pandemic influenza vaccines stockpile; access to vaccines for developing countries; technology transfer; and financial support.

The Way Forward

National Level

Pandemic preparedness activities take place within the context of national priorities, competing activities and limited resources. Joint approaches that foster closer multilateral cooperation and promote cross-sectoral participation of the government, policy, academic and civil society commuities will generate a more comprehensive, efficient and cost-effective strategy to prevent future crisis situations. Addressing additional common regional challenges, and finding optimized solutions, will help tackle not only the symptoms but also the underlying causes of pandemics. This should include increasing the focus on farming practices, environmental conservation, long-held lifestyle traditions, public misconceptions, media misrepresentations, poverty-line economics and novel compensation funds such as supplementary farm insurance. Plans and procedures should also be reassessed and updated as new technologies and increased information become available, and as the endemic status of infections alters.

Regional Level

In summary, ASEAN countries, predisposed due to social, economic, demographic, environmental and behavioural determinants of an outbreak, and because of their close geographical location to each other, have great incentives to work together to improve individual and combined strategies for preparedness. There may be a need to evaluate and streamline the regional framework to harmonize current approaches, although keeping in mind variations in local settings. For instance, there may be a need for the Mekong Basin Disease Surveillance (MBDS) system to be plugged into the ASEAN and the Global Outbreak Alert and Response Network (GOARN) surveillance frameworks since people move frequently across borders.

Although there seems to be no "one-size-fits-all" solution, national responses should be plugged into existing regional frameworks, which in turn represent international guidelines and protocols. There is currently a rising window of opportunity within pandemic preparedness activities that should be seized, in order to strengthen essential response capacities required for a growing number of public health emergencies.

The region would benefit from working towards a broader framework that does not just focus on pandemic preparedness, but on an EID framework or a disaster management framework. By doing so, all nations involved would be building up capacity for multi-sectoral preparedness not limited to pandemics but extending to mitigate the threat of other EIDs, natural disasters and other emergencies. This would optimize limited resources and is very relevant for ASEAN and Asia on the whole, considering the frequency of earthquakes, floods, cyclones, landslides and other similar events.

While effectiveness remains the key, the role of ethical and sustainable preparedness and response should guide the preparedness plans and governments ought to strive to include equity, efficiency, solidarity and liberty in all policies. Although the economic cost of these commitments cannot be underestimated, failure to do so may result in much greater social costs including the breakdown of health security for rich and poor alike.

Concluding, one should bear in mind that in any urgent or emergent public health situation, conflicting individual and population interests should be balanced. To assess and balance these competing interests and values, policy-makers can draw on sound ethical principles. Such an ethical approach does not provide a prescribed set of policies; instead it applies principles such as equity, utility, efficiency, liberty, reciprocity and solidarity, in light of local context and cultural values. Policy-makers can use these principles as a framework to assess and balance a range of interests and to ensure that overarching concerns, such as protecting human rights, are addressed. Any measures that limit individual rights and civil liberties should be shown to be necessary, reasonable, proportional, equitable, non-discriminatory and in full compliance with national and international laws.

In conclusion, it is clear that pandemic preparedness and, more broadly, global public health security have improved substantially over the past decade, albeit from a very low starting point. However, in spite of efforts to highlight the severity of pandemic diseases, national strategic goals remain somewhat unclear and underdeveloped. While the pandemic outbreaks in the 2000s have highlighted that governments are now both willing and able to report outbreaks, many nations, including some within the Southeast Asian region, have considerable and indeed expanding gaps between strategic focus and real-time surveillance, response and operational capacities, particularly in the animal health sector. Bridging this gap and going beyond discourse to action remains a monumental task which will require deeper institutionalism and a more integrated, multi-sectoral and comprehensive approach to pandemic preparedness and health security. This will undoubtedly improve the organization, resource management, technical guidance, capacity, monitoring, evaluation and overall mechanics of health care delivery and promote health and human security not only in Asia but across the world.

Notes

1   UNDP, *Human Development Report: New Dimensions of Human Security* (UNDP, 1994), available at <http://hdr.undp.org/en/reports/global/hdr1994/>.
2   Ibid.
3   Christian Enemark, "Is Pandemic Flu a Security Threat?" *Survival* 51, no. 1 (2009).
4   Tracey Churchill-Page, "The Global is the Local: Global Health in Southeast Asia", in *Culture, Religion and Identity in Southeast Asia*, edited by A.D.B. Cook (Cambridge Scholars Publishing, 2007).
5   Ibid.
6   Ibid.
7   D.P. Fidler, "Emerging Trends in International Law Concerning Global Infectious Disease Control", *Emerging Infectious Diseases* 9, no. 3 (2003).
8   Ibid.
9   Ibid.
10 GATT, Article XX[b] in Fidler (2003).
11 Muthiah Alagappa, *Comprehensive Security: Interpretations in ASEAN Countries* (Honolulu, Hawaii: International Relations Program, East-West Center of California, 1989).
12 Mely Caballero-Anthony, "SARS in Asia: Crisis, Vulnerabilities, and Regional Responses", *Asian Survey* 45, no. 3 (2005).
13 Desmond Ball, *The Council for Security Cooperation in the Asia-Pacific: Its Record and Prospects* (Canberra: Strategic and Defense Studies Centre, Australian National University, 2000).
14 CSCAP, *Memorandum No. 3: The Concepts of Comprehensive and Cooperative Security* (Kuala Lumpur: Institute of Strategic and International Studies, 1995).
15 Mely Caballero-Anthony, "SARS in Asia: Crisis, Vulnerabilities, and Regional Responses", *Asian Survey* 45, no. 3 (2005).

[16]   For discussion on the merits of human security as global security, see Ralph Pettman, "Human Security as Global Security: Reconceptualising Strategic Studies", *Cambridge Review of International Affairs* 18, no. 1 (2005).

[17]   UNAIDS, *HIV in Asia and the Pacific: Getting to Zero* (Geneva: UNAIDS, 2011), available at <http://www.unaids.org/en/media/unaids/contentassets/documents/unaidspublication/2011/20110826_APGettingToZero_en.pdf>.

[18]   Ibid.

[19]   International Crisis Group, *HIV/AIDS as a Security Issue*, Issues Report no. 1 (Washington, D.C./Brussels, 2001).

[20]   Colin McInnes and Simon Rushton, "HIV, AIDS and Security: Where Are We Now?" *International Affairs* 86, no. 1 (2010): 225–45.

[21]   UNAIDS, "UNAIDS Report on the Global AIDS Epidemic" (Geneva: UNAIDS, 2010), available at <http://www.unaids.org/globalreport/Global_report.htm> (accessed 11 October 2011).

[22]   H.S.B. Yudhoyono, "Sambutan Pembukaan the 9th International Congress on AIDS in Asia and Pacific (ICAAP)", Presidential webpage, 2009, available at <http://www.presidenri.go.id/index.php/pidato/2009/08/09/1202.html>.

[23]   UNAIDS, *HIV in Asia and the Pacific: Getting to Zero* (Geneva: UNAIDS, 2011), available at <http://www.unaids.org/en/media/unaids/contentassets/documents/unaidspublication/2011/20110826_APGettingToZero_en.pdf>.

[24]   Ibid.

[25]   D. Altman, "The Political Dimensions to HIV/AIDS Responses in Southeast Asia", *ASCI Research Report*, no. 5 (Melbourne, Australia: LaTrobe, 2008), available at <http://tlweb.latrobe.edu.au/humanities/profiles/ss/altman/asci-08.pdf>.

[26]   Colin McInnes and Kelley Lee, "Health, Security and Foreign Policy", *Review of International Studies* 32 (2006).

[27]   WHO, *Weekly Epidemiological Record*, no. 38, 2006, available at <http://www.who.int/wer/2006/wer8138.pdf>.

[28]   WHO, "Summary of Probable SARS Cases with Onset of Illness from 1 November 2002 to 31 July 2003", available at <http://www.who.int/csr/sars/country/table2004_04_21/en/index.html>.

[29]   Melissa Curley and Nicholas Thomas, "Human Security and Public Health in Southeast Asia: The SARS Outbreak", *Australian Journal of International Affairs* 58, no. 1 (2004).

[30]   Mely Caballero-Anthony, "Combating Infectious Diseases in East Asia: Securitization and Global Public Goods for Health and Human Security", *Journal of International Affairs* 59, no. 2 (2006).

References

Alagappa, Muthiah. *Comprehensive Security: Interpretations in ASEAN Countries.* Honolulu, Hawaii: International Relations Program, East-West Center of California, 1989.

Altman, D. "The Political Dimensions to HIV/AIDS Responses in Southeast Asia". *ASCI Research Report No. 5*. Melbourne, Australia: LaTrobe, 2008. Available at <http://tlweb.latrobe.edu.au/humanities/profiles/ss/altman/asci-08.pdf>.

Ball, Desmond. *The Council for Security Cooperation in the Asia-Pacific: Its Record and Prospects*. Canberra: Strategic and Defense Studies Centre, Australian National University, 2000.

Caballero-Anthony, Mely. "Combating Infectious Diseases in East Asia: Securitization and Global Public Goods for Health and Human Security". *Journal of International Affairs* 59, no. 2 (2006).

———. "SARS in Asia: Crisis, Vulnerabilities, and Regional Responses". *Asian Survey* 45, no. 3 (2005).

Churchill-Page, Tracey. "The Global is the Local: Global Health in Southeast Asia". In *Culture, Religion and Identity in Southeast Asia*, edited by A.D.B Cook. Cambridge Scholars Publishing, 2007.

CSCAP. *Memorandum No. 3: The Concepts of Comprehensive and Cooperative Security*. Kuala Lumpur: Institute of Strategic and International Studies, 1995.

Curley, Melissa and Nicholas Thomas. "Human Security and Public Health in Southeast Asia: The SARS Outbreak". *Australian Journal of International Affairs* 58, no. 1 (2004).

Enemark, Christian. "Is Pandemic Flu a Security Threat?" *Survival* 51, no. 1 (2009).

Fidler, D.P. "Emerging Trends in International Law Concerning Global Infectious Disease Control". *Emerging Infectious Diseases* 9, no. 3 (2003).

International Crisis Group. *HIV/AIDS as a Security Issue*. Issues Report no. 1. Washington, D.C./Brussels, 2001.

McInnes, Colin and Kelley Lee. "Health, Security and Foreign Policy". *Review of International Studies* 32 (2006).

McInnes, Colin and Simon Rushton. "HIV, AIDS and Security: Where Are We Now?" *International Affairs* 86, no. 1 (2010): 225–45.

Pettman, Ralph. "Human Security as Global Security: Reconceptualising Strategic Studies". *Cambridge Review of International Affairs* 18, no. 1 (2005).

UNAIDS. *HIV in Asia and the Pacific: Getting to Zero*. Geneva: UNAIDS, 2011. Available at <http://www.unaids.org/en/media/unaids/contentassets/documents/unaidspublication/2011/20110826_APGettingToZero_en.pdf>.

———. "UNAIDS Report on the Global AIDS Epidemic". Geneva: UNAIDS, 2010. Available at <http://www.unaids.org/globalreport/Global_report.htm> (accessed 11 October 2011).

UNDP. *Human Development Report: New Dimensions of Human Security*. UNDP, 1994. Available at <http://hdr.undp.org/en/reports/global/hdr1994/>.

Yudhoyono, H.S.B. "Sambutan Pembukaan the 9th International Congress on AIDS in Asia and Pacific (ICAAP)". Presidential webpage, 2009. Available at <http://www.presidenri.go.id/index.php/pidato/2009/08/09/1202.html>.

3

FOOD

Irene A. Kuntjoro, Sofiah Jamil and
Arpita Mathur

The global food price shocks in 2007/2008 have demonstrated the need to effectively address food insecurity in Southeast Asia — both at the national and regional level. This chapter goes beyond issues of supply and demand of food, and provides greater insight into the role of Human Security in understanding the issue of food security in a holistic manner. The rising price of rice in recent years has caught the attention of both people and policy-makers in the ASEAN region. According to the Asian Development Bank, Indonesia and Vietnam are amongst the Asian countries that have experienced double digit food price inflation during the 2007–08 food price crisis. Needless to say, food price inflation has also been on the rise in their neighbouring countries as well. At the time, global stocks of major cereals fell significantly, showing the growing disparity between production and consumption. With the stock-to-use ratios at their lowest for rice in 2006 and wheat in 2007. While stocks have improved since the food price crisis, they remained at 400 million metric tonnes in 2010 as compared to 547 million metric tonnes of grain in 1999.[1] The impact of this on the region has been crippling as rice is considered as a primary commodity — both economically and socially — in Southeast Asia. It distinguishes itself from other commodities such as corn and wheat that are considered to have "multi-end-use". For many Asian countries, rice has no substitute in many diets. This is reinstated in the fact that Asia was noted as both the producer and consumer of approximately 96 per cent of the world's rice in 2009/10 by the U.S.

Department of Agriculture.[2] Countries like Vietnam and Thailand are the top two largest rice exporters in the world in 2010/11, whereas the Philippines was listed as the world's top importer in the world rice trade in 2010/11.[3]

While the functions of the ASEAN member states may differ, one factor remains constant even after the 2007–08 global food crisis, which is that the poor and marginalized are the worst affected. This is significant in ASEAN member states as the overwhelming majority of its member states are developing countries. However it should also be remembered that the issue of food security is not new but rather has been re-ignited due to the high food prices. While these price shocks may be useful in highlighting the urgency of the issue and hopefully spur governments to act responsibly and effectively, the issue of food security must be addressed holistically, encompassing not just matters of demand and supply of food, but broader human security aspects such as health and environmental concerns.

WHAT IS FOOD SECURITY?

The concept of Food Security has evolved considerably over the last three decades. Initially, the food security framework emphasized an economic approach in which food was seen as a commodity. This was evident during the 1974 World Food Summit where food security was defined as the "availability at all times of adequate world food supplies of basic foodstuffs to sustain a steady expansion of food consumption and to offset fluctuations in production and prices".[4] Concerns raised in this regard are — transitory food insecurity (cyclical/seasonal such as rice gaps during "lean season") and temporary food insecurity (unpredictable shocks, natural or man-made disasters).

However, this definition, which indicated the role of maintaining just the supply of food resources, gradually evolved to include demand-side factors as well as the extent to which these demands are met. The principle of "Freedom from Want" — as espoused by Prof Amartya Sen, co-chair of the UN Commission for Human Security — also received more emphasis in this regard, as it noted the importance of development in ensuring the security of the individual. In addition to this, the 1994 Human Development Report[5] made mention of food security as one of the seven pillars of ensuring human security. It was only in 1996 during the World Food Summit in Rome, where the definition of food security reflected a truly holistic approach to the problem. According to the Food and Agricultural Organisation (FAO),

Food Security "[is] a situation that exists when all people, at all times, have physical, social and economic access to sufficient, safe and nutritious food that meets their dietary needs and food preferences for an active and healthy life."[6]

While the definition is holistic and takes into account the various needs of an individual, it is also much more complex and tedious to achieve. According to Figure 3.1, it is seen that at the household level, the narrow economic approach of food security is a subset of the larger and more comprehensive approach that includes health and environmental among other concerns. Gross et al. noted that the difficulty in addressing the problem occurs when the link between a causal factor of malnutrition and the nutritional status is less direct, wherein more time is required to improve the situation.[7] This therefore raises problems faced by governments in coordinating policies at different levels and ministries in trying to address the problem.

Figure 3.1
Conceptual Framework of Nutrition Security at Household

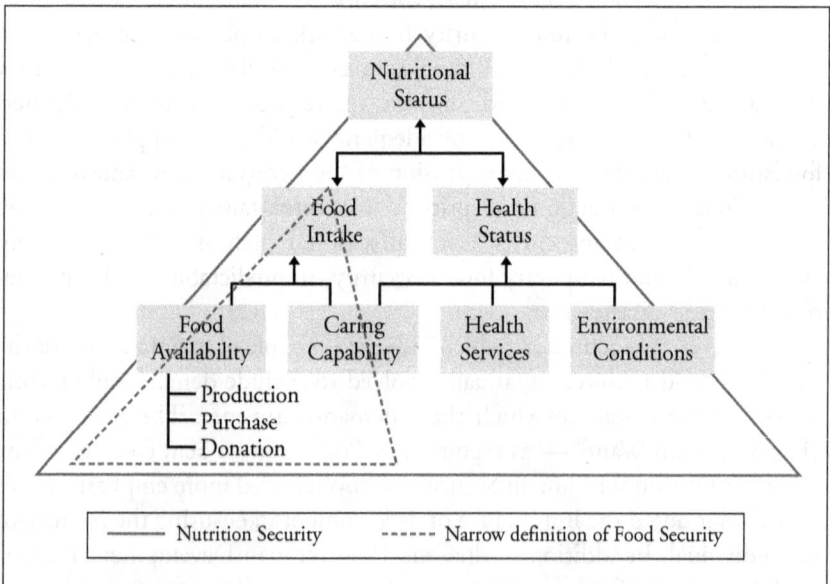

Source: Extracted from Rainer Gross, Hans Schoeneberger, Hans Pfeifer, and Hans-Joachim A. Preuss, "Four Dimensions of Food and Nutrition Security: Definitions and Concepts", April 2000, available at <http://www.unsystem.org/scn/Publications/SCNNews/scnnews20.pdf>.

This is further complicated by the range of issues that have contributed to rising food prices such as (1) higher fuel prices; (2) the demand for biofuels as an alternative energy source, which has put a strain and competition on the use of agricultural lands for food and cash crops; (3) the increasing demand for food by major developing countries such as China and India and; (4) weather related disasters that have destroyed resources for the production of food crops.

Food insecurity, as a result of high food prices, has several repercussions on other aspects of human security. Most significant is the fact that food insecurity threatens individuals' survival, especially the poor and marginalized. Soaring food prices has a significant weakening impact to their purchasing power. According to Robert Zoellick, President of the World Bank, there is no margin for survival in regions where food comprises from half to three quarters of household purchasing power. Asia is home to two-thirds of the world's poor, for whom food takes up 30 to 50 per cent of their household budget. High food prices could also threaten to reverse the gains in poverty reduction in the Asia-Pacific region, and thereby, undermine the global fight against poverty. International organizations such as the ADB and FAO have noted that if high food prices persist, the Millennium Development Goal of halving poverty by 2015 could be jeopardized.[8]

Furthermore, Southeast Asian countries are developing countries with a large trend of urbanization that has created wider disparities between the urban and rural population. Not only would the rise in food prices have adverse impacts on the poor rural populations, but it would also raise the likelihood of increased rural-urban migration, as many flock to the cities in hope of better livelihood opportunities. Such trends are evident worldwide. According to a survey conducted by the IFAD, rural families are sending their children to the cities or abroad to look for work in ever greater numbers due to the dire need to support their rural relatives. In doing so, these poor rural children may run the risk of further jeopardizing their own security — such as falling prey to human traffickers, as is the case in various parts of Southeast Asia.

Food insecurity also has grave implications for public health. The lack of food would give rise to increased incidents of malnutrition, which could exacerbate the spread of infectious diseases — such as diarrhoeal diseases and acute respiratory diseases — especially in developing countries. This would inevitably affect the productivity levels of the populations. As seen in Figure 3.1, the need to effectively engage public health services would be essential to support efforts in addressing food security, as the latter requires a multidisciplinary approach to the problem.

From the perspective of state security, food security also has implications on their political stability, both as a cause and an effect. Food security can be jeopardized by the lack of political or social stability. Likewise, food insecurity can lead to political and social instability and, in turn, a regime's survival. The food riots in Indonesia and the Philippines are prime examples of this in the ASEAN region. Many Asian governments nevertheless recognize food security as an essential element of their national security. This is reflected in their protectionist agricultural policies such as securing new agreements on imports, increasing the budget to boost rice production and also curbing rice exports and other policies that reflect a sense of "national vulnerability" towards the availability and access to food supplies.

In the Philippines, for example, the government mobilized the military to guard the distribution of cheap rice to rice distribution stations and poorer areas of Manila and ordered authorities to charge rice hoarders with economic sabotage, a crime that carries a life sentence. This clearly reflects the significance of food security as a political issue, and to a further extent, as a matter of regime survival.

Apart from its implications on domestic stability, food security could destabilize regional security. The policy to curb food exports in order to secure national food supply in one country could have a negative impact on other countries. An example was the proposal by Thailand's Prime Minister Samak Sundaravej on 30 April 2008 of an Organization of Rice Exporting Countries, as rice was seen as a political threat to the region as it might hamper the economic cooperation built among ASEAN countries but this was later dropped because the countries involved were unlikely to be able to coordinate their prices or control farmers' production.[9]

Food Security as Human Security in ASEAN

The soaring prices and its effects (as mentioned above) also threaten the progress towards the Millennium Development Goals in halving the poverty rate by 2015. Jonathan Pincus, chief economist for the UN Development Programme (UNDP) in Hanoi argued similarly that the gains made in meeting the UN Millennium Development Goals are under threat as higher rice prices will certainly mean a number of households that had risen above the poverty line will fall back below it.[10]

While some ASEAN governments claim to have the problem under control at the macro level — via securing domestic food supply and price, especially rice commodity — the problem that requires greater attention is ensuring proper access to food for a large percentage of the population that cannot afford it. In Indonesia, despite the government's efforts to reduce poverty following the crises in 1997–98, over 50 per cent of the population still live on less than US$2 per day and an estimation of 37 million people live below poverty line. The situation is similar in the Philippines, where 68 million people live on less than $2 per day and over 50 per cent of the population in the region is living below the national poverty line of 60 cents per person per day.

The spiking price of rice also threatens the Accelerated Hunger-Mitigation Programme (AHMP) of the Philippines government, which seeks to address both the supply and demand side by increasing food production and food delivery while at the same time putting more money into people's pockets. The high prices have also forced the government to scale down efforts to address malnutrition among children.

There also seems to be a vicious cycle where chronic poverty — the main factor contributing to the lack of food accessibility and malnutrition — has also resulted in slow human development and poor health and living conditions. Apart from the lack of food, the limited access to safe water, proper sanitation and health services are prime contributors to the levels of malnutrition. Since 1990, ASEAN has been home to about 80 million undernourished people, with the bulk of them residing in Vietnam, Indonesia, Thailand and Philippines (as seen from Table 3.1).

Table 3.1
Undernourished People in ASEAN
(millions)

	1990–92	1995–97	2001–03
Brunei	0.0098	0.0093	0.0117
Cambodia	4.4	5.4	4.6
Indonesia	16.4	11.8	13.8
Laos	1.2	1.3	1.2
Malaysia	0.5	na	0.6
Myanmar	4	3.1	2.7
Philippines	16.2	15.4	15.2
Thailand	16.8	13.7	13.4
Vietnam	20.6	16.7	13.8
Total	80.1	67.4	65.3

* Statistics on Singapore unavailable.
Source: FAO, Food Security Statistics, by Country, available at <http://www.fao.org/faostat/foodsecurity/Cous_en.htm> (last updated 3 March 2006).

This seems somewhat ironic as most of these countries are prime producers of rice in the region. Half of Cambodia's population (in 1990) was undernourished, with its neighbours trailing not too far behind (as seen in Table 3.2).

Rising food prices thereby only serves to exacerbate the situation by putting a strain on the poor's expenses. To ensure sufficient levels of food, many poor families opt to either spend less on other essentials, such as healthcare and education, or resort to "stinting", which is the act of buying cheaper (and likely less nutritious) food products.

This situation is amplified in regions that have poor infrastructure or have been destroyed by the calamity of natural disasters. The increasing incidents of weather related disasters such as floods and droughts, as a result of climate change, would put a further strain on states' emergency response capacities and their ability to adapt to changing climates — some of which have been insufficient to begin with.

In the case of Myanmar, the level of food insecurity continues. In the aftermath of effects Cyclone Nargis that hit southern Myanmar it is estimated that about 924,000 people needed food assistance until the November 2008 harvest, while around 300,000 needed relief until April

Table 3.2
Proportion of Populations that Are Undernourished in ASEAN
(percentage)

	1990–92	1995–97	2001–03
Brunei	4	3	3
Cambodia	43	46	33
Indonesia	9	6	6
Laos	29	28	21
Malaysia	3	<2.5	3
Myanmar	10	7	5
Philippines	26	22	19
Thailand	30	23	21
Vietnam	31	23	17

* Statistics on Singapore unavailable.

Source: FAO, Food Security Statistics, by Country, available at <http://www.fao.org/faostat/foodsecurity/Cous_en.htm> (last updated 3 March 2006).

2009. According to the Post-Nargis Joint Assessment (PONJA), 42 per cent of all food stocks were destroyed and 55 per cent of families only had stocks for one day or less.[11]

Beyond National Response

According to the FAO, several initiatives have been made by individual member states in ASEAN to ameliorate the effects of the high prices (as seen in Table 3.4). However, national responses are hardly enough as there may be a clash of interests, which would impede development and the overall security in the region. Regional mechanisms are therefore vital to ensure that states are headed towards the same goal without jeopardizing the security of its neighbour.

Food security has gained more political weight and become the focal point for discussion and cooperation as a non-traditional security issue. In the ASEAN Ministerial Meeting in Singapore on 21 July 2008, ministers agreed that rising food prices posed a serious challenge to the region, which was the beginning of food security significantly making its way up the policy agenda. They also reaffirmed the importance of regional and international efforts in addressing the issue of having access to adequate and reliable supply of staple foods and stable prices. In 1979 ASEAN took action concerning food security in the region by agreeing to an ASEAN Food Security Reserve Agreement. Under the ASEAN+ 3 framework, ASEAN has implemented two food security projects namely the East Asia Rice Reserve (EAERR) and the ASEAN Food Security Information System, the latter which was a result of the first Strategic Plan of Action (SPA) on ASEAN Cooperation in Food, Agriculture and Forestry (1999–2004). This plan was to be consistent with the first phase of the Hanoi Plan of Action to implement the ASEAN Vision 2020. In reviewing the progress of the SPA (1999–2004), a research project commissioned by the ASEAN Australia Development Cooperation Programme (AADCP) was undertaken.

This study alongside consultations and meetings of ASEAN officials concluded that the overall ASEAN Cooperation in Food, Agriculture and Forestry has made considerable progress in accordance to the stated objectives. The review also concluded that the current strategic trusts, as stated in the SPA (1999–2004), were still consistent and relevant with the trends and issues for cooperation then led to the adoption of the SPA on ASEAN Cooperation in Food, Agriculture and Forestry (2005–10).

Most recently, states in the region agreed to the ASEAN Integrated Food Security (AIFS) Framework and Strategic Plan of Action on Food Security in the ASEAN region (SPA-FS) 2009–13 aims to increase food production, reduce post-harvest losses, promote conducive market and trade for agriculture commodities and inputs, ensure food stability, promote availability and accessibility to agriculture inputs and operationalize regional food emergency relief arrangements.[12] While there is significant added value in these multilateral agreements to enhance cooperation in the region, there still remain gaps and challenges in implementing these agreements across the region.

The Way Forward

As mentioned at the World Summit on Food Security in 2009, the means to address the challenges to food security should be tailored to fit a country's specific needs. Especially by bearing in mind that the issue of food security does not stand alone, as it is a major determinant of nutritional status that relates to other aspect of human security such as health and the environment. One option for ASEAN is to strategize its role by assisting countries to fulfil its food security and at the same time creating conducive regional trade on food.

Another avenue for ASEAN to pursue as a collective is to effectively utilize the Agreement on the ASEAN Food Security Reserve as a framework for regional emergency food aid. With the high level of inflation that threatened food security in the region, this agreement could provide a safeguard that encourage ASEAN states to cooperate in overcoming emergency food supply deficits. As it has been discussed above, in a state of emergency, states will exert any policies that will improve their own food security that oftentimes is at the expense of their neighbouring countries' food security. This situation could destabilize regional security. Therefore effectively utilizing this agreement can coordinate ASEAN states to overcome their food insecurity by avoiding negative impacts to overall regional security.

Likewise, the SPA has provided an avenue that will pave a way to more effective planning of food production and trade in the region. When this is implemented well, ASEAN is in a position to assist its member states by providing an ASEAN food security database and information that could benefit the region in two ways. First, it encourages the increase of food and agriculture production of member states in order to reach self-sufficiency and at the same time share information and analysis on other member states' food security policies as well as investment on food production in the region in order to create a positive regional food trade. The SPA is an venue for sharing of agricultural technology in order to support agricultural state-sufficiency.

Lastly, the ASEAN Community is a gateway to further galvanize and synchronize initiatives from various ministries (such as health, environment, agriculture and trade) to effectively address the issue of food security. Empowering the ASEAN Community is expected to alleviate the risk of liberalization of food that can disrupt food security. Sharing information on agricultural technology, investment, and also policies could help each member states to set up food security policies that suit them best. Moreover, ASEAN Community could also be a framework to maintain conducive economic cooperation on food liberalization.

While Southeast Asia as a whole still seems to fair rather well compared to Asia more broadly in addressing poverty and food security (see Table 3.3), the issue of food security still needs to be carefully addressed in the region. With a number of developing countries residing in the region, the problem of food security becomes a pertinent element of human security as it is closely related with issues of individual survival, poverty, malnutrition, health and the environment. These issues, themselves, have the potential to generate a ripple effect on neighbouring countries. While it is undeniable that the issue of food security is complex and has no immediate solution, it is hoped that ASEAN states further garner and strengthen their political will to reduce the adverse impact on their people. Effectively utilizing the regional initiatives and mechanisms, would be the first step.

FOOD PRICE RISE AND ITS CONSEQUENCES

There has been at once a speedy and simultaneous rise in prices for all food crops — soyabeans, corn, wheat, rice and oilseeds — even though prices have fallen from their 2008 peak. According to the FAO (2010) "Food Outlook — Global Market Analysis 2010", the cost of a typical food basket is about 80 per cent higher than it was in 2002–04. While the impact of spiralling food prices varies across countries as well as social groups, some common outcomes can easily be delineated, more so amongst vulnerable groups which face universal problems arising from poverty and social systems.

Table 3.3

Policy Measures taken by Governments to Reduce the Impact of Soaring Prices in 2007/8

| | Consumer oriented | | | | | | | Producer oriented | | Trade oriented | | |
| | Tax | Social | | | Market | | | Production Support | Market Management | Import | Export | |
	Taxes/ customs	Food assistance	Food subsidies	Safety net & other	Price controls	Release stocks	Food procurement & other	Producer credit & other	Minimum producer prices & other	Import tariffs & other	Quantitative export control	Export price control & tax measures
Afghanistan	✓								✓			
Azerbaijan			✓					✓		✓		
Bangladesh					✓						✓	
Cambodia						✓	✓				✓	
China	✓							✓		✓	✓	
India									✓		✓	✓
Indonesia			✓		✓			✓	✓	✓	✓	✓
Iran (Islamic Republic of)										✓	✓	
Jordan	✓											
Kazakhstan												
Kyrgyzstan											✓	✓
Malaysia					✓	✓		✓	✓			
Mongolia	✓								✓			
Nepal									✓		✓	
Pakistan			✓					✓		✓		
Philippines			✓					✓	✓	✓		✓
Republic of Korea									✓			
Saudi Arabia		✓										
Sri Lanka					✓							
Syrian Arab Republic				✓								
Thailand						✓						
Vietnam											✓	

Source: Food and Agricultural Organisation (FAO), July 2008, Crop Prospects and Food Situation, No. 3, available at <http://www.fao.org/docrep/010/ai470e/ai470e05.htm> (accessed 23 November 2012).

Table 3.4

Index of Projected Real Food Crop Prices (2004 = 100)

	2007	2008	2009	2010	2015
Maize	139	175	165	155	148
Wheat	154	215	191	166	140
Rice	130	243	208	183	160
Soyabeans	119	156	147	139	115
Soyabean oil	136	187	173	160	110
Sugar	133	157	167	176	182

Source: World Bank (2008*a*, p. 3).

Individual Level

At the individual level, a hike in food basket bills translates into different impacts on constituent members of a family. In most cases, individuals falling into the at-risk bracket are women and girls. There is a domino effect with lifelong impact on children born to expectant and lactating mothers who go through food deprivation. Older children are also likely to be impacted if there is a need to divert funds from education and preventive healthcare to food for sustenance. Every individual from the lower-income group who has to compromise on the number of meals and a nutritious diet (quality of food grains in their diet becomes lower) due to higher cost of food is on the receiving end. This in turn translates into increasing physical vulnerability to diseases. Socially, this also means early age marriages for girls, for instance, in parts of South Asia where they are considered a "burden" on the family. In extreme cases, individuals might resort to unlawful and criminal activities. A recent NDTV news report from a village in Madhya Pradesh (India) is perhaps witness to such "crimes of compulsion" — a daily wage tribal labourer was pushed to commit theft of a sack of wheat from his neighbour to which he remarked, "There was nothing to eat, I stole in desperation." All these consequences of the food crisis will coalesce to increase the number of food-insecure individuals, that is, those consuming less than the nutritional target of 2,100 calories a day as recommended by the United States Department of Agriculture in 2010. The poor fall further into the mire of poverty.

Household Level

Food security of the household as a unit relies on variables such as price of food consumed, income and size of the family. Income in turn is affected by other factors such as taxes payable to the government. The impact of the food crisis encompassed compromises on the dietary intake of women and girls, in the form of an overall less nutritious and diversified diet, and diversion of funds from sectors such as sanitation, education, clean water and health. An International Food Policy Research Institute (IFPRI) study entitled "Global Food Crises: Monitoring and Assessing Impact to Inform Policy Responses" notes that much also depended on the kind of household analysed.[13] While a food-selling household might actually gain from a price rise, the hardest hit were food-buying households, whose income might not have kept pace with the price rise. Impoverishment and the compelling need for food — even though it had become more expensive — might also lead poor households to sell off assets such as houses, cattle and even their land (which increases in value giving them greater incentive to sell with rise in food prices) to feed the family. In many cases, households also obtained loans from moneylenders at high rates of interest, thus entering the vicious circle of poverty and debt. Indebtedness has often led poor farmers to commit suicide, leaving families without an earning member. This situation was reported in East Kenya, where nearly 2,000 farmers committed suicide in the wake of poor harvests caused by drought. Some even killed their families to save them from suffering after their land was taken away.[14]

National Level

At the national or state level, several challenges emerge. Of course, the first direct effect can be seen in the rise of domestic prices of food in tandem with a global increase in prices. In the case of food exporting countries which may impose export bans to secure their own markets, there is less revenue earned. Governments will also have to deal with the increased costs of developing social security mechanisms and bolstering existing ones to cushion the impact of rising food prices on the population. The ordeal for developing, low-income and food importing countries will be far greater, as they have to grapple with an inflated import bill. There is an overall decline in the quality of human resource available in the country due to reduction in critical inputs such as robust health and literacy. Social unrest and demonstrations stemming from high food prices disturbed smooth governance in many places from Bangladesh to Indonesia. There was also an augmented tendency towards migration to cities and urban areas following landlessness.

THE 2008 FOOD CRISIS

The period up to the last decade (apart from 1973–75) was relatively favourable in terms of food pricing, in keeping with the positive impact of the Green Revolution which began in the 1950s. The beginning of the 2000s, however, brought about a gradual hike in food prices which accelerated around 2006. The crisis which surfaced around 2005 started with an increase in the prices of wheat. This was followed by a rise in price of maize, and then rice. Similarly, prices of dairy products, poultry and beef also shot up. The magnitude of the crisis is shown in an United Nations Conference on Trade and Development (UNCTAD) G-24 Discussion Paper which stated that wheat prices increased 127 per cent and rice a whopping 170 per cent, making a cumulative increase of 83 per cent in global food prices.[15] According to FAO (2009) estimates in "The State of Food Insecurity in the World 2009", rising food prices and high unemployment have pushed the number of undernourished to a pinnacle of 1.02 billion in 2009.

What multiplied the recent debacle manifold was the global financial crisis. Not only did the crisis shrivel the resources which could otherwise have been pumped into the agricultural sector, but rising unemployment and reduction in wages also clearly diminished the already limited capacity of the poor to sustain their livelihood. Remittances from migrant workers to their home countries also fell. South Asian countries have high dependence on these remittances as do countries such as the Philippines where as many as 17 per cent of households survive on them. Joachim von Braun (2008a) of IFPRI succinctly noted, "Although the food and financial crises developed from different underlying causes, they are becoming intertwined in complex ways through their implications for financial and economic stability, food security, and political security."[16] The ones suffering were developing countries which faced high domestic food price inflation due to their economies being increasingly interwoven with the international economy.

The Drivers of the 2008 Food Crisis

This begs the larger question of what pushed the world to the brink of such a catastrophe. Before attempting to delineate the drivers, it would be imperative to mention that not only are these drivers many and complicated, but analysts have also allocated diverse weightage to each one of them. Some basic issues such as population growth and changes in consumption patterns are commonly agreed upon, but there were other specifics painting the picture red. Some of the major drivers of the price rise are enumerated below.

The first critical factor was a rise in oil and energy prices, which had an impact in primarily two ways. One, both are essential components of fertilizers which ended up absorbing the cost hike, and two, they are also an integral part of the mechanized agriculture system as well as the food processing and transportation systems of today. The moment this increase in production costs of agricultural products occurred there was an automatic transfer of costs to food commodities.

There is also the related factor of increasing demand for biofuels, also known as agro-fuels, spurred by the ever-increasing cost of fuels such as petroleum. Biofuels are primarily derived from agricultural products such as grains and oilseeds, for example, maize is used for the production of ethanol and palm oil for diesel. Other food crops also used to produce biofuels include sugarcane, soya and canola. Usage of crops for fuel results in both less land and crops for food. The U.S. and the European Union (E.U.) have been tagged as culprits by analysts in such diversion of crops for fuel. Both have subsidies and tax incentives in place for the production of biofuels. There have been estimates pointing towards the possibility of nearly one-third of U.S. corn production being diverted towards production of ethanol over the next decade. Considering that the U.S. is both the largest producer and exporter of corn, this would have an impact on the maize available for consumption as food as well as the price of this corn.

The third factor to which price rise can be attributed is an overall decline in the growth rate of agricultural production. An UNCTAD discussion paper cites the fact that the annual growth rate of production of aggregate grains and oilseeds was 2.2 per cent per year in the period 1970–90, falling to about 1.3 per cent thereafter, with predictions for 2009–17 standing at 1.2 per cent.[17] Apart from this, there are problems stemming from natural calamities, deforestation, less cultivable land due to development, and construction.

Speculation in financial markets and hoarding within states due to corrupt practices have had an impact on the price rise as well. Due to the financial crisis on the global front, speculators found it more comforting to turn to commodities which were experiencing rising prices. Climate change and natural disasters have contributed directly towards the problem. For example, in Australia, there were unusually high temperatures and forest fires. Similarly, the cyclones Sidr and Nargis wreaked havoc in Bangladesh and Myanmar respectively. According to Oxfam Canada in 2008, Cyclone Sidr killed over 1 million livestock, destroyed shrimp enclosures and decimated 2 million acres of crops. Financial speculation and hoarding when combined with poor stocks of food grains have had a cumulative effect on price rise.[18]

Domestic barriers put in place by different governments at the national level — as a result of the price rise and as a means to "secure" domestic markets — have had an unfavourable impact on the already spiking prices. Countries such as India, Pakistan, Vietnam and Russia responded to the crisis by imposing export restrictions on grains such as rice. According to a World Bank working paper by Donald Mitchell in 2008 which cites the United States Department of Agriculture (USDA), there was a noticeable and distinct increase in rice prices following the Indian and Vietnamese bans. Such bans led to less supply worldwide. There was also panic buying by countries such as Hong Kong and Vietnam. The Philippines imported 1.3 million tons of rice in January–April 2008, which was more than they had imported in the whole of 2007. Hoarding of food grains only added to the problem.[19]

Changing food consumption patterns all over the world, and especially amongst countries such as China and India, have also had an impact on food prices. There is an increasing demand for meat and poultry amongst the growing middle-class, which in turn means an added demand for commodities such as soyabeans and corn used to feed these animals. The fact that it takes as much as 7 kilogrammes of grain to produce 1 kilogramme of beef explains the phenomenon.

Finally, the devaluation of the US dollar at the time of the food crisis contributed to an increase in food prices. There was also overall less aid and investment at the international level as economies were hard hit by the financial crisis.

IMPACT OF THE CRISIS ON ASIA

According to the FAO (2008*b*) "The State of Food Insecurity in the World 2008" statistics on the number of additional undernourished in the world as a result of rising prices, it was evident that in regional terms, besides sub-Saharan Africa, Asia was the most impacted, with an additional 41 million people going below the hunger threshold. The Asia-Pacific region is home to over half of the world's population and an unenviable 63 per cent of the world's undernourished.[20] This was in part because most regional countries are increasingly linked to trade at the global level, while others are members of the low-income food deficit countries, even as the region is home to a formidable population. Even food exporting countries within Asia did not remain insulated from the crisis.

In analysing the impact of the food crisis on Asia, it has to be remembered that the two food commodities most affected by the cancerous price rise were the staples of rice and wheat. Rice is the staple food of over 2 billion

Table 3.5

**2009 Global Hunger Index (GHI) by Severity and
Overall Vulnerability to the Global Downturn**
(Some Asian Countries)

	Severity				
	Less than 4.9 (Low)	5.0 to 9.9 (Moderate)	10.0 to 19.9 (Serious)	20.0 to 29.9 (Alarming)	More than 30.0 (Extremely Alarming)
High Vulnerability			Lao PDR Vietnam		
Medium Vulnerability			Sri Lanka	Bangladesh Cambodia India Pakistan	
Low Vulnerability			Myanmar Nepal		

Note: Vulnerability data are from IMF (2009) as cited in the 2009 Global Hunger Index. For the 2009 GHI, data on the proportion of undernourished are for 2003–05, data on child mortality are for 2007, and data on child malnutrition are for the latest year, that is, 2002–07, for which data is available. Table includes only countries for which both 2009 GHI and IMF vulnerability data are available.
Source: 2009 Global Hunger Index (Von Grebmer et al., 2009, p. 18).

Asians while wheat is the staple for 1 billion people according to the Asian Development Bank.[21] On the production parameter, the Asia-Pacific produces 90 per cent of the world's rice. These statistics are both critical pointers to as well as variables in understanding the mammoth impact of the price rise and the food crisis on the region as a whole. In many ways, the current ongoing scare over wheat price rise has something in common with the 2008 crisis.

Social Impact

The first social impact was related to the vicious cycle of poverty, rising food prices and food insecurity. The urban poor and migrants were the ones to feel the heat from the price rises as they were more affected by global price rise being that they were also consumers of processed food (which began to incorporate higher prices of oil) and ingredients of processed food such as wheat for bread. A large chunk of the middle-class in Asia felt the tremors, with those bordering on poverty falling further into the trap. For instance small farmers and poor agriculturalists in Cambodia felt the pressure from the rising oil prices. This contrasted with relatively well-off countries like Singapore where people spend only about 8 per cent of their income on food. A World Bank study in 2008 entitled "Double Jeopardy" also reveals that spiking food prices have not only increased poverty, but has raised the Gini index of inequality by 5 per cent in countries such as Bangladesh.[22]

Malnutrition, a phenomenon which already plagues Asia, was aggravated, increasing in sync with the rise in food prices. Countries such as India which otherwise experienced high economic growth had to deal with double the rate of stunted children, which at 47 per cent was five times that of China. There was a change in consumption patterns as well as quantity of food consumed in India as prices of wheat and rice inflated by 15 and 21 per cent respectively. According to case studies of countries affected by the economic crisis in the FAO (2009) "The State of Food Insecurity in the World 2009" report, households in Bangladesh had to resort to eating fewer and low-quality meals, slashing expenses on health and making a shift towards new income sources such as casual labour.[23]

Reports of food riots and social unrest arising out of mounting food prices came from various quarters in the region — Pakistan, Indonesia and Malaysia. In Pakistan in January 2008, troops had to be called in to guard vehicles transporting food.[24] There was also widespread panic in countries such as Vietnam where stockpiling and hoarding led to an unprecedented four-hour live broadcast by the Prime Minister and other leaders to allay fears.[25] In the Philippines, the National Bureau of Investigation was called in to conduct raids on traders suspected of hoarding rice. The Agricultural Secretary of the Philippines Arthur Yap instructed food chains such as KFC to reduce by half the rice served per meal to avoid wastage. In Indonesia, the rise in price of soyabeans brought forth sharp protests.[26]

In sum, all of these meant a fall in human resource quality as well as the food security of Asians. The impact of self-regulatory and government-initiated steps to ameliorate the situation meant that people had to trade off good quality food, healthcare and education for the basic inputs of survival. A 2008 World Bank study cites the case of Bangladesh where a survey revealed that about half of all households reduced spending on education to cope with the rise in food prices. Such a fall in terms of health, education, etc., considered essential for development means that the young workforce and children lost out on these integral inputs.[27]

Economic Impact

The most damaging impact on Asian countries was the rapid rise of domestic food prices leading to inflation. A 2008 ADB Special Report points out Asian countries such as Bangladesh, China, Vietnam, Indonesia and Pakistan experienced double-digit inflation. This trend cuts across both exporting and importing countries.[28]

Inflation of food prices pushed overall inflation higher in countries such as China, India, Indonesia and Vietnam. For instance, the inflation rate in Cambodia touched 20 per cent in 2008.[29] According to the Central Bank of Indonesia in 2008, annual inflation growth in Indonesia touched 8.17 per cent in March 2008. This meant that basic food commodities went out of the reach of not just the poor, but also the marginally middle-class. Primary food importing countries such as the Philippines struggled to obtain supplies of rice. Bills of food importing countries such as Lao PDR went up. There was an increased pressure on regional governments to respond by increasing food subsidies and undertaking other social security measures to salvage the situation. In Indonesia the government increased allocation for food support by US$290 million. Similarly, in the Philippines President Arroyo made efforts to ensure that there was enough subsidized rice for the poor.[30]

Countries considered major exporters of food produce such as India and Vietnam placed export restrictions. Indonesia banned the export of popular medium grade rice till national stocks were more than 3 million tons and domestic prices low. China imposed price controls on certain food items such as grain, cooking oil and eggs; and India banned the export of all rice except basmati. This might have been done to secure domestic supplies and prices, but also had the simultaneous negative impact of discouraging agricultural produce and trade. There was also a loss in terms of the opportunity to earn foreign exchange. The domestic situation in food exporting countries was also not entirely positive. For instance, even though the rice-producing farmers in Cambodia benefitted from the price rise, there were other sections of the population which responded to the situation by reducing expenditure on goods and services. Also, livestock and fish production declined due to a shift in focus towards rice production.

Political Impact

There was significant fallout from price rises on the domestic and regional political stages of Asia. Amongst the worst hit was of course war-ravaged

Afghanistan which bore not just the brunt of political problems but also faced natural disasters. The price of wheat which is the staple food grain in Afghanistan rose sharply during the period as did other commodities such as cereals, oils and fats. According to the USDA "Food Security Assessment 2008–09",[31] grain production declined by 37 per cent due to a drought in 2008. This only added to public discontent and strife in daily life there.

Elsewhere, *New York Times* cited a survey conducted by the Merdeka Center in the post-election period in Malaysia.[32] The voters clearly cited rising food and fuel prices as "the most important problem in the country", and nearly voted out the ruling coalition party in the elections. President Arroyo of the Philippines threatened to throw hoarders into jail in the face of threats of food riots.

At the regional level, the food price rise exposed the weaknesses of Asian regional mechanisms in handling and finding a remedy for such crises. The Association of Southeast Asian Nations (ASEAN) mechanism proved to be ineffective, and efforts to form a "rice cartel" following a proposal by Thailand to form an Organization of Rice Exporting Countries were quashed due to fears that it might create bad blood amongst ASEAN members. The crisis has spurred these countries to work towards evolving a safety valve mechanism as well as strengthening existing ones. Examples of such mechanisms are the ASEAN Integrated Food Security Framework and the Strategic Plan of Action on Food Security in the ASEAN Region.

Policy Response

Food insecurity arising out of rising food prices has eaten into the very sacrosanct concept of human security in the world, especially in developing countries, and even more so in Asia. The world of course responded to the crisis in myriad ways and at different levels. Individual countries responded at one level. The United Nations (U.N.) Secretary-General set up a High Level Task Force on the Global Food Security Crisis which produced a Comprehensive Framework for Action. The G-8 called for greater investment in the agricultural sector. Countries such as Cambodia, China, Indonesia and Korea imposed price controls and introduced consumer subsidies, while others such as Bangladesh, Indonesia and India distributed food rations and stamps. At the regional and multilateral levels, several steps were taken. The World Bank set up the Global Food Crisis Response Program while the ADB initiated a plan of assistance and financial help for the poor impacted by rising food prices which included food subsidies, incentives for agriculture and investments in improving infrastructure. In addition, food aid was pledged and social safety nets strengthened as well as efforts made to bolster agricultural produce.

However, much needs to be done in terms of alleviating the discomfort and struggle of several poor and vulnerable groups. At the national level, governments have to handle problems such as hoarding and corruption which are rampant in many parts of the world. Also avoidance of wastage of food is essential, as is having effective storage facilities for food grains. At the regional level, more coordinated efforts are needed to ride through such a crisis in the future. An effective response may come not just from sub-regional groupings such as ASEAN, ASEAN+3 or the South Asian Association for Regional Cooperation (SAARC) but also effective interaction and coordination amongst these groupings. At the international level, the multilateral donors which pledge funds and assistance have to also ensure that these are effectively implemented and do not go to waste. Food security can only be achieved if food becomes available and accessible to the most vulnerable sections of society.

Notes

[1]   Asian Development Bank, *Global Food Price Inflation and Developing Asia* (Philippines: ADB, 2011), available at <http://www.adb.org/documents/reports/global-food-price-inflation/food-price-inflation.pdf>.

[2]   USDA, "Table 09 Rice Area, Yield, and Production" (USDA: Foreign Agricultural Service, 2011), available at <http://www.fas.usda.gov/psdonline/psdgetreportaspx?hidReportRetrievalName=BVS&hidReportRetrievalID=893&hidReportRetrievalTemplateID=1>.

[3]   USDA, "World Rice Trace", in *Grain: World Markets and Trade* (USDA: Office of Global Analysis, 2010), available at <http://www.fas.usda.gov/grain/circular/2010/12-10/grainfull12-10.pdf>.

[4]   FAO, "Food Security: Concepts and Measurement", in *Trade Reforms and Food Security: Conceptualizing the Linkages* (FAO: Economic and Social Development Department, 2003), available at <http://www.fao.org/docrep/005/y4671e/y4671e06.htm>.

[5]   UNDP, "New Dimensions of Human Security", in *Human Development Report*, 1994, available at <http://hdr.undp.org/en/reports/global/hdr1994/>.

[6]   World Food Summit, "Rome Declaration on World Food Security", Rome, Italy, 13–17 November 1996, available at <http://www.fao.org/docrep/003/w3613e/w3613e00.htm>.

[7]   R. Gross, H. Schoeneberger, H. Pfeifer, and H.J. Preuss, "Four Dimensions of Food and Nutrition Security: Definitions and Concepts", 2000, available at <http://www.foodsec.org/DL/course/shortcourseFA/en/pdf/P-01_RG_Concept.pdf>.

8   B. Quigley, "30 Years Ago Haiti Grew All the Rice It Needed. What Happened?" *News, Views, Essays and Reflections*, 2008, available at <http://www.margueritelaurent.com/pressclips/foodcrisis.html>.

9   "Thailand Drops Idea for Rice Cartel", *New York Times*, 6 May 2008, available at <http://www.nytimes.com/2008/05/06/business/worldbusiness/06iht-baht.4.12621295.html>.

10 IRIN, "Vietnam: Rising Inflation Hurting Poor, Undermining Poverty Gains", Humanitarian News and Analysis, 11 June 2008, available at <http://www.irinnews.org/InDepthMain.aspx?indepthid=72&reportid=78685>.

11 UNDP, "Post-Nargis Joint Assessment Final Report", 10 July 2008, available at <http://www.mm.undp.org/UNDP_Publication_PDF/PONJA%20full_report.pdf>.

12 ASEAN, "ASEAN Integrated Food Security (AIFS) Framework and Strategic Plan of Action on Food Security in the ASEAN Region (SPA-FS) 2009–2013", 2009, available at <www.aseansec.org/22338.pdf>.

13 Todd Benson, Nicholas Minot, John Pender et al., *Global Food Crises: Monitoring and Assessing Impact to Inform Policy Responses* (Washington, D.C.: International Food Policy Research Institute [IFPRI], 2008), available at <http://www.ifpri.org/publication/global-food-crises>.

14 Gitonga Njeru, "Climate-related Farmer Suicides Surging in Eastern Kenya", Alertnet, 12 July 2010, available at<http://www.alertnet.org/db/an_art/60167/2010/06/12-130113-1.htm>.

15 Anuradha Mittal, "The 2008 Food Price Crisis: Rethinking Food Security Policies", UNCTAD G-24 Discussion Paper No. 56 (2009), available at <http://www.oaklandinstitute.org/pdfs/G24_DiscussionPaper56.pdf>.

16 Joachim Von Braun, *Food and Financial Crises: Implications for Agriculture and the Poor* (Washington, D.C.: International Food Policy Research Institute [IFPRI], 2008*a*), available at <http://www.ifpri.org/publication/food-and-financial-crises>.

17 Anuradha Mittal, "The 2008 Food Price Crisis: Rethinking Food Security Policies", UNCTAD G-24 Discussion Paper No. 56 (2009), available at <http://www.oaklandinstitute.org/pdfs/G24_DiscussionPaper56.pdf>.

18 Oxfam Canada, "Bangladesh Cyclone 2007", 16 January 2008, available at <http://69-64-72-92.dedicated.abac.net/what-we-do/emergencies/bangladesh-cyclone-2007>.

19 Donald Mitchell, "A Note on Rising Food Prices", Policy Research Working Paper 4682 (Washington, D.C.: The World Bank (WB) Development Prospects Group, 2008), available at <http://www-wds.worldbank.org/external/default/WDSContentServer/IW3P/IB/2008/07/28/000020439_20080728103002/Rendered/PDF/WP4682.pdf>.

20 Food and Agriculture Organization of the United Nations (FAO), *The State of Food Insecurity in the World 2008: High Food Prices and Food Security — Threats*

and Opportunities, 2008*b*, available at <http://ftp.fao.org/docrep/fao/011/ i0291e/i0291e00.pdf>.

21   Asian Development Bank (ADB), *Special Report — Food Prices and Inflation in Developing Asia: Is Poverty Reduction Coming to an End?* Metro Manila, 2008, available at <http://www.adb.org/Documents/reports/food-prices-inflation/food-prices-inflation.pdf>.

22   World Bank (WB), "Double Jeopardy: Responding to High Food and Fuel Prices", G8 Hokkaido-Toyako Summit, Japan, 2008*a*, available at <http://web. worldbank.org/WBSITE/EXTERNAL/NEWS0,,contentMDK:21827681~pag ePK:64257043~piPK:437376~theSitePK:4607,00.html>.

23   Food and Agriculture Organization of the United Nations (FAO), *The State of Food Insecurity in the World 2009: Economic Crises — Impacts and Lessons Learned*, Rome, 2009, available at <http://www.fao.org/docrep/012/i0876e/ i0876e00.htm>.

24   "Pakistan Army Guards Scarce", *BBC News*, 14 January 2008, available at <http://news.bbc.co.uk/2/hi/south_asia/7187719.stm>.

25   Randall Arnst, "Business as Usual: Responses within ASEAN to the Food Crisis", Occasional Papers 4 (Bangkok: Focus on the Global South, 2009), available at <http://focusweb.org/pdf/occasionalpaper4.pdf>.

26   Federation of Malaysian Consumers Associations (FOMCA), *Food Crisis in Southeast Asia: The Political-Economic Impact of the Rise of Commodity Prices*, Selangor, 2008.

27   World Bank (WB), "Rising Food and Fuel Prices: Addressing the Risks to Future Generations", Washington, D.C., 2008*b*, available at <http://siteresources. worldbank.org/DEVCOMMEXT/Resources/Food-Fuel.pdf>.

28   Asian Development Bank (ADB), *Special Report — Food Prices and Inflation in Developing Asia: Is Poverty Reduction Coming to an End?* Metro Manila, 2008, available at <http://www.adb.org/Documents/reports/food-prices-inflation/food-prices-inflation.pdf>.

29   Cambodia Development Resource Institute (CDRI), "Impact of High Food Prices in Cambodia: Survey Report", 2008, available at <http://home.wfp. org/stellent/groups/public/documents/ena/wfp189739.pdf>.

30   Central Bank of Indonesia, "Indonesia Inflation, March 2008", 8 April 2008, available at <http://www.bi.go.id/web/en/Publikasi/Investor+Relation+Unit/ Government+Press+Release/Inflation+March+2008.htm>.

31   Shahla Shapouri, Stacey Rosen, Birgit Meade et al., "Food Security Assessment, 2008–09", GFA-20 (Washington, D.C.: Economic Research Service/USDA, 2009), available at <http://www.ers.usda.gov/Publications/GFA20/GFA20. pdf>.

32   Thomas Fuller, "Asian Food Crisis has Political and Civil Implications", *New York Times*, 18 April 2008, available at <http://www.nytimes.com/2008/04/18/ world/asia/18iht-food.1.12130435.html?_r=1>.

References

Arnst, Randall. "Business as Usual: Responses within ASEAN to the Food Crisis". Occasional Papers 4. Bangkok: Focus on the Global South, 2009. Available at <http://focusweb.org/pdf/occasionalpaper4.pdf>.

ASEAN. "ASEAN Integrated Food Security (AIFS) Framework and Strategic Plan of Action on Food Security in the ASEAN Region (SPA–FS) 2009–2013", 2009. Available at <www.aseansec.org/22338.pdf>.

Asian Development Bank (ADB). *Global Food Price Inflation and Developing Asia*. Philippines: ADB, 2011. Available at <http://www.adb.org/documents/reports/global-food-price-inflation/food-price-inflation.pdf>.

———. *Special Report — Food Prices and Inflation in Developing Asia: Is Poverty Reduction Coming to an End?* Metro Manila, 2008. Available at <http://www.adb.org/Documents/reports/food-prices-inflation/food-prices-inflation.pdf>.

Benson, Todd, Nicholas Minot, John Pender et al. *Global Food Crises: Monitoring and Assessing Impact to Inform Policy Responses*. Washington, D.C.: International Food Policy Research Institute (IFPRI), 2008. Available at <http://www.ifpri.org/publication/global-food-crises>.

Cambodia Development Resource Institute (CDRI). "Impact of High Food Prices in Cambodia: Survey Report", 2008. Available at <http://home.wfp.org/stellent/groups/public/documents/ena/wfp189739.pdf>.

Central Bank of Indonesia. "Indonesia Inflation, March 2008", 8 April 2008. Available at <http://www.bi.go.id/web/en/Publikasi/Investor+Relation+Unit/Government+Press+Release/Inflation+March+2008.htm>.

Federation of Malaysian Consumers Associations (FOMCA). *Food Crisis in Southeast Asia: The Political-Economic Impact of the Rise of Commodity Prices*. Selangor, 2008.

Food and Agriculture Organization of the United Nations (FAO). *The State of Food Insecurity in the World 2009: Economic Crises — Impacts and Lessons Learned*. Rome, 2009. Available at <http://www.fao.org/docrep/012/i0876e/i0876e00.htm>.

———. *The State of Food Insecurity in the World 2008: High Food Prices and Food Security — Threats and Opportunities*, 2008b. Available at <http://ftp.fao.org/docrep/fao/011/i0291e/i0291e00.pdf>.

———. "Food Security: Concepts and Measurement". In *Trade Reforms and Food Security: Conceptualizing the Linkages*. FAO: Economic and Social Development Department, 2003. Available at <http://www.fao.org/docrep/005/y4671e/y4671e06.htm>.

Fuller, Thomas. "Asian Food Crisis has Political and Civil Implications". *New York Times*, 18 April 2008. Available at <http://www.nytimes.com/2008/04/18/world/asia/18iht-food.1.12130435.html?_r=1>.

Gross, R., H. Schoeneberger, H. Pfeifer, and H.J. Preuss. "Four Dimensions of Food and Nutrition Security: Definitions and Concepts", 2000. Available at

<http://www.foodsec.org/DL/course/shortcourseFA/en/pdf/P-01_RG_Concept. pdf>.

IRIN. "Vietnam: Rising Inflation Hurting Poor, Undermining Poverty Gains". IRIN: Humanitarian News and Analysis, 11 June 2008. Available at <http://www. irinnews.org/InDepthMain.aspx?indepthid=72&reportid=78685>.

Mitchell, Donald. "A Note on Rising Food Price". Policy Research Working Paper No. 4682. Washington, D.C.: The World Bank (WB) Development Prospects Group, 2008. Available at <http://www-wds.worldbank.org/ external/default/WDSContentServer/IW3P/IB/2008/07/28/000020439_ 20080728103002/Rendered/PDF/WP4682.pdf>.

Mittal, Anuradha. "The 2008 Food Price Crisis: Rethinking Food Security Policies". UNCTAD G-24 Discussion Paper No. 56 (2009). Available at <http://www. oaklandinstitute.org/pdfs/G24_DiscussionPaper56.pdf>.

Njeru, Gitonga. "Climate-related Farmer Suicides Surging in Eastern Kenya". Alertnet, 12 July 2010. Available at <http://www.alertnet.org/db/an_ art/60167/2010/06/12-130113-1.htm>.

Oxfam Canada. "Bangladesh Cyclone 2007", 16 January 2008. Available at <http://69-64-72-92.dedicated.abac.net/what-we-do/emergencies/bangladesh-cyclone-2007>.

"Pakistan Army Guards Scarce". BBC News, 14 January 2008. Available at <http:// news.bbc.co.uk/2/hi/south_asia/7187719.stm>.

Quigley, B. "30 Years Ago Haiti Grew All the Rice It Needed. What Happened?" News, Views, Essays and Reflections, 2008. Available at <http://www.margueritelaurent. com/pressclips/foodcrisis.html>.

Shapouri, Shahla, Stacey Rosen, Birgit Meade et al. "Food Security Assessment, 2008–09". GFA-20. Washington, D.C.: Economic Research Service/USDA, 2009. Available at <http://www.ers.usda.gov/Publications/GFA20/GFA20. pdf>.

"Thailand Drops Idea for Rice Cartel". New York Times, 6 May 2008. Available at <http://www.nytimes.com/2008/05/06/business/worldbusiness/06iht-baht.4.12621295.html>.

UNDP. "Post-Nargis Joint Assessment Final Report", 10 July 2008. Available at <http://www.mm.undp.org/UNDP_Publication_PDF/PONJA%20full_report. pdf>.

———. "New Dimensions of Human Security". Human Development Report, 1994. Available at <http://hdr.undp.org/en/reports/global/hdr1994/>.

USDA. "Table 09 Rice Area, Yield, and Production". USDA: Foreign Agricultural Service, 2011. Available at <http://www.fas.usda.gov/psdonline/psdgetreport. aspx?hidReportRetrievalName=BVS&hidReportRetrievalID=893&hidReport RetrievalTemplateID=1>.

———. "Grain: World Markets and Trade". USDA: Office of Global Analysis, 2010. Available at <http://www.fas.usda.gov/grain/circular/2010/12-10/grainfull12-10.pdf>.

Von Braun, Joachim. *Food and Financial Crises: Implications for Agriculture and the Poor*. Washington, D.C.: International Food Policy Research Institute (IFPRI), 2008*a*. Available at <http://www.ifpri.org/publication/food-and-financial-crises>.

World Bank (WB). "Double Jeopardy: Responding to High Food and Fuel Prices". G8 Hokkaido-Toyako Summit, Japan, 2008*a*. Available at <http://web.worldbank.org/WBSITE/EXTERNAL/NEWS/0,,contentMDK:21827681~pagePK:64257043~piPK: 437376~theSitePK:4607,00.html>.

———. "Rising Food and Fuel Prices: Addressing the Risks to Future Generations". Washington, D.C., 2008*b*. Available at <http://siteresources.worldbank.org/DEVCOMMEXT/Resources/Food-Fuel.pdf>.

World Food Summit. "Rome Declaration on World Food Security". Rome, Italy, 13–17 November 1996. Available at <http://www.fao.org/docrep/003/w3613e/w3613e00.htm>.

4

WATER

Mely Caballero-Anthony and
Pau Khan Khup Hangzo

INTRODUCTION

Water is essential for all socio-economic development and for maintaining healthy ecosystems. As population increases and development calls for increased allocations of groundwater and surface water for the domestic, agriculture and industrial sectors, the pressure on water resources intensifies, leading to tensions, conflicts among users, and excessive pressure on the environment. Over the last decades, there has been a growing speculation about the likelihood of an acute conflict or even war over freshwater resources. Scholars increasingly point out that the twenty-first century might see the battles fought due to water scarcity. Indeed, water is the only resource having no substitute and its distribution is uneven, with some nations suffering severe droughts every year and the others blessed with water abundance. And although history shows that full-scale wars over water, proving to be neither strategically rational nor hydrographically effective, have never been fought, water continues to be a source of intense disputes worldwide. The problem grows harder when it comes to the relationships between two or more countries over river water as a result of the "internationalization" of a basin through political change. This chapter examines the growing water security challenges in Asia and argues that existing mechanisms for water management are inadequate to address the challenges. Using the Hindukush-Himalayan region as a case study, the chapter pointed out the deficiencies in water cooperation and offers a way forward to sustainably manage shared water resources.

CURRENT STATE OF WATER SECURITY

Total water availability on earth is estimated at 1,360 million cubic kilometres.[1,2] Of this, 97.5 per cent is in the oceans and is unsuitable for human consumption. Freshwater accounted for 2.5 per cent out of which 70 per cent is in the form of glaciers and icebergs, 30 per cent is stored in groundwater, and 0.3 per cent is accounted for by lakes and rivers. See Figure 4.1.

An estimated 4,500 cubic kilometres of water are withdrawn annually for use in agriculture, industry, and domestic sectors.[3] As of 2010, agriculture accounted for 71 per cent of global water withdrawals; industry accounted for 16 per cent; and domestic use accounted for 14 per cent. By 2030, under an average economic growth scenario and if no efficiency gains are assumed, global water requirements would increase by 40 per cent grow i.e. from the current 4,500 cubic kilometers to 6,900 cubic kilometers.[4] See Table 4.1.

Figure 4.1   Water Resources

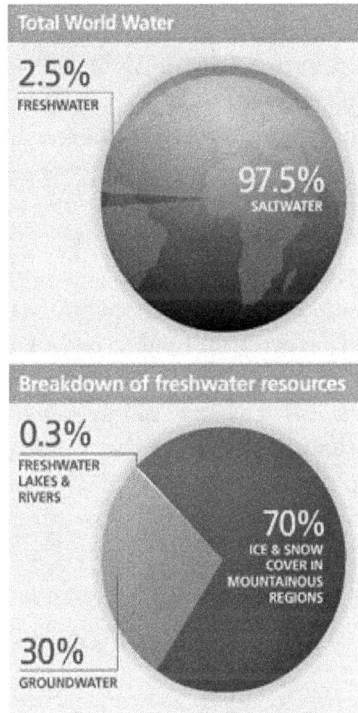

Source: UN Water, "Water Resources", undated, <http://www.unwater.org/statistics_res.html>.

Table 4.1

Estimates of Current and Future Water Use

Water Use by Sectors	2010 Withdrawals (in cubic kilometres)	2030 Withdrawals (in cubic kilometres)
Municipal & Domestic	600	900
Industry	800	1,500
Agriculture	3,100	4,500
Total	4,500	6,900

Source: The Barilla Group et al., 2009.

The growing water resource challenge was driven by population growth, urbanization, and growing affluences. It was estimated that the world's population will reach 9.1 billion by 2050, 34 per cent higher than today. At the same time urbanization will continue at an accelerated pace and about 70 per cent of the world's population will be urban by 2050 compared to 49 per cent today. In order to feed this larger, more urban and richer population, food production must increase by 70 per cent.[5] The growing pressure on water resources has led to water scarcity in some parts of the world. Water scarcity is defined as the point at which the aggregate impact of all users impinges on the supply or quality of water under prevailing institutional arrangements to the extent that the demand by all sectors, including the environment, cannot be satisfied fully.[6] Specifically, water scarcity occurs where water availability in a country or in a region is below 1,000 cubic meters per person per year.[7] Water availability of between 1,000–1,600 cubic meters per person per year on the other hand is characterized as water stress. In all, around 1.2 billion people, or almost one-fifth of the world's population are estimated to live in areas of physical scarcity[8] and 500 million people approaches this situation.[9] Another 1.6 billion people face economic water shortages[10] and about 1.6 billion people live in water-scarce basins.[11]

TRANSBOUNDARY RIVER AND CONFLICT

"Transboundary waters" is defined as "any surface or ground waters which mark, cross or are located on boundaries between two or more states".[12] Transboundary waters, be they rivers, groundwater or lakes, linked states together in a complex system of interdependence in spheres as diverse as economics, politics, environmental policies, and security. Hydrological interdependence especially in water-scarce river basins creates both a potential for conflicts between riparian states and incentives for interstate cooperation. An assessment by the United Nations of shared international rivers in 1958 identified 166 major international river basins.[13] By 2002, this number has increased to 263 due to the internationalization of national basins through political changes, such as the breakup of the Soviet Union and Yugoslavia, as well as access to better mapping sources and technology.[14] See Table 4.2.

The river basins discussed above covered nearly one-half of the earth's surface area and accounted for an estimated 60 per cent of global freshwater flow and approximately 40 per cent of the world's population lives in these basins. Even more striking than the total number of basins is the number of countries with territory within these watersheds. Approximately one-third

Table 4.2
The World's Transboundary River Basins

Regions	Transboundary River Basins	
	Number	Percentage of Continental Area
Africa	59	62
Asia	57	40
Europe	69	55
North and Central America	40	37
South America	38	59
Total	263	48

Source: Adapted from Cooley et al., 2009.[15]

of the 263 international basins are shared by more than two countries, and 19 involve five or more sovereign states. Of these 19, one basin, the Danube, has 17 riparian nations. Five basins — the Congo, Niger, Nile, Rhine and Zambezi — are shared by between nine and eleven countries. The remaining thirteen basins — the Amazon, Ganges-Brahmaputra-Meghna, Lake Chad, Tarim, Aral Sea, Jordan, Kura-Araks, Mekong, Tigris-Euphrates, Volga, La Plata, Neman, and Vistula — have between five and eight riparian countries.

It has been argued that the conflict of the future will be over the control of shared water resources. Gleick (1993)[16] for example noted that where water is scarce, competition for limited supplies can lead nations to see access to water as a matter of "national security" thereby heightening the potential for conflict. Homer-Dixon (1995)[17] went further and outlines the circumstances that could led upstream and downstream neighbours to go to war: the downstream country must be highly dependent on the water for its national well-being; the upstream country must be able to restrict the river's flow; there must be a history of antagonism between the two countries; and, most importantly, the downstream country must be militarily much stronger than the upstream country. Others however argued for the possibilities of cooperation between co-riparian. According to Wolf et al. (2003),[18] no nations have gone to war specifically over water resources for thousands of years. The only recorded incident of an outright war over water occurred more than 4,000 years ago between two Mesopotamian city-states, Lagash and Umma, in modern-day Iraq. Conversely, between the years 805 and 1984, countries signed more than 3,600 water-related treaties.[19] It was observed that cooperative relations centres primarily on navigation, flood control, water allocation, water quality, joint management, information sharing, joint monitoring, hydropower etc.

HINDU-KUSH HIMALAYA (HKH) REGION: TOWARDS CONFLICT OR COOPERATION?

The Hindu-Kush Himalaya (HKH), also known as the "Third Pole" or "Asia's water tower" because it hosts the largest areas of glaciers, snow and permafrost outside the North Pole and the South Pole, extends some 3,500 km from Afghanistan in the west to Myanmar and China in the east, and runs through Pakistan, Nepal, India, Bangladesh and Bhutan. The region

Figure 4.2
HKH Map with Major River Basins

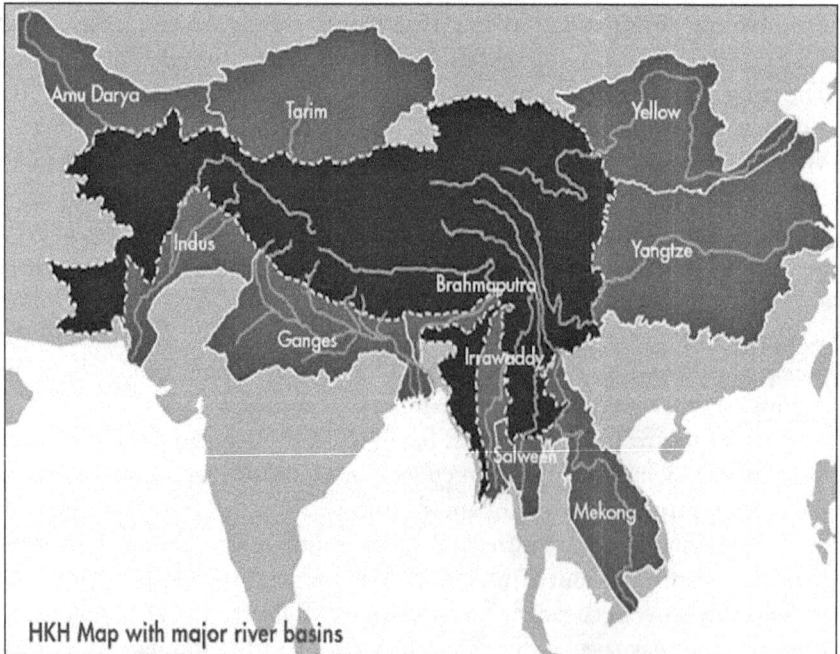

HKH Map with major river basins

Note: The dark shade indicates mountain ranges whereas the light shade indicates river systems of the HKH region.
Source: ICIMOD, u.d.

is the source of ten huge Asian river systems providing irrigation, power and drinking water for an estimated 1.3 billion people, or around 20 per cent of the world's population (China Dialogue et al., 2009).[20] These river systems include the Tarim (Dayan), Amu Darya, Indus (including Sutlej), Ganges, Brahmaputra (Yarlung Tsangpo–Brahmaputra), Irrawaddy, Salween (Nu), Mekong (Lancang), Yangtze (Jinsha), and the Yellow (Huang He).[21] See Figure 4.2.

A good gauge of the transboundary significance of rivers originating from the KHK region is the water dependency ratio. Water dependency ratio is an index that measures the amount of water resources originating outside a country and highlighted the potential vulnerability of shared waters to competing interests. Bangladesh and Pakistan have the highest dependency ratios with 91 and 77 per cent of their freshwaters originating from outside their borders respectively. Kyrgyzstan and China on the other hand has a dependency ratio of zero and 1 per cent because all or most of their water comes from within their respective borders.[22] See Table 4.3.

It is important to note that no wars have been fought over rivers in the HKH region. This however does not mean that tensions are absent. The current hydro-politics in the HKH region is characterized by various degrees of conflict and cooperation. The absence of a region-wide strategy

Table 4.3
Water Dependency Ratio in Selected Countries of the Hindukush-Himalayan Region

Central and South Asia	Water Dependency Ratio (%)	East and Southeast Asia	Water Dependency Ratio (%)
Afghanistan	15	Cambodia	75
Bangladesh	91	China	1
India	34	Laos PDR	43
Kazakhstan	31	Myanmar	16
Kyrgyzstan	0	Thailand	49
Nepal	6	Vietnam	59
Pakistan	77		
Uzbekistan	77		

Source: The Asia Society, 2009.

to address and manage water in a way that balances not only social and economic needs but also the protection of ecosystems could have adverse impact in the region. What exists is an assemblage of agreements between riparian states. Primary focus of transboundary water agreements adopted during the twentieth century focus almost exclusively on water quality, water quantity, water allocation, navigation, flood control, hydropower, pollution, fishing, border issues, joint management, technical cooperation, and economic development.[23] Bilateral agreements however may not always be the most effective way of resolving disputes, especially where the parties are unequal.[24] One party may deny that a dispute existed, advance unreasonable claims or simply drag its feet. Parties may also have uneven bargaining powers or unequal legal and technical expertise in the matters involved.

TRANSBOUNDARY WATER MANAGEMENT IN THE HKH REGION

Most of the rivers of the HKH region lack any treaty among riparian countries and each has different and conflicting plans for development in the basin. When countries do cooperate, it is done largely through bilateral cooperation. Here we review existing cooperative frameworks in the four sub-regions of the HKH region namely South and Central Asia, and East and Southeast Asia. South Asia is home to a number of bilateral agreements and most of them involved India owing to its hydro-hegemonic status in the region. Due to the consequences of partition in 1947, the Indus River basin was divided between India and Pakistan with the headwaters in India and the lower basin in Pakistan thereby creating the potential for major conflict. To avoid conflict over the Indus water, India and Pakistan, with the help of the World Bank signed the Indus Water Treaty in 1960. The Treaty divides the Indus waters equally between the two countries: India was granted the primary use of the eastern rivers (Beas, Ravi, and Sutlej) and Pakistan the same rights to the western rivers (Chenab, Indus and Jhelum) of the Indus River basin.[25] Both sides are also permitted non-consumptive rights to the other country's three rivers — Pakistan was allotted agricultural use on the Ravi, while India was given restricted storage capacity for hydropower development on all three Pakistan rivers, minding that large amounts of water are not retained or redirected.

The history of water sharing between India and Bangladesh is long-standing and has often been turbulent particularly over the Ganges River. The dispute over the sharing of the waters of the Ganges River erupted in 1951 because India decided to construct the Farakka Barrage/dam in the state of West Bengal, about ten miles from the border with Bangladesh. India contended that construction of the Farakka Barrage was needed in order to divert waters from the Ganges River to the Hooghly River for a variety of reasons. These include the need to maintain the flow in the Hooghly River so that the river would remain navigable. India also maintained that more water was needed in the Hooghly River in order to flush out the silt that deposited in the Calcutta Port to ensure that the port would remain accessible. India also maintained that additional water was needed in the Hooghly River to counteract a high concentration of salinity in the water and to provide Calcutta with water for irrigation, domestic, and municipal purposes. Bangladesh however contended that any decrease in the flow of the Ganges River would negatively affect irrigation, decrease the water supply, inhibit fishery production, reduce groundwater tables, aggravate the salinity problem, and restrict river navigation, which is the most frequently used mode of transportation in Bangladesh. To address the issue of equitable distribution of the waters of the Ganges River during low-flow months, India and Bangladesh concluded a treaty on 12 December 1996. Cooperation on shared water resources between India and Nepal centred on the Mahakali and the Kosi rivers and the two countries have signed treaties in 1996 and 1954 respectively. These treaties addressed concerns regarding the regulation of the flow of the river and ensure flood management. There have been various disputes over the specific issue of dam construction; hydro power generation; irrigation development; flood control/management; and navigation. Crucially, cooperation between the two hydro-hegemons, China and India, remains limited. The two countries have not entered into any agreements on their shared waters and cooperation is limited to Memorandum of Understandings (MOU) such as one on the Brahmaputra which was signed in 2002. Also, the two countries held Joint Expert Level meetings on Trans-Border Rivers annually since 2008.[26] India and China have also begun to discuss cooperation over monitoring the melting of glaciers in the Himalayas.

Besides bilateral treaties, there is also limited multilateral cooperation in the HKH region notably in Southeast Asia and Central Asia. The Mekong River Basin Commission (MRC) is one of the rare examples of successful multilateral cooperation. See Figure 4.3. The river originates in Yunnan Province in China and flows through Myanmar, Laos, Thailand, Cambodia, and Vietnam where it finally empties in the South China Sea. The Mekong River Commission (MRC), formed on 5 April 1995 by an agreement between the governments of Cambodia, Lao PDR, Thailand

Figure 4.3

Characteristics of the Mekong River Basin

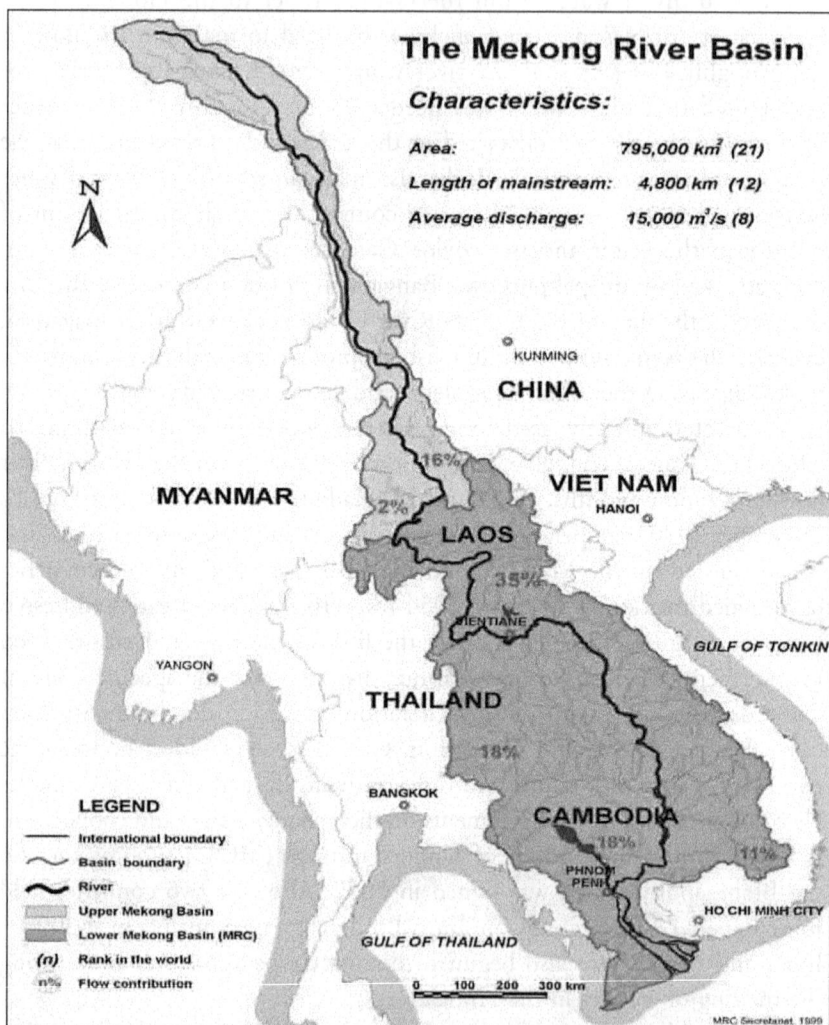

The Mekong River Basin

Characteristics:

Area: 795,000 km² (21)
Length of mainstream: 4,800 km (12)
Average discharge: 15,000 m³/s (8)

N

KUNMING
CHINA

MYANMAR   VIET NAM
                          HANOI
16%
2%   LAOS
35%
VIENTIANE
                          GULF OF TONKIN
YANGON

THAILAND

18%

LEGEND   BANGKOK
                                CAMBODIA
──── International boundary   18%   11%
∼   Basin boundary   PHNOM
∼   River   PENH
     Upper Mekong Basin   HO CHI MINH CITY
     Lower Mekong Basin (MRC)
(n) Rank in the world   GULF OF THAILAND
n%   Flow contribution   0   100   200   300 km

                                                    MRC Secretariat, 1999

Source: Bach et al., 2011.[28] Base Data/Data provided by Mekong River Commission and reproduced with permission.

and Vietnam is an international organization that provides the institutional framework to promote regional cooperation among riparian states.[27] The MRC's goal is to encourage balanced and coordinated developments and investments in irrigation and drought management, navigation, hydropower, flood management, fisheries, watershed management, environment, and tourism. China and Myanmar became Dialogue Partners of the MRC in 1996. China in particular has agreed to share information on its river flows and dam operations.

Since the collapse of the Soviet Union, Central Asia has become a tangle of unresolved transboundary water disputes. The Aral Sea Basin which comprises parts of Afghanistan, Kazakhstan, Kyrgyzstan, Tajikistan, Turkmenistan, and Uzbekistan is the dominant hydro-geographic features in Central Asia. See Figure 4.4. Melt water from extensive permanent snow fields and glaciers in the Tien Shan and Pamir mountain ranges feeds the major rivers of the Aral Sea Basin, the Syr Darya and the Amu Darya rivers. Much of the region's water flows originated from the mountains of Kyrgyzstan and Tajikista.[29] In managing their shared water, Aral Basin countries still relied on a complex system of quotas and barter deals that were established under the former Soviet Union. Under the quota system, downstream cotton producing countries namely Uzbekistan, Turkmenistan and Kazakhstan are given the largest quotas and the upstream countries were given much smaller quotas due to their smaller populations and low cotton production. Restrictions were imposed on irrigated agriculture in the latter two to maximize cotton output in their neighbours. Under the barter deals, Kyrgyzstan and Tajikistan, which have only limited gas and coal deposits, are provided with huge amounts of Turkmen and Uzbek gas as well as coal and *mazut* (a heavy fuel oil made from refinery residues) from Kazakhstan to satisfy their domestic energy consumption needs. After independence, the need for all riparian to enter into an agreement regulating water allocation in the Basin has become apparent. As such, countries of the Aral Sea Basin established the Almaty Agreement on 18 February 1992. The agreement further formalized the water allocation schemes of the Soviet era and has now caused intense grievances. Since independence, all the riparian countries expanded their irrigated agriculture to compensate for a sharp industrial decline following the collapse of the Soviet Union leading to increased water consumption which is 1.5 times more water than recommended leading to shortages. Besides, Uzbekistan and Kazakhstan has introduced world prices for their gas, coal and *mazut*. Kyrgyzstan and Tajikistan could not afford to pay and therefore increased electric production in the rivers. This increased electricity production caused considerable problems for downstream countries as it not only disrupted the flow of water but also reduced the water available to them for irrigation.

Figure 4.4
The Central Asian Region and the Aral Sea Basin

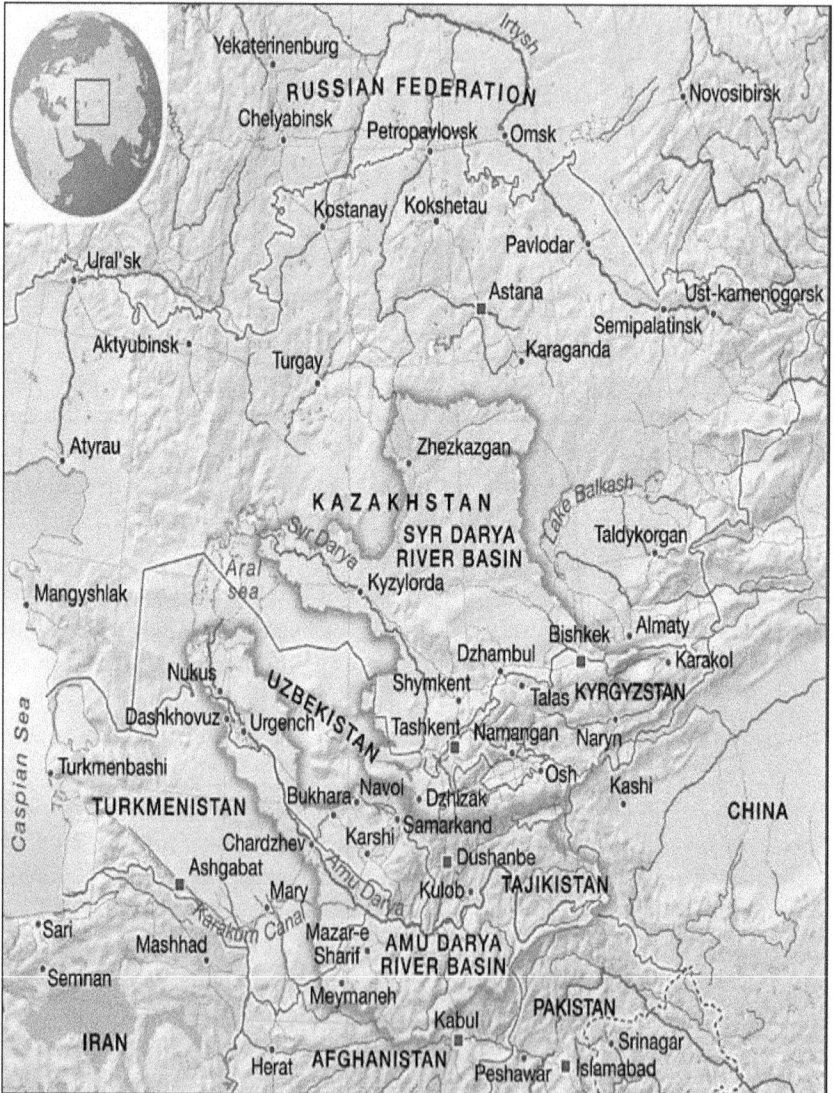

Source: Granit et al., "Regional Water Intelligence Report: Central Asia", Stockholm International Water Institute (SIWI), March 2010, <http://www.watergovernance.org/documents/WGF/Reports/Paper-15_RWIR_Aral_Sea.pdf>.

INTEGRATED WATER RESOURCES MANAGEMENT (IWRM): A WAY TO SUSTAINABILITY

Existing treaties and frameworks are not sufficient to sustainably address the challenges of water security challenges in the HKH region as they focus almost exclusively on water quality, water quantity, navigation, hydropower, border issues, joint management, technical cooperation, and economic development. What is required is a comprehensive region-wide cooperation that addresses water security at the basin level. This is especially important in light of climate change that could significantly impact water resources of the HKH region. Higher temperatures associated with climate change threaten to plunge river basins into further water scarcity due to its dependence on melt waters from declining Himalayan glaciers. Himalayan glaciers cover about three million hectares or 17 per cent of the mountain area as compared to 2.2 per cent in the Swiss Alps forming the largest body of ice outside the polar caps. In all, there are an estimated 15,000 glaciers in the Himalayas storing 12,000 cubic kilometres of freshwater which supports perennial rivers of the HKH region.[30] The Intergovernmental Panel on Climate Change's (IPCC) noted in its fourth assessment report in 2007 that "glaciers in the Himalaya are receding faster than in any other part of the world" and that the total glacial area will likely shrink from the present 500,000 to 100,000 square kilometres by the year 2035. This assessment however has been criticized as inaccurate and was accused of using figures from a non-peer reviewed journal.[31] Despite this, the prediction has heaped more attention on the state of glaciers in the HKH region. Subsequent studies concluded that 30 per cent of Himalayan glaciers will disappear by 2030, 40 per cent by 2050, and 70 per cent by the end of the century.[32]

It is widely accepted that the most appropriate geographical entity for the planning and management of water resources is the river basin. A river basin is the portion of land drained by a river and its tributaries. It encompasses the entire land surface dissected and drained by many streams and creeks that flow downhill into one another, and eventually into one river. Water management at the basin level is done through the Integrated Water Resource Management (IWRM) approach which is defined as "a process which promotes the coordinated development and management of water, land and related resources, in order to maximize the resultant economic and social welfare in an equitable manner without compromising the sustainability of vital ecosystems".[33] This approach views the hydrographic basin as the basic water management unit and calls for a comprehensive, participatory planning and implementation tool for managing and developing water resources in a way that balances social and economic needs, and that ensures the protection of ecosystems. The idea of taking an integrated approach to water development and management originated from the 1992 Earth Summit in Rio de Janeiro.[34] While there are no set IWRM rules, the Dublin Conference (International Conference on Water and Environment, 1992) set out four guiding principles associated with water use. These are:

Fresh water is a finite and vulnerable resource, essential to sustain life, development and the environment. Since water sustains life, effective management of water resources demands a holistic approach, linking social and economic development with protection of natural ecosystems. Effective management links land and water uses across the whole of a catchment area or groundwater aquifer.

Water development and management should be based on a participatory approach, involving users, planners and policy-makers at all levels. The participatory approach involves raising awareness of the importance of water among policy-makers and the general public. It means that decisions are taken at the lowest appropriate level, with full public consultation and involvement of users in the planning and implementation of water projects.

Women play a central part in the provision, management and safeguarding of water. This pivotal role of women as providers and users of water and guardians of the living environment has seldom been reflected in institutional arrangements for the development and management of water resources. Acceptance and implementation of this principle requires positive policies to address women's specific needs and to equip and empower women to participate at all levels in water resources programmes, including decision-making and implementation, in ways defined by them.

Water has an economic value in all its competing uses and should be recognized as an economic good. Within this principle, it is vital to recognize first the basic right of all human beings to have access to clean water and sanitation at an affordable price. Past failure to recognize the economic value of water has led to wasteful and environmentally damaging uses of the resource. Managing water as an economic good is an important way of achieving efficient and equitable use, and of encouraging conservation and protection of water resources.

Notes

1   Each cubic kilometre is equivalent to 1,000 billion litres (1 billion tonnes) of water.

2   Mark W. Rosegrant, *Water Resources in the Twenty-First Century: Challenges and Implications for Action*, Food, Agriculture, and the Environment Discussion Paper 20 (Washington, D.C.: International Food Policy Research Institute [IFPRI], March 1997), available at <http://www.ifpri.org/sites/default/files/publications/pubs_2020_dp_dp20.pdf>.

3   The Barilla Group et al., *Charting Our Water Future Economic Frameworks to Inform Decision-Making*, 2030 Water Resources Group, 2009, available at <http://www.mckinsey.com/App_Media/Reports/Water/Charting_Our_Water_Future_Exec%20Summary_001.pdf>.

4   The Barilla Group et al., *Charting Our Water Future Economic Frameworks to Inform Decision-Making*, 2030 Water Resources Group, 2009, available at <http://www.mckinsey.com/App_Media/Reports/Water/Charting_Our_Water_Future_Exec%20Summary_001.pdf>.

5   Food and Agriculture Organization (FAO), "How to Feed the World in 2050", High-Level Expert Forum, Rome, 12–13 October 2009, available at <http://www.fao.org/fileadmin/templates/wsfs/docs/expert_paper/How_to_Feed_the_World_in_2050.pdf>.

6   Food and Agriculture Organization (FAO), "Coping with Water Scarcity: Challenge of the Twenty-first Century", 22 March 2007, available at <http://www.fao.org/nr/water/docs/escarcity.pdf>.

7   Luis S. Pereira, Ian Cordery, and Iacovos Iacovides, *Coping With Water Scarcity*, Technical Documents in Hydrology, no. 58 (Paris: UNESCO, 2002), available at <http://unesdoc.unesco.org/images/0012/001278/127846e.pdf>.

8   *Physical water scarcity* (water resources development is approaching or has exceeded sustainable limits): more than 75 per cent of river flows are withdrawn.

9   *Approaching physical water scarcity*: more than 60 per cent of river flows are withdrawn. These basins will experience physical water scarcity in the near future.

10 *Economic water scarcity* (human, institutional, and financial capital limit access to water even though water in nature is available locally to meet human demands): water resources are abundant relative to water use, with less than 25 per cent of water from rivers withdrawn for human purposes, but malnutrition exists.

11 Earthscan/International Water Management Institute (IWMI), *Water for Food, Water for Life: A Comprehensive Assessment of Water Management in Agriculture* (London; Colombo, 2007), available at <http://www.fao.org/nr/water/docs/Summary_SynthesisBook.pdf>; Food and Agriculture Organization (FAO), "Coping with Water Scarcity: Challenge of the Twenty-first Century", 22 March 2007, available at <http://www.fao.org/nr/water/docs/escarcity.pdf>.

[12]   United Nations, "Convention on the Protection and Use of Transboundary Watercourses and International Lakes", Helsinki, 17 March 1992, available at <http://live.unece.org/fileadmin/DAM/env/water/pdf/watercon.pdf>.

[13]   River basin, also known as watershed or catchment, is defined as the area which contributes hydrologically (including both surface and groundwater) to a first order stream, which, in turn, is defined by its outlet to the ocean or to a terminal (closed) lake or inland sea.

[14]   Cooley et al., *Understanding and Reducing the Risks of Climate Change for Transboundary Waters* (Oakland: Pacific Institute, December 2009), available at <http://www.pacinst.org/reports/transboundary_waters/transboundary_water_and_climate_report.pdf>; Meredith A. Giordano and Aaron T. Wolf, "Sharing Waters: Post-Rio International Water Management", Natural Resources Forum 27 (2003): 163–71, available at <http://www.transboundarywaters.orst.edu/publications/abst_docs/narf_051_Giordano.pdf>.

[15]   Cooley et al., *Understanding and Reducing the Risks of Climate Change for Transboundary Waters* (Oakland: Pacific Institute, December 2009), available at <http://www.pacinst.org/reports/transboundary_waters/transboundary_water_and_climate_report.pdf>.

[16]   Peter H. Gleick, "Water and Conflict: Fresh Water Resource and International Security", *International Security*, vol. 18, no. 1 (1993): 79–112, available at <http://www.pacinst.org/reports/international_security_gleick_1993.pdf>.

[17]   Thomas Homer-Dixon, "The Myth of Global Water Wars", *Toronto Globe and Mail*, 9 November 1995, available at <http://www.homerdixon.com/download/the_myth_of_global.pdf>.

[18]   Aaron T. Wolf, Shira B. Yoffe, and Mark Giordano, *International Waters: Indicators for Identifying Basins at Risk*, Technical Documents in Hydrology, PCCP series, no. 20, UNESCO, 2003, available at <http://unesdoc.unesco.org/images/0013/001333/133306e.pdf>.

[19]   Aaron Wolf, "Conflict and Cooperation along International waterways", *Water Policy*, vol. 1, no. 2 (1998): 251–65, available at <http://www.cawater-info.net/bk/water_law/pdf/wolf_e.pdf>.

[20]   China Dialogue et al., *The Water of the Third Pole: Sources of Threat, Sources of Survival*, 2009, available at <http://www.chinadialogue.net/UserFiles/File/third_pole_full_report.pdf>.

[21]   International Centre for Integrated Mountain Development (ICIMOD), "Hindu Kush-Himalayan Region", undated, available at <http://www.icimod.org/?page=43>.

[22]   The Asia Society, *Asia's Next Challenge: Securing the Region's Water Future*, New York, April 2009, available at <http://asiasociety.org/files/pdf/WaterSecurity Report.pdf>.

[23]   Cooley et al., *Understanding and Reducing the Risks of Climate Change for Transboundary Waters* (Oakland: Pacific Institute, 2009), available at <http://www.pacinst.org/reports/transboundary_waters/transboundary_water_

and_climate_report.pdf>; Aaron Wolf, "Conflict and Cooperation along International Waterways", *Water Policy*, vols. 1 and 2 (1998): 251–65, available at <http://www.cawater-info.net/bk/water_law/pdf/wolf_e.pdf>.

24   Sergei Vinogradov, Patricia Wouters, and Patricia Jones, *Transforming Potential Conflict into Cooperation Potential: The Role of International Water Law*, UNESCO/IHP/WWAP, Technical Documents in Hydrology, PCCP Series, no. 2 (2003), available at <http://www.gwptoolbox.org/images/stories/Docs/unceso%20intwaterlaw.pdf >.

25   Government of India/Government of Pakistan, *The Indus Waters Treaty 1960*, 10 September 1960, available at <http://www.circleofblue.org/waternews/wp-content/uploads/2010/11/IndusWatersTreaty1960.pdf>; Kishor Uprety and Salman M.A. Salman, "Hydro-Politics in South Asia: A Comparative Analysis of the Mahakali and the Ganges Treaties", *Natural Resources Journal*, vol. 39, no. 2 (1999), available at <http://lawlibrary.unm.edu/nrj/39/2/05_salman_ganges.pdf>.

26   Ministry of External Affairs, "Q.533 Chinese Dams on Upper Reaches of Brahmaputra", Ministry of External Affairs, Rajya Sabha, 4 August 2011, available at <http://www.mea.gov.in/mystart.php?id=220117963>.

27   Mekong River Commission (MRC), "Agreement on the Cooperation for the Sustainable Development of the Mekong River Basin", Chiang Rai, 5 April 1995, available at <http://www.mrcmekong.org/download/agreement95/agreement_Apr95.pdf>.

28   Hanne Bach et al., *From Local Watershed Management to Integrated River Basin Management at National and Transboundary Levels* (Vientiane: Mekong River Commission [MRC], 2011), available at <http://www.mpowernetwork.org/Knowledge_Bank/Key_Reports/PDF/Dialogue_Reports/Watershed_Management.pdf>.

29   Bruce Pannier, "Battle Lines Drawn in Central Asian Water Dispute", Radio Free Europe/Radio Liberty, 19 April 2009, available at <http://www.rferl.org/content/Battle_Lines_Being_Drawn_In_Central_Asian_Water_Dispute/1611679.html>.

30   Intergovernmental Panel on Climate Change (IPCC), *Climate Change 2007: Working Group II: Impacts, Adaption and Vulnerability*, IPCC Fourth Assessment Report (AR4), 2007, available at <http://www.ipcc.ch/publications_and_data/ar4/wg2/en/ch10s10-6-2.html#>.

31   Jonathan Leake and Chris Hastings, "World Misled over Himalayan Glacier Meltdown", *The Times*, 17 January 2010, available at <http://www.timesonline.co.uk/tol/news/environment/article6991177.ece>.

32   Keith Schneider, "70 Per Cent of Himalayan Glaciers Gone by Next Century, Studies Say", Circle of Blue, 29 June 2010, available at <http://www.circleofblue.org/waternews/2010/world/70-percent-of-himalayan-glaciers-gone-by-next-century-studies-say/>.

[33]   Global Water Partnership (GWP)/Technical Advisory Committee (TAC), *Integrated Water Resources Management*, TAC Background Paper no. 4, Stockholm, 2000, available at <http://www.unep.org/civil_society/GCSF8/pdfs/IWRM_water_efficiency_eng.pdf>.

[34]   United Nations, Agenda 21, "Section II: Conservation and Management of Resources for Development, Chapter 18: Protection of the Quality & Supply of Freshwater Resources: Application of Integrated Approaches to the Development, Management and Use of Water Resources", Official outcome of the United Nations Conference on Environment and Development (UNCED), Rio de Janeiro, 3–14 June 1992, available at <http://www.un.org/esa/dsd/agenda21/res_agenda21_18.shtml>.

References

The Asia Society. *Asia's Next Challenge: Securing the Region's Water Future*. New York, April 2009. Available at <http://asiasociety.org/files/pdf/WaterSecurityReport.pdf>.

Bach, Hanne et al. *From Local Watershed Management to Integrated River Basin Management at National and Transboundary Levels*. Vientiane: Mekong River Commission (MRC), 2011. Available at <http://www.mpowernetwork.org/Knowledge_Bank/Key_Reports/PDF/Dialogue_Reports/Watershed_Management.pdf>.

The Barilla Group et al. *Charting Our Water Future Economic Frameworks to Inform Decision-Making*. 2030 Water Resources Group, 2009. Available at <http://www.mckinsey.com/App_Media/Reports/Water/Charting_Our_Water_Future_Exec%20Summary_001.pdf>.

China Dialogue et al. *The Water of the Third Pole: Sources of Threat, Sources of Survival*, 2009. Available at <http://www.chinadialogue.net/UserFiles/File/third_pole_full_report.pdf>.

Cooley et al. *Understanding and Reducing the Risks of Climate Change for Transboundary Waters*. Oakland: Pacific Institute, December 2009. Available at <http://www.pacinst.org/reports/transboundary_waters/transboundary_water_and_climate_report.pdf>.

Earthscan/International Water Management Institute (IWMI). *Water for Food, Water for Life: A Comprehensive Assessment of Water Management in Agriculture*. London; Colombo, 2007. Available at <http://www.fao.org/nr/water/docs/Summary_SynthesisBook.pdf>.

Food and Agriculture Organization (FAO). "How to Feed the World in 2050". High-Level Expert Forum, Rome, 12–13 October 2009. Available at <http://www.fao.org/fileadmin/templates/wsfs/docs/expert_paper/How_to_Feed_the_World_in_2050.pdf>.

————. "Coping with Water Scarcity: Challenge of the Twenty-first Century", 22 March 2007. Available at <http://www.fao.org/nr/water/docs/escarcity.pdf>.

Giordano, Meredith A. and Aaron T. Wolf. "Sharing Waters: Post-Rio International Water Management". *Natural Resources Forum* 27 (2003): 163–71. Available at <http://www.transboundarywaters.orst.edu/publications/abst_docs/narf_051_Giordano.pdf>.

Gleick, Peter H. "Water and Conflict: Fresh Water Resource and International Security". *International Security*, vol. 18, no. 1 (1993): 79–112. Available at <http://www.pacinst.org/reports/international_security_gleick_1993.pdf>.

Global Water Partnership (GWP)/Technical Advisory Committee (TAC). *Integrated Water Resources Management*. TAC Background Paper no. 4. Stockholm, 2000. Available at <http://www.unep.org/civil_society/GCSF8/pdfs/IWRM_water_efficiency_eng.pdf>.

Government of India/Government of Pakistan. *The Indus Waters Treaty 1960*, 10 September 1960. Available at <http://www.circleofblue.org/waternews/wp-content/uploads/2010/11/IndusWatersTreaty1960.pdf>.

Homer-Dixon, Thomas. "The Myth of Global Water Wars". *Toronto Globe and Mail*, 9 November 1995. Available at <http://www.homerdixon.com/download/the_myth_of_global.pdf>.

Intergovernmental Panel on Climate Change (IPCC). *Climate Change 2007: Working Group II: Impacts, Adaption and Vulnerability*. IPCC Fourth Assessment Report (AR4), 2007. Available at <http://www.ipcc.ch/publications_and_data/ar4/wg2/en/ch10s10-6-2.html#>.

International Centre for Integrated Mountain Development (ICIMOD). "Hindu Kush-Himalayan Region". Undated. Available at <http://www.icimod.org/?page=43>.

Leake, Jonathan and Chris Hastings. "World Misled over Himalayan Glacier Meltdown". *The Times*, 17 January 2010. Available at <http://www.timesonline.co.uk/tol/news/environment/article6991177.ece>.

Mekong River Commission (MRC). "Agreement on the Cooperation for the Sustainable Development of the Mekong River Basin". Chiang Rai, 5 April 1995. Available at <http://www.mrcmekong.org/download/agreement95/agreement_Apr95.pdf>.

Ministry of External Affairs. "Q.533 Chinese Dams on Upper Reaches of Brahmaputra". Ministry of External Affairs, Rajya Sabha, 4 August 2011. Available at <http://www.mea.gov.in/mystart.php?id=220117963>.

Pannier, Bruce. "Battle Lines Drawn In Central Asian Water Dispute". Radio Free Europe/Radio Liberty, 19 April 2009. Available at <http://www.rferl.org/content/Battle_Lines_Being_Drawn_In_Central_Asian_Water_Dispute/1611679.html>.

Pereira, Luis S., Ian Cordery, and Iacovos Iacovides. *Coping With Water Scarcity*. Technical Documents in Hydrology, no. 58. Paris: UNESCO, 2002. Available at <http://unesdoc.unesco.org/images/0012/001278/127846e.pdf>.

Rosegrant, Mark W. *Water Resources in the Twenty-First Century: Challenges and Implications for Action*. Food, Agriculture, and the Environment Discussion Paper 20. Washington, D.C.: International Food Policy Research Institute (IFPRI), March 1997. Available at <http://www.ifpri.org/sites/default/files/publications/pubs_2020_dp_dp20.pdf>.

Schneider, Keith. "70 Percent of Himalayan Glaciers Gone by Next Century, Studies Say". Circle of Blue, 29 June 2010. Available at <http://www.circleofblue.org/waternews/2010/world/70-percent-of-himalayan-glaciers-gone-by-next-century-studies-say/>.

United Nations. "Convention on the Protection and Use of Transboundary Watercourses and International Lakes". Helsinki, 17 March 1992. Available at <http://live.unece.org/fileadmin/DAM/env/water/pdf/watercon.pdf>.

Uprety, Kishor and Salman M. A. Salman. "Hydro-Politics in South Asia: A Comparative Analysis of the Mahakali and the Ganges Treaties". *Natural Resources Journal*, vol. 39, no. 2 (1999). Available at <http://lawlibrary.unm.edu/nrj/39/2/05_salman_ganges.pdf>.

Wolf, Aaron. "Conflict and Cooperation along International Waterways". *Water Policy*, vol. 1, no. 2 (1998): 251–65. Available at <http://www.cawater-info.net/bk/water_law/pdf/wolf_e.pdf>.

Wolf, Aaron T., Shira B. Yoffe, and Mark Giordano. *International Waters: Indicators for Identifying Basins at Risk*. Technical Documents in Hydrology, PCCP series, no. 20. UNESCO, 2003. Available at <http://unesdoc.unesco.org/images/0013/001333/133306e.pdf>.

Vinogradov, Sergei, Patricia Wouters, and Patricia Jones. *Transforming Potential Conflict into Cooperation Potential: The Role of International Water Law*. UNESCO/IHP/WWAP, Technical Documents in Hydrology, PCCP Series, no. 2 (2003). Available at <http://www.gwptoolbox.org/images/stories/Docs/unceso%20intwaterlaw.pdf>.

5

NATURAL DISASTERS

Mely Caballero-Anthony, Irene A. Kuntjoro,
Sofiah Jamil, Pau Khan Khup Hangzo and
Sadhavi Sharma

Southeast Asia witnesses a number of natural disasters and did so through-out 2010, highlighting variable levels of national preparedness in dealing with disasters and illustrating the need for greater regional cooperation. This chapter looks at how governments in this disaster-prone region respond to the impact of these large scale events.

WHAT ARE NATURAL DISASTERS?

The Centre for Research on the Epidemiology of Disasters (CRED) defines a disaster as "a situation or event which overwhelms local capacity, necessitating a request to a national or international level for external assistance; an unforeseen and often sudden event that causes great damage, destruction and human suffering".[1] For a disaster to be entered into its Emergency Events Database or EM-DAT, at least one of the following criteria must be fulfilled: 10 or more people reported killed; 100 or more people reported affected; declaration of a state of emergency; and calls for international assistance.

The EM-DAT distinguishes two generic categories for disasters: natural and technological. The natural disaster category was further divided into five sub-groups, which in turn cover twelve disaster types and more than thirty sub-types, as can be found on Table 5.1.

As in previous years, in 2008 Asia remained the most affected continent by natural disasters. The region accounted for 40 per cent of all reported natural disasters and more than 80 per cent of all reported victims. Economic

Table 5.1
Classification of Natural Disasters

Disaster Sub-Group	Definition	Disasters: Main Types
Geophysical	Events originating from solid earth.	• Earthquakes • Volcanic eruptions • Mass movements (dry): rockfall, landslide, avalanche, subsidence
Meteorological	Events caused by short-lived/small to meso scale atmospheric processes (in the spectrum from minutes to days).	• Storms: tropical cyclone, extra-tropical cyclone, local storm
Hydrological	Events caused by deviations in the normal water cycle and/or overflow of bodies of water caused by wind set-up.	• Floods: general flood, flash flood, storm surge/coastal flood • Mass movements (wet): rockfall, landslide, avalanche, subsidence
Climatological	Events caused by long-lived/meso to macro scale processes (in the spectrum from intra-seasonal to multi-decadal climate variability).	• Extreme temperatures: heat wave, cold wave, extreme weather conditions • Droughts • Wildfires: forest fire, land fire
Biological	Disaster caused by the exposure of living organisms to germs and toxic substances.	• Epidemics: viral infectious disease, bacterial infectious disease, parasitic infectious disease, fungal infectious disease, prion infectious disease • Insect infestation • Animal stampede

Source: Adapted from *Annual Disaster Statistical Review 2008: The Numbers and Trends* (CRED, June 2009).

damage costs in Asia almost doubled from 34 per cent in the period 2000–07 to 62 per cent in 2008. Looking at the patterns of natural disaster in Asia, one can observed all types of natural disasters. This is particularly true in Southeast Asia. The most common forms of natural disasters in Cambodia, Indonesia, Philippines and Vietnam for the period 1900 to 2009 are:

Indonesia   : Earthquakes, volcanic eruptions, floods, droughts, storms, epidemics and wildfires.
Philippines : Earthquakes, volcanic eruptions, floods, droughts and storms.
Vietnam   : Floods, droughts, storms and epidemics.
Cambodia : Floods, droughts, storms and epidemics.

What is EM-DAT?

Since 1988 the World Health Organization (WHO) Collaborating Centre for Research on the Epidemiology of Disasters (CRED) has been maintaining an Emergency Events Database or EM-DAT. EM-DAT was created with the initial support of the WHO and the Belgian government. The main objective of the database is to serve the purposes of humanitarian action at national and international levels. It is an initiative aimed to rationalise decision-making for disaster preparedness, as well as providing an objective base for vulnerability assessment and priority setting.

EM-DAT contains essential core data on the occurrences and effects of over 16,000 mass disasters in the world from 1900 to present. The database is compiled from various sources, including UN agencies, non-governmental organisations, insurance companies, research institutes and press agencies. Find out more at <http://www.emdat.be/>.

ANALYSING A RANGE OF DISASTERS

During the final quarter of 2009, Southeast Asia was afflicted by a number of natural disasters that have caused infrastructural damage and human insecurities in several places in the region. Between September and early November alone, a number of earthquakes affected different areas along the Indonesian archipelago (see Table 5.2), of which the earthquakes that struck West Java and West Sumatra are considered the two major ones. Between 26 September and 31 October, the Philippines witnessed three devastating tropical storms. While the country is used to an average of twenty typhoons a year, storms continuously test its disaster response plans to the limit, forcing it to seek international help. The first of the three tropical storms, Typhoon Ketsana, locally known as "Ondoy", swept across Metro Manila and parts of Central Luzon on 26 September, drenching the island nation with its heaviest rainfall in forty years — a month's worth in just twelve hours — which flooded about 80 per cent of Manila. After creating a calamity in the Philippines, Ketsana lashed the central and northern provinces of Cambodia and central and highland provinces of Vietnam on 29 October. Typhoon Parma, also known as "Pepeng", struck the Philippines a week later on 3 October. This was followed by Typhoon Mirinae, also known as "Santi", on 30 October. On 8 November, this typhoon made landfall in Vietnam. An overview of the extent of damage caused by these disasters can be seen in Table 5.2.

Looking Beyond Numbers and Figures

The Padang earthquake accounted for damage to 85 per cent of public infrastructure in West Sumatra. Among the victims were those found trapped in the rubble; shoddy infrastructure often causes increased death tolls in disasters. The government of West Sumatra admitted that they had not been strict in applying building codes and regulations to ensure quake-proof construction. They hence promised to increase supervision in meeting these standards, by setting up a construction council tasked with ensuring that construction plans meet government standards.

The quake and the subsequent landslides had cut access to several remote areas, particularly the inland mountainous areas. It has hindered aid distribution during periods of relief efforts and could further slow down the reconstruction and rehabilitation process. Essential aid has only reached most isolated villages nearly four weeks after an earthquake. The Indonesian National Agency for Disaster Management (Badan Nasional Penanggulangan Bencana or BNPB) has stated that rebuilding of roads and bridges are one of the main priorities of the reconstruction and rehabilitation process. These efforts will be supported by the Indonesian Military (TNI), which have agreed to deploy 500 soldiers to rebuild roads or create new access routes to affected areas.[2]

In the disaster's aftermath, the threat of fresh landslides in affected areas becomes imminent with the coming of the monsoon season. Therefore, there is a need to relocate the people from emergency shelters to transitional shelters that are stronger. There is a shortage of water for thousands of survivors, with contaminated wells and damage to water pumps in many houses. More than a month following the earthquake, the survivors are still

Table 5.2

List of Major Natural Disasters and Its Impacts in Southeast Asia from September to November 2009

Date	Disaster Event	Locations Affected	Deaths	Injured	Houses Damaged	Other Damages
2 Sep	Earthquake 7.3 on Richter Scale	Tasikmalaya, West Java	81	1,287	243,000	• 12,000 damaged infrastructures and public facilities • Over 194,000 people displaced
26 Sep	Typhoon Ketsana (Ondoy)	Metro Manila & Central Luzon, the Philippines (total of 16 cities)	464	529	185,004	• 4,901,234 persons affected
29 Sep	Typhoon Ketsana	Central and northern provinces of Cambodia	43	67	1,783 (as of 7 Oct)	• 40,000 hectares of paddy fields damaged
29 Sep	Typhoon Ketsana	Vietnam (total of 15 central & highland provinces)	163 (two highest: 47 in Kon Tum; 33 in Quang Ngai — as of 4 Oct 09)	616 (as of 4 Oct 09)	400,000	• 3,000,000 people affected destroyed crops across central Vietnam
30 Sep	Earthquake 7.6 Richter Scale	Padang, West Sumatra	1,117 (two highest: 675 in Pariaman; 313 in city of Padang)		279,000	• 8,800 damaged infrastructures and public facilities
3 Oct	Typhoon Parma (Pepeng)	The Philippines (total of 36 cities)	456	207	54,373	• 4,478,284 people affected
30 Oct	Typhoon Mirinae (Santi)	The Philippines (total of 8 cities)	18	6	75	• 13,456 people affected
8 Nov	Typhoon Mirinae	Vietnam (total of 9 provinces)	123 (Highest: 78 in Phu Yen — as of 8 Nov 09)	145	50,755	• 19,000 hectares of paddy field damaged • 2,400 hectares of fish and shrimp aquaculture damaged

Sources: Various media and government reports.

Table 5.3
List of Earthquakes in Indonesia, September–November 2009

Date	Area Affected	Magnitude (on Richter Scale)
2 Sep	Tasikmalaya, West Java	7.3
30 Sep	Padang, West Sumatra	7.6
4 Oct	Papua	5.5
24 Oct	Maluku	7.3
25 Oct	Maluku	5.3 and 5.0
29 Oct	Jayapura, Papua	5.8
29 Oct	Bitung, North Sulawesi	5.6
9 Nov	Bima, West Nusa Tenggara	6.7
10 Nov	Maluku	5.2
10 Nov	Mentawai, West Sumatra	4.8
11 Nov	Mentawai, West Sumatra	5
12 Nov	Tanahmasa, North Sumatra	5

grappling with lack of clean water and sanitation. Approximately 600,000 people in Padang are projected to be dependent on water trucks until the end of 2009.

In the Philippines, survivors living in the presence of flood waters and in shelters are at risk of infectious disease outbreaks caused by the lack of safe water and clean sanitation. Among the victims of Mirinae, there were 167 people who suffer from leptospirosis, a flood-borne disease caused by exposure to water contaminated with rat and other animal urine.

In the case of Cambodia, even before the advent of Ketsana, the country had experienced heavy rains since 8 September, and the resultant flood waters had inundated thirty-nine communes in six districts of Kampong Thom Province. In addition to the existing flooding, the tropical storm brought more flood water and havoc to at least three provinces. It has brought long-term impacts due to destroyed rice, vegetables and other cash crops. According to Agriculture Minister Chan Sarun, out of 2,331 million hectares of land under paddy cultivation, the tropical storm had damaged between 2 to 4 per cent, or 40,000 hectares. As a result, both farmers who own farmlands and those who sell their labour to work on farms are deprived of their livelihoods. International aid organizations like Oxfam are warning of a looming food crisis with 15,000 households waiting for immediate food assistance, with the number increasing rapidly as floodwaters continue to recede slowly. Many more families have used up their food stocks. Many in hard-hit regions have resorted to dangerous practices to feed their families. Some farmers, for example, have been selling their cattle at rock-bottom prices. Others who have no assets are borrowing money, promising to pay it back with cheap labour at 2,000 riels (US$0.48) a day. This makes them increasingly vulnerable to labour exploitation.

An Important Milestone, Yet Not Enough

In response to the frequent disasters, governments in the region have established or appointed a dedicated national body as the focal point for natural disaster management. Under the Law No. 24/2007 on Disaster Management, the Indonesian government formed the BNPB in 2008. It is tasked with disaster prevention, relief effort coordination and overseeing post-disaster reconstruction. Following the Indian Ocean tsunami in 2004, the Indonesian government is increasingly capable of leading the disaster response operations, with the BNPB as its spearhead. The government plays a coordinating role in both domestic and international responses.

In the aftermath of the Tasikmalaya earthquake in West Java, the government promised to cover 80 per cent of the total rehabilitation funds, equalling to 1.5 trillion rupiah. The remaining 20 per cent was covered by the relevant provincial and municipal governments. Considering the relatively modest magnitude of the disaster and its increasing disaster management capacity, the Indonesian government did not appeal for international assistance. In a different case, the severity of the West Sumatra earthquake has compelled Indonesia to appeal for international assistance. The government estimates that the reconstruction process in West Sumatra will cost up to US$700 million, including a proposed US$300 million to rebuild damaged houses and the remaining used to reconstruct damaged public facilities and other infrastructure. The government is planning to adopt the combination of the reconstruction model used for the tsunami-affected Aceh and the 2006 Yogyakarta earthquake by taking into consideration cultural values in West Sumatra. President Yudhoyono noted that the reconstruction and rehabilitation process have to be seen as an opportunity to build more resilient communities and infrastructure for future disasters.

The National Disaster Coordinating Council (NDCC), chaired by the Secretary of National Defense, is the focal point for disaster management in the Philippines. The NDCC comprises eighteen heads of departments or agencies as members. These include the Chief of Staff of the Armed Forces of the Philippines, Secretary-General of the Philippine National Red Cross, the head of the Philippine Information Agency, Executive Secretary and the Administrator of the Office of Civil Defense. Disaster preparedness, prevention, mitigation and response are carried out under the NDCC system. At the national level, the NDCC serves as the President's advisor on disaster preparedness programmes, disaster operations and rehabilitation efforts undertaken by the government and the private sector.

The Philippine government has come in for scathing criticism for its response, with many calling it inadequate and delayed. The government has so far not responded directly to the accusations that it has not been doing enough, although it acknowledged that it had been overwhelmed by the disaster. Survivors, while thankful for the relief goods that have been coming their way, have criticized the government for not warning residents early enough about the floods or for not having enough resources to deal with the calamity. The storms also exposed the government's poor urban planning that has allowed sprawling shanty towns to be established beside flood pathways and riverbanks.

Responding to earlier criticism during the aftermath of Ketsana, government agencies responded swiftly to the remaining storms, launching extensive search and rescue operations and releasing emergency relief stocks. The military also provide help in relief efforts. Pre-emptive evacuation of people living in vulnerable areas has been undertaken. However, the extensive damage caused by flood waters has meant that the capacities of many local and national response agencies have been exhausted. On 28 September, the Chair of the NDCC requested through the United Nations Resident Coordinator for the assistance of the international community in responding to the effects of storms.

In Cambodia, the National Committee for Disaster Management, a ministerial-level agency chaired by the prime minister, is at the forefront in responding to disasters. The government, in partnership with international agencies, assesses the damage to and needs of affected communities in the aftermath of Ketsana. Food, relief supplies, and medicines have been provided. The Cambodian Ministry of Health (MOH) has provided flood kits, diarrhoea kits and anti-malaria medicines to affected areas. Mobile health teams have been sent to affected areas. Water purification tablets have also been supplied by the MOH. Further damage assessment is underway.

In Vietnam, the People's Aid Coordinating Committee serves as the focal point for coordination of relief support. During the recent typhoons, the Vietnamese government was prepared to distribute food and non-food aid to affected communities and to work together with international agencies. The government was also able to monitor the coming typhoons. The early warning mechanism was functioning and evacuations were successful in minimizing casualties. More than 200,000 people had been evacuated from the path of Ketsana before it struck central Vietnam. The military and the police also helped the authorities to conduct evacuations down to the local level. Although more than 370,000 people were evacuated from the typhoon's path, it remains a challenge for the government to provide shelter and food for the evacuees. Floods and mudslides have also made it difficult to deliver aid to the survivors in several areas.

Moreover, unexpected sustained heavy rains and having to recover from the impact of Ketsana compounded the impact of Mirinae in Vietnam, overwhelming the resilience of communities and the government's capacity to respond. Despite progress shown in the country, the Vietnamese government is expected to further improve its preparedness to cope with storms and flooding, especially with the increasing magnitude and frequency of these storms. Bui Minh Tang, the Director of the National Centre for Hydro-Meteorological Forecasting, argued that Vietnam needs to improve its capacity, infrastructure, equipment and technology in meteorological forecasting. It would be useful to support public early warning systems that have been put in place.[3]

Minimizing Casualties and Humanitarian Risk

In responding to the earthquake in West Java, BNBP spokesperson, Priyadi Kardono, admitted that there was lack of resources and coordination. Even though there were adequate amounts of aid, it was unevenly distributed and did not reach the survivors in a timely manner. Limited human resources and other means such as transportation caused the delay. Learning from this experience, the provincial government of West Java is planning to establish a Local Agency for Disaster Management, to be operational by early 2010 to effectively address and coordinate future disaster management activities.

This case reflects general concern regarding weak coordination of recovery efforts and slow assistance to the victims. In disaster relief, time is essential to minimize casualties. Logistical delay should be cut to deliver help in time. Yet, Dr Syamsul Ma'arif, the Chairman of BNBP argued that the success of relief and recovery efforts should be proportionally assessed in a wider perspective. Delayed in immediate response on the ground could be caused by the collapse of local authorities which also will find themselves as disaster victims.

This is where a people-centred disaster management approach should be further advanced. According to Indonesian law, local communities should be at the front lines of disaster prevention and responses. Looking at the developments surrounding Typhoon Ketsana's landfall in the Philippines, civil society has become the forefront of relief efforts when the government is overwhelmed. Strengthening community capacity to prevent and cope with disasters is a concrete way to save lives. Developing early-warning systems is crucial. The Vietnamese government and Vietnam's communities have set a good example in implementing early warning mechanisms in the wake of the two typhoons. Disaster preparedness awareness and skills for emergency situations should be fostered among communities living in disaster-prone areas.

Observing experiences in dealing with disasters, some countries are better prepared than others. Nevertheless, improvements in disaster management capacity are pertinent for all states in the region. Scientific findings have indicated that the region would see an increasing magnitude and frequency of natural disasters. Disaster management should be seen as a cycle of prevention and emergency relief, to rehabilitation and reconstruction. Rehabilitation and reconstruction processes should aim to strengthen the resilience of the communities as a means of prevention, so that when the next disaster hits, both states and communities in the region would be better prepared.

INTEGRATING ADAPTATION INTO DEVELOPMENT POLICY IN SOUTHEAST ASIA

Southeast Asia is potentially one of the more vulnerable regions to climate change impacts, as many of the countries in the region have relatively low levels of development, weak infrastructure, long coastlines, and a significant percentage of the population is still dependent on agriculture, a sector which is more climate-sensitive. Recognizing this, developing countries in the region have been vociferous in their support for adaptation. This section looks at three countries — Indonesia, Thailand and the Philippines — to examine the place of adaptation in government policy.

Countries in Southeast Asia are already more susceptible to extreme weather events. Climate change increases their potential vulnerability to natural hazards; coastal geography means that these countries are more likely to be affected by sea-level rise, tropical storms and cyclones. Similarly, the agricultural sector in the region is also more likely to be affected on account of changes in the climate. Agriculture is the main source of livelihood in nearly all the countries in the region and the 2009 Economics of Adaptation to Climate Change (EACC) Report shows that changes in temperature will significantly affect crop yields and production, necessitating adaptation in the sector.[4] While climate change could also potentially have implications for areas such as health, water supply and business, infrastructure and agriculture will prove to be key areas in the region that demand greater attention. The EACC Report suggests that the costs of adaptation could be US$75–100 billion a year, and East Asia and the Pacific are expected to face the highest costs with infrastructure accounting for the largest share. Growing population and the high concentration of human and economic activities in this mostly coastal region is also an important factor in adaptation needs and capacities.[5]

As seen previously, adaptation can either be planned or reactive. Often reactive adaptation takes place at an individual and local level, and is thus difficult to monitor or record. Planned adaptation, however, can be undertaken as part of an international agenda, regionally and, as is more common, by national governments. Increasingly, planned adaptation at a local level is also being undertaken by community-based and non-governmental organizations. Many international organizations and aid agencies such as the United States Agency for International Development (USAID), Oxfam, International Institute for Environment and Development (IIED), and the United Nations are playing an increasing role in driving local adaptation programmes.

According to the Institute of Social and Environmental Transition's (ISET) study of existing adaptation knowledge and measures in Southeast Asia, all policy and research approaches to adaptation in the region largely fall under the following categories: (1) national efforts to meet obligations of the United Nations Framework Convention on Climate Change (UNFCCC); (2) assessment of climate change impacts and vulnerabilities, particularly around water and agriculture; (3) community-based adaptation strategies; (4) disaster management and disaster risk reduction; and (5) economic analyses and adaptation research.[6]

In this section, we provide an overview of national policy plans and of measures that address key concern areas for most countries in terms of vulnerabilities. These are adaptation needs in agriculture such as changes in crop management, water use, the use of new types of seeds and disaster management, something which includes preparedness, building flood defences and efficient response systems.

The National Communication to the United Nations Framework Convention on Climate Change (UNFCCC) is a useful indication of a country's strategy and policy on climate change. Ninety-one countries, including Indonesia, the Philippines and Thailand, have ratified the UNFCCC. As per Article 4.1b of the Framework, all member parties are to "formulate, implement, publish and regularly update national, and where appropriate, regional programmes containing measures to ... facilitate adaptation to climate change".[7]

The initial national communications to the UNFCCC were submitted by Indonesia (1999), Thailand (2000), and the Philippines (2000). While presenting plans for mitigating Green House Gas (GHG) emissions, the communications have placed relatively less attention to adaptation, only acknowledging its importance but lacking a coherent and detailed policy on it.

Indonesia

Indonesia submitted its initial national communication to the UNFCCC in 1999. The document does not state a clear adaptation policy or a strategy for it. However, it recognizes the importance of adaptation and technology in agriculture as well as other areas such as forestry, energy, and coastal resources. It states the need for a long-term adaptation strategy for the possibility of sea-level rise and the need for improving technology and innovation, and for information transfer in order to speed up adaptation. Its stated policy on adaptation in the 1999 document focused only on the Clean Development Mechanism (CDM).[8]

Indonesia's National Action Plan (RAN-PI) for addressing climate change was formulated in 2007 with the aim of it serving as a guideline for various government institutions in carrying out coordinated and integrated efforts for tackling climate change, including adaptation. Along with the RAN-PI, it also formulated Indonesia's Climate Change Adaptation Plan or ICCAP, which is based conceptually on the interaction between society, ecology and economy and "aims to embed a climate risk and opportunity management mechanism within national, provincial and local development plans"[9] and is supported by the United Nations Development Programme (UNDP). In addition, Indonesia has proposed the Presidential Regulation, which will function as an umbrella to all activities related with climate change impact in terms of both mitigation and adaptation. As per the RAN-PI, adaptation to climate change is a key aspect of the national development agenda with its integration into the national development plans as the long-term objective. It also suggests that the adaptation agenda should be linked to the National Action Plan on Reduction of Disaster Risk (RAN-PRB). The RAN-PI as a policy instrument aims to integrate both adaptation and mitigation into various policy areas such as health, agriculture, disaster management, science and technology. It has a clear strategy for integrating the adaptation agenda in its development goals, which includes mainstreaming adaptation into the infrastructure planning and design — maintaining drains, building regulations for coastal development — as well as into other sectors' policy such as agriculture, health and industry.

Thailand

Thailand has so far only submitted its first national communication to UNFCCC,[10] which articulates its policy on climate change, both with regard to mitigation and adaptation. The communication includes information on vulnerabilities and adaptation, research and development, technology transfer and financial resources. It also expresses the need for greater institutional, technological and financial assistance in the areas of vulnerability assessment and adaptation planning. Further, Thailand has incorporated climate change issues into its social and economic development strategies. Thailand's initial communication identifies adaptation options, although in more general terms, in the various sectors of concern, mainly agriculture and coastal management because of potential sea-level rises. The Thai government's stated adaptation objective is "to enhance the research and development capacity" in water resources conservation and agricultural practices. The key constraints in formulating an effective adaptation programme, according to the national communication, are the lack of sufficient research and development in climate and economic modelling as well as in specific areas such as new agricultural technology. There is particular emphasis on the need for technology improvement, research and development, and the need for the transfer of technology from developed countries to developing countries. This is mainly to facilitate vulnerability assessments and climate modelling in order to predict climate impacts.

In January 2008, the Council of Ministers passed a resolution acknowledging national strategies dealing with climate change management for 2008–12, which includes the creation of adaptation ability to address and lessen vulnerability to climate impacts.

Philippines

The Philippines submitted its first national communication to the UNFCCC in December 1999.[11] Its second communication is still in progress. For its national communication, the Philippines conducted detailed vulnerability assessments, especially in the agricultural sector. It includes detailed investigations into and options for adaptation in agriculture and the management of coastal resources, with a stress on the need for increased research in order to design and implement carefully planned adaptation strategies. A number of government bodies such as the National Economic and Development Authority (NEDA) Board, the Department of Environment and Natural Resources (DENR) and National Water Resources Board are involved in mapping an adaptation strategy. The communication recognizes and addresses adaptation needs in much detail.

Other bodies have been created in order to deal with climate change and related areas. In 2007, the Presidential Task Force on Climate Change

Table 5.4

Climate Change Adaptation Initiatives in Southeast Asia

Countries	State/Non-State Policy and Action
Indonesia	UNFCCC: First National Communication with adaptation component National Plan Addressing Climate Change (RAN-PI) Draft National Strategy on Adaptation (ICCAP) EcoSecurities: carbon trading Nestle: water management REDD: Reducing Emissions from Deforestation and Degradation
Thailand	UNFCCC: First National Communication National Strategy on Adaptation
Philippines	UNFCCC: First National Communication (section on adaptation) Second National Communication draft in progress IACCC: Climate Change Adaptation Project (WB-GEF and UNDP/MDG-F) Three national bodies: IACCC, PTFCC and DENR Advisory Group on climate change Philippine Network on Climate Change Manila Observatory/klima: local adaptive management SMART cell phone service provider for warning devices Unilever: aquatic resources restoration Provincial Government of Albay: mainstreaming CC-A COPE (Christian Aid) Oxfam

Source: "Climate Adaptation in Asia: Knowledge Gaps and Research Issues in South East Asia", ISNET Report, June 2008.

was created to conduct climate impact assessments, especially on the most vulnerable sectors such as water, agriculture and coastal areas. Another body, the Inter-Agency Committee on Climate Change was created in 1992 to serve as a national mechanism to coordinate all activities related to climate change. The Environment Management Bureau of the DENR has initiated the Climate Change Adaptation Phase 1, with the aim of developing sector-responsive adaptation activities.[12]

Governments in the region are aware of their adaptation needs, and while there are a number of impacts assessment studies and research underway, comprehensive national plans on adaptation are lacking. As Resurreccion et al. note in their 2008 ISET report, national plans on adaptation are still in the preparatory or planning stages in all countries in the region. These are being prepared by several different departments and sometimes inter-department government bodies although this coordination tends to be in a more ad hoc fashion. For a list of state and non-state initiatives related to climate change and adaptation, see Table 5.4.

POLICY STRATEGIES

Agriculture

Agriculture is an important sector in the region. Despite rapid economic growth and structural transformation, a significant percentage of the populations in most Southeast Asian countries are employed in agriculture. Most Southeast Asian poor live in rural areas and still rely on agriculture for their livelihoods. Poor subsistence farmers are also the most vulnerable to climate change. In many Southeast Asian countries, farmers have traditionally observed a number of practices to adapt to climate variability, for example intercropping, mixed cropping, agro-forestry, animal husbandry, and developed new seed varieties to cope with local climate shifts. Governments in the region are conducting vulnerability assessments in the sector and most of them are working closely with agricultural ministries.

Many agriculture ministries frame adaptation as a way of improving agriculture or crop production systems. Indonesia has stated the need for research and technology to make agriculture more resilient and has suggested food diversification and the local dissemination of agricultural technology to farmers for locally-focused adaptation. In the framework of the RAN-PI, the Ministry of Agriculture in Indonesia has formulated a national strategy. The Agency of Agricultural Research and Development has identified and evaluated adaptive technologies, including the development of crop varieties that are high yielding, drought and inundation tolerant, as well as resistant to pests and diseases. The Agency has also identified and developed production technologies through appropriate crop, water and soil management, water conservation and its efficient utilization, a cropping calendar for Java and a blueprint for drought and flood anticipation.[13]

The agriculture sector in Thailand has adapted to developments in domestic and international economic and social environments. The Thai government's adaptation plan includes a slow shift to organic agriculture. It has conducted impact studies to determine the effects of climate change on crop yields. The studies reflect a number of uncertainties, which present a number of constraints in applying an adaptation model. As an initial measure, the government has noted the usefulness of intensifying the conservation of drought resistant varieties; by improving crop varieties to drought tolerant types; by improving cropping practices to conserve water; and by promoting crop diversification. It also points out the need for an improvement in climate scenarios and achieving more suitable crop models.

Agriculture in Thailand also has adapted to local environmental conditions. According to Thailand's initial national communication to UNFCCC, it has promoted soil conservation, reduction in the application of chemical pesticides and fertilizers, and even chemical-free or organic agriculture. Significantly, it admits that in the long-term it is difficult to study the effectiveness of adaptation measures adopted by individuals and communities locally.

Some precautionary measures suggested as adaptation options, while research and development are ongoing, include:

- Conservation and improvement of local drought resistant varieties
- Improvement of cropping practices to minimize water use
- Application of risk averse cropping systems
- Analysis of potential crop substitution in different regions
- Promotion of crop diversification programme[14]

Agriculture is one of the major sectors for adaptation in the Philippines that has been identified by the government (the others include water and coastal resources). The country's national communication stresses the need for support to farmers and an increase in the adoption of modern technology. The government has conducted vulnerability and adaptation studies in the agricultural sector and has identified a number of gaps that require attention. These include:

- Vulnerability and assessment of production of other important crops (i.e. sugar cane, coconut, cash crops, etc.) and of livestock
- Assessment of the changes in geographical and seasonal distribution of thermal and water resources which are important to crop and livestock production
- Assessment of reduction in GHG emissions with the implementation of the Balanced Fertilisation Programme
- Assessment of reduction in GHG emission from different mixes of adaptation strategies
- Development of management methods from adaptation of agriculture systems to the predicted increased CO_2 concentrations and associated climate change
- Assessment of impacts of intensive farming systems, especially because rice production needs to meet demands of increasing population
- Assessment of long-term effects of climate change on soil fertility and effectiveness of fertilizers and chemicals[15]

Coastal and Disaster Risk Management

Coastal geography in the region means that many cities could potentially be affected by sea-level rise. Coastal infrastructure is an important component of adaptation in these countries and is recognized by governments as an important area because of the level of urbanization and economic activities in some of the coastal cities.

The Philippines ranks high among the most disaster-prone countries and is exposed to several powerful tropical cyclones or storms annually. In 2009 for instance, the tropical storms Ketsana and Parma caused hundreds of casualties and severe damage to housing and other property. In response to concerns about increasing disaster risks arising from climate change, the Philippines Government enacted a new legislation, called the Climate Change Act of 2009, which will integrate disaster risk reduction measures into climate change adaptation plans, development and poverty reduction programmes.[16] The Act also aims to invite foreign funding for adaptation and disaster risk reduction.[17] The primary function of the commission is to "ensure the mainstreaming of climate change, in synergy with disaster risk reduction, into national, sectoral and local development plans and programmes".[18]

In a joint project by the NEDA and UNDP and the Australian Agency for International Development (AusAID), another project, which recognizes the importance of adaptation and disaster risk reduction, was unveiled in 2009. The project "Integrating Disaster Risk Reduction and Climate Change Adaptation (DRR/CCA) in Local Development Planning and Decision-making Processes" aims to mainstream the related concerns of disaster risk reduction and climate change adaptation into local decision-making and planning processes.

According to Smith Dharmasaroja, chair of the Thai Government's National Disaster Warning Administration, Bangkok's land subsidence coupled with rising sea-levels put the city at risk. To counter this threat, disaster prevention experts are now advocating the construction of a 100 billion baht (US$3 billion) flood prevention wall to protect Bangkok.[19] Thailand has conducted a number of vulnerability assessments identifying impacts on inundation of coastal areas and existing drainage and flood control facilities. However, in its national communication it expresses the inadequacy of these when it comes to drawing conclusions or formulating policy recommendations with regard to adaptation options. The Communication states the need for more research, while suggesting some options for adapting to sea-level rise:

- Establishing a coastal hazard management subcommittee to develop policies, strategies and guidelines for coastal hazard management
- Providing guidelines on management and development of coastal areas
- Improving drainage and flood control facilities
- Improving cropping systems suitable to such environmental change, using organic matter to improve salty soil conditions
- Improving crop cultural practices[20]

Local Adaptive Strategies

A number of non-government actors are facilitating adaptation measures in the region, especially in rural areas. Most community-based adaptation projects are being run by international organizations, NGOs and civil society. There are a few projects where the government is aided by international donor bodies and development organizations to work jointly with local bodies and civil society organizations.

The UNFCCC documents local adaptive strategies in its database, which intends to facilitate the transfer of coping strategies, practices and local knowledge. Some examples of local autonomous coping strategies include integrated community-based risk reduction in Indonesia, which is a Red Cross project aimed to develop capacities and "to learn about integrating risk reduction, climate change adaptation, and micro-finance in one holistic project" (UNFCCC adaptation database). This includes community organization and mobilization, formation and training of volunteer groups, self-help groups and availability of micro-credit to complement these activities among others.

In Thailand, in the Lower Songkram River Basin, indigenous forecasting methods — ants removing their eggs from the nest is seen as a sign of rain while a decrease in mushrooms can signal drought — is seen as a community-based case of autonomous adaptation. Other coping mechanisms in the agricultural sector include the ability to grow two different types of rice for dry and wet seasons, respectively, and the diversification of livelihoods. In the Philippines, according to the UNFCCC coping strategies database, indigenous communities of the Philippines use drums and horns to alert their communities against storms and cyclones. Local elderly people in the community, based on abnormal behaviour of animals and the appearance of particular clouds, forecast and predict cyclones and storms.

Other examples of community-based adaptation, where international actors and non-government organizations and players are involved, include crop selection, alternative cultivation methods, soil conservation, dissemination of knowledge and information, capacity building and improved low-cost housing designs that are more flood resistant.

Integrating Adaptation into Development Policy

An overview of government adaptation policies in some countries in the region show that these are largely still in the planning stages, and while governments have conducted some vulnerability assessments and identified risk areas and some adaptation options, concrete strategies and ground-based measures are still absent from national policies. The primary reasons cited for this in national communications are the lack of adequate research support, technology and resources. There is also a considerable uncertainty expressed in the risk assessments, making it difficult to plan ahead.

On the other hand, many local community-based strategies are being encouraged and recognized by international organizations and NGOs. These concentrate largely on agriculture and natural disaster amelioration. According to Herminia Francisco in 2008, measures that entail big investments, like infrastructure for flood protection and retreat strategies, warrant a central role for the national governments. Further, local governments and civil society can work together in areas such as disaster management, early warning systems and capacity building.[21]

A common approach to adaptation, however, is that of continued and sustained development, be it at a national or a local level. At a national level, governments recognize the need for incorporating adaptation goals into national development agendas. Using this approach, different government ministries are working in tandem in terms of adaptation. However, the means to put concrete adaptation measures in place is still a challenge for most governments on account of the lack of financial resources and access to technology, as well as competing development goals.[22]

It is too early to assess the effectiveness of adaptation programmes and instruments in the region, as these are still in a preparatory stage with limited research capacity and many programmes are yet to be implemented. However, in terms of the needs of specific sectors, the local governments often respond to areas that fall within their normal developmental mandate without approaching it specifically as adaptation. This is especially the case for disaster preparedness. In the absence of adequate research and accurate climate risk assessments, it would serve governments well to continue their development strategies taking into consideration adaptation needs.

Regional Support for Southeast Asia Disaster Preparedness

The previous section highlighted the level of preparedness of governments in Southeast Asia whose countries had been struck by natural disasters from September to early November 2009. This section seeks to map out the development of regional initiatives, to support national efforts, on disaster management in Southeast Asia.

A comprehensive approach is pertinent to minimize risks of disasters in Southeast Asia. In a book titled *Disaster and Development*, Dr Andrew E. Collins offers a framework for looking at comprehensive disaster management, which he referred to as the "disaster management cycle". It is called a cycle to highlight that lessons learnt from one disaster should be applied to improve future disaster preparedness, thus minimizing risks. This cycle incorporates the aspects of preparedness, early warning, mitigation, relief, recovery and rehabilitation. Dr Collins defined these as the following:

- Preparedness — Having an adequate level of development in disaster reduction;
- Early warning — The ability to predict a disaster event and build community awareness about potential disasters;
- Mitigation — The reduction of the impact of potential disasters up until and whilst they occur;
- Relief — The immediate responses that reduce the impact of a disaster after it had happened;
- Recovery — The process of restoring lives, livelihoods and infrastructures to a locally acceptable standard; and
- Rehabilitation — The process in dealing with the longer-term effects of a disaster and a full restoration to development.[23]

Dr Collins based his arguments on the principle that disaster management forms part of a larger sustainable development context. Regarding the abovementioned cycle, he argued that rehabilitation, preparedness and early warning could be considered development-oriented activities, whereas mitigation, relief and recovery are considered emergency-oriented ones. Moreover, preparedness, early warning and mitigation could be categorized as prevention activities while rehabilitation, recovery and relief could be categorized as response activities. A cyclic framework is expected to make disaster prevention the key in avoiding or minimizing the impact of disasters, while response activities play a part to prevent further and future disasters (see Figure 5.1).

Implementing a comprehensive disaster management framework requires strong local and national-based preparedness. A regional framework renders support to strengthening the capacity of national and locally-based disaster preparedness mechanisms. Based in a region prone to natural disasters, ASEAN and the ASEAN Regional Forum (ARF) have started a number of initiatives on disaster management.

Figure 5.1

Proposed Cyclical Framework on dealing with Natural Disasters

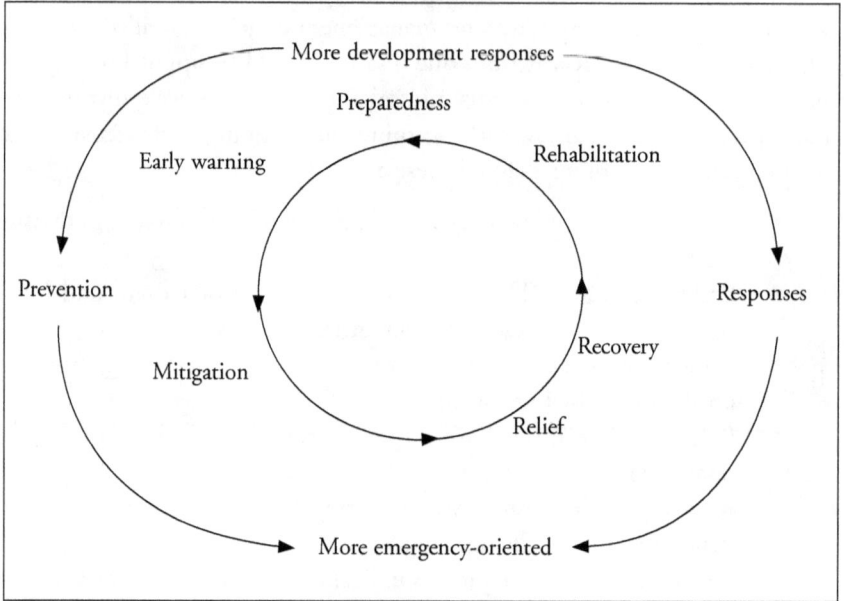

Source: Andrew E. Collins, *Disaster and Development* (London and New York: Routledge, 2009).

The Development of ASEAN Disaster Management Mechanisms

Disaster management is not a new issue for ASEAN; it was one of the first areas of cooperation for the bloc. The ASEAN Expert Group on Disaster Management, as the focal point to enhance cooperation in disaster management, first met in 1971. Disaster management has been one of the eight principles and objectives of regional cooperation since as early as the Declaration of the ASEAN Concord, adopted in February 1976. Initially formed as a regional socio-economic bloc, ASEAN member states believe that vulnerability to disasters would affect economic and social conditions in the region and hinder the development of member states, which in turn could pose a challenge to regional stability.

Further cooperation on this area was marked by the adoption of the ASEAN Declaration on Mutual Assistance on Natural Disasters in Manila in 1976. The Declaration called for ASEAN member states to cooperate in the area of disaster-warnings communication, and the exchange of experts, training, information and documents. It also called for states to establish a national agency to coordinate national disaster preparedness and to be the focal point for regional cooperation. These efforts were strengthened only in 2003 by the forming of the ASEAN Committee on Disaster Management (ACDM). The ACDM consists of the heads of national disaster management agencies.

The ACDM launched an ASEAN Regional Programme on Disaster Management (ARPDM) in May 2004 to foster more tangible regional cooperation from 2004 to 2010. Moreover, this programme also aimed to expand the scope of cooperation to engage ASEAN dialogue partners and relevant international organizations. The ARPDM has outlined twenty-nine activities under five major components which were the result of an assessment of member states' needs and capacities. The five major components with their objectives are as follows:

- The establishment of an ASEAN Regional Disaster Framework. This component aims to promote regional cooperation through a number of joint projects;
- Capacity building to support member countries on disaster management priority areas;
- Sharing of information and resources through networks and research;
- Promoting, collaboration and strengthening partnerships among various stakeholders on sub-state, state and international levels; and
- Promoting public education, awareness and advocacy.[24]

The ARPDM basically establishes two types of activities, namely multi-stakeholders cooperation on sub-national, national and international levels, as well as supporting national capacity.

The ASEAN Agreement on Disaster Management and Emergency Responses (AADMER) is a product of the priority areas implemented through the ARPDM. The AADMER will enter into force by the end of 2009 after being ratified by the Philippines, the last of the ten ASEAN states to do so. Signed by all ASEAN Foreign Ministers in July 2005, AADMER is a legally-binding agreement for ASEAN member states to foster regional cooperation in disaster management. It is a framework to develop operational procedures for a concerted effort to respond swiftly to disasters. These include arrangements for relief assistance, custom and immigration exemptions, a coordinating centre, funding, standby emergency response, and civil-military cooperation. It is also a form of regional commitment to the Hyogo Framework for Action (HFA) on disaster reduction.

Hyogo Framework for Action 2005–2015: Building the Resilience of Nations and Communities to Disasters

HFA was adopted at the World Conference on Disaster Reduction that was held from 18 to 22 January 2005 in Kobe, Hyogo, Japan. The Conference's expected outcome was to pursue substantial reduction of disaster losses in lives and in the social, economic and environmental assets of communities and countries. Hence, three strategic goals were set as follows:

- The integration of disaster risk reduction into sustainable development policies at all levels.
- The development and strengthening of institutions, mechanisms and capacities at all levels.
- The systemic incorporation of risk reduction approaches into the design and implementation of emergency preparedness, response and recovery programmes.

There are five areas of priority for practices to be implemented from 2005 to 2015. They are to:

- Ensure that disaster risk reduction is a national and local priority with strong institutional basis for implementation.
- Identify, assess and monitor disaster risks and enhance early warning.
- Use knowledge, innovation and education to build a culture of safety and resilience at all levels.
- Reduce the underlying risk factors.
- Strengthen disaster preparedness for effective response at all levels.

Source: UNISDR, "Hyogo Framework for Action 2005–2015: Building the Resilience of Nations and Communities to Disasters", extracted from the final report of the World Conference on Disaster Reduction (A/CONF.206/6). Available at <http://www.unisdr.org/eng/hfa/docs/Hyogo-framework-for-action-english.pdf>.

In between its signing and full ratification, ASEAN has begun to implement a number of provisions under the AADMER. A number of simulations and joint exercises on disaster preparedness have taken place. An example is the ASEAN Regional Disaster Emergency Response Simulation Exercise, or ARDEX, held annually to test joint regional emergency response and humanitarian assistance capacity. The first exercise, ARDEX-05, was held in 2005 using a scenario of an earthquake in Selangor, Malaysia. Subsequent ones were held in Cambodia, Singapore and Thailand. Ironically, the Philippines was expected to host ARDEX-09 by the end of October 2009, which was during the height of the series of typhoons such as Ketsana and Parma that struck the country.

A Shift of Focus to Disaster Risk Reduction

The AADMER accommodates various stages of the disaster management cycle in its provisions, namely the element of preparedness, early warning, mitigation, relief, recovery and rehabilitation. Incorporating a comprehensive approach to disaster preparedness is a valuable lesson learnt from the tsunami in 2004, as indicated in the ASEAN Declaration on Action to Strengthen Emergency Relief, Rehabilitation, Reconstruction and Prevention on the Aftermath of Earthquake and Tsunami Disaster adopted in December 2004. ASEAN is trying to evolve from mainly focusing on information exchange and strengthening regional relief efforts to building capacity, so as to conduct appropriate rehabilitation and reconstruction. This will contribute to the prevention and mitigation of future calamities caused by disasters. In March 2005, Ambassador Ong Keng Yong as then-ASEAN Secretary General noted the importance of a people-centred approach in disaster management in order to reduce vulnerabilities. He also acknowledged the need for ASEAN states to shift their paradigms to disaster risk reduction, where investments should be made in the area of pre-disaster preparedness.

The importance of sustainable development in disaster risk reduction has also been mentioned in the ARPDM 2004–10. In line with this aspiration, ASEAN announced in May 2009 a joint effort geared at disaster risk reduction and disaster management in Southeast Asia with the United Nations International Strategy for Disaster Reduction (UNISDR) and the World Bank. Moreover, the ACDM is currently developing a platform similar to that of ARPDM, to be implemented from 2010 to 2015. The main objective of this new platform would be to implement disaster risk reduction initiatives in order to build disaster-resilient nations in Southeast Asia.

Role of the ASEAN Regional Forum in Regional Disaster Management

Complementing disaster management efforts in ASEAN, the ARF has been looking at disaster management as one of the security concerns in the region. Hence, it has developed a number of initiatives among its members. The

ARF, established in 1994, is the principal forum for security dialogue in the Asia Pacific. It provides a setting in which members can discuss current regional security issues and develop cooperative measures to enhance peace and security in the region. The forum draws together twenty-seven countries which have a bearing on the security of the Asia-Pacific region, including the ten ASEAN member states (Brunei, Cambodia, Indonesia, Laos, Malaysia, Myanmar, Philippines, Singapore, Thailand and Vietnam), the ten ASEAN dialogue partners (Australia, Canada, China, the European Union, India, Japan, New Zealand, Republic of Korea, Russia and the United States), one ASEAN observer (Papua New Guinea), as well as the Democratic People's Republic of Korea, Mongolia, Pakistan, Timor-Leste, Bangladesh and Sri Lanka. The objectives of the ASEAN Regional Forum are outlined in the First ARF Chairman's Statement (1994), namely:

- To foster constructive dialogue and consultation on political and security issues of common interest and concern; and
- To make significant contributions to efforts towards confidence building and preventive diplomacy in the Asia-Pacific region.[25]

Disaster relief is an important aspect of comprehensive security, and a valuable confidence building measure for the ARF. Disasters cause serious damage to local economies and social stability, and hence affect the security of states. Moreover, major disasters do not respect political boundaries, but are a common problem for all states in the region. As indicated in Table 5.5,

Table 5.5

Relative Intensity of Natural Hazards Faced by Countries in Southeast Asia

Country	Typhoon	Flood	Drought	Landslide	Tsunami	Earthquake	Volcano	Fire
Cambodia	L	S	L					L
Indonesia	L	M	M	L	L	S	M	M
Lao PDR	L	S	M					M
Malaysia	M	S*	S	L	M			L
Myanmar	M	M	M	M		S		S
Philippines	S	S	L	S	S	S	M	S
Thailand	L	S*	S	L		L		L
Vietnam	M	M	L	S	S	L		L

Legend: S–severe; M–moderate; L–low; * coastal flooding.
Source: Lolita Bildan, *Disaster Management in Southeast Asia: An Overview*, Asian Disaster Preparedness Center (ADPC), 2003.

Southeast Asia is prone to natural disasters. Scientific findings have also indicated that the region will see an increasing intensity and frequency of these disasters in the coming year. Regional cooperation among states is thus essential in dealing with natural disasters. Cooperation of this nature could enhance mutual confidence and hence regional security, as well as reinforce the sense of good neighbourliness among ARF participants. This point was reiterated at the 16th ASEAN Regional Forum held in Phuket, Thailand on 23 July 2009. Participants recognized that natural disasters pose an increasing threat to the peoples of the Asia-Pacific region, and emphasized the urgency of developing effective prevention, relief, mitigation and rehabilitation measures and arrangements in the region, so as to complement and reinforce existing mechanisms, including those of the United Nations.

ASEAN Regional Forum Inter-Sessional Meeting on Disaster Relief

The ASEAN Regional Forum Inter-Sessional Meeting on Disaster Relief (ARF-ISMDR) is the framework which facilitates discussions on natural disasters. The aim of the ISMDR is to enhance confidence and mutual trust among ARF participants through practical cooperation in disaster relief. Nine meetings have been held so far. The first meeting was held in Wellington, New Zealand in February 1997 and the ninth meeting was held in Hawaii in September 2009. These meetings brought together ARF members, represented by their respective Ministries of Foreign Affairs and Defence, as well as additional agencies like the Asian Disaster Preparedness Center (ADPC), the Asian Disaster Reduction Center (ADRC) and the International Federation of Red Cross and Red Crescent Societies (IFRC). The Meetings took up a wide range of issues which mainly focus on the following:

Mechanisms for Regional Cooperation in Disaster Management in Southeast Asia

• **ASEAN Experts Group on Disaster Management**

First called in 1971. The 11th meeting in August 2000 adopted the guidelines for disaster relief assistance and the development of the ASEAN Region Program on Disaster Management. The *ADMIN Newsletter* promotes awareness and information exchange.

- **ASEAN Regional Forum Inter-Sessional Meeting on Disaster Relief**

The 4th meeting in May 2000 agreed on information sharing on disaster data and early warning, mutual assistance for disaster preparedness and relief, training in disaster management, and promotion of greater awareness in disaster preparedness and relief.

- **ASEAN Regional Cooperation on Trans-boundary Haze Pollution**

Started in 1995. The Regional Haze Action Plan sets out cooperative measures among member countries. Inter-governmental negotiation meetings in September 2001 agreed on monitoring, assessment and prevention, and the immediate deployment of people and goods across borders in case of environmental disaster. Set up an ASEAN Fire Danger Rating System for quantitative measurements of level of risk of fire and haze.

- **Mekong River Commission (or MRC)**

Established in 1995, replacing the Mekong Committee that was set up in 1957. The MRC Flood Management and Mitigation Strategy provides technical products and services on flood preparedness measures, addresses differences and facilitation involving structural measures, and capacity building and technology transfer in emergency response measures.

- **Asian Disaster Preparedness Center Regional Consultative Committee on Regional Cooperation in Disaster Management (or ADPC-RCC)**

Established in 2000. The November 2001 meeting identified priorities for capacity building for national disaster management systems, regional initiatives for disaster management and new action areas for ADPC-RCC members.

- **UNESCAP Typhoon Committee**

Established in 1967. The July 2001 meeting reviewed the Regional Cooperation Program Implementation Plan and identified five priority activities: forecasting technology, public information and education, institutional development, network development and communication network.

- **Asian Disaster Reduction Center**

  Established in 1998. Areas of concern include exchange of disaster reduction experts from each country, gathering and provision of disaster reduction information, and research for multinational disaster reduction cooperation.

  Source: Lolita Bildan, *Disaster Management in Southeast Asia: An Overview* (ADPC, 2003).

- Enhancement of early warning capabilities on emergencies such as earthquakes, floods and severe storms;
- Mutual assistance;
- Creation of a regional database;
- Information exchange and experience-sharing;
- Networking among agencies directly involved in disaster management should be further enhanced. For this purpose, a List of Contact Points for disaster management among the ARF participants was updated and circulated;
- Disaster relief training; and
- Promoting awareness.

One important culmination of these meetings was the inaugural joint humanitarian exercise called the ARF Voluntary Demonstration of Response (VDR) on Disaster Relief which was conducted in the Philippines from 4 to 8 May 2009. The ARF-VDR is a robust civilian-led, military supported exercise designed to demonstrate ARF national capabilities in response to an affected country's request for assistance, and build regional assistance capacity for major, multinational relief operations. Following a hypothetical super-typhoon, participating countries offered assistance in response to a Philippine government request for international humanitarian relief. Areas covered in the demonstration include land, air and maritime search and rescue operations, medical assistance/evacuation and engineering reconstruction. Civil-military projects include reconstruction of a school building, construction of a bridge, installation of a water supply system and the medical treatment of approximately 8,000 Filipinos in the Central Luzon area. The effort was commended by a senior US diplomat and was judged successful enough to warrant renewal in 2010.

These exercises constitute the first major effort on the part of the ARF to develop an operational arm. A focus on responses to natural disasters

— the most politically neutral of crises — is commendable, and reflects the inclination of ASEAN member states to view non-traditional security threats, rather than more conventional military conflicts, as better prospects for regional cooperation.

Disaster management provides an opportunity to strengthen cooperation among member states of ASEAN and the ARF, where disaster management initiatives have been evolving. Regional institutions have begun to realize the importance of mainstreaming comprehensive disaster management initiatives in the region. Documents and statements within both regional arrangements show promising progress towards building a region more resilient to natural disasters. Yet, it remains to be seen whether actual improvements can be realized in the region, beyond the published declarations and agreements.

Notes

1. For more information on the Centre for Research on the Epidemiology of Disasters (CRED), available at <http://www.cred.be/>.
2. For more information on Badan Nasional Penanggulangan Bencana, available at <http://www.bnpb.go.id/website/asp/index.asp>.
3. For more information on the National Centre for Hydro-Meteorological Forecasting, available at <http://www.nchmf.gov.vn/web/en-US/43/Default.aspx>.
4. World Bank, Economic of Adaptation to Climate Change [EACC] Report, 2009, available at <http://climatechange.worldbank.org/content/economics-adaptation-climate-change-study-overview>.
5. Ibid.
6. Bernadette P. Resurreccion, Edsel E. Sajor with Elizabeth Fajber, *Climate Adaptation in Asia: Knowledge Gaps and Research Issues in South East Asia*, ISET-International and IST-Nepal, 2008, available at <http://www.i-s-e-t.org/images/pdfs/Climate%20Adaptation%20SEA%20Sept08.pdf>.
7. UNFCCC, *Compendium on Methods and Tools to Evaluate Impact of, and Vulnerability and Adaptation to, Climate Change*, Final Draft Report, 2005, available at <http://unfccc.int/files/adaptation/methodologies_for/vulnerability_and_adaptation/application/pdf/consolidated_version_updated_021204.pdf>.
8. Government of Indonesia, First Submission to the UNFCCC, Jakarta, Indonesia, 1999, available at <http://unfccc.int/resource/docs/natc/indonc1.pdf>.
9. Bernadette P. Resurreccion, Edsel E. Sajor with Elizabeth Fajber, *Climate Adaptation in Asia: Knowledge Gaps and Research Issues in South East Asia*, ISET-International and IST-Nepal, 2008, available at <http://www.i-s-e-t.org/images/pdfs/Climate%20Adaptation%20SEA%20Sept08.pdf>.
10. Government of Thailand, First Submission to the UNFCCC, Bangkok, Thailand, 1999, available at <http://unfccc.int/resource/docs/natc/thainc1.pdf>.

[11]   Government of the Philippines, First Submission to the UNFCCC, Manila, Philippines, available at <http://unfccc.int/resource/docs/natc/phinc1.pdf>.

[12]   Bernadette P. Resurreccion, Edsel E. Sajor with Elizabeth Fajber, *Climate Adaptation in Asia: Knowledge Gaps and Research Issues in South East Asia*, ISET-International and IST-Nepal, 2008, available at <http://www.i-s-e-t.org/images/pdfs/Climate%20Adaptation%20SEA%20Sept08.pdf>.

[13]   Las, Isral, "Indonesia Boosts R&D to Cope with Climate Change", *Jakarta Post*, 6 December 2007.

[14]   Government of Thailand, First Submission to the UNFCCC, Bangkok, Thailand, 1999, available at <http://unfccc.int/resource/docs/natc/thainc1.pdf>.

[15]   Government of the Philippines, First Submission to the UNFCCC, Manila, Philippines, available at <http://unfccc.int/resource/docs/natc/phinc1.pdf>.

[16]   United Nations International Strategy for Disaster Reduction, "Hyogo Framework for Action 2005–2015: Building the Resilience of Nations and Communities to Disasters", extracted from the final report of the World Conference on Disaster Reduction (A/CONF.206/6), available at <http://www.unisdr.org/eng/hfa/docs/Hyogo-framework-for-action-english.pdf>.

[17]   Paulo Romero, "GMA signs Climate Change Act", *Philippine Star*, 24 October 2009, available at <http://www.philstar.com/article.aspx?articleid=517009&publicationsubcategoryid=63>.

[18]   "Global Assessment Report on Disaster Risk Reduction", United Nations International Strategy for Disaster Reduction Secretariat, 2009, available at <http://www.preventionweb.net/english/hyogo/gar/report/index.php?id=9413&pid=34&pil:1>.

[19]   Corrine Kisner, "Climate Change in Thailand: Impacts and Adaptation Strategies", Climate change case study, Climate Institute, July 2008, available at <http://www.climate.org/topics/international-action/thailand.htm>.

[20]   Government of Thailand, First Submission to the UNFCCC, Bangkok, Thailand, 1999, available at <http://unfccc.int/resource/docs/natc/thainc1.pdf>.

[21]   Arief Anshory Yusuf and Herminia Francisco, *Climate Change Vulnerability Mapping for Southeast Asia* (Singapore: Economy & Environment Program for Southeast Asia [EEPSEA], 2009).

[22]   Arief Anshory Yusuf and Herminia Francisco, *Climate Change Vulnerability Mapping for Southeast Asia* (Singapore: Economy & Environment Program for Southeast Asia [EEPSEA], 2009).

[23]   Andrew E. Collins, *Disaster and Development* (London and New York: Routledge, 2009).

[24]   ASEAN, "The ASEAN Regional Programme on Disaster Management: A Regional Strategy for Disaster Reduction" (Jakarta: ASEAN Secretariat, 2004), available at <http://www.asean.org/18455.htm>.

[25]   ASEAN, "Chairman's Statement: The First Meeting of the ASEAN Regional Forum" (Jakarta: ASEAN Secretariat, 1994), available at <http://www.aseansec. org/3621.htm>.

References

ASEAN. "The ASEAN Regional Programme on Disaster Management: A Regional Strategy for Disaster Reduction". Jakarta: ASEAN Secretariat, 2004. Available at <http://www.asean.org/18455.htm>.

————. "Chairman's Statement: The First Meeting of the ASEAN Regional Forum". Jakarta: ASEAN Secretariat, 25 July 1994. Available at <http://www.aseansec. org/3621.htm>.

Collins, Andrew E. *Disaster and Development*. London and New York: Routledge, 2009.

Government of Indonesia. First Submission to the UNFCCC. Jakarta, Indonesia, 1999. Available at <http://unfccc.int/resource/docs/natc/indonc1.pdf>.

Government of Thailand. First Submission to the UNFCCC. Bangkok, Thailand, 1999. Available at <http://unfccc.int/resource/docs/natc/thainc1.pdf>.

Government of the Philippines. First Submission to the UNFCCC. Manila, Philippines, 1999. Available at <http://unfccc.int/resource/docs/natc/phinc1. pdf>.

Kisner, Corrine. "Climate Change in Thailand: Impacts and Adaptation Strategies". Climate change case study. Climate Institute, July 2008. Available at <http:// www.climate.org/topics/international-action/thailand.htm>.

Las, Isral. "Indonesia Boosts R&D to Cope with Climate Change". *Jakarta Post*, 6 December 2007.

Resurreccion, Bernadette P., Edsel E. Sajor with Elizabeth Fajber. *Climate Adaptation in Asia: Knowledge Gaps and Research Issues in South East Asia*. ISET-International and IST-Nepal, 2008. Available at <http://www.i-s-e-t.org/images/ pdfs/Climate%20Adaptation%20SEA%20Sept08.pdf>.

Romero, Paulo. "GMA signs Climate Change Act". *Philippine Star*, 24 October 2009. Available at <http://www.philstar.com/article.aspx?articleid=517009&p ublicationsubcategoryid=63>.

UNFCCC. *Compendium on Methods and Tools to Evaluate Impact of, and Vulnerability and Adaptation to, Climate Change*. Final Draft Report, 2005. Available at <http://unfccc.int/files/adaptation/methodologies_for/ vulnerability_and_adaptation/application/pdf/consolidated_version_updated_ 021204.pdf>.

United Nations International Strategy for Disaster Reduction Secretariat (UNISDR). *Global Assessment Report on Disaster Risk Reduction*, 2009. Available at <http:// www.preventionweb.net/english/hyogo/gar/report/index.php?id=9413&pid:3 4&pil:1>.

————. "Hyogo Framework for Action 2005–2015: Building the Resilience of Nations and Communities to Disasters". Extracted from the final report of the World Conference on Disaster Reduction (A/CONF.206/6), 2005. Available at <http://www.unisdr.org/eng/hfa/docs/Hyogo-framework-for-action-english.pdf>.

World Bank. "Economics of Adaptation to Climate Change (EACC) Report", 2009. Available at <http://climatechange.worldbank.org/content/economics-adaptation-climate-change-study-overview>.

Yusuf, Arief Anshory and Herminia Francisco. *Climate Change Vulnerability Mapping for Southeast Asia*. Singapore: Economy & Environment Program for Southeast Asia (EEPSEA), 2009.

6

INTERNAL CONFLICT

Mely Caballero-Anthony, Alistair D.B. Cook,
Pau Khan Khup Hangzo, Lina Gong and
Manpavan Kaur

Asia is a region where internal conflicts continue to plague state and human security, despite the decline of interstate conflicts since the end of the Cold War. Moreover, studies on the patterns of internal conflicts have also been confined to armed insurgencies, secessionism and civil conflicts, while less attention has been given to other forms of internal conflicts such as religious and/or ethnically-motivated communal violence, violent political clashes among competing political forces, and political uprisings. In recent years, the dimensions of internal conflict in Asia have also become more complex due to the growing challenges posed by religious radicalism and terrorism.

To be sure, the multiplicity of patterns of internal conflicts in Asia has dramatically increased the human costs of conflicts and violent threats faced by people within states. These have also resulted in an array of human insecurities, from poverty and human deprivation, mass population displacement, worsening human rights abuses, particularly among women and children, marginalization, threats of infectious diseases, and forced migration to a host of transnational crimes. In Southeast Asia for example, internal conflicts within individual member states have had actual and potential cross-border implications. The secessionist and insurgency problems in the Philippines, the violence in the Muslim provinces in Southern Thailand, the ethnic tensions in Myanmar and restive provinces in Indonesia could all affect regional security and stability. Indeed, while many Asian states have moved up the global rankings of economic development, there still remain internal conflicts within many of these states. As a result, while some areas of

one individual state prosper other areas with a higher prevalence of violence
have fallen behind.

> If we are to break the cycles of violence and lessen the stresses that drive
> them, countries must develop more legitimate, accountable and capable
> national institutions that provide for citizen security, justice and jobs.
>
> — Robert B. Zoellick,
> World Bank President
> Washington, 11 April 2011

> While much of the world has made rapid progress in reducing poverty
> over the past 60 years, areas suffering from political instability and
> criminal violence are being left far behind and face stagnation, both
> in terms of economic growth and disappointing human development
> indicators.
>
> — Justin Lin,
> World Bank Chief Economist and Senior Vice-President,
> Development Economics, Washington, 11 April 2011

As documented in the World Development Report 2011, countries with
internal conflicts are developing at a slower pace, and those regions home to
these conflicts maybe falling permanently behind.[1] Indeed, throughout the
periods of internal conflict, there has been a significant impact on national
budgets of Asian states. For example, in the Philippines, the government
has stationed half of the armed forces in the conflict-affected regions of
Mindanao and the Sulu Archipelago. The Thai government is spending
$2.1 billion over four years on special development assistance in the
conflict-affected southern border region — figures that are extraordinary to
everyday governance.[2] This prevalence of internal conflicts negatively affects
the international relations of Asian states, as governments shy away from
internal dynamics within the region so that, in turn, they expect the same
reciprocal relationship. This has a significant impact on the regional security
arrangements, which impacts the level of influence Asian states on global
security concerns and the ability within the region to address the internal
conflicts and in turn human security across Asia.

This chapter approaches the issue of internal conflict in Asia in two
complementary ways. In the first instance it investigates the prevalence of
small arms and light weapons (SALWs), which form a significant dynamic
to the internal conflicts. Through understanding their extent and reach this
chapter will demonstrate that in order to combat the underlying causes and
consequences of internal conflicts, the availability of SALWs needs to be

addressed, not just in supply but in demand as well, which will require a comprehensive approach to the peaceful resolution of conflict in the region. In the second half of the chapter, there is an application of the Risk Assessment Model and Ethnic Rebellion Model to the internal conflict in Myanmar — home to one of the most notable and protracted conflicts in Asia. As 2011 drew to a close the domestic situation in Myanmar has shown some improvements, which has led to cautious optimism across Asia, culminating in a visit by the US Secretary of State, Hilary Clinton and the agreement by ASEAN member states to grant Myanmar the ASEAN Chair in 2014. Both of these gestures are recognition and encouragement to the reforms announced by the nominally civilian government. While there have been several announcements and a shift in tactic by the government that to address issues of national reconciliation there needs to be a political solution, there also remains many areas that are home to political violence. With a focus on prevalence of SALWs and on applying early warning systems to the conflict in Myanmar, this chapter addresses both of the myriad root causes of conflict — the availability and desirability of weapons — and evaluates the use of early warning systems in systematically analysing internal conflicts.

SMALL ARMS AND LIGHT WEAPONS

Although weapons of mass destruction (WMDs) are considered to pose the gravest threat to international peace and security, in practice, small arms and light weapons (SALWs) kill more people than WMDs. However, SALWs have been largely ignored in arms control discussions. This section argues that regulating the proliferation of SALWs will contribute towards the peaceful resolution of internal armed conflicts in Southeast Asia. Weapons of mass destruction (WMDs) are considered to pose the gravest threat to international security and are defined as "chemical, biological, radiological, or nuclear weapons capable of a high order of destruction or causing mass casualties" (US Department of Defense 2010). The threat of WMD use and their proliferation resulted in the establishment of a number of legally binding multilateral treaties such as the Nuclear Non-Proliferation Treaty (NPT), the Chemical Weapons Convention (CWC), the Biological Weapons Convention (BWC) and the Comprehensive Test Ban Treaty (CTBT), as well as bilateral treaties such as the Strategic Arms Reduction Treaty (START) and the Strategic Offensive Reductions Treaty (SORT). Although the threat of WMD use declined with the end of the Cold War, there are renewed concerns over the possibility of rogue states and non-state actors acquiring WMD capabilities. The possibility of terrorists obtaining WMD capabilities, for example, is considered to be "one of the most serious contemporary threats".[3]

The preoccupation with WMDs has led the international community to pay less attention to the one weapons category that kills more people than WMDs: SALWs. The United Nations (UN) defines small arms as weapons manufactured to military specifications for use by one person as lethal instruments of war and these include revolvers and self-loading pistols, rifles and carbines, sub-machine guns, assault rifles and light machine guns. Light weapons, on the other hand, are designed for use by several persons working in a crew and these include heavy machine guns, hand-held under-barrel and mounted grenade launchers, portable anti-aircraft guns, portable anti-tank guns, recoilless rifles, portable launchers of anti-tank missile and rocket systems, portable launchers of anti-aircraft missile systems and mortars of calibres of less than 100 millimetres (mm).[4]

SALWs kill people in a variety of situations such as wars, civil conflicts, gang fights or government-condoned violence. Small arms, in particular, are also the weapons of choice for suicide, homicide or random violence. On the whole, SALWs cause more conflict-related deaths than any other type of conventional weapons. For example, an estimated 200,000 to 400,000 people are killed annually by SALWs, accounting for between 60 to 90 per cent of 500,000 conflict-related deaths each year.[5] SALWs, therefore, are the real "WMDs".

GLOBAL AND REGIONAL ESTIMATES OF SMALL ARMS AND LIGHT WEAPONS

There is an estimate of at least 875 million SALWs in the world. Of these, an estimated 350,000 belong to non-state armed groups — insurgents and militias — that were actively fighting in 2009.[6] An unspecified number of these arms were in circulation in Southeast Asia due to several reasons.[7] Firstly, the ongoing internal armed conflicts in Myanmar, the Philippines and Thailand draw demand for SALWs from both state and non-state actors alike. Although information on the total number of SALWs in circulation in Southeast Asia is limited, a large proportion of them are either imported arms or arms manufactured under license. Secondly, Southeast Asia has several post-conflict states such as Cambodia and Vietnam where vast numbers of military SALWs can be easily obtained. Thirdly, the region also has long maritime and continental frontiers that are difficult to monitor, thereby providing opportunities for traffickers. Lastly, most countries in the region have poor storage facilities, making theft, loss and smuggling of SALWs possible coupled with a lack of adequate enforcement of domestic gun control legislation.

Table 6.1

Gun Ownership in Southeast Asia

Country	Civilian Guns		Government Guns	
	Number of Privately owned Firearms (2007)	Rate of Civilian Firearm Possession (No. of firearms per 100 people) (2007)	Military Firearms (2006)	Law Enforcement Firearms (2006)
Thailand	10,000,000	15.6	1,957,500	175,000
Philippines	3,900,000	4.7	449,350	164,326
Cambodia	273,000–600,000	4.3	187,912–190,000	93,800
Myanmar	2,000,000	4.0	503,500	100,800
Vietnam	1,100,000	1.7	9,849,600	229,476
Malaysia	370,000	1.5	440,250	70,000
Brunei	5,400	1.4	9,690	2,450
Lao PDR	71,000	1.2	104,690	16,089
Singapore	22,000	0.5	563,750	46,200
Indonesia	–	0.5	2,057,700	392,000
Timor-Leste	3,000	0.3	–	–

Source: Compiled from Gunpolicy.org.

THE MISUSE OF SMALL ARMS AND
LIGHT WEAPONS IN SOUTHEAST ASIA AND ITS
SOCIOECONOMIC IMPACTS

The acquisition of SALWs does not by itself incite the conflicts in which SALWs are used.[8] The degree of SALW proliferation and their misuse depend upon the underlying nature of the conflicts. Stewart (2003, 2004) identifies the existence of severe "horizontal inequalities" as the primary source of internal armed conflict. Horizontal inequalities refer to inequalities between culturally defined (ethnic) groups with regard to access to economic, social and political resources. Such inequalities cause certain groups to suffer deprivation, and they fuel resentment and violent conflicts.[9] SALWs are often the weapons of choice in such conflicts because they are "widely available, low in cost, extremely lethal, simple to use, durable, highly portable, easily concealed, and possess legitimate military, police, and civilian uses". As a result, "they are present in virtually every society".[10] The presence of horizontal inequalities in Southeast Asia, coupled with easily accessible arms, exacerbates violent conflicts in the region. For example, the resurgence of violence in southern Thailand is attributed to the theft of more than 300 guns — including AK-47s and M-16 assault rifles — from a military camp in Narathiwat province on 4 January 2004.[11] The uncontrolled proliferation of SALWs has exacted a huge toll on Southeast Asia. The following section analyses both the human and economic costs of SALW proliferation and its misuse.

Human Cost

SALWs cause conflict-related deaths in two ways: direct and indirect. Direct deaths are the result of fatal wounds and injuries caused by bullets or other projectiles. As mentioned earlier, 60 to 90 per cent of an estimated 500,000 conflict-related deaths each year are directly attributed to SALWs.[12] Indirect deaths are caused by, for example, disease, starvation and the destruction of health infrastructure. Table 6.2 provides estimates of armed conflict-related deaths in countries with ongoing armed conflicts in Southeast Asia.

Economic Cost

Internal armed conflicts, exacerbated by the proliferation of SALWs, impose a significant economic burden on both states and societies. Armed conflicts such as civil wars are therefore characterized as "development in reverse".[13]

Table 6.2
Armed Conflict-Related Deaths in Southeast Asia

Countries	Parties to Conflict	Fatalities

Myanmar	• **State parties:** Government of Myanmar
	• **Non-state parties:**
	  ○ All Burma Students Democratic Front
	  ○ United Wa State Army (UWSA)
	  ○ Mon National Liberation Army (MNLA)
	  ○ Mong Thai Army (MTA)
	  ○ Democratic Karen Buddhist Army (DKBA)
	  ○ Palaung State Liberation Army (PSLA)
	  ○ Kachin Independence Army (KIA)
	  ○ Karen National Liberation Army (KNLA)
	  ○ Karenni National Progressive Party Army
	  ○ Shan State Army-South (SSA-South)
	  ○ Chin National Army (CNA)
	  ○ Myanmar National Democratic Alliance Army (MNDAA)
		More than 14,970 killed since 1985

Philippines	• **State parties:** Government of the Philippines
	• **Non-state parties:**
	  ○ New People's Army (NPA)
	  ○ Moro Islamic Liberation Front (MILF)/
	  Moro National Liberation Front (MNLF)
	  ○ Abu Sayyaf Group (ASG)
		Involving NPA: More than 41,070 killed since 1969
		Involving MILF/MNLF: At least 100,000 killed since 1971
		Involving ASG: Less than 1,680 killed since 1991

| Thailand | • **State parties:** Government of Thailand
• **Non-state parties:**
   ○ Bersatu — United Front for the Independence of Pattani
   ○ Barasi Revolusi Nasional (BRN)
   ○ Gerakan Mujahideen Islam Pattani (GMIP)
   ○ Pattani United Liberation Organization (PULO)
   ○ Runda Kumpulan Kecil (RKK) | More than 3,000 people killed since 2004 |

Note: The table includes only countries with active internal armed conflicts.
Source: Compiled from IISS (n.d.)[14] and Project Ploughshares (2010).[15]

According to Collier (1999), civil wars affect the gross domestic product (GDP) of a country through five main channels: destruction, disruption, diversion within country, diversion abroad and dissaving. With regards to destruction, the Labour force is reduced through death and injury, and physical capital such as infrastructure is destroyed. Secondly, productive activities are disrupted and social order breaks down thereby increasing the risk and cost of doing business. Thirdly, government resources are diverted away from productive investment to destructive expenditures thus allowing for internal diversion. Fourthly, the economic assets as well as human capital move abroad as a result of war. The final channel is through people out of desperation are forced to use their financial savings or sell their assets at very low returns.[16]

Drawing on data for 92 countries worldwide, 19 of which are facing civil war, Collier concludes that, on average, a civil war reduces the growth of real GDP per capita by 2.2 per cent for every conflict year. Despite the difficulty in estimating the economic costs of internal armed conflicts in Southeast Asia, we can nonetheless conclude that armed conflicts do impose significant economic costs. According to the few existing estimates, the Philippines loses at least 1 per cent of GDP per year as a result of the ongoing armed conflict in Mindanao through the destruction of assets, lost production, lost investments and loss in tourism.[17] Economic losses from the conflict in southern Thailand on the other hand are estimated to have amounted to more than US$3.1 billion since 2004.[18]

Pathways Forward

Despite the carnage caused by the uncontrolled proliferation of SALWs, countries in Southeast Asia have been slow in taking effective action. ASEAN's approach, for example, has so far been limited as it addresses arms proliferation in the region only in the context of transnational crime.[19] This however has several implications. SALW proliferation or illegal arms trafficking is often overshadowed by other transnational crime issues such as human trafficking, human smuggling and drug trafficking. The criminalization of SALWs leads to the sidelining of the destabilizing effects of SALWs outside the context of transnational crime, such as increased societal violence. It also contributes to the avoidance of economic, political and diplomatic solutions to the numerous armed insurgencies within the region. It is therefore essential that ASEAN addresses the proliferation of SALWs not only within the context of transnational crime but also within the context of conflict resolution and peacebuilding. This would require the adoption of a comprehensive approach with efforts made at all levels — global, regional and national.

At the global level, negotiations are now underway to establish a comprehensive, legally binding Arms Trade Treaty (ATT). An agreement is expected to be reached in 2012. Under the ATT, each state will remain in control of its arms export control arrangements but will be legally obliged to assess arms exports on a case-by-case basis against the criteria agreed under the treaty. These criteria would be based on existing obligations and commitments to prevent human rights abuses, uphold international humanitarian law, and promote stability, prosperity and security. In line with the global momentum, ASEAN, at the regional level, is well-placed to establish regional standards on the import and export of conventional weapons including SALWs. Such standards will help ASEAN monitor the import and export of arms by member states, and promote transparency and greater responsibility in the transfer of conventional arms. Finally, at the national level, Southeast Asian countries need to improve their implementation of gun control laws. There is no dearth of gun control legislation in Southeast Asia. The Philippines, for example, has twenty-one individual executive orders, laws, acts, memorandums, presidential decrees, directives and amendments. Likewise, Thailand has the 1947 and 1967 Acts on Controlling Firearms, Ammunition, Explosives, Fireworks and Imitation of Firearms. However, due to weak implementation, SALWs continue to proliferate in both countries. Effective implementation of existing legislation thus constitutes an important first step towards the control of the proliferation and use of SALWs which fuel conflict. In the second section of this chapter it turns to analysing the internal conflict in Myanmar to provide some grounded research that we are able to determine the ability to evaluate some of the leading early warning systems for internal conflict as a policy solution.

CONFLICT PREVENTION — INTERNAL CONFLICT IN MYANMAR

Applying the Ethnic Rebellion Model and Risk Assessment Model

One of the salient policy recommendations for conflict and genocide prevention is the use of early warning models. This section investigates and applies two well-known models used for conflict and genocide risk assessments to test the impact of Myanmar's Border Guard Force (BGF) policy on the ongoing internal ethnic conflict. The two models used are the

Ethnic Rebellion Model (ERM)[20] and the Risk Assessment Model (RAM) for Genocides or Politicides.[21] The application of these models shows that the internal ethnic conflict is likely to continue and there exist trigger or accelerating factors for genocide to occur. While there is utility in applying these models, this NTS Insight also identifies some gaps in and challenges with these models, which need to be addressed if they are to become effective conflict and genocide prevention assessments.

Myanmar is a culturally diverse state with one third of its population classified as ethnic nationalities, minority ethnic groups mainly found in the border areas. According to Minority Rights Group International (MRGI), the largest ethnic groups are the Shan and Karen.[22] Myanmar is experiencing protracted internal conflict with its eastern ethnic nationalities, especially the conflict in Karen State which began in 1948 and continues to intensify.[23] Up to 2007, the conflicts have displaced an estimated 503,000 people in eastern Myanmar.[24] Immediately after the 7 November 2010 general elections, over 20,000 fled to Thailand to escape fighting between government troops and armed ethnic groups.[25]

The ongoing internal conflict is reflective of the inability of the government and ethnic nationalities to reach a sustainable political solution over the past sixty years. Ethnic nationalities had administered their own territories from the colonial period to the formation of the Union of Burma following the Panglong Agreement in 1947.[26] However, this autonomy began to be reduced following General Ne Win's 1962 coup d'etat, generating further internal instability. However, by 1988 most ethnic groups had made ceasefire agreements. Under these agreements, they were still allowed to develop their territories until a new constitution was formulated and their armies were able to retain their arms.[27]

Ethnic nationalities' autonomy was further reduced in 2005 with the increased presence of the government's military — the Tatmadaw — in eastern ethnic areas.[28] Presently, the government is implementing its Border Guard Force (BGF) policy. The BGF policy is included in Section 337 of Myanmar's 2008 Constitution, which requires that Myanmar have only one national army. The BGF Policy Blueprint gives the Tatmadaw greater control over ethnic armed groups by transferring the governance of security affairs along the border to regional military commanders.[29] The ethnic nationalities largely reject the BGF policy as seen in the armed clashes between the Tatmadaw and the Myanmar National Democratic Alliance Army in Shan State.[30] Indeed, previous negotiations have illustrated that ethnic nationalities are not open to bringing their armies under the command of the Tatmadaw as this arrangement is negatively perceived.[31] The limited success of previous ceasefire negotiations with the government was based on a "peace-through-development policy of mutual trust building"[32] as such a policy did not undermine their aspiration for federalism. In the following sections, two early warning models are used to assess the effects of the BGF policy on the ongoing internal conflict in Myanmar and the potential for mass atrocities, particularly genocide.

Conceptual Overview of Early Warning Models

An early warning model "includes data collection, analysis and/or formulation of recommendations, including risk assessment and information sharing".[33] Its purpose is to assist in decision-making so as to enable timely response with the aim of the prevention, reduction, resolution or transformation of a crisis.[34] In this section, an early warning model specifically refers to a system that monitors escalatory developments which occur prior to the onset of genocide stemming from ethnic conflicts. The effectiveness of early warning and response depends not only on the accuracy of the analysis, but also on the communication of the information to an appropriate actor. In the context of genocide prevention, the state is considered the primary actor responding to early warning signals and preventing potential genocide. However, there have been cases where the state itself has committed mass atrocities, such as during the Rwandan genocide in 1994. In such circumstances, the international community needs to be aware of developments in conflict situations, as they bear the responsibility of assisting in the prevention of genocide. This division of responsibility between the state and the international community has been reinforced by the emerging norm of the responsibility to protect (commonly referred to as the RtoP norm).[35]

Early warning models use either quantitative or qualitative methods to evaluate a situation. The qualitative approach is based on expert judgment of information from several sources, including media coverage, open-source data, and embassy and intelligence reports.[36] Qualitative analysis may be biased as the analyst's prior knowledge and perception of an issue are subjective and can influence the assessment. Supplementary to qualitative analysis is quantitative analysis which assesses situations through statistical analysis. As quantitative models are derived from data analysis of a large number of cases, it is arguably more objective and applicable than qualitative analysis. Moreover, it has been shown that quantitative models can be highly accurate. The Political Instability Task Force (PITF) project, for instance, found that PITF models which do not involve many variables and complex interactions accurately classify 80 per cent of the instability onsets and stables in the historical data[37] (for a detailed account of the PITF project, go to <http://globalpolicy.gmu.edu/pitf/>. One drawback of quantitative models is the time lag between data collection, data analysis and the release of results.[38]

This section will use two predictive models based on quantitative analysis — the Ethnic Rebellion Model[39] (ERM) for the Minorities at Risk (MAR) project[40,41] and Harff's 2003 Risk Assessment Model (RAM) which is part of the PITF project[42] — to assess the prospects of continuing ethnic rebellions and the intensified risks of genocide as a result of the adoption of the BGF policy. The two models are selected on the basis of two criteria — their authoritativeness and the hypothesized link between ethnic rebellion and genocide. With regard to their authoritativeness, both models are recommended tools of genocide prevention for the UN Secretary-General's Special Adviser on the Prevention of Genocide.[43] The link between ethnic rebellion and genocide is explained by Moore (2000) and Saxton (2005) in the following way: strong ethnic rebellion will provoke the government to adopt further harsher policies to curb resistance with the potential to ultimately end in genocide.[44] However, it is also important to recognize that conflict situations and genocide can be mutually exclusive; genocide can also occur during peacetime, which poses a significant challenge to these models.[45] Based on the link between ethnic rebellion and genocide, the two models remain applicable to the Myanmar case — the failure of the BGF policy to accommodate the ethnic nationalities further incentivises them to rebel, which in turn leads to harsher retaliation by the Tatmadaw with the potential for genocide to occur. In the next section, the ERM is applied to identify factors that have caused and will continue to cause ethnic rebellions in Myanmar, and to examine how the BGF policy ill reinforce these factors.

Assessing Myanmar's Internal Ethnic Conflict Using the Ethnic Rebellion Model

For this analysis, the PITF project definition of ethnic war as a proxy for ethnic conflict is used (see Box 1).

The cause of the prolonged ethnic conflict in Myanmar has its roots in the tension found between the monopoly of state power by the military government and the aspiration of ethnic nationalities for federalism, greater autonomy and more equality in the exercise of civil rights, as envisioned in the 1947 Panglong Agreement.

BOX 1: Definition of Ethnic Conflict

Episodes of violent conflict between governments and national, ethnic, religious, or other communal minorities (ethnic challengers) in which the challengers seek major changes in their status ... rioting and warfare between rival communal groups is not coded as [ethnic conflict] unless it involves conflict over political power or government policy (Esty et al., cited in Sambanis 2001, p. 262).

Despite the differences in their specific claims, most of the ethnic nationalities share the common aspiration for greater autonomy rather than independence.[46] The Karen National Union (KNU) officials assert that their ultimate goal is to achieve the right to self-determination of the Karen people with the guarantee of ethnic equality within "a genuine union of Burma".[47] The Shan militant organizations desire the right to self-determination, or at the very least, widespread autonomy in Shan State. They are also concerned with economic development and protecting their culture.[48] Similarly, the Chin National Front (CNF) has been committed to the aspirations of militant groups of other ethnic nationalities.[49]

The Government's Solution — Reification of the Ethnic Political Identity

The military government adopted two major policies to resolve the protracted ethnic conflicts — ceasefire agreements and border guard forces. However, it has not been able to reach an agreement with every ethnic militant group with regard to the two policies. This has led to increased ethnic conflicts. In December 2003, the KNU brokered a "gentleman's agreement" with the military government to cease the fighting but little progress has been made subsequently. Since early 2006, the military government has launched major operations against the KNU and its civilian support base, displacing at least 20,000 people in northern Karen State.[50] In addition, between 2009 and 2010, the conflict between the government forces and the KNU escalated to level 43 in conflict intensity, indicating a severe crisis.[51] With regard to the BGF policy, only the Democratic Karen Buddhist Army (DKBA) and the National Democratic Army-Kachin (NDA-K) have joined the BGF. In November 2010, there was an outbreak of violence between the Tatmadaw and a breakaway faction of the DKBA that opposed the group's decision to join the BGF.[52] It is clear that these policies have failed to yield substantial progress on the peace process because they did not make sufficient concessions to meet the claims of these groups, particularly on the political front. However, whilst there has been recognition that a political solution needs to be found, recent negotiations to broker an interim ceasefire have not produced any results in late 2011 after meetings between the KNU and government representative.

MAR Ethnic Rebellion Model

The ERM assesses the risk of future ethnic conflict. It hypothesises that ethnic rebellion is a joint function of variables that are categorized into three groups — group incentives, group capacity and group opportunities.[53] This section will apply group-level data from the 2009 MAR dataset4 to the ERM to assess the likelihood of continuing ethnic rebellion against the Myanmar military government. The BGF policy and its impact will be incorporated into the analysis. Ethnic nationalities evaluated in this analysis include the Mon, Shan, Rohingya, Chin, Kachin and Karen.

Group Incentives

"Group incentives" are higher if members are, or perceive themselves to be, more disadvantaged compared to other groups.[54] The four variables in this group include: lost autonomy, as well as economic, political and cultural discrimination.

Despite the relatively low scores of these groups on "lost autonomy", all groups are still considered to have strong incentives for rebellion as they have suffered severe economic, political and cultural discrimination. According to a United Nations Children's Fund (UNICEF) analysis on women and children, between 1997 and 2000 most of the border regions fell significantly below the national average on socioeconomic indicators.[55] In addition to economic insecurity, ethnic nationalities are also politically underprivileged. Most recently, refusals by ethnic nationalities to join the government's BGF led to the cancellation of voting in ethnic areas.[56] Therefore, the BGF policy has increased rather than decreased the incentives for rebellion.

Group Capacity

> "Group capacity" for collective action depends on, first, the sense of cultural identity and the extent to which that identity is shared, and second, the existence of organisations that give expression to group aspirations and objectives.[57]

"Cultural identity" is a variable that is assessed primarily through four indicators as shown in Table 6.2. The higher the score, the more distinct the group is. The scores of the ethnic nationalities vary from one indicator to another, but overall, the indicators show that these nationalities have distinct cultural identities. Furthermore, the persistence of the military government in imposing the notion of nationhood has created a sustained sense of alienation among ethnic nationalities.[58]

"Militant mobilization" is a variable that reveals the number of militant organizations pursuing group interests. The level of "militant mobilization" is very high among all the ethnic nationalities, with the Karen and Rohingya scoring the highest (see Table 6.3). The KNU was noted to be the "largest, most powerful and influential, most visible and best-organized ethnic political/military organization in Burma".[59] In addition, several other breakaway factions of the KNU, such as the DKBA, have also claimed to speak for the Karen constituency. Nevertheless, despite the KNU being debilitated by the loss of its stronghold to the government and its breakaway factions, it remains the primary organization representing Karen interests.

With regard to the Rohingya, which has been severely discriminated against, the main militant groups include the Rohingya Solidarity Organization (RSO) and the Arakan Rohingya Islamic Front (ARIF), which formed the Arakan Rohingya National Organisation (ARNO) in 1999.[60] Although there are other political organizations that have claimed to represent the interests of the Rohingya, the RSO and the ARIF are the most influential. The BGF policy is an attempt by the military government to disarm militant groups, but it has been unsuccessful. Only the DKBA and the NDA-K have accepted the deal; and the DKBA has since experienced a split between those who are pro-engagement and those who are not.

Group Opportunities

"Group opportunities" refers to political environments that shape the chances of successful rebellion.[61] Two variables are analysed in order to assess "group opportunities". The first is whether there has been any "recent changes in regime structure". This analysis determines that there has not been any major political change in Myanmar since 2009.[62] Although the country conducted a general election in 2010 and convened its first meeting of parliament in January 2011, its political space is limited. The reason for this is that 25 per cent of seats in parliament and in key ministries (home, defence and border affairs) are reserved for the military, and the largest party in parliament — the Union Solidarity and Development Party (USDP) — was established, and is still heavily influenced, by the military. In view of this, "group opportunities" remain slim. The second variable in analysing "group opportunities" is whether "support from kindred groups" exists. It measures the extent of support for the ethnic nationalities from the Myanmarese diaspora and kindred groups in neighbouring states. Support can be political, military and non-military in nature. All six ethnic nationalities scored a figure of zero on this, indicating that these groups are not receiving substantial support from kindred groups.

Assessment by the ERM

The assessment of the future of ethnic conflict based on the ERM reveals that the ethnic nationalities are very likely to continue their rebellion against the military government — they registered high scores for most of the variables under "group incentives", with slim "group opportunities" for successful rebellion. "Group capacity" varies among the militant groups of all ethnic nationalities. Large militant groups such as the KNU are capable of continuing their rebellion against the government. As of 2006, the Shan and Karen are rated as the ethnic nationalities most likely to rebel based on the 2009 MAR dataset, scoring five out of seven on the possibility of rebellion, the highest among the investigated ethnic nationalities. Therefore, the BGF policy has fuelled rather than defused the incentives for rebellion. The cancellation of voting in the national election in ethnic areas due to their resistance to the BGF policy triggered waves of fighting in November 2010.

Existence of internal armed conflict, primarily due to ethnic rebellion, is a widely recognized risk factor of genocide.[63] The following section undertakes an assessment of the structural risk factors of genocide in pursuit of the posited link between continuing ethnic rebellion and genocide.

Assessing the Probability of Genocide in Myanmar Using the Risk Assessment Model

The Risks of Genocide

BOX 2: UN Definition of Genocide

Article 2 of the Convention on the Prevention and Punishment of the Crime of Genocide defines the crime as:

Acts committed with the intent to destroy, in whole or in part, a national, ethnical, racial or religious group by either of the following: (a) killing members of the group; (b) causing serious bodily or mental harm to members of the group; (c) deliberately inflicting on the group, conditions of life calculated to bring about its physical destruction in whole or in part; (d) imposing measures intended to prevent births within the group; or (e) forcibly transferring children of the group to another group (UN 1948).

International criminal law recognizes the following mass atrocity crimes: genocide, crimes against humanity and war crimes. However, early warning indicators have been developed to monitor only the crime of genocide (for definition, see Box 2). The model used to assess the probability of genocide is Harff's RAM. The RAM uses six risk factors to assess the probability of genocide: (1) existence of political upheaval; (2) prior genocide; (3) ethnic character of the ruling elite; (4) regime type of the ruling elite; (5) nature of ideological orientation of the ruling regime; and (6) trade openness of the country.[64] The RAM is premised on the finding that all episodes of genocide and political mass murder of the last half-century have been carried out in the context of internal conflict and regime instability.[65] Therefore, the RAM assesses the probable onset of genocide from a situation of escalated political instability by considering a number of factors invoked by the historical and present conditions within the country (see Harff [2003] for further information on the model's methodology). The model has 74 per cent accuracy in identifying prospective genocides.[66]

The RAM risk factors are widely recognized structural risk factors of genocide.[67] Structural factors refer to the underlying incompatibilities, whereas triggers or accelerators are more proximate factors that can cause a conflict to escalate into genocide. Structural factors need to be addressed to eradicate the possibility of genocide in the longer term because monitoring and tackling these factors allow for a reversal of the development of trigger or accelerating events of genocide.[68] As shown in Figure 6.1, the risk

Figure 6.1
Process of Violence: A Military Planning Tool

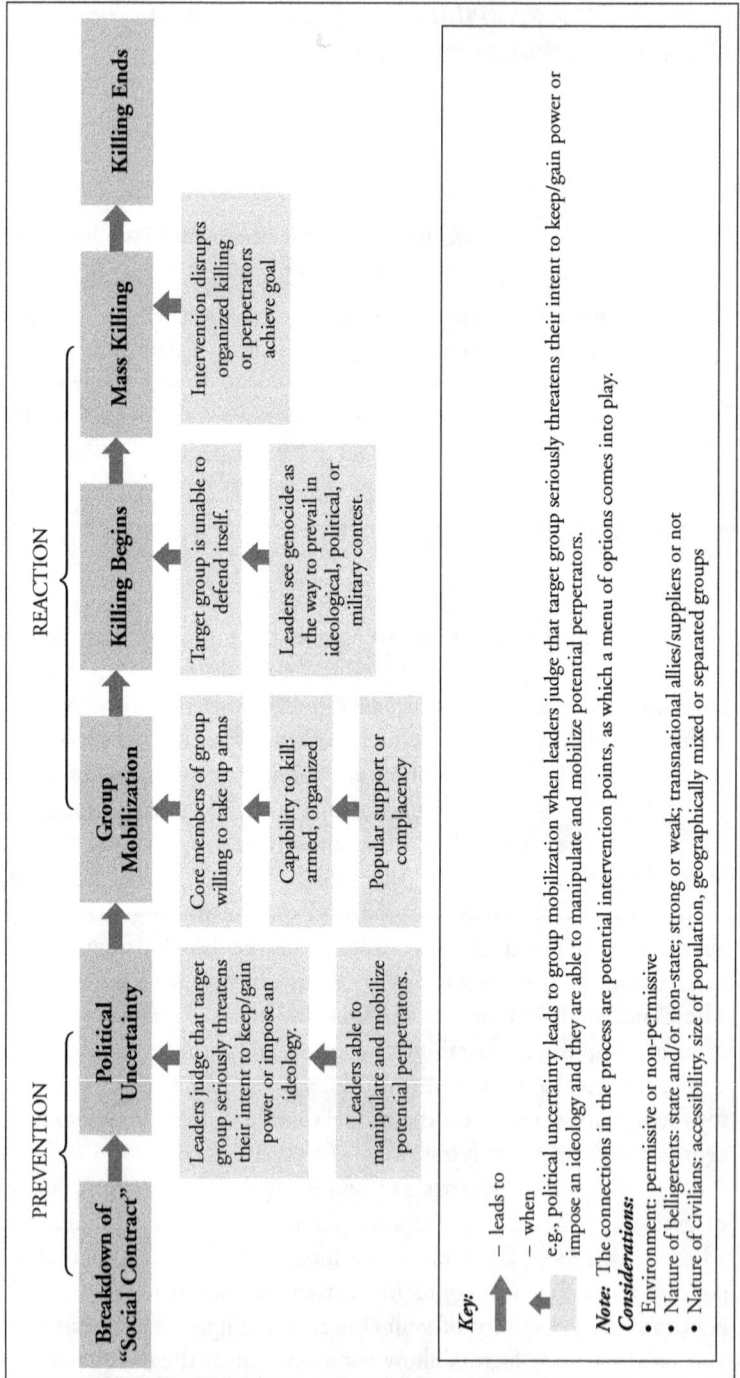

PREVENTION

Breakdown of "Social Contract"

Political Uncertainty

Leaders judge that target group seriously threatens their intent to keep/gain power or impose an ideology.

Leaders able to manipulate and mobilize potential perpetrators.

Group Mobilization

Core members of group willing to take up arms

Capability to kill: armed, organized

Popular support or complacency

REACTION

Killing Begins

Target group is unable to defend itself.

Leaders see genocide as the way to prevail in ideological, political, or military contest.

Mass Killing

Intervention disrupts organized killing or perpetrators achieve goal

Killing Ends

Key:

→ – leads to

→ – when

e.g., political uncertainty leads to group mobilization when leaders judge that target group seriously threatens their intent to keep/gain power or impose an ideology and they are able to manipulate and mobilize potential perpetrators.

Note: The connections in the process are potential intervention points, as which a menu of options comes into play.

Considerations:

• Environment: permissive or non-permissive
• Nature of belligerents: state and/or non-state; strong or weak; transnational allies/suppliers or not
• Nature of civilians: accessibility, size of population, geographically mixed or separated groups

Source: Albright and Cohen (2008, p. 107).

assessment undertaken in Table 6.4 addresses the early stages of genocide prevention — the overall assessment of the risk factors for genocide in Myanmar considers the government's attempts at internal democratization in recent years, examining in particular its BGF policy. As discussed above, the government's continued insistence on implementing the BGF policy is worsening Myanmar's internal security and political instability. The purpose of the assessment in this section is the prevention of genocide or mass atrocities in the future by highlighting signs of preparation for genocide to enable more detailed monitoring and analysis of fault lines along which genocide and mass atrocities could develop.[69]

Table 6.4
Myanmar's Performance on the Risk Factors for Genocide Based on PITF Coding Method, 1995–2009

Risk Factor	Score*	Note
(1) Political upheaval excluding genocide	25 (2009)	1–9 = low 10–20 = medium 21–34 = high 35–60 = very high
(2) Prior genocide	1 (2008)	Dummy variable: 0 = no prior genocide 1 = prior genocide exists
(3) Ethnic character of ruling elite	1 (2008)	0 = elite ethnicity is not salient 1 = elite ethnicity is very salient
(4) Regime type of ruling elite	–6 (2009)	–10–0 = autocracy 1–7 = partial democracies 8–10 = democracies
(5) Ideological orientation of ruling elite	1 (2008)	0 = no exclusionary ideology 1 = exclusionary ideology
(6) Trade openness	37.4 (2009)	<20 = very low 21–40 = low 41–70 = medium 71–100 = high >100 = very high

Note: * year in bracket represents the most recent available data. The data are collected from multiple sources but coded in accordance with the PITF coding method.
Source: Compiled from PITF (2009*b*), Harff and Gurr (2008), Polity IV (2009), EU Trade Statistics (2011).

Myanmar's performance on six risk factors — political upheaval excluding genocide, prior genocide, ethnic character of the ruling elite, regime type of the ruling elite, ideological orientation of the ruling elite, trade openness — between 1995 and 2009 is shown in Table 6.4. These factors will then be further assessed by drawing on the current research and the latest information on developments in Myanmar.

Political Upheaval and Prior Genocides

This section discusses Myanmar's experience of over sixty years of internal political instability and instances of prior genocide. The factor of "political upheaval" is closely linked to the effect of the BGF policy in exacerbating the political stability within Myanmar. According to the RAM, the greater the magnitude of previous internal political upheavals, the more likely a new state failure will lead to genocide.[70] Myanmar's internal political instability dates back to its independence in 1948.[71] Between 1961 and 2009, this instability was mostly due to ethnic conflicts.[72] Table 6.4 shows that the existence of political upheaval in Myanmar was high in 2009. In 2010, as a consequence of the implementation of the BGF policy, tensions with ethnic militant groups that had previously agreed to a ceasefire with the government — such as the Kachin Independence Organization (KIO) and the United Wa State Army (UWSA) — increased. Therefore, the persistent internal political instability could mean that current clashes over the BGF policy could act as a trigger event, and lead to genocide. In any case, the above suggests that the variable "political upheaval" remains high in Myanmar. A prior instance of genocide increases the risks of genocide recurring by more than three times.[73] As noted in Table 6.4, genocide had previously occurred in Myanmar, in 1978, claiming an estimated 5,000 victims.[74] It is clear that Myanmar ranks high on the risk factor of "political upheaval", and performs positively on the factor of "prior genocide" in the RAM. In the following, the factors of "ethnic character", "regime type" and "ideological orientation" of the ruling elite are considered.

Ethnic Character, Regime Type and Ideological Orientation of the Ruling Elite

The RAM predicts that an ethnically salient ruling elite and an autocratic regime increase the probability of genocide, but when accompanied by an exclusionary ideology, increase the probability of genocide by two and a half times.[75] As far as analysing the regime type, while there is evidence of a positive shift — Myanmar held elections in 2010 — the political space available is still limited.[76] The military secured 25 per cent of the total parliamentary seats through direct appointment and the USDP (the military-backed dominant political party in Myanmar) won 80 per cent of the contested parliamentary seats, retaining the military's dominant influence in internal politics.[77] As voting was not conducted in some ethnic border areas, ethnic nationalities comprise a very small number among the parliamentarians.[78]

As far as analysing the ethnic saliency of the ruling elite and its exclusionary ideology, a study by the Centre for Peace and Conflict Studies revealed shared experiences of ideological exclusion among ethnic nationalities that reinforced feelings of discrimination by the government.[79] Ethnic groups deemed the government unsupportive of the development of ethnic national identities, culture and language. Indeed, education in ethnic states is heavily "burmanised" and publication of non-Burmese language newspapers and books has been banned since 1995.[80] Since independence, all main national political institutions including the army have been dominated by the Burmans and traditional ethnic nationality leaders have been excluded from positions of power in local areas.[81] Freedom House reports in 2010 that political rights and civil liberties in Myanmar were ranked at the lowest levels.[82] As there are few ethnic nationality parliamentarians, it is unlikely that the ethnic character and ideological orientation of the ruling elites will undergo substantive changes towards these groups after the 2010 election and further into 2011. This analysis reveals that Myanmar has not moved significantly away from the indicators reflected in Table 6.4. There remains a prevalence of ideological exclusion of non-Burman ethnic nationalities, and a high degree of polarization between the ruling elite and the ethnic nationalities.

Trade Openness

According to the RAM, countries with low openness to trade are two and a half times more at risk of genocide. The RAM further suggests that although international economic linkages inhibit gross human rights violations, political linkages increase the prospects of countries responding to pressures to minimize violations.[83] Although Myanmar has been assessed to score at 8.15 on trade openness in 1989 which is very low according to the PITF coding method, this has changed in recent years as seen by the elevation of the score to 37.4 in 2009 (see Table 6.4). Myanmar is economically dependent on its neighbours as revealed by the junta's engagement over the last two years with India, China and ASEAN, as the military government transitioned to a civilian one as part of the 2008 Constitution.[84] While such interactions do increase prospects of the country responding to external pressure to minimize violations, the fact that foreign policies in the region are premised on the principle of non-interference in internal affairs and constructive engagement could lessen the impact of any pressure.[85] As there is limited interaction on human rights in the region, current political linkages may not be strong enough to significantly pressure Myanmar.

Assessment by the RAM

This section demonstrates that all six risk factors of the RAM are present in Myanmar, with political upheaval remaining high under present conditions, triggered by the BGF policy. The RAM indicates that there are genocide-conducive conditions present in Myanmar, also as a result of the BGF policy. The Genocide Prevention Project's Mass Atrocity Watch List 2008–09 ranked Myanmar in Tier 1. Tier 1 countries have the highest risk of suffering mass atrocity crimes and require immediate diplomacy as well as increased civilian protection.[86] In 2010, Myanmar, with its ethnic nationalities, particularly, the Kachin, Karenni, Karen, Mon, Rakhine, Rohingya, Shan, Chin and Wa, was ranked the country that is fifth highest at risk of mass atrocity crimes.[87] In the following section, the chapter identifies some links between the two models that reinforce their combined use in the analysis undertaken in this NTS Insight. The challenges faced by these models are also highlighted.

Challenges and Ways Forward for the ERM and the RAM

The ERM and the RAM are both risk assessment models that highlight potentials and probabilities of continuing ethnic rebellions and the onset of genocide in Myanmar.[88] As such, they do not adequately provide incremental early warning signals, inhibiting policy-makers from recognizing early warning signs and implementing counter-measures at each stage of the escalation of ethnic rebellions and genocidal situations.[89]

However these models can establish a baseline for the assessment of tension if used in conjunction with one another. Firstly, there is an overlap in the risk factors identified by the ERM and the RAM. For instance, the

ERM's "economic, political, and cultural discrimination" overlaps with the RAM's "exclusionary ideology of the ruling elite". In essence, both models highlight the role of state-led discrimination against ethnic nationalities in intensifying ethnic tensions which could lead to ethnic rebellion. These create unstable political environments that spur on the risk factors for genocide. Secondly, the assessment of the continuation of ethnic conflict sets the baseline for the subsequent analysis on the prospect of genocide using the RAM. The difference between them is that they look at the state-ethnic group relationship from different levels. The ERM model adopts a bottom-up approach that identifies ethnic groups that are likely to initiate rebellions against the government. The RAM is a top-down approach that examines the existence of risk factors of genocide against these groups against the backdrop of ethnic rebellions. While this combination establishes a baseline for tension in a country, it does not provide incremental early warning signals and this remains a significant challenge to the effectiveness of these two models in providing early warning.

By using the ERM, this NTS Insight tests the BGF policy to see whether it will fuel incentives for ethnic nationalities to rebel rather than reduce their militant activities; the analysis shows that the BGF policy has heightened Myanmar's internal ethnic conflict. The ERM also shows that this ethnic rebellion will in turn create domestic conditions conducive to the genocide risk factors specified by the RAM. Due to the time lag in the availability of the data, the application of the two models in the analysis is complemented by qualitative analysis based on the latest available news articles and reports. It is argued that while the two models can establish a baseline for assessing the continuation of conflict and the existence of conditions conducive to the occurrence of genocide, there is a need for these and other models to develop the capacity to identify incremental early warning signs if these models are to be effective in providing policy-makers with useful signals.

CONCLUSION

Whilst Asian states have their own individual experiences with internal conflict some have the conditions for mass atrocities to occur, whilst others will remain simmering but both having significant implications for human security in Asia. This chapter looked at the experiences in Asia broadly in terms of the small arms and light weapons sector and more specifically with the case study of Myanmar and the potential for mass atrocities to occur to illustrate two significant dynamics of internal conflict in Asia. Southeast Asian states have long been subject to extra-regional influences, be they cultural, economic, linguistic, military or political in nature. The substantial religious diversity of the region, both in affiliation and practice, is one example: Hindu, Buddhist, Islam and Christian traditions. These religious traditions are practised in substantial numbers within Southeast Asia, a result of both external influences and intra-regional development. While heterogeneous states are hardly unique to Southeast Asia, this diversity continues to have important implications for the development of conflict within and between states. In particular, the application of the Westphalian model of statehood to such diverse polities requires the consideration of how this diversity impacts upon the development and continuing problem of internal conflict. The shared experiences in Southeast Asia of internal conflict allow for a greater understanding of intra-regional interactions. This chapter provided insight into the underlying dynamics of internal conflict in Asia and provided two detailed analysis of how to understand two complex and multifaceted aspects of internal conflict and its impact on human security.

Notes

1   World Bank, World Development Report 2011 (Washington, D.C.: World Bank, 2011), available at <http://wdr2011.worldbank.org/>.
2   D. David Arnold and Thomas I. Parks, "Are Internal Conflicts Holding Asia Back?", in Asia: Weekly Insight and Analysis from The Asia Foundation, The Asia Foundation, 19 October 2011, available at <http://asiafoundation.org/in-asia/2011/10/19/are-internal-conflicts-holding-asia-back/>.
3   U.S. Army Training and Doctrine Command (U.S. Army TRADOC), Terrorism and WMD in the Contemporary Operational Environment, TRADOC G2 Handbook no. 1.04, Fort Leavenworth, Kansas, 2007, available at <http://www.fas.org/irp/threat/terrorism/sup4.pdf>.
4   United Nations General Assembly (UNGA), "Report of the Panel of Governmental Experts on Small Arms", New York, 1997, available at <http://www.un.org/Depts/ddar/Firstcom/SGreport52/a52298.html>.
5   Small Arms Survey, Small Arms Survey 2001: Profiling the Problem (Geneva: Graduate Institute of International and Development Studies, 2001), available at <http://www.smallarmssurvey.org/publications/by-type/yearbook/small-arms-survey-2001.html>; Small Arms Survey, Small Arms Survey 2005: Weapons at War (Geneva: Graduate Institute of International and Development Studies, 2005), available at <http://www.smallarmssurvey.org/publications/by-type/yearbook/small-arms-survey-2005.html>; Phillip Killicoat, Weaponomics: The Global Market for Assault Rifles, Policy Research Working Paper 4202 (Washington, D.C.: The World Bank, 2007), available at <http://www-wds.worldbank.org/external/default/WDSContentServer/IW3P/IB/2007/04/13/000016406_20070413145045/Rendered/PDF/wps4202.pdf>.

6   Small Arms Survey, *Small Arms Survey 2010: Gangs, Groups, and Guns* (Geneva: Graduate Institute of International and Development Studies, 2010), available at <http://www.smallarmssurvey.org/publications/by-type/yearbook/small-arms-survey-2010.html>.

7   International Action Network on Small Arms (IANSA), n.d., "South East Asia & the Pacific".

8   United Nations General Assembly (UNGA), "Report of the Panel of Governmental Experts on Small Arms", New York, 1997, available at <http://www.un.org/Depts/ddar/Firstcom/SGreport52/a52298.html>.

9   Frances Stewart, "Horizontal Inequalities: A Neglected Dimension of Development", CRISE Working Paper no. 1 (Oxford: Centre for Research on Inequality, Human Security and Ethnicity [CRISE], University of Oxford, 2003), available at <http://www.crise.ox.ac.uk/pubs/workingpaper1.pdf>; Frances Stewart, "Development and Security", CRISE Working Paper no. 3 (Oxford: Centre for Research on Inequality, Human Security and Ethnicity [CRISE], University of Oxford, 2004), available at <http://www.crise.ox.ac.uk/pubs/workingpaper3.pdf>.

10   Boutwell and Klare, cited in Phillip Killicoat, *Weaponomics: The Global Market for Assault Rifles*, Policy Research Working Paper 4202 (Washington, D.C.: The World Bank, 2007), available at <http://www-wds.worldbank.org/external/default/WDSContentServer/IW3P/IB/2007/04/13/000016406_20070413145045/Rendered/PDF/wps4202.pdf>.

11   International Crisis Group (ICG), "Southern Thailand: Moving towards Political Solutions?", Crisis Group Asia Report no. 181, 8 December 2009, available at <http://www.crisisgroup.org/~/media/Files/asia/south-east-asia/thailand/181%20Southern%20Thailand%20Moving%20towards%20Political%20Solutions.ashx>; "Gun Culture Booming in the Troubled South", *Bangkok Post*, 6 September 2009, available at <http://www.bangkokpost.com/news/investigation/23379/gun-culture-booming-in-the-troubled-south>.

12   Small Arms Survey, *Small Arms Survey 2001: Profiling the Problem* (Geneva: Graduate Institute of International and Development Studies, 2001), available at <http://www.smallarmssurvey.org/publications/by-type/yearbook/small-arms-survey-2001.html>; Small Arms Survey, *Small Arms Survey 2005: Weapons at War* (Geneva: Graduate Institute of International and Development Studies, 2005), available at <http://www.smallarmssurvey.org/publications/by-type/yearbook/small-arms-survey-2005.html>.

13   Paul Collier, Lani Elliott, Håvard Hegre, Anke Hoeffler et al., *Breaking the Conflict Trap: Civil War and Development Policy* (Washington, D.C.: The World Bank and Oxford University Press, 2003), available at <http://homepage.mac.com/stazon/apartheid/files/BreakingConflict.pdf>.

14   International Institute for Strategic Studies (IISS), n.d., IISS Armed Conflict Database, available at <http://acd.iiss.org/armedconflict/MainPages/dsp_WorldMap.asp>.

[15]   Project Ploughshares, Armed Conflicts Report 2010, Ontario, Canada, 2010, available at <http://www.ploughshares.ca/libraries/ACRText/ACR-TitlePage. html>.

[16]   Paul Collier, "On the Economic Consequences of Civil War", Oxford Economic Papers, vol. 51, no. 1 (1999): 168–83, available at <http://oep.oxfordjournals. org/content/51/1/168.abstract>.

[17]   Paul Oquist, Peacebuilding and Human Security: A Compilation of Policy Assessment Papers on Peace and Development in Southern Philippines (Philippines: United Nations Development Programme [UNDP], 2009), available at <http://www.undp.org.ph/Downloads/knowledge_products/Peace%20Building %20and%20Human%20Security%20UNDP-policy_book.pdf>.

[18]   Srisompob Jitpiromsri, "Updated Statistics: Thailand's Southern Violence from January 2004 through March 2009", Deep South Watch, blog, 20 April 2009, available at <http://www.deepsouthwatch.org/node/287>.

[19]   Association of Southeast Asian Nations (ASEAN), "ASEAN Declaration on Transnational Crime", 20 December 1997, available at <http://www.aseansec. org/5640.htm>.

[20]   Barbara Harff and Ted Robert Gurr, Countries at Risk of Genocide and Politicide in 2008, available at <http://globalpolicy.gmu.edu/genocide/CurrentRisk2008. pdf>.

[21]   Barbara Harff, "No Lessons Learned from the Holocaust? Assessing Risks of Genocide and Political Mass Murder since 1955", American Political Science Review, vol. 97, no. 1 (2003), available at <http://www.brynmawr.edu/Acads/ GSSW/schram/harff.pdf>.

[22]   Chizom Ekeh and Martin Smith, "Minorities in Burma", MRGI Briefing Papers (UK: Minority Rights Group International, 2007), available at <http://www. minorityrights.org/3546/briefing-papers/minorities-in-burma.html>.

[23]   Heidelberg Institute for International Conflict Research (HIIK), Conflict Barometer 2010, 19th Annual Conflict Analysis (Heidelberg: Department of Political Science, University of Heidelberg, 2010), available at <http://www. hiik.de/en/konfliktbarometer/pdf/ConflictBarometer_2010.pdf>; James Milner, "Refugees and the Regional Dynamics of Peacebuilding", paper presented at the seminar series on Refugees in International Relations, Oxford, 5 December 2008, available at <http://www.globaleconomicgovernance.org/ wp-content/uploads/MT%20Week%208%20Milner.pdf>.

[24]   Chizom Ekeh and Martin Smith, "Minorities in Burma", MRGI Briefing Papers (UK: Minority Rights Group International, 2007), available at <http://www.minorityrights.org/3546/briefing-papers/minorities-in-burma. html>.

[25]   "20,000 Flee Myanmar Fighting: Thai Officials", Channel NewsAsia, 9 November 2010, available at <http://www.channelnewsasia.com/stories/ afp_asiapacific/view/1092278/1/.html>.

[26] Centre for Peace and Conflict Studies (CPCS), *Listening to Voices from Inside: Ethnic People Speak: Myanmar*, Cambodia, 2010, available at <http://www. centrepeaceconflictstudies.org/fileadmin/downloads/pdfs/Ethnic_People_Speak. pdf>; Chao-Tzang Yawnghwe, "Burma and National Reconciliation: Ethnic Conflict and State-Society Dysfunction", *Legal Issues on Burma Journal*, no. 10 (2001), available at <http://www.ibiblio.org/obl/docs/LIOB10-cty. htm>.

[27] Marie Lall, "The 2010 Myanmar Elections", *Heinrich Böll Stiftung — The Green Political Foundation*, 4 January 2011, available at <http://www.boell.de/ worldwide/asia/promotion-of-democracy-the-2010-myanmar-elections-10885. html>.

[28] Thailand Burma Border Consortium (TBBC), *Protracted Displacement and Militarisation in Eastern Burma*, Bangkok, 2009, available at <http://www.tbbc. org/resources/resources.htm>.

[29] International Crisis Group (ICG), "China's Myanmar Strategy: Elections, Ethnic Politics and Economics", Crisis Group Asia Briefing, no. 112 (2010), available at <http://www.crisisgroup.org/~/media/Files/asia/north-east-asia/ B112%20Chinas%20Myanmar%20Strategy%20%20Elections%20Ethnic% 20Politics%20and%20Economics.ashx>; "Myanmar: Border Guard Plan Could Fuel Ethnic Conflict", IRIN, 29 November 2010, available at <http://www. irinnews.org/Report.aspx?ReportID=91221>.

[30] Brian McCartan, "China, Myanmar Border on a Conflict", *Asia Times*, 10 September 2009, available at <http://www.atimes.com/atimes/ Southeast_Asia/KI10Ae01.html>; "Myanmar: Border Guard Plan Could Fuel Ethnic Conflict", IRIN, 29 November 2010, available at <http://www.irinnews. org/Report.aspx?ReportID=91221>; Saw Yan Naing, "Tatmadaw Reinforces Troops in Ethnic Areas", *The Irrawaddy*, 6 January 2011, available at <http:// www.irrawaddy.org/article.php?art_id=20476>.

[31] Carnegie Council, "Ethnic Reconciliation and Political Reform before Justice in Burma", *Human Rights Dialogue: Transitional Justice in East Asia and Its Impact on Human Rights*, vol. 1, no. 8 (1997), available at <http:// www.carnegiecouncil.org/resources/publications/dialogue/1_08/articles/556. htmlL>; Linn Zin, "Burma Junta Bids to Quash the 'Panglong Spirit'", Asian Correspondent, 8 December 2010, available at <http://asiancorrespondent. com/43481/burma%E2%80%99s-junta-blame-on-the-coming-of-second-panglong-conference/>.

[32] Ardeth Maung Thawnghmung, *The Karen Revolution in Burma: Diverse Voices, Uncertain Ends*, Policy Studies 45 (Washington, D.C.: East-West Center, 2008), available at <http://www.eastwestcenter.org/publications/search-for-publications/browse-alphabetic-list-of-titles/?class_call=view&mode=view&pub_ ID=2718>.

[33] Austin, cited in Herbert Wulf and Tobias Debiel, "Systemic Disconnects: Why Regional Organisations Fail to Use Early Warning and Response Mechanisms",

Global Governance, vol. 16, no. 4 (2010): 525–47, available at <http://www. gsdrc.org/go/display&type=Document&id=4017>.

34   Herbert Wulf and Tobias Debiel, "Systemic Disconnects: Why Regional Organisations Fail to Use Early Warning and Response Mechanisms", *Global Governance*, vol. 16, no. 4 (2010): 525–47, available at <http://www.gsdrc. org/go/display&type=Document&id=4017>.

35   For more information on the Responsibility to Protect norm in Asia, see Alistair D.B. Cook and Lina Gong, "Cambodia's Legacy and the Responsibility to Protect in Asia", *Peace Review: A Journal of Social Justice* 23 (2011): 447–55; Mely Caballero-Anthony, "The Responsibility to Protect: Opening Up Spaces for Advancing Human Security", *The Pacific Review*, vol. 25, no. 1 (2012): 113–34.

36   Jack A. Goldstone, *Using Quantitative and Qualitative Models to Forecast Instability*, Special Report 204 (Washington, D.C.: United States Institute of Peace, 2008), available at <http://www.usip.org/publications/using-quantitative-and-qualitative-models-forecast-instability>.

37   Jack A. Goldstone, Robert H. Bates, Ted Robert Gurr et al., "A Global Forecasting Model of Political Instability", paper presented at the Annual Meeting of the American Political Science Association, Washington, D.C., 1–4 September 2005, available at <http://globalpolicy.gmu.edu/pitf/PITFglobal.pdf>.

38   Lawrence Woocher, "Developing a Strategy, Methods and Tools for Genocide Early Warning", report prepared for the Office of the Special Adviser to the UN Secretary-General on the Prevention of Genocide (New York: Center for International Conflict Resolution, Columbia University, 2006), available at <http://www.un.org/en/preventgenocide/adviser/pdf/Woocher%20Early%20w arning%20report,%202006-11-10.pdf>.

39   "Ethnic rebellion" is a concerted campaign of violent action used by organisations claiming to represent an ethnic group to make claims against the state (Gurr and Moore 1997, p. 1083). It is discussed as one form of "ethnic conflict" in this chapter, and will be used interchangeably with "ethnic conflict".

40   For details of the project, please go to <http://www.cidcm.umd.edu/mar/>.

41   Barbara Harff and Ted Robert Gurr, "Systematic Early Warning of Humanitarian Emergencies", *Journal of Peace Research*, vol. 35, no. 5 (1998): 551–79, available at <http://jpr.sagepub.com/content/35/5/551.short>.

42   Barbara Harff, "No Lessons Learned from the Holocaust? Assessing Risks of Genocide and Political Mass Murder since 1955", *American Political Science Review*, vol. 97, no. 1 (2003), available at <http://www.brynmawr.edu/Acads/ GSSW/schram/harff.pdf>.

43   Lawrence Woocher, "Developing a Strategy, Methods and Tools for Genocide Early Warning", report prepared for the Office of the Special Adviser to the UN Secretary-General on the Prevention of Genocide (New York: Center for International Conflict Resolution, Columbia University, 2006), available at <http://www.un.org/en/preventgenocide/adviser/pdf/Woocher%20Early%20w arning%20report,%202006-11-10.pdf>.

44 Will H. Moore, "The Repression of Dissent: A Substitution Model of Government Coercion", *Journal of Conflict Resolution*, vol. 44, no. 1 (2000): 107–27; Gregory D. Saxton, ed., "Repression, Grievances, Mobilization, and Rebellion: A New Test of Gurr's Model of Ethnopolitical Rebellion", *International Interactions*, vol. 31 (2005): 1–30, available at <http://www.acsu.buffalo.edu/~gdsaxton/papers/International%20Interactions.pdf>.

45 Alex J. Bellamy, "Mass Atrocities and Armed Conflict: Links, Distinctions, and Implications for the Responsibility to Prevent", Policy Analysis Brief (Muscatine, IA: The Stanley Foundation, 2011), available at <http://www.stanleyfoundation.org/publications/pab/BellamyPAB22011.pdf>.

46 Carnegie Council, "Ethnic Reconciliation and Political Reform before Justice in Burma", *Human Rights Dialogue: Transitional Justice in East Asia and Its Impact on Human Rights*, vol. 1, no. 8 (1997), available at <http://www.carnegiecouncil.org/resources/publications/dialogue/1_08/articles/556.html>.

47 Saw Kwe Htoo, Naw May Oo, Saw Htoo Htoo Lay et al., "From Political Aspiration to National Consensus: The Need for a National Consultative Conference in Karen Context", n.d., available at <http://www.karen.org/news2/messages/112.html>.

48 Minorities at Risk (MAR) Project, "Assessment for Shans in Burma" (College Park, MD: Center for International Development and Conflict Management, University of Maryland, 2006), available at <http://www.cidcm.umd.edu/mar/assessment.asp?groupId=77507>.

49 Physicians for Human Rights (PHR), *Life under the Junta: Evidence of Crimes against Humanity in Burma's Chin State* (MA: Cambridge, 2011), available at <http://physiciansforhumanrights.org/library/documents/reports/Burma-full-rpt-Chin-state.pdf>.

50 Ashley South, *Ethnic Politics in Burma: States of Conflict* (London: Routledge, 2008), available at <http://www.routledge.com/books/details/9780415410083/>.

51 Heidelberg Institute for International Conflict Research (HIIK), *Conflict Barometer 2010*, 19th Annual Conflict Analysis (Heidelberg: Department of Political Science, University of Heidelberg, 2010), available at <http://www.hiik.de/en/konfliktbarometer/pdf/ConflictBarometer_2010.pdf>.

52 "Myanmar: Border Guard Plan Could Fuel Ethnic Conflict", IRIN, 29 November 2010, available at <http://www.irinnews.org/Report.aspx?ReportID=91221>.

53 Lawrence Woocher, "Developing a Strategy, Methods and Tools for Genocide Early Warning", report prepared for the Office of the Special Adviser to the UN Secretary-General on the Prevention of Genocide (New York: Center for International Conflict Resolution, Columbia University, 2006), available at <http://www.un.org/en/preventgenocide/adviser/pdf/Woocher%20Early%20warning%20report,%202006-11-10.pdf>.

54 Barbara Harff and Ted Robert Gurr, *Countries at Risk of Genocide and Politicide in 2008*, available at <http://globalpolicy.gmu.edu/genocide/CurrentRisk2008.pdf>.

55 Morten B. Pedersen, "Burma's Ethnic Minorities: Charting Their Own Path to Peace", *Critical Asian Studies*, vol. 40, no. 1 (2008): 45–66, available at <http://criticalasianstudies.org/issues/vol40/no1/burmas-ethnic-minorities.html>.

56 "Myanmar Cancels Voting in More Minority Areas", *Washington Post*, 2 November 2010, available at <http://www.washingtonpost.com/wp-dyn/content/article/2010/11/02/AR2010110202043.html>.

57 Barbara Harff and Ted Robert Gurr, "Systematic Early Warning of Humanitarian Emergencies", *Journal of Peace Research*, vol. 35, no. 5 (1998): 559, available at <http://jpr.sagepub.com/content/35/5/551.short>.

58 Chao-Tzang Yawnghwe, "Burma and National Reconciliation: Ethnic Conflict and State-Society Dysfunction", *Legal Issues on Burma Journal*, no. 10 (2001), available at <http://www.ibiblio.org/obl/docs/LIOB10-cty.htm>.

59 Petry, cited in Ardeth Maung Thawnghmung, *The Karen Revolution in Burma: Diverse Voices, Uncertain Ends*, Policy Studies 45 (Washington, D.C.: East-West Center, 2008), available at <http://www.eastwestcenter.org/publications/search-for-publications/browse-alphabetic-list-of-titles/?class_call=view&mode=view&pub_ID=2718>.

60 Andrew Selth, "Burma's Muslims: Terrorists or Terrorised?", Canberra Papers on Strategy and Defence no. 150 (Canberra: Strategic Defence Studies Centre, Australian National University, 2003), p. 15.

61 Barbara Harff and Ted Robert Gurr, *Countries at Risk of Genocide and Politicide in 2008*, p. 560, available at <http://globalpolicy.gmu.edu/genocide/CurrentRisk2008.pdf>.

62 Polity IV, "Polity IV: Regime Authority Characteristics and Transitions Datasets", Center for Systemic Peace, Colorado State University, 2009, available at <http://www.systemicpeace.org/inscr/inscr.htm>.

63 Madeleine K. Albright and William S. Cohen, *Preventing Genocide: A Blueprint for U.S. Policymakers* (U.S.: United States Holocaust Memorial Museum, American Academy of Diplomacy and United States Institute of Peace, 2008), p. 25, available at <http://www.ushmm.org/genocide/taskforce/report.php>; Michael Freeman, "Never Again! Genocide and the International Community", *Papeles del CEIC*, vol. 1, no. 27 (2007): 11–12, <http://redalyc.uaemex.mx/pdf/765/76500703.pdf>.

64 Barbara Harff, "No Lessons Learned from the Holocaust? Assessing Risks of Genocide and Political Mass Murder since 1955", *American Political Science Review*, vol. 97, no. 1 (2003): 66–67, available at <http://www.brynmawr.edu/Acads/GSSW/schram/harff.pdf>.

65 Ibid., p. 70.

66 Ibid., p. 66.

67 United States Agency for International Development (USAID), *Measuring Fragility: Indicators and Methods for Rating State Performance* (Washington, D.C., 2005), available at <http://pdf.usaid.gov/pdf_docs/PNADD462.pdf>; Madeleine K. Albright and William S. Cohen, *Preventing Genocide: A*

Blueprint for U.S. Policymakers (U.S.: United States Holocaust Memorial Museum, American Academy of Diplomacy and United States Institute of Peace, 2008), available at <http://www.ushmm.org/genocide/taskforce/report.php>; Gregory H. Stanton, "Building an Anti-Genocide Regime", in *The Prevention and Intervention of Genocide — Genocide: A Critical Bibliographic Review*, vol. 6, edited by Samuel Totten (New Jersey: Transaction Publishers, 2008), available at <http://books.google.com.sg/books?hl=en&lr=&id=mSHY4X3PkCQC&oi=fnd&pg=PA63&dq=harff%2Bgenocide+risk+assessment+model+2003%2Bcritique&ots=SVH3ZDsRqj&sig=9R-sIghtI5UI0_JU8nQRTVbu6xo#v=onepage&q&f=false>.

68   Madeleine K. Albright and S. Cohen William, *Preventing Genocide: A Blueprint for U.S. Policymakers* (U.S.: United States Holocaust Memorial Museum, American Academy of Diplomacy and United States Institute of Peace, 2008), pp. 60–63, available at <http://www.ushmm.org/genocide/taskforce/report.php>.

69   Madeleine K. Albright and S. Cohen William, *Preventing Genocide: A Blueprint for U.S. Policymakers* (U.S.: United States Holocaust Memorial Museum, American Academy of Diplomacy and United States Institute of Peace, 2008), p. 19, available at <http://www.ushmm.org/genocide/taskforce/report.php>.

70   Barbara Harff, "No Lessons Learned from the Holocaust? Assessing Risks of Genocide and Political Mass Murder since 1955", *American Political Science Review*, vol. 97, no. 1 (2003): 66, available at <http://www.brynmawr.edu/Acads/GSSW/schram/harff.pdf>.

71   Renaud Egreteau, "Burma (Myanmar) 1930–2007", Online Encyclopedia of Mass Violence (Paris: SciencesPo, 2009), available at <http://www.massviolence.org/IMG/article_PDF/Burma-Myanmar-1930-2007.pdf>.

72   Political Instability Task Force (PITF), "PITF State Failure Problem Set 1995–2009 — Excel Ethnic Wars", Integrated Network for Societal Conflict Research (INSCR) Data Page, 2009*b*, available at <http://www.systemicpeace.org/inscr/PITF%20Ethnic%20Wars%202009.xls>.

73   Barbara Harff, "No Lessons Learned from the Holocaust? Assessing Risks of Genocide and Political Mass Murder since 1955", *American Political Science Review*, vol. 97, no. 1 (2003): 66–67, available at <http://www.brynmawr.edu/Acads/GSSW/schram/harff.pdf>.

74   Ibid.

75   Ibid.

76   Marie Lall, "The 2010 Myanmar Elections", *Heinrich Böll Stiftung — The Green Political Foundation*, 4 January 2011, available at <http://www.boell.de/worldwide/asia/promotion-of-democracy-the-2010-myanmar-elections-10885.html>.

77   Thomas Maung Shwe, "Ban 'Hopes' New Government Means Change in Burma", Mizzima, 8 February 2011, available at <http://www.mizzima.com/

edop/analysis/4856-ban-hopes-new-government-means-change-in-burma. html>; Patrick Pierce, "Impunity or Reconciliation in Burma's Transition", ICTJ Briefing (New York: International Center for Transitional Justice, 2010), available at <http://www.ictj.org/static/Publications/ICTJ_MMR_transition_ pb2010.pdf>.

[78] Thomas Maung Shwe, "Ban 'Hopes' New Government Means Change in Burma", Mizzima, 8 February 2011, available at <http://www.mizzima.com/ edop/analysis/4856-ban-hopes-new-government-means-change-in-burma. html>.

[79] Centre for Peace and Conflict Studies (CPCS), *Listening to Voices from Inside: Ethnic People Speak: Myanmar* (Cambodia, 2010), available at <http://www. centrepeaceconflictstudies.org/fileadmin/downloads/pdfs/Ethnic_People_Speak. pdf>.

[80] Morten B. Pedersen, "Burma's Ethnic Minorities: Charting Their Own Path to Peace", *Critical Asian Studies*, vol. 40, no. 1 (2008): 45–66, available at <http://criticalasianstudies.org/issues/vol40/no1/burmas-ethnic-minorities.html>; Centre for Peace and Conflict Studies (CPCS), *Listening to Voices from Inside: Ethnic People Speak: Myanmar* (Cambodia, 2010), available at <http://www. centrepeaceconflictstudies.org/fileadmin/downloads/pdfs/Ethnic_People_Speak. pdf>.

[81] Morten B. Pedersen, "Burma's Ethnic Minorities: Charting Their Own Path to Peace", *Critical Asian Studies*, vol. 40, no. 1 (2008): 45–66, available at <http:// criticalasianstudies.org/issues/vol40/no1/burmas-ethnic-minorities.html>.

[82] Freedom House, "Freedom in the World — Burma (Myanmar) (2010)", Washington, D.C., 2010, available at <http://www.freedomhouse.org/template. cfm?page=22&year=2010&country=7792>.

[83] Barbara Harff, "No Lessons Learned from the Holocaust? Assessing Risks of Genocide and Political Mass Murder since 1955", *American Political Science Review*, vol. 97, no. 1 (2003): 68, available at <http://www.brynmawr.edu/ Acads/GSSW/schram/harff.pdf>.

[84] Trevor Wilson, Leslie Teo, and Masahiro Hori, "The Impact of Globalization on Economic Development in Myanmar", in *Globalization and Development in the Mekong Economies*, edited by Leung Suiwah, Benedict F.W. Bingham and Matt Davies (UK: MPG Books Groups, 2010), pp. 133–50, available at <http://books.google.com.sg/books?hl=en&lr=&id=wtJmkEA0tcEC&oi=fnd&p g=PA133&dq=myanmar+%2Btrade+openness%2B2010&ots=9uTq0NXhNE&s ig=5IqcD1ORUfVg-qXygzf3vHEajVM#v=onepage&q&f=false>.

[85] Oo Zaw and Win Min, *Assessing Burma's Ceasefire Accords*, Policy Studies 39 (Washington, D.C.: East-West Center, 2007); John Arendshorst, "The Dilemma of Non-interference: Myanmar, Human Rights, and the ASEAN Charter", *Northwestern University Journal of International Human Rights*, vol. 8, no. 1 (2009), available at <http://www.law.northwestern.edu/journals/jihr/v8/ n1/5/>.

[86]   Genocide Prevention Project (GPP), "More than an Ounce Required: Summon-
       ing the Political Will to Prevent Genocide and Mass Atrocity Crimes in the
       21st Century" (New York: Public Interest Projects, 2009), available at <http://
       www.preventorprotect.org/overview/report.html>.
[87]   Minority Rights Group International (MRGI), "Peoples under Threat 2010
       Table 1", United Kingdom, Table 1, 2010, available at <http://www.minority
       rights.org/download.php?id=794>.
[88]   Ted Robert Gurr, "A Risk Assessment Model of Ethnopolitical Rebellion",
       in *Preventing Measures: Building Risk Assessment and Crisis Early Warning
       Systems*, edited by John L. Davies and Robert Gurr (Maryland: Rowman and
       Littlefield Publishers, 1998), pp. 15–26.
[89]   Gregory H. Stanton, "Building an Anti-Genocide Regime", in *The Prevention
       and Intervention of Genocide — Genocide: A Critical Bibliographic Review*,
       vol. 6, edited by Samuel Totten (New Jersey: Transaction Publishers, 2008),
       p. 284, available at <http://books.google.com.sg/books?hl=en&lr=&id=mSHY4
       X3PkCQC&oi=fnd&pg=PA63&dq=harff%2Bgenocide+risk+assessment+mode
       l+2003%2Bcritique&ots=SVH3ZDsRqj&sig=9R-sIghtI5UI0_JU8nQRTVbu6
       xo#v=onepage&q&f=false>.

References

"20,000 Flee Myanmar Fighting: Thai Officials". Channel NewsAsia, 9 November
    2010. Available at <http://www.channelnewsasia.com/stories/afp_asiapacific/
    view/1092278/1/.html>.
Albright, Madeleine K. and William S. Cohen. *Preventing Genocide: A Blueprint
    for U.S. Policymakers*. U.S.: United States Holocaust Memorial Museum,
    American Academy of Diplomacy and United States Institute of Peace, 2008.
    Available at <http://www.ushmm.org/genocide/taskforce/report.php>.
Arendshorst, John. "The Dilemma of Non-interference: Myanmar, Human Rights,
    and the ASEAN Charter". *Northwestern University Journal of International
    Human Rights*, vol. 8, no. 1 (2009). Available at <http://www.law.northwestern.
    edu/journals/jihr/v8/n1/5/>.
Arnold, David D. and Thomas I. Parks. "Are Internal Conflicts Holding Asia
    Back?" In *Asia: Weekly Insight and Analysis from The Asia Foundation*. The
    Asia Foundation, 19 October 2011. Available at <http://asiafoundation.org/
    in-asia/2011/10/19/are-internal-conflicts-holding-asia-back/>.
Association of Southeast Asian Nations (ASEAN). "ASEAN Declaration on Trans-
    national Crime", 20 December 1997. Available at <http://www.aseansec.
    org/5640.htm>.
Bellamy, Alex J. "Mass Atrocities and Armed Conflict: Links, Distinctions,
    and Implications for the Responsibility to Prevent". Policy Analysis Brief.
    Muscatine, IA: The Stanley Foundation, 2011. Available at <http://www.
    stanleyfoundation.org/publications/pab/BellamyPAB22011.pdf>.

Caballero-Anthony Mely. "The Responsibility to Protect: Opening Up Spaces for Advancing Human Security". *The Pacific Review*, vol. 25, no. 1 (2012): 113–34.

Carnegie Council. "Ethnic Reconciliation and Political Reform before Justice in Burma". *Human Rights Dialogue: Transitional Justice in East Asia and Its Impact on Human Rights*, vol. 1, no. 8 (1997). Available at <http://www.carnegiecouncil.org/resources/publications/dialogue/1_08/articles/556.html>.

Centre for Peace and Conflict Studies (CPCS). *Listening to Voices from Inside: Ethnic People Speak: Myanmar*. Cambodia, 2010. Available at <http://www.centrepeaceconflictstudies.org/fileadmin/downloads/pdfs/Ethnic_People_Speak.pdf>.

Collier, Paul. "On the Economic Consequences of Civil War". Oxford Economic Papers, vol. 51, no. 1 (1999): 168–83. Available at <http://oep.oxfordjournals.org/content/51/1/168.abstract>.

Collier, Paul, Lani Elliott, Håvard Hegre, Anke Hoeffler et al. *Breaking the Conflict Trap: Civil War and Development Policy*. Washington, D.C.: The World Bank and Oxford University Press, 2003. Available at <http://homepage.mac.com/stazon/apartheid/files/BreakingConflict.pdf>.

Cook, Alistair D.B. and Lina Gong. "Cambodia's Legacy and the Responsibility to Protect in Asia". *Peace Review: A Journal of Social Justice* 23 (2011): 447–55.

Egreteau, Renaud. "Burma (Myanmar) 1930–2007". Online Encyclopedia of Mass Violence. Paris: SciencesPo, 2009. Available at <http://www.massviolence.org/IMG/article_PDF/Burma-Myanmar-1930-2007.pdf>.

Ekeh, Chizom and Martin Smith. "Minorities in Burma". MRGI Briefing Papers. UK: Minority Rights Group International, 2007. Available at <http://www.minorityrights.org/3546/briefing-papers/minorities-in-burma.html>.

Freedom House. "Freedom in the World — Burma (Myanmar) (2010)". Washington, D.C., 2010. Available at <http://www.freedomhouse.org/template.cfm?page=22&year=2010&country=7792>.

Genocide Prevention Project (GPP). "More than an Ounce Required: Summoning the Political Will to Prevent Genocide and Mass Atrocity Crimes in the 21st Century". New York: Public Interest Projects, 2009. Available at <http://www.preventorprotect.org/overview/report.html>.

Goldstone, Jack A. *Using Quantitative and Qualitative Models to Forecast Instability*. Special Report 204. Washington, D.C.: United States Institute of Peace, 2008. Available at <http://www.usip.org/publications/using-quantitative-and-qualitative-models-forecast-instability>.

Goldstone, Jack A., Robert H. Bates, Ted Robert Gurr et al. "A Global Forecasting Model of Political Instability". Paper presented at the Annual Meeting of the American Political Science Association. Washington, D.C., 1–4 September 2005. Available at <http://globalpolicy.gmu.edu/pitf/PITFglobal.pdf>.

"Gun Culture Booming in the Troubled South". *Bangkok Post*, 6 September 2009. Available at <http://www.bangkokpost.com/news/investigation/23379/gun-culture-booming-in-the-troubled-south>.

Gurr, Ted Robert. "A Risk Assessment Model of Ethnopolitical Rebellion". In *Preventing Measures: Building Risk Assessment and Crisis Early Warning Systems*, edited by John L. Davies and Robert Gurr. Maryland: Rowman and Littlefield Publishers, 1998.

Harff, Barbara. "No Lessons Learned from the Holocaust? Assessing Risks of Genocide and Political Mass Murder since 1955". *American Political Science Review*, vol. 97, no. 1 (2003). Available at <http://www.brynmawr.edu/Acads/GSSW/schram/harff.pdf>.

Harff, Barbara and Ted Robert Gurr. *Countries at Risk of Genocide and Politicide in 2008*. Available at <http://globalpolicy.gmu.edu/genocide/CurrentRisk2008.pdf>.

——. "Systematic Early Warning of Humanitarian Emergencies". *Journal of Peace Research*, vol. 35, no. 5 (1998): 551–79. Available at <http://jpr.sagepub.com/content/35/5/551.short>.

Heidelberg Institute for International Conflict Research (HIIK). *Conflict Barometer 2010*. 19th Annual Conflict Analysis. Heidelberg: Department of Political Science, University of Heidelberg, 2010. Available at <http://www.hiik.de/en/konfliktbarometer/pdf/ConflictBarometer_2010.pdf>.

International Action Network on Small Arms (IANSA), n.d. "South East Asia & the Pacific".

International Crisis Group (ICG). "China's Myanmar Strategy: Elections, Ethnic Politics and Economics". Crisis Group Asia Briefing, No. 112 (2010). Available at <http://www.crisisgroup.org/~/media/Files/asia/north-east-asia/B112%20Chinas%20Myanmar%20Strategy%20%20Elections%20Ethnic%20Politics%20and%20Economics.ashx>.

——. "Southern Thailand: Moving towards Political Solutions?" Crisis Group Asia Report No. 181, 8 December 2009. Available at <http://www.crisisgroup.org/~/media/Files/asia/south-east-asia/thailand/181%20Southern%20Thailand%20Moving%20towards%20Political%20Solutions.ashx>.

International Institute for Strategic Studies (IISS), n.d. IISS Armed Conflict Database. Available at <http://acd.iiss.org/armedconflict/MainPages/dsp_WorldMap.asp>.

Jitpiromsri, Srisompob. "Updated Statistics: Thailand's Southern Violence from January 2004 through March 2009". Deep South Watch, blog, 20 April 2009. Available at <http://www.deepsouthwatch.org/node/287>.

Killicoat, Phillip. *Weaponomics: The Global Market for Assault Rifles*. Policy Research Working Paper 4202. Washington, D.C.: The World Bank, 2007. Available at <http://www-wds.worldbank.org/external/default/WDSContentServer/IW3P/IB/2007/04/13/000016406_20070413145045/Rendered/PDF/wps4202.pdf>.

Lall, Marie. "The 2010 Myanmar Elections". *Heinrich Böll Stiftung: The Green Political Foundation*, 4 January 2011. Available at <http://www.boell.de/worldwide/asia/promotion-of-democracy-the-2010-myanmar-elections-10885.html>.

McCartan, Brian. "China, Myanmar Border on a Conflict". *Asia Times*, 10 September 2009. Available at <http://www.atimes.com/atimes/Southeast_Asia/KI10Ae01.html>.

Milner, James. "Refugees and the Regional Dynamics of Peacebuilding". Paper presented at the seminar series on Refugees in International Relations, Oxford, 5 December 2008. Available at <http://www.globaleconomicgovernance.org/wp-content/uploads/MT%20Week%208%20Milner.pdf>.

Minorities at Risk (MAR) Project. "Assessment for Shans in Burma". College Park, MD: Center for International Development and Conflict Management, University of Maryland, 2006. Available at <http://www.cidcm.umd.edu/mar/assessment.asp?groupId=77507>.

Moore, Will H. "The Repression of Dissent: A Substitution Model of Government Coercion". *Journal of Conflict Resolution*, vol. 44, no. 1 (2000): 107–27.

"Myanmar: Border Guard Plan Could Fuel Ethnic Conflict". IRIN, 29 November 2010. Available at <http://www.irinnews.org/Report.aspx?ReportID=91221>.

"Myanmar Cancels Voting in More Minority Areas". *Washington Post*, 2 November 2010. Available at <http://www.washingtonpost.com/wp-dyn/content/article/2010/11/02/AR2010110202043.html>.

Oquist, Paul. *Peacebuilding and Human Security: A Compilation of Policy Assessment Papers on Peace and Development in Southern Philippines*. Philippines: United Nations Development Programme (UNDP), 2009. Available at <http://www.undp.org.ph/Downloads/knowledge_products/Peace%20Building%20and%20Human%20Security%20UNDP-policy_book.pdf>.

Pedersen, Morten B. "Burma's Ethnic Minorities: Charting Their Own Path to Peace". *Critical Asian Studies*, vol. 40, no. 1 (2008): 45–66. Available at <http://criticalasianstudies.org/issues/vol40/no1/burmas-ethnic-minorities.html>.

Physicians for Human Rights (PHR). *Life under the Junta: Evidence of Crimes against Humanity in Burma's Chin State*. MA: Cambridge, 2011. Available at <http://physiciansforhumanrights.org/library/documents/reports/Burma-full-rpt-Chin-state.pdf>.

Pierce, Patrick. "Impunity or Reconciliation in Burma's Transition". ICTJ Briefing. New York: International Center for Transitional Justice, 2010. Available at <http://www.ictj.org/static/Publications/ICTJ_MMR_transition_pb2010.pdf>.

Political Instability Task Force (PITF). "PITF State Failure Problem Set 19952009 — Excel Ethnic Wars". Integrated Network for Societal Conflict Research (INSCR) Data Page, 2009*b*. Available at <http://www.systemicpeace.org/inscr/PITF%20Ethnic%20Wars%202009.xls>.

Polity IV. "Polity IV: Regime Authority Characteristics and Transitions Datasets". Center for Systemic Peace, Colorado State University, 2009. Available at <http://www.systemicpeace.org/inscr/inscr.htm>.

Project Ploughshares. Armed Conflicts Report 2010. Ontario, Canada, 2010. Available at <http://www.ploughshares.ca/libraries/ACRText/ACR-TitlePage.html>.

Saw, Kwe Htoo, Naw May Oo, Saw Htoo Htoo Lay et al. "From Political Aspiration to National Consensus: The Need for a National Consultative Conference in Karen Context". n.d. <www.karen.org>. Available at <http://www.karen.org/news2/messages/112.html>.

Saw, Yan Naing. "Tatmadaw Reinforces Troops in Ethnic Areas". The Irrawaddy, 6 January 2011. Available at <http://www.irrawaddy.org/article.php?art_id=20476>.

Saxton, Gregory D. "Repression, Grievances, Mobilization, and Rebellion: A New Test of Gurr's Model of Ethnopolitical Rebellion". International Interactions, vol. 31 (2005): 1–30. Available at <http://www.acsu.buffalo.edu/~gdsaxton/papers/International%20Interactions.pdf>.

Selth, Andrew. "Burma's Muslims: Terrorists or Terrorised?" Canberra Papers on Strategy and Defence no. 150. Canberra: Strategic Defence Studies Centre, Australian National University, 2003.

Shwe, Thomas Maung. "Ban 'Hopes' New Government Means Change in Burma". Mizzima, 8 February 2011. Available at <http://www.mizzima.com/edop/analysis/4856-ban-hopes-new-government-means-change-in-burma.html>.

Small Arms Survey. Small Arms Survey 2010: Gangs, Groups, and Guns. Geneva: Graduate Institute of International and Development Studies, 2010. Available at <http://www.smallarmssurvey.org/publications/by-type/yearbook/small-arms-survey-2010.html>.

———. Small Arms Survey 2005: Weapons at War. Geneva: Graduate Institute of International and Development Studies, 2005. Available at <http://www.smallarmssurvey.org/publications/by-type/yearbook/small-arms-survey-2005.html>.

———. Small Arms Survey 2001: Profiling the Problem. Geneva: Graduate Institute of International and Development Studies, 2001. Available at <http://www.smallarmssurvey.org/publications/by-type/yearbook/small-arms-survey-2001.html>.

South, Ashley. Ethnic Politics in Burma: States of Conflict. London: Routledge, 2008. Available at <http://www.routledge.com/books/details/9780415410083/>.

Stanton, Gregory H. "Building an Anti-Genocide Regime". In The Prevention and Intervention of Genocide – Genocide: A Critical Bibliographic Review, vol. 6, edited by Samuel Totten. New Jersey: Transaction Publishers, 2008. Available at <http://books.google.com.sg/books?hl=en&lr=&id=mSHY4X3PkCQC&oi=fnd&pg=PA63&dq=harff%2Bgenocide+risk+assessment+model+2003%2Bcritique&ots=SVH3ZDsRqj&sig=9R-sIghtI5UI0_JU8nQRTVbu6xo#v=onepage&q&f=false>.

Stewart, Frances. "Development and Security". CRISE Working Paper No. 3.
    Oxford: Centre for Research on Inequality, Human Security and Ethnicity
    (CRISE), University of Oxford, 2004. Available at <http://www.crise.ox.ac.
    uk/pubs/workingpaper3.pdf>.
———. "Horizontal Inequalities: A Neglected Dimension of Development".
    CRISE Working Paper No. 1. Oxford: Centre for Research on Inequality,
    Human Security and Ethnicity (CRISE), University of Oxford, 2003.
    Available at <http://www.crise.ox.ac.uk/pubs/workingpaper1.pdf>.
Thailand Burma Border Consortium (TBBC). *Protracted Displacement and
    Militarisation in Eastern Burma*. Bangkok, 2009. Available at <http://www.tbbc.
    org/resources/resources.htm>.
Thawnghmung, Ardeth Maung. *The Karen Revolution in Burma: Diverse Voices,
    Uncertain Ends*. Policy Studies 45. Washington, D.C.: East-West Center,
    2008. Available at <http://www.eastwestcenter.org/publications/search-for-
    publications/browse-alphabetic-list-of-titles/?class_call=view&mode=view&pub_
    ID=2718>.
United Nations General Assembly (UNGA). "Report of the Panel of Governmental
    Experts on Small Arms". New York, 1997. Available at <http://www.un.org/
    Depts/ddar/Firstcom/SGreport52/a52298.html>.
United States Agency for International Development (USAID). *Measuring Fragility:
    Indicators and Methods for Rating State Performance*. Washington, D.C., 2005.
    Available at <http://pdf.usaid.gov/pdf_docs/PNADD462.pdf>.
US Army Training and Doctrine Command (US Army TRADOC). *Terrorism and
    WMD in the Contemporary Operational Environment*. TRADOC G2 Handbook
    No. 1.04. Fort Leavenworth, Kansas, 2007. Available at <http://www.fas.org/
    irp/threat/terrorism/sup4.pdf>.
Wilson, Trevor, Leslie Teo, and Masahiro Hori. "The Impact of Globalization on
    Economic Development in Myanmar". In *Globalization and Development in
    the Mekong Economies*, edited by Leung Suiwah, Benedict F.W. Bingham and
    Matt Davies. UK: MPG Books Groups, 2010. Available at <http://books.
    google.com.sg/books?hl=en&lr=&id=wtJmkEA0tcEC&oi=fnd&pg=PA133&dq=
    myanmar+%2Btrade+openness%2B2010&ots=9uTq0NXhNE&sig=
    5IqcD1ORUfVg-qXygzf3vHEajVM#v=onepage&q&f=false>.
Woocher, Lawrence. "Developing a Strategy, Methods and Tools for Genocide Early
    Warning". Report prepared for the Office of the Special Adviser to the UN Secretary-
    General on the Prevention of Genocide. New York: Center for International
    Conflict Resolution, Columbia University, 2006. Available at <http://www.un.org/
    en/preventgenocide/adviser/pdf/Woocher%20Early%20warning%20report,
    %202006-11-10.pdf>.
World Bank. World Development Report 2011. Washington, D.C.: World Bank,
    2011. Available at <http://wdr2011.worldbank.org/>.
Wulf, Herbert and Tobias Debiel. "Systemic Disconnects: Why Regional Organisations
    Fail to Use Early Warning and Response Mechanisms". *Global Governance*,

vol. 16, no. 4 (2010): 525–47. Available at <http://www.gsdrc.org/go/display& type=Document&id=4017>.

Yawnghwe, Chao-Tzang. "Burma and National Reconciliation: Ethnic Conflict and State-Society Dysfunction". *Legal Issues on Burma Journal*, no. 10 (2001). Available at <http://www.ibiblio.org/obl/docs/LIOB10-cty.htm>.

Zaw, Oo and Win Min. *Assessing Burma's Ceasefire Accords*. Policy Studies 39. Washington, D.C.: East-West Center, 2007.

Zin, Linn. "Burma Junta Bids to Quash the 'Panglong Spirit'". Asian Correspondent, 8 December 2010. Available at <http://asiancorrespondent.com/43481/ burma%E2%80%99s-junta-blame-on-the-coming-of-second-panglong-conference/>.

7

FORCED MIGRATION

Mely Caballero-Anthony, Alistair D.B. Cook
Priyanka Bhalla and Pau Khan Khup Hangzo

Since 2008 there have been numerous reports in the international media of Rohingya, a Muslim minority group from Myanmar, attempting to escape to Thailand and Malaysia, via perilous boat journeys. After being "pushed back" by Thai authorities, there was pressure on ASEAN and the Bali Process for People Smuggling, Trafficking in Persons and Related Transnational Crime, to address the root cause of statelessness. The aim of this chapter is to survey the current status of forced migration in Asia drawing on contemporary examples to illustrate the various manifestations of the concept. There is a particular focus on the issue of statelessness as it is a prevalent concern in the region, where post-colonial states have split ethnic groups across artificial borders and displaced many who are not recognized by the national government as part of the state. The first section of this chapter gives an overview at both global and regional levels and tracing the issue of statelessness, its causes and consequences. In addition, this chapter explains the significance of statelessness under international law, highlights cases in Southeast and South Asia, and concludes by reviewing the types of solutions that have potential for being effective.

Between 18 and 30 December 2008, the Royal Thai Navy pushed out to sea at least 992 Rohingyas who attempted to enter Thailand after fleeing Myanmar. *TIME* reported that the first group of 412 people sailed for twelve days in a contingent of two boats. The Thai navy intercepted them and moved them to a barren isle off the Thai mainland. They were later towed back to sea in a boat, which drifted for ten days and ten nights. The Indian coast guard rescued 107 of them on December 27 whereas more than 300 of them were believed to have drowned. Another group of 580, arrested around December 30, was put into four boats whose engines were removed, then towed together and abandoned at sea. Of this group, one boat with 193 onboard was rescued in Indonesia's Sabang Island in Aceh on January 7, and another boat with 150 onboard was rescued in Tillanchang Island, Andaman and Nicobar of India, on January 10. Two boats with a total of 237 people are reportedly missing.

Rohingyas as well as other ethnic groups fleeing Myanmar to escape oppression or to find a better life elsewhere is not a new phenomenon. What was new, according to Human Rights Watch, was that between January and February 2009, the plight of Rohingyas was for the first time captured on camera and disseminated widely. These pictures captured by tourists showed hundreds of Rohingya men lying, head first, in rows along the beach guarded by armed Thai authorities, including police, navy and national park service officials. They appeared first in the *South China Morning Post* on 15 January 2009 and later in the BBC and then CNN. What followed was an international condemnation of Thailand's "push-back" policy. The Thai government, however, stood by its official policy of deporting Rohingyas, as they arrived illegally, and refused to recognize them as refugees or asylum seekers.

While issues like migration, human trafficking and transnational crime have been discussed at great length by regional multilateral forums like the Association of South East Asian Nations (ASEAN), the issue of statelessness itself has not been adequately addressed and is still poorly understood in the region. According to the United Nations High Commission for Refugees (UNHCR) in 2008, Southeast Asia has the world's largest stateless population. 4.3 million of the world's 6.6 million stateless population are to be found in the region with Thailand alone hosting an estimated 3 million stateless people. The Rohingyas are just one group of stateless people in the region.[1]

THE PROBLEM OF STATELESSNESS

Who are the Stateless?

For the majority of the world's population, citizenship and nationality are taken for granted. Owning a birth certificate and/or passport gives many of us access to precious economic, political and social rights, which are *supposed* to be available for all. Article 15 of the Universal Declaration of Human Rights (UDHR) states that everyone has a right to nationality and that no one shall be deprived of having a nationality or changing their nationality.

Stateless people lack identity documentation, and often live in a precarious situation, on the margins of society.

A stateless person is defined by the UNHCR as someone without nationality or citizenship. The majority of stateless persons **are not** refugees or asylum seekers, however, in some cases they can be if a state decides to recognize them as such. Often they are part of a repressed minority group within a state, for example Rohingyas in Myanmar, the Roma in Romania or the Bidun in Jordan. There are two types of stateless persons, the *de jure* and *de facto* stateless. The *de jure* stateless are not recognized as nationals under the laws of any country, whereas *de facto* stateless persons have legal nationality, but they cannot prove it either due to lack of documentation or because it is not effective.[2] *De jure* stateless persons could be members of repressed minority groups, who may have been nationals of the country they inhabit, at one time, but had their citizenship revoked during a time of political change in that country. *De facto* stateless persons are often children who were never registered at birth. *De facto* stateless persons also have problems in proving their former nationality, for lack of proper documentation or certificates. It should be noted that there are often situations when it is difficult to distinguish between *de jure* and *de facto* statelessness. UNHCR further emphasizes:

> Stateless people face numerous difficulties in their daily lives: they lack access to health care, education, property rights and the ability to move freely. They are also vulnerable to arbitrary treatment and crimes like trafficking. Their marginalisation can create tensions in society and lead to instability at an international level, including, in extreme cases, conflict and displacement.

Why are They Stateless?

1. *Political change and discrimination*:   The persecution of ethnic nationalities in Myanmar started during the 1962 coup d'etat. It took place for two primary reasons: (1) The Myanmar military was afraid of a state break up and (2) it wanted to strengthen the socialist and economic base in Myanmar by getting rid of foreign dominance.[3] One of the ethnic groups most severely affected by this policy were *Rohingyas*, who have been systematically discriminated against to this day. As a result of the harsh treatment they face, hundreds of thousands of Rohingyas have fled to Bangladesh, Thailand or Malaysia. Within Myanmar, they are restricted to the North Arakan region, and remain stateless, as the government of Myanmar refuses to issue them citizenship.

2. ***Trafficking***:   In 2001, the United Nations Educational, Cultural and Scientific Organization (UNESCO) in Thailand identified the lack of citizenship as the "single greatest risk factor for highland minority girls and women in Thailand".[4] When a person is stateless, it is only possible to find work in the informal sector, which creates more risk, exploitation and vulnerability. In the 2009 U.S. Department of State Trafficking in Persons Report, the link between statelessness and trafficking is further elaborated upon:[5]

> Stateless populations are easy targets for forced labor, land confiscation, displacement, and other forms of persecution and exploitation. Without a nationality or legal citizenship, they may lack protection from police or access to systems of justice. In their desperate struggle for survival, stateless people often turn to human smugglers and traffickers to help them escape discrimination or government persecution. They become victims again and again as the problems of statelessness, refugee issues, and trafficking intersect.

3.   Rohingyas are a prime example, as they have been victims of traffickers, while trying to escape repression in Myanmar.

4. ***Laws regulating marriage***:   In Vietnam, many women had to renounce their Vietnamese citizenship when marrying a foreigner, usually Taiwanese, South Korean or Chinese men. If the marriage resulted in divorce, they would find themselves stateless, as the old law did not require these women to gain another nationality before they had to renounce their Vietnamese one. However, a law was been passed in Vietnam, which allows dual citizenship and does not allow a Vietnamese person to renounce their own citizenship, unless they have gained a new one.[6]

5. ***Failure to register children at birth***:   There are an estimated one million stateless children in Thailand. Previously, Thai law did not allow migrants to register their children, if they were born in Thailand. However, in 2008 the Thai government amended this law, stating that all children born in Thailand, regardless of the parents' legal status, could be registered.[7]

6. ***Nationality based solely on descent***:   In some countries, such as the United States, nationality at birth is based on *jus solis*. This means that if a child is born in the U.S., they receive American nationality, regardless of the parents' nationality. In other countries, however,

nationality is based on *jus sanguine*, meaning that a child receives nationality based on descent and not on place of birth. Before the Nepal Citizenship Act was instated in 2006, Nepali nationality could only be passed on by the Nepali father. This rendered millions of children stateless. However, since 2006, nationality can be passed on through the Nepali mother as well, reducing some of the numbers of stateless persons in Nepal.[8]

Table 7.1
Typologies of Statelessness

Denial and Deprivation of Citizenship	Withdrawal and Loss of Citizenship
Methods: The intentional and unintentional use of or interpretation of provisions in nationality laws so as to discriminate between groups; removal from census; gender-based legislation that prevents women from transmitting nationality. **Cases:** Bangladesh, Dominican Republic, Federal Republic of Germany, Georgia, Kashmir, Kazakhstan, Kenya, Myanmar, Nepal, Russia	**Methods:** The revocation of laws; forced removals following xenophobic campaigns. **Cases:** Bhutan, Ivory Coast, DRC, Germany (1933–45), Kuwait, Lebanon, Mauritania (pre-2007), Syria
State Succession/State Restoration	**Lack of Access**
Methods: Ill-defined nationality laws following conflict, de-federation, secession, state succession and state restoration in multinational situations. **Cases:** Bosnia and Herzegovina, Croatia, Estonia, Ethiopia, Eritrea, Latvia, Lithuania, Former Yugoslav Republic of Macedonia, Montenegro, Serbia, Former USSR, Yemen	**Methods:** Lack of opportunities to register births and marriages, the use of high fees for documents, requirements regarding the presence of witnesses to certify documents. **Cases:** Croatia, Ecuador, Fiji, India, Israel, Kyrgyzstan, Former Yugoslav Republic of Macedonia, Nepal, Panama, Russia, Serbia, Slovenia, Sri Lanka

Source: Brad K. Blitz, "Statelessness, Protection and Equality", Forced Migration Policy Briefing 3, Oxford Refugees Studies Centre, 2009, p. 16.

Statelessness as a Problem Under International Law

Which International Legal Definitions and Instruments are Related to Statelessness?

One of the areas, rarely understood, is the standing of statelessness in the framework of international law. If the below mentioned legal instruments were more widely ratified, it would make a big difference in the status and protection of the stateless. It is important to mention that Southeast Asia has a history of rejecting international refugee law and, therefore, international law related to statelessness.[9] Scholar Sarah Davies argues in her book *Legitimising Rejection: International Refugee Law in Southeast Asia* that Southeast Asian nations have consistently been able to reject the use of international refugee law as:

- The Conventions are eurocentric in their content and do not take into account the Southeast Asian context of refugee and migrant flows.
- During the Indochinese refugee crisis (1975–96), Southeast Asian states received both material assistance and resettlement offers from the international community for individuals who were only granted temporary asylum.
- Throughout the Indochinese refugee crisis, Southeast Asian states claimed that Indochinese refugees were not "genuine" refugees, but individuals who were fleeing economic hardship, rather than widespread persecution. Till the mid-1980s the international community rejected this claim, however, in 1989, as a result of "compassion fatigue", the US, Australia and France began to accept the term of "illegal migrants" for the Indochinese asylum seekers. It also helped that states such as Thailand used the framework of international refugee law to explain their claims in pushing back Rohinghyas.

It is important to understand this background when trying to understand why Southeast Asian states not only reject the international law framework associated with refugees, but also that with stateless persons. Stateless persons, like refugees, are often labelled as "illegal migrants". The inaction of Southeast Asian states in the area of statelessness does not just have to do with the fact that statelessness, as an issue, is not widely understood, but also with the historical rejection of Southeast Asian states harbouring refugees and asylum seekers, who would potentially place a financial burden on them.

International Conventions on Statelessness

There are two major international conventions on statelessness: **the 1954 Convention relating to the Status of Statelessness and the 1961 Convention on the Reduction of Statelessness**. Unfortunately, both conventions do not have many signatories. The 1954 convention has 65, including the Philippines as the only signatory from the Southeast Asia region (UNHCR 2009). The 1961 convention only has 37 and none are from Southeast Asia (UNHCR 2009).

1. **The 1954 convention**, while not widely ratified, especially in countries where the problem of statelessness is the greatest, this convention does provide a definition of statelessness, accepted as international customary law. It also has provisions for stateless persons to be protected, like nationals in the country they inhabit, under certain categories such as "wage earning employment", "rationing", "public education" and "public relief".[10]

2. **The 1961 convention** added some important provisions, including that one cannot be born stateless (though only individual countries national law can decide this), that one cannot lose one's citizenship because of state successions and that one should not become stateless due to renouncing one's citizenship, losing it or being deprived of it (Blitz 2009). However, both the 1954 Convention and the 1964 Convention only refer to *de jure* statelessness; there is no definition or mention of *de facto* statelessness.

   Professor Brad K. Blitz, Director of the International Observatory on Statelessness, elaborates:

   > One important failing of this convention is that it does not prohibit the possibility of revocation of nationality under certain circumstances nor does it retroactively grant citizenship to all currently stateless persons.

3. **The 1951 Convention relating to the Status of Refugees and the 1967 Protocol** has 141 signatories, including Cambodia, Timor Leste and the Philippines from the Southeast Asia region. It is technically also applicable to stateless persons. The Convention's definition of a refugee is:

   > As a result of events occurring before 1 January 1951 and owing to well-founded fear of being persecuted for reasons of race, religion, nationality, membership of a particular social group or political

opinion, is outside the country of his nationality and is unable or, owing to such fear, is unwilling to avail himself of the protection of that country; or who, not having a nationality and being outside the country of his former habitual residence as a result of such events, is unable or, owing to such fear, is unwilling to return to it.

However, it remains a problematic definition, as the person "not having a nationality" has to be "outside the country of his former habitual residence". This is why only some stateless persons are considered refugees or asylum seekers. In addition, when a person is applying for asylum status, the first step is determining and verifying nationality. In Bangladesh, for example, 28,000.[11] Rohingyas live in refugee camps, as they are considered to be fleeing from a well-founded fear of persecution and they are outside their habitual country, Myanmar. Stateless persons do not have a country they can be repatriated to as is the case with refugees.

Other Examples of International Legal Instruments

Internationally binding legal instruments worth mentioning are (1) **The UN Convention on the Rights of the Child (CRC)**, (2) **The 1966 International Covenant on Civil and Political Rights (ICCPR)**, (3) **The 1966 (ICESR)**, (4) **The 1965 Convention on the elimination of all forms of racism**, and (5) **The Convention on Elimination of all forms of Discrimination Against Women (CEDAW)**. These international legal instruments can aid in protection and social assistance measures for stateless persons including:

1. **The CRC** came into force on 2 November 1990 and has been ratified by 193 countries. All ASEAN member states are party to the CRC. It is article 7 of the CRC that is of particular importance to stateless persons, as it stipulates child registration and a right to a nationality, thus providing a child with statehood.
2. **The ICCPR** came into force on 23 March 1976, but has only been ratified by Laos and the Philippines. Cambodia, Indonesia and Thailand have all signed but not ratified. Brunei, Malaysia, Myanmar and Singapore have not signed the agreement. The ICCPR emphasizes that rights should be granted to all, regardless of nationality and citizenship. It also reiterates the importance of non-discrimination and a child's right to nationality thus providing a child with statehood.
3. **The ICESR** came into force on 3 January, 1976, and has 160 state parties. Cambodia, Indonesia, the Lao People's Democratic Republic,

the Philippines, Thailand and Vietnam are parties to the ICESR. This Covenant underlines the right to take part in cultural life, reflected in article 15.

4. **The 1965 Convention on the elimination of all forms of racism** came into force on 4 January 1969 and has 173 state parties, including Cambodia, Indonesia, Lao People's Democratic Republic, Thailand, Vietnam and the Philippines (the only Southeast Asian country to ratify). Article 2 and Article 5 are particularly significant for statelessness. Article 2 calls for state parties to not engage in any act of racial discrimination against "persons", "groups of persons", or "institutions". Article 5 lists the "right to nationality" as one of the rights that should be guaranteed by all state parties.

5. **CEDAW** came into force on 3 September 1981, and has 186 state parties. All ASEAN member states are party to CEDAW. Article 9 in CEDAW underlines that women should be granted equal rights with men to "acquire, change or retain" their nationality. In addition, this article calls for women to have equal rights to men "with respect to the nationality of their children".

Notably, in the context of Southeast Asia's rejection of international refugee law and in some cases international human rights law, the Southeast Asian countries that have signed onto the ICCPR and ICESR did not do so until the late 1990s and post 2000 — Cambodia (1992) signed post Paris Peace Accords, The Lao Peoples Democratic Republic signed the ICESR in 2007 and the ICCPR in 2009. Author Philip John Eldridge comments in his book *The Politics of Human Rights in Southeast Asia*:[12]

> Civil society groups have become stronger and better organised in the past decade. International pressures, strengthened by the economic crisis, have pushed governments towards greater formal and rhetorical accommodation with international standards, while resisting or obscuring their operational requirements. Accession by ASEAN states to UN Human Rights instruments, though improving in the 1990s, remains weak and uneven. Governments are often slow in following up policy declarations with necessary legal and administrative action (2002).

Developments in National Law of Asian Countries

For the purposes of length, only developments in Thailand and Bangladesh shall be highlighted. In both 2008 and 2009, there have been legal developments, which will help some stateless persons receive citizenship and prevent statelessness in other cases. In 2008, Thai law was amended so all children born in Thailand, regardless of their parents' nationality, can be registered at birth. Currently, Thailand is in the process of amending its Citizenship Act to provide citizenship to some stateless populations, such as populations living in southern provinces along the Thai-Burma border, including Ranong, Prachoub, Kirikham and Chumporn.[13] This still leaves many stateless persons out of the process, as UNHCR's most current population estimate of stateless persons in Thailand is 3.5 million.

In Bangladesh, around 300,000 Urdu-speaking Biharis, who fled to Bangladesh (then "East Pakistan") after the India-Pakistan partition in 1947, lived in 66 camps in Dhaka.[14] In 1971, when Bangladesh was formed, there was resentment by Bengalis towards the Biharis, as they had supported the West Pakistan army and were from then on referred to as "stranded Pakistanis". In 1974, Pakistan accepted 170,000 Bihari refugees.[15] However, the remaining Biharis in Bangladesh remained stateless, until recently. In 1993, an additional 300 Biharis were repatriated to Pakistan. In a landmark Bangladesh Supreme Court decision in 2003, ten Biharis were granted citizenship, on the grounds that they were either born in the camps or had been residing in Bangladesh since the time of partition.[16] This Supreme Court decision gave precedence for this ruling in May 2008, when 150,000 Biharis were granted citizenship, on the grounds that they were either born after 1971 or were minors during Bangladesh's war of independence.[17]

OVERVIEW OF GLOBAL AND REGIONAL TRENDS

Global Estimates of Statelessness

There has been a gradual expansion in coverage and knowledge of stateless persons. Giving due importance to the identification and reduction of statelessness, UNHCR has expanded its data collection mechanism in 2004, aiming at the more systematic identification of stateless persons. As such, UNHCR was able to identify 42 countries hosting stateless populations, out of which there were data for 30 countries with an estimated 1.5 million stateless persons on 31 December 2004. By the end of 2005, UNHCR reported the existence of stateless populations in 62 countries. For the 48 countries where data are available at the end of that year, the total number was estimated to be 2.4 million. For 2006, the number of countries with reliable estimates increased marginally to 49. However, the number of identified stateless populations more than doubled to 5.8 million.

In 2007, the total number of stateless persons reported in UNHCR statistics dropped by roughly 3 million as a result of the major breakthroughs achieved in Nepal and Bangladesh. In Nepal, new legislation was adopted, which facilitates the issuance of citizenship certificates to approximately 2.6 million people. In Bangladesh, the process of registration of adults of Bihari/Urdu-speaking communities and the issuance of national identity cards has been undertaken. There are an estimated 250,000 to 300,000 Bihari/Urdu-speaking communities in that country whose rights as Bangladeshi citizens had not been recognized following the separation of what is now Bangladesh from Pakistan in 1971. As a consequence, the number of stateless persons in UNHCR statistics dropped from 5.8 million in 2006 to slightly under 3 million people by the end of 2007. By the end of 2008, statistics on statelessness are available for 58 countries, with an estimated 6.6 million stateless persons.

It is important to note that the actual population of stateless people is expected to be much higher because UNHCR's statistics include data only on countries for which reliable official statistics or estimates of stateless populations are available. The overall global estimates of stateless population are 12 million, including countries that have significant stateless populations, but for which no reliable figures could be provided.

However, despite the expansion in coverage and knowledge of stateless persons, the number of States party to the 1954 Convention relating to the Status of Stateless Persons (the 1954 Convention) and the 1961 Convention on the Reduction of Statelessness (the 1961 Convention), two key instruments for the protection of stateless people and the prevention

Table 7.2

Number of Countries Reporting Statistics on Stateless Persons

Year	Number of Countries Reporting Statistics on Stateless Persons	Total Numbers of Stateless Persons
2004	30	1.5 million
2005	48	2.4 million
2006	49	5.8 million
2007	54	3 million
2008	58	6.6 million

Source: UNHCR, *2008 Global Trends: Refugees, Asylum-seekers, Returnees, Internally Displaced and Stateless Persons*, 16 June 2009.

and reduction of statelessness remained limited. In some cases, questions relating to nationality were viewed as sensitive and falling solely within the realm of national sovereignty, despite the legitimate interest of the international community in this issue.

Regional Estimates of Statelessness

Southeast Asia is home to the world's largest stateless population. Of the estimated 6.6 million stateless people worldwide, Southeast Asia accounted for 4.3 million of them, with Thailand alone hosting 3 million stateless people. As noted earlier, the actual numbers of stateless population could be higher because UNHCR's statistics include data only on countries for which reliable official statistics or estimates of stateless populations are available.

As Table 7.3 indicates, in Southeast Asia, there are no reliable figures for Brunei, Cambodia, Indonesia and Philippines although significant stateless

Table 7.3
Stateless Population in Southeast Asia

Country of Residence	Description/Origin	Population End-2008	Of Who: UNHCR Assisted**
Brunei Darussalam	Stateless	*	–
Cambodia	Stateless	*	–
Indonesia	Stateless	*	–
Malaysia	Stateless	40,001	–
Myanmar	Stateless	723,571	200,000
Philippines	Stateless	*	–
Thailand	Stateless	3,500,000	–
Vietnam	Former Cambodian refugees	7,200	–
Southeast Asia Total		4,270,772	200,000
Global Total		6,572,167	225,488

Notes: * Significant stateless populations but no reliable figures existed.
        ** The majority of stateless people are still beyond the reach of UNHCR.
Source: UNHCR, *2008 Global Trends: Refugees, Asylum-seekers, Returnees, Internally Displaced and Stateless Persons*, 16 June 2009.

populations exist in these countries. However, with the expansion in coverage and knowledge of stateless persons increases this gap was expected to narrow in the future.

Regional Cases

Rohingyas in Myanmar and the hill tribes in Thailand shall be highlighted in this section, as the Rohingyas are among the most vulnerable and the hill tribes of Thailand form the largest population of stateless persons worldwide, estimated at 3.5 million according to the latest UNHCR statistics. The stateless hill tribes themselves are estimated at 400,000.[18]

1. **Rohingyas in Burma**

    It is estimated that around 725,000 Rohingyas live in the North Rakhine region, along the Myanmar Bangladesh border. They are related to the Chittagonian Bangladeshis, but were conquered by the Burmese in the early nineteenth century. Of South Asian descent and practising Sunni Islam, Rohingyas have increasingly been discriminated against since Myanmar's independence in 1948. After military rule commenced in Myanmar in 1962, numerous policies against residents of Indian and Chinese descent were instituted, causing a mass exodus, including of Rohingyas. Hundreds of thousands of Rohingyas fled to neighbouring Bangladesh in 1978 and were stripped of their Burmese citizenship under the 1982 Burmese Citizenship Act. While 28,000 Rohingyas have been accepted as refugees in Bangladesh and live in UNHCR supported camps in the Cox Bazaar district, it is estimated that 200,000 Rohingyas, who do not have refugee status and remain stateless, live in surrounding areas.[19] Rohingyas who still live in the North Rakhine region suffer under the repressive policies of the Myanmar state. Sean Garcia and Camilla Olson of *Refugees International* write:

    > The Rohingya need authorisation to leave their villages and are not allowed to travel beyond the Northern Rakhine State. They need official permission to marry and must pay exorbitant taxes on births and deaths. Religious freedom is restricted, and the Rohingya have been prohibited from maintaining or repairing crumbling religious buildings.

Increasingly, Rohingyas are also fleeing to Malaysia and Thailand by sea. However, in Thailand they have been turned away most notably in December 2008, when Thailand was criticized for its "push-back" policy. According to Thailand, Rohingyas are a "national security threat"[20] and only want to enter Thailand in order to "volunteer with Thai Muslim separatist militants".[21] In the March 2009 fact finding report on the Thai push-back phenomenon, by the Thai Action Committee for Democracy in Burma (TACDB) and the Lawyers Council of Thailand, General Manu Kongpant, Director of Internal Security Operations Command (ISOC) is quoted as saying: "Rohingyas migration is involved with human smuggling and trafficking from the beginning, during journey, until they reach the destination, which sometimes [is] connected with terrorists, drug trafficking and weapon trade."

Malaysia, which is not a signatory to the 1951 Convention Relating to the Status of Refugees or the 1954 Convention Relating to the Status of Statelessness, often targets Rohingyas for deportation under the auspice of being "illegal migrants". Approximately 13,000 Rohingyas are registered in Malaysia, but only 400 have access to primary education opportunities.[22]

A bilateral development between Myanmar and Bangladesh in December 2009, led to Bangladesh handing Myanmar a list with names of the 28,000 Rohingya refugees living in its Cox Bazaar district. Myanmar has accepted that 9,000 of the 28,000 on the list are its citizens and has stated that it will begin the process of repatriation "as soon as possible".[23] However, there are concerns by organizations advocating for the rights of the Rohingya, such as the Arakan Project, that the repatriation process may not be voluntary and, therefore, an infringement of international law.[24] This development also begs the question of what will happen to the remaining refugees in the Cox Bazaar camps and the approximately 200,000 stateless Rohingyas, who live in surrounding areas.

2. **Hill tribes in Thailand**

The hill tribes in Thailand are made up of many different ethnic minorities, originating from Myanmar, China, Laos and Tibet. The following nine groups are recognized by the Thai government: Karen, Mong, Yao, Lisu, Akha, Thin, Lua and Khamu. The most populous of these groups are the Karen, who fled political change and persecution in Myanmar, and the Hmong, who fled the Indo-China conflict in the 1970s. Even though hill tribes, including the nine groups mentioned above, have resided in Thailand for multiple generations, a little more than half of them have

Table 7.4

Organizations Working on Preventing and Reducing Statelessness

Type and Name of Organization	What Issues They Work on Connected to Statelessness
International Organizations	
UNHCR	Since 1974, UNHCR has been the lead agency working with and providing assistance and protection for the stateless. A 2006 document by the UNHCR Executive Committee (now comprising 76 states) titled "Conclusion on Identification, Prevention and Reduction of Statelessness and Protection of Stateless Persons", gave UNHCR new ground to expand its work on statelessness, including a focus on: • Research and statistics related to statelessness, development of a systematic method for information gathering; • Working more closely and in partnership with other UN agencies such as the United Nations Fund for Children — UNICEF (for birth registration) and the United Nations Population Fund — UNFPA (for population data); • Advocating strongly with countries who have still not ratified the 1954 and 1961 Conventions.
United Nations Secretariat	UN Special Rapporteur on Non-Citizens, Human Security Commission, Office of the High Commissioner for Human Rights (OHCHR).
UNICEF	Specializes in facilitating birth registrations, in conjunction with PLAN international.
UNFPA	Specializes in collecting population data, gives technical assistance on how to e.g. include stateless persons in census data.
UNESCO	Focuses on the link between statelessness and trafficking in Southeast Asia, with an emphasis on Thailand.
United Nations Development Program (UNDP)	Runs an "equal access to justice" programme worldwide, which has helped some stateless persons attain legal status.

Table 7.4 *(Cont'd)*

Type and Name of Organization	What Issues They Work on Connected to Statelessness
Asian Development Bank (ADB)	Conducted a study on the impact of birth registration campaigns in Asia.

International NGOs and Think-Tanks

Refugees International	Refugees International advocates lifesaving assistance and protection for displaced people, and promotes solutions to displacement crises, which includes a programme on statelessness. It published the *Global Survey on Statelessness* in March 2009.
Open Society Institute (OSI)	The OSI seeks to shape public policies that assure greater fairness in political, legal, and economic systems and safeguard fundamental rights. It has a programme on statelessness, but currently focuses more on statelessness in African countries.
The Equal Rights Trust	The Equal Rights Trust is an independent international organization whose purpose is to combat discrimination and to promote equality as a fundamental human right and a basic principle of social justice. Within this mission, it addresses the issue of statelessness.
The International Observatory on Statelessness (IOS)	Created by Oxford Brookes University and the Oxford Refugees Studies Centre, the IOS focuses on collating national data on patterns, types and conditions of statelessness and promotes research on patterns and causes of statelessness by gathering data on a range of issues.
Plan International	A children's organization aiming to alleviate poverty, Plan International worked on a large birth registration campaign with UNICEF in 2006.
Human Rights Watch	Has written several reports on stateless persons, the most recent is "Perilous Plight: Burma's Rohingya take to the Seas".
Amnesty International	Has also written numerous reports and raised the issue of statelessness.

Table 7.4   *(Cont'd)*

Type and Name of Organization	What Issues They Work on Connected to Statelessness
National Organizations in the Southeast Asia Region	
The Arakan Project	Based in Bangkok, the Arakan Project focuses on raising awareness and advocacy for Rohingyas.
The Legal Assistance Center	Focuses on education for stateless children in the Mae Ai town of Thailand.

Thai nationality, while the rest remain stateless.[25] It is a complicated and time-consuming procedure for hill tribe people to obtain citizenship in Thailand, as they have to follow the Central Registration on nationality acquisition regulations, based on the 1996 House Registration for Hill Tribe People.[26] As mentioned in the international law section, the proposed amendment of the Thai Citizenship Act, under the current interim government, may change some of this.

From the preceding discussion, it is clear that there is an increasing awareness of statelessness in Southeast Asia and some efforts are underway to address the issue. There are still many roadblocks ahead in finding solutions to the various problems related to statelessness. With increasing cooperation between the UNHCR, affected countries, regional bodies and civil society organizations, the plight of stateless people can become better understood.

However, it is important to note that there remains confusion over the status of stateless persons, depending on whether they are in a territory where they are supposed to be citizens versus in a territory where they are considered under a different status, such as: (a) refugees (b) asylum-seekers or (c) illegal migrants. The status that stateless persons receive considerably affects the treatment they receive under international law. For example, the majority of Rohingya are stateless, however, some are regarded as refugees in Bangladesh and others are labelled as "illegal migrants" in Thailand.

While the "stateless", "refugees" and "illegal migrants" have needs and issues that are specific to only them, they also have many cross-sectional similarities with each other, which are not analysed enough. The cross-sectional similarities between the above mentioned categories and the policy relevance of the many faces of statelessness in Southeast Asia will be analysed in the next section.

THE MANY FACES OF STATELESSNESS

December 2009, 4,300 Laotian Hmongs in Thailand were involuntarily repatriated to Laos. Their status in Thailand has often been disputed, as some have officially been recognized by UNHCR as "refugees", others are considered "economic migrants" or "illegal migrants" by Thailand and as a result, many of their children are "stateless". The label they receive decides the treatment they get under national and international law. In the previous section the aim was to better understand the issue of statelessness, why it occurs and what it means under international law. This section aims to analyse the difference between stateless persons in their habitual residence and stateless persons on the move, explaining the many faces of statelessness within Southeast Asia.

Article 1 of the 1955 Convention Relating to the Status of Stateless Persons defines a stateless person as one "who is not considered as a national by any state under the operation of its law". However, this definition does not distinguish the different dimensions of statelessness which is two-fold: "stateless persons in their habitual residence" and "stateless persons on the move". The below quotation attempts to depict the many faces of statelessness with particular attention to cases in Southeast Asia.

> [The view towards stateless persons] varies from government to government. In general, these are individuals who are not claimed by any country. They are considered foreigners, they are discriminated against, they are simply individuals who are unwanted.
>
> — Maureen Lynch,
> Senior Advocate on Stateless Initiatives,
> Refugees International

Lives of Stateless Persons in their Habitual Residence: Indigenous Minorities and Children of Undocumented Migrant Workers

This section gives examples of "Stateless persons in their habitual residence", referring to individuals who are stateless in their country of residence. Specifically, this section shall focus on two types of stateless groups: indigenous minorities and stateless children of undocumented migrant workers.

Indigenous Peoples and Minorities

Rohingyas

The Rohingyas are an ethnic and religious minority group of Myanmar. Human Rights Watch estimated the total population, as of 2009, at about two million, of which approximately 800,000 remain in Myanmar, primarily in western Rakhine State and Yangon. About 200,000 live in Bangladesh, of which 30,000 live in squalid refugee camps. An estimated half million have migrated to the Middle East and 50,000 to Malaysia. Others are scattered throughout the region.[27] They lost their political and constitutional identity when the military government, led by General Ne Win, promulgated the Citizenship Act of Burma in 1982.[28] The Act specifically stated that:

> Nationals such as the Kachin, Kayah, Karen, Chin, Burman, Mon, Rakhine or Shan and ethnic groups as have settled in any of the territories included within the State as their permanent home from a period anterior to 1185 BE, 1823 AD are Burma citizens.

Moreover, it was also stated that the Council of State "may decide whether any ethnic group is national or not" and "may, in the interest of the State, revoke the citizenship or associate citizenship or naturalised citizenship of any person except a citizen by birth". The Act effectively denies Rohingyas recognition of their status as a Burmese ethnic minority group. They are subsequently not listed among the 135 officially recognized "ethnic nationalities", consequently rendering them stateless.

Deprivation of citizenship has served as a key strategy to justify arbitrary treatment and discriminatory policies against Rohingyas. Severe restrictions on their movements are increasingly applied. They are banned from employment in the civil service, including in the education and health sectors. In 1994, the authorities stopped issuing Rohingya children with birth certificates. By the late 1990s, official marriage authorizations were made mandatory. Infringement of these stringent rules can result in long prison sentences. Other coercive measures such as forced labour, arbitrary taxation and confiscation of land, also practised elsewhere in the country, are imposed on the Rohingya population in a disproportionate manner.

The UNHCR is actively involved in Rakhine State trying to reduce incidence of statelessness among Rohingyas. Its primary objective is to promote the integration of persons without citizenship into Myanmar society and improve their livelihoods. The UNHCR estimated that approximately

750,000 residents of Rakhine State still remain stateless.[29] The first step towards reducing statelessness among Rohingyas is to issue them with some form of identity cards, which have been denied to them since 1982. Even when the colour-coded Citizens Scrutiny Cards (CRCs) were issued to all Myanmar people in 1982, Rohingyas were not issued any cards. In 1995, the authorities started issuing Temporary Registration Cards (TRC) to Rohingyas. This process was stalled from 1998 to 2007. When it was restarted in 2007, more than 30,000 people registered to obtain TRCs just between March and June. Noor Hakim, recipient of TRC under that programme, commented that he could not only travel now but could also "apply for marriage permission". Under the renewed effort of the UNHCR, issuance of TRCs to all Rohingyas over the age of ten continued on 22 August 2009. By the end of that year, more than 75 per cent of those who are eligible are in possession of TRCs. The TRCs, however, do not mention a birthplace for the registered person. Moreover, Rohingyas' ethnicity is referred to as "Bengali" on the card and their religion as "Islam".

Despite the issuance of TRCs, the question of the legal status of Rohingyas still remains unclear. Former UNHCR representative in Yangon, Jean-Francois Durieux, observed that "They (the Rohingyas) are not citizens by law. We do not say this document exists in law. Under international law, it is a temporary document, proving residence not citizenship."[30] The Myanmar government needs to build up its constituency among Rohingyas, even though they are considered "non-citizens".[31]

The Integrated Regional Information Network (IRIN) reported on 24 February 2010 that UN agencies and NGOs in Myanmar began the ongoing process of consolidating humanitarian efforts in assisting needs of Rohingyas, for the first time, by working on the Common Humanitarian Action Plan (CHAP). The CHAP will be a one-year plan, with the possibility of extension, and is geared towards all residents in the Rakhine State, including Rohingyas. Bhairaja Panday, Country Representative for UNHCR in Myanmar, was quoted as saying:

> We are confident that the situation will improve [for Rohingyas] in some measure; we don't know exactly how much ... I think the government feels they need to address the problem now, and they do not want it to linger like this for a long time.

The final solution, however, lies in amending or repealing the 1982 Citizenship Act and granting Rohingyas full citizenship and accompanying rights. This is a long-term objective and the international community must work together to put pressure on the Myanmar Government to amend its citizenship law; the current CHAP process may be a start towards it.

Hill Tribes of Thailand

The major hill tribes of Northern Thailand are Karen, Lahu, Lisu, Hmong, Akha, Lawa, Yao and Paduang. Thailand's Ministry of Interior estimated in June 2000 that there are about one million hill tribes and minority people in Thailand, of which nearly half have already obtained Thai nationality. Of the remaining, about 100,000 have qualified for Thai citizenship; about 90,000 entitled to permanent residency; an estimated 120,000 are children, who are also entitled to Thai citizenship. The remaining 190,000 tribal and minority people are permitted to stay temporarily in the country pending government's final decision on how to deal with them.

The origin of the stateless status of these hill tribes goes back to 1956 when the first country-wide national census failed to register them because in the words of Yindee Lertcharoenchok, a consultant to UNESCO, "the presence of highland people in remote mountainous regions was overlooked by the authorities". Thus, the hill tribes became "stateless minorities" in their own country. Their Thai status was recognized only when the first census of highland population was conducted in 1969–70. Nearly 120,000 hill tribe people in 16 provinces were covered in the survey. Between 2 January 1975 and 20 March 1992, a total of 182,065 highland people in 20 provinces were registered as Thai nationals. In 1985–88, the second census of highland population was conducted in 18 provinces and nearly 580,000 people were covered. Following the survey, the government decided to register their personal record certificates and issue a highland identity card, commonly known as a "blue card". In 1990–91, nearly 250,000 were registered and given a blue card. Under the Ministry of Interiors 1992/1996 regulation handbook on Thai citizenship registration for highland people, 46,555 were registered as Thai citizens.

In May 1999, the Thai government decided to set up a committee to study the problems in categorizing hill tribe and other ethnic minorities, and the process of granting legal status to these different groups. Following recommendations by the committee, the Thai Government decided on 29 August 2000 to grant Thai citizenship or "alien status", which constitutes permanent residency, to hundreds of thousands of hill tribes and other minority groups of people in Thailand. It decided to confer Thai citizenship on hill tribe children, who were born between 14 December 1972 and 25 February 1992. The Government also agreed to allow about 190,000 hill tribe and minority people, who entered Thailand after 3 October 1985 until 15 September 1999, to stay in the country for one year pending studies on how to deal with them.

On 28 August 2001, the government of former prime minister Thaksin Shinawatra decided to grant Thai citizenship to hill tribe children, whose parents were registered as "alien" with permanent residency, regardless of when they were born. It also allowed those 190,000 tribal and highland minorities to stay in Thailand for another year.

To further speed up the process, UNESCO launched the "Highland Birth and Citizenship Registration Promotion Project" in 2006. The project resulted in the most extensive study ever undertaken in Thailand of the relationship between birth registration, legal status and access to social services. The study includes approximately 11,000 (out of 18,000) highland households in Chiangmai, Chiangrai, and Mae Hongson. However, UNESCO's project is still very small. In order to account for all stateless population and also to make sure that the chance of leaving anyone behind is remote, the project needs to be expanded through the infusion of more funds, professional staffs as well as more cooperation from local NGOs and relevant government agencies.

Children of Undocumented Migrant Workers

Decades of irregular migration to Sabah in eastern Malaysia have resulted in large numbers of undocumented children of migrants from the Philippines and Indonesia who are potentially at risk of statelessness. The estimated numbers of these stateless children is between 10,000 and 30,000.

Undocumented migrants in Malaysia are frequently targeted for arrest and deportation. This resulted in the deportation of the parents leaving their children homeless and to fend for themselves. Children of migrants who are born in Malaysia may be undocumented if they do not possess a birth certificate. In addition, if a child's parents have been deported and they have no other family ties in Malaysia, it may be difficult for them to trace their roots back to their parents' country of origin in order to apply for a passport. If no government recognizes these undocumented children as nationals, then the children are vulnerable to statelessness.

However, under the UN Convention relating to the Status of Stateless Persons, the term "stateless person" refers to anyone who is not considered a national by any State under the operation of its law. The absence of a birth certificate does not mean that a child is stateless. However, when a child does not have a birth certificate and he/she has no other way of tracing her family's country of origin to apply for a passport, then the child may indeed be stateless or at risk of statelessness.

In order to obtain a birth certificate in Malaysia, it is necessary to produce a valid passport for each parent and a certificate of marriage, documents which many migrants do not possess. In addition, those who work in rural areas are sometimes not able to travel to the national registration authority to apply for a birth certificate.

Malaysia is a signatory to the Convention on the Rights of the Child, which states in Article 7 that all children have a right to acquire nationality at birth. However, Malaysia does not grant citizenship by birth, choosing not to adhere to the principle of *jus soli*. Individuals can only apply for citizenship if one parent is a citizen of Malaysia. Foreign parents can register their children for birth certificates, but the certificates are stamped *orang asing* (foreigner), reflecting the fact that the parents are not citizens of Malaysia.

Lives of Stateless Persons on the Move: Malaysia and Thailand

This section gives examples of the problems and opportunities stateless persons on the move face, specifically in Malaysia and Thailand. "Stateless persons on the move" refers to those who cross the border in the hope of escaping persecution and finding asylum.

Problems

Malaysia

One of the biggest and least reported problems for a stateless person on the move is the threat of getting arrested for illegally entering another country and being indefinitely detained.[32] The *2008 UN Working Group on Arbitrary Detention Report* also states that "a straight analysis of the statistics indicates that in some countries the numbers of non-citizens in administrative detention exceeds the number of sentenced prisoners or detainees, who have or are suspected of having committed a crime". In Malaysia, for example, Rohingyas are considered to be "illegal migrants" once they are on their territory. Approximately 20,000–25,000 Rohingyas live in Malaysia. Of these, 16,662 Rohingyas have registered with the UNHCR as of 1 July 2009 (UNHCR Malaysia). Malaysia does not distinguish between refugees, asylum seekers and illegal migrants under its national law. In a report *Trapped in a Cycle of Flight: Stateless Rohingya in Malaysia* by the Equal Rights Trust

(January 2010), raids on "illegal migrants" by the Malaysian Royal Police, Immigration Department and Ikatan Relawan Rakyat (RELA — the People's Volunteer Corps assisting the Immigration department), are described as:

> Raids are generally conducted either by the police, Immigration Department or more frequently as a joint RELA-Immigration operation. They do not differentiate between refugees, stateless persons and illegal migrants and generally disregard any UNHCR refugee documentation when making arrests. Such raids are known to take place in the middle of the night and without warrants, when RELA volunteers typically bang on people's doors demanding entry and break into their lodgings … Rohingya have also been arrested in markets, work places, tea shops, metro stations etc.

It is important to explain that the RELA is a group of "volunteer vigilantes",[33] originally created in the 1960s to guard against communists and transformed into a group for tracking down "illegal immigrants" in 2005.[34] According to the *New Straits Times*, RELA membership went up from 340,000 in 2006 to 475,000 members in 2007. Malaysia's official law enforcement in comparison has only 200,000 members nationwide.[35] Zaidoun Asmuni, RELA's Director-General in 2007 aptly expressed why this volunteer corps has grown so much in popularity: "We have no more Communists at the moment, but we are now facing illegal immigrants … as you know, in Malaysia illegal immigrants are enemy No. 2 [after drugs]".[36]

Raids, like the one described above, are legally permissible under article 51(1) of the Malaysian Immigration Act. Once detained, Rohingyas are unable to return to Myanmar, as they are not legally considered citizens and Myanmar does not readily want to welcome them back. Most Rohingyas also do not want to return to the persecution they are bound to face in Myanmar. With illegal status in Malaysia and no country to return to, stateless, detained Rohingyas face the challenge of being indefinitely detained or being trafficked, especially since article 34(1) of the Malaysian Immigration Act does not state a maximum detention period. The danger of being trafficked is specific to Rohingyas, as they are not formally deported back to Myanmar, but either handed over to Thai immigration officials or left at the Malay-Thai border, where they are picked up by human traffickers.[37]

Agence France Press reported in July 2009 that Malaysian Police arrested five immigration officials for being part of an international trafficking syndicate, which "sold" Rohingyas into forced labour or handed them over to traffickers who would charge them between 300 and 600 Ringgit for their illegal journey back into Malaysia. Criminal Investigation Department head Mohammed Bakri Zinin was quoted as saying:

> According to a victim, the suspects were directly involved in human trafficking, starting from the Malaysia-Thailand border [to other] exit points to international countries … upon reaching the exit point, the victims were handed over to a syndicate before being taken to a neighbouring country.

Since this scandal, the Malaysian government has requested UNHCR to assist in screening and determining the status of Myanmar nationals (including Rohingyas) in detention centres.[38] It is too recent a development to predict what effect it will have on the numbers and treatment of "illegal immigrants" in Malaysian detention centres.

Thailand

Thailand, like Malaysia, often does not distinguish between refugees, asylum seekers and illegal migrants. Thailand has a stronger relationship with UNHCR than Malaysia does, due to its history of hosting Burmese refugees on the Thailand-Myanmar border since the Indo-Chinese refugee crisis. However, since Thailand is not a signatory to the 1951 Refugee Convention, its domestic definition for refugees is restrictive, stating that they are "people fleeing fighting". Like Malaysia, it would rather give the label of "illegal migrant" than "refugee" or "asylum seeker" to groups outside of its official refugee camps, such as the Hmong, Rohingya and Shan. In addition, the Hmong and Rohingya are also considered as "national security threats".[39]

When, amid much international criticism, 4,300 Laotian Hmongs were involuntarily repatriated to Laos in December 2009, the Thai Foreign Ministry stated: "Thai authorities managed the safe and orderly return of some 4,300 Laotian Hmong illegal migrants in the shelter at Nam Khao in Patchaboon Province and in the Immigration Detention Centre in Nong Khai Province to the Lao People's Democratic Republic, in accordance with the Thai Immigration Act."

The Hmong are a complicated case in terms of status in Thailand, as some of them have officially been recognized as refugees by UNHCR, while others, who were born in Thailand, are considered stateless. Many of the Hmong originally fled from Laos to Thailand in the 1970s. The

American Central Intelligence Agency (CIA) had trained thousands of Hmongs between 1960 and 1973 to fight communists in Laos. However in 1975, after the Communist takeover in Laos, the government has been accused of purposefully discriminating against ethnic Hmongs and Hmong families associated with the CIA from 1960–73, creating an environment of persecution.[40] Author Brian McCartan writes in the *Asia Times*:

> There is longstanding controversy over the Hmong's status in Thailand. Both the Thai and Lao governments claim they are mainly economic migrants, an assessment that some human rights workers and observers of the Hmong situation confirm. However, they say several hundred from the Huay Nam Khao camp, and certainly the 158 people held in Nong Khai already recognised by the UNHCR, would be at a clear risk of government reprisals if they were repatriated to Laos (2010).

On 28 December 2009, the Thai military deported 4,371 Hmong from the Huay Nam Khao camp and 158 Hmong, who had been in Thai detention since 2006. These individuals were forcibly repatriated to Laos by 4 January 2010.[41] While some Hmongs successfully resettled in the United States in the 1990s and in 2003, during this event, international concerns and requests for resettlement by the United Nations, several governments and NGOs were blatantly ignored.

Opportunities

Being granted refugee status is better than being stateless, but it is hard to acquire. According to the 1951 Convention Relating to the Status of Refugees, the term "refugee" applies to any person who...

> ... owing to well-founded fear of being persecuted for reasons of race, religion, nationality, membership of a particular social group or political opinion, is outside the country of his nationality and is unable or, owing to such fear, is unwilling to avail himself of the protection of that country; or who, not having a nationality and being outside the country of his former habitual residence as a result of such events, is unable or, owing to such fear, is unwilling to return to it.

In theory, stateless persons who qualify as a refugee within this definition must be eligible for protection under this Convention. However, in Southeast Asia, stateless persons often do not enjoy the status of refugee under the Refugee Convention.

For example, in response to its widely criticized "push-back policy", the Thai government on 5 February 2009 announced its official policy of deporting Rohingyas, who illegally arrive in Thailand by boat, emphasizing that refugee camps would not be opened to accept them.[42] *Mizzima* quoted the Deputy Prime Minister, Suthep Thaugsuban, as saying that "we have no plan to open refugee camps for them. We cannot afford to shoulder the extra burden of accommodating 300,000 refugees on our soil. We will deport them to Burma, which is their country of origin." Thailand's position contrasted with that of UNHCR, which considers Rohingyas as refugees and hence urged the Thai government to offer them protection. Moreover, Thailand, just like most Southeast Asian countries, is not party to the Convention relating to the Status of Refugees.[43]

Authors Katherine Perks and Jarlath Clifford write in their article "The legal limbo of detention":

> When a stateless person is a refugee, he or she cannot be penalised for illegal entry or presence. Stateless persons who are not refugees do not enjoy such protection under the 1954 Convention relating to the Status of Stateless Persons and are therefore potentially at greater risk of detention for breach of immigration regulations.[44]

For example, in Bangladesh, 28,000 Rohingyas have refugee status and live in formal UNHCR run camps, where they have access to basic rights and services they would not have if they were stateless. Living in refugee camps, Rohingyas have access to healthcare, education, food and shelter because they are registered as an existing person. There is no danger of being indefinitely detained. However, for the approximately 200,000 Rohingyas in Bangladesh, who do not have refugee status and live in squatter camps near the formal refugee camps, life is even more complicated as they do not exist on paper anywhere. Their names, which may have been on family lists in Myanmar at some point in time, are no longer there, and in Bangladesh, they are also undocumented persons. In an interview with Chris Lewa, Founder and Coordinator of The Arakan Project, an organization advocating on behalf of the Rohingyas, Lewa expressed:

> [The] main problem with Rohingya outside of the camp ... if they are abused, they cannot seek redress, because that means they have to enter the justice system and they would then be charged for illegal entry ... Once in jail, they are likely to remain there indefinitely as Bangladesh does allow access to UNHCR and Burma would not re-admit them ... so some of these individuals remain in jail for nearly 20 years!

It is clear from the forgoing discussion that the problems of refugees and statelessness often overlap. If a person is forced to leave a country of habitual residence because of well-founded fears of persecution, as laid down in the Refugee Convention, they are eligible to apply for refugee status. However, there are stateless people who do not have a well-founded fear of persecution, as well as many who never leave their long-term homes and are therefore not categorized as refugees. Similarly, some refugees may be stateless, but most are.[45]

Small legislative and administrative changes can make a big difference, however there is potential for more. Malaysia and Thailand have made some small legislative and administrative changes, regarding the status, situation and treatment of stateless persons. This section highlights both the positive and negative aspects of these decisions.

Malaysia: Article 14 in the Constitution and the IMM13 Permit

Even though Article 14 in the Malaysian Constitution entitles any person born within the Malaysian Federation citizenship, including individuals who were not born citizens of any other country, the implementation of this article has been partial at best.[46] For example, children of mixed Malaysian-Rohingya marriages have been able to receive citizenship on a much more consistent basis than stateless Rohingya born in Malaysia.[47]

Malaysia is also supposed to issue birth certificates to the children of refugees and undocumented migrant workers. However, in the case of stateless children in Sabah, eastern Malaysia, whose parents are undocumented Philippino and Indonesian migrant workers, it has been a complicated situation. In the 2009 report by the Asia-Pacific Mission for Migrants titled *Narrative Report: Fact Finding Mission on Undocumented Migrant Workers and Their Families in Sabah, Malaysia*, it is pointed out:

> Public health services are not allocated to undocumented [migrant workers] while private hospitals charge very high. For children born in private clinics, they have to pay RM 1000 for a birth certificate. Migrant workers with legal documents only need to pay RM 60.

In addition, children born to undocumented Philippino and Indonesian migrant workers in Sabah, who have received birth certificates, are categorized by the Malaysian government as *orang asing* (foreigner) and, therefore, do not have access to public education.[48] In many instances, it is not easy for the parents of stateless children in Sabah to obtain birth certificates for their children, as:

- They are undocumented migrant workers and fear being detained if they try to register their child.
- Birth certificates are expensive.
- Birth registration sites are difficult to reach.

While far from a durable solution, **Malaysia also has temporary residence permits called IMM13**, permissible under section 55(1) of its Immigration Act, which states that the Home Minister can exempt "any person or group of persons from the provisions of the Act".[49] These permits are renewable on an annual basis for 90RM and allow access to public services, including healthcare and public education. Most importantly, permit holders are allowed to work. However, these permits can also be cancelled anytime at the Home Minister's dicretion[50] and according to the International Observatory on the Status of Statelessness:

> The government issued temporary stay permits in the form of the IMM13 document, an immigration pass for stateless people. These documents do not represent a durable solution for ending the Rohingyas' statelessness. The government has not fulfilled its promise to grant the Rohingyas identity cards and temporary work permits.

Thailand: The Administrative Court System

As the Thai National Human Rights Commission does not have access to the national court system, an alternate legal space for stateless persons to have their voices heard is in the Thai Administrative Courts. Thai Administrative courts were set up by the 1997 Constitution and officially created in March 2001. They are composed of a Supreme Administrative Court and Administrative Courts of First Instance. Their mission from 2005–08 was:

- To try and adjudicate administrative cases impartially and swiftly, in order to assure the protection of rights, liberties, and administer justice to the parties in dispute;
- To set precedents in the area of administrative law as the guidelines for good practice in public administration for State agencies and officials.[51]

There are two specific cases, when decisions by the Administrative courts made a difference to stateless persons. In 2002, the District Chief,

Table 7.5
Lessons and Good Practice for Effective Birth Registration

Lessons Learnt	Examples
Changes in policy and legislation by governments	In 2008, Thailand passed a legislation so that all children born in Thailand, regardless of their parents' nationality can be registered.
Partnering with a diverse range of organizations at different levels	Civil society organizations, UN agencies, government, community based organizations, can all be valuable partners in different steps of the process.
Involving children and communities	Young volunteers in Cambodia have educated friends and elders by holding children's fairs and explaining the importance of birth registration through posters.
Birth registrations systems need to be flexible	In Thailand, Plan International has helped create a network of local authorities, NGOs and community representatives in provinces with large hill tribe populations.
Free registration and birth certification	Indonesia provides free birth registration.
Retrospective registration may be necessary	Some countries' governments facilitate retrospective court hearings through free local court hearings, reducing the number of unregistered children.
Integration of birth registration into the broader child rights agenda	Belgium has successfully linked the child registration issue to child soldiers and child trafficking.
Integration of birth registration into existing public services	Linking it to primary healthcare, immunization and school enrollment.
Training and capacity building of birth registration officials	Sri Lanka has developed a toolkit to help officials carry out mobile registration.
Monitoring is essential	National governments should have information systems for birth registration.

Sustainability is best ensured by government ownership.

Source: Adapted from the article, Simon Heap and Claire Cody, "The Universal Birth Registration Campaign", *Forced Migration Review*, no. 32 (2009).

Thongchai Setthapat, of Mae Ai province in Chiang Mai, Thailand revoked the citizenship of 1,143 of its residents, rendering them stateless.[52] However, Thai administrative courts overturned this decision and reinstated citizenship for these particular individuals.[53]

In September 2009, Thong Mongdee, a stateless boy of Burmese origin and residing in Thailand, received a temporary Thai passport so he could attend an origami competition in Japan. This one-time travel permission was granted by the Administrative Court.[54] This particular decision did not offer a durable solution, but may set precedence for future court cases involving statelessness.

The Prevention and Reduction of Statelessness in Southeast Asia

Despite Southeast Asia's historical rejection of international legal instruments relating to UNHCR's "persons of concern" including refugees, asylum seekers, returnees, the internally displaced and the stateless,[55] it would be wrong to claim that there have not been some positive developments for stateless persons in this region. **A key aspect in preventing and reducing statelessness is to distinguish between problems of statelessness** that can be easily solved, such as ensuring that a child is registered at birth, versus problems of statelessness that are more protracted and complex, such as the situation of the Rohingyas.

> Resolving more protracted situations of statelessness is almost easier for governments. In most cases what is lacking is political will. It can be done. It is just a matter of a government initiative to resolve the problem ... it is not that one situation is easier than the other ... taking an example of integration such as the Bangladesh High Court decision, which granted citizenship to thousands of stateless Biharis, is a great one. These individuals now need to be integrated fully into society, which is happening very slowly. Regional processes, such as the Bali Forum on Trafficking or the ASEAN Intergovernmental Commission on Human Rights, can be useful in calling attention to the issue, but one must not forget to work with particular governments.
>
> — Maureen Lynch,
> Senior Advocate on Stateless Initiatives,
> Refugees International

In the area of increasing birth registrations globally, UNICEF and Plan International have managed to have worldwide impact with their Universal

Birth Registration Campaign, which started as a pilot project in 1998 but was continued by Plan International till 2009. For example, in Cambodia, Plan International managed to facilitate the registration of 12.14 million children between 2005 and 2009.[56] In Indonesia, birth registration increased from 3 per cent to 72 per cent in one year, thanks to a major change in legislation in 2004.[57] Birth certificates were made free of charge for children less than eighteen years and the birth registration process was simplified by making it less bureaucratic and allowing for it to be carried out at the village level.

Another key aspect in preventing and reducing statelessness is change in legislation. For example, Malaysia and Thailand should re-examine the period of detention listed in their Immigration Acts.

A third key aspect in preventing and reducing statelessness is advocacy for more bi-lateral and multi-lateral agreements between states in the Southeast Asia region. For example, in December 2009, Myanmar agreed to repatriate 9,000 Rohingyas, who have refugee status in Bangladesh.[58] However, it should be noted that this particular bi-lateral agreement deals with involuntary repatriation, which is illegal under international law. It has often been suggested by scholars and practitioners that multi-lateral agreements may be more successful for problems of statelessness that are more protracted. In the case of the Rohingyas, it has been suggested that an agreement among Bangladesh, Myanmar, Thailand, the U.S. and the UN, may lead to a more durable solution.[59]

A fourth key aspect in preventing and reducing statelessness is the potential for a solution emerging from a regional body such as the Association of Southeast Asian Nations (ASEAN), the ASEAN Intergovernmental Body on Human Rights or the Bali Process for People Smuggling, Trafficking in Persons and Related Transnational Crime. With the establishment of the ASEAN Intergovernmental Commission on Human Rights, it is hoped that international human rights issues, such as statelessness, would be part of its mandate.

The treatment of stateless persons in their habitual residence versus stateless persons on the move needs to be further analysed. Particularly the issue of indefinite detainment and successful best practices on how to reduce and prevent statelessness, deserve more attention.

REGIONAL CHAMPIONS — EXAMINING THE COMPARATIVE ADVANTAGES OF AICHR AND ACWC

Since 2009 Southeast Asia has witnessed the emergence of several new and promising policy entry points for the advancement of the protection of civilians (POC) in Southeast Asia. On 23 October 2009, the ASEAN Inter-governmental Commission on Human Rights (AICHR) was launched. This was followed six months later, on 7 April 2010, by the inauguration of the ASEAN Commission on the Promotion and Protection of the Rights of Women and Children (ACWC). This section investigates how current regional institutional developments could affect and advance the general POC agenda in the ASEAN region. It also provides some key recommendations for how the AICHR and ACWC might collaborate and coordinate more effectively with one another, thus maximizing the benefits of these institutional developments for the security and well being of peoples/populations across the region.

There have been significant prospects for further regional integration through the signing of the ASEAN Charter in Southeast Asia. However, there have also been significant challenges that have dampened these prospects. The development of AICHR was widely welcomed, but when its mandate was unveiled there was widespread disappointment that it was a "toothless tiger" that did not have a mandate equally balanced between promotion and protection of human rights.[60] That said, it did provide a wake-up call for stakeholders in the region on how much power ASEAN member states are willing to invest in a regional commission.

In November 2004, ASEAN leaders met and adopted the "Vientiane Action Programme 2004–10", which established the "strategic thrusts" of the three ASEAN communities — the ASEAN Security Community to "enhance peace, stability, democracy and prosperity in the region through comprehensive political and security cooperation"; the ASEAN Economic Community to "enhance competitiveness for economic growth and deve-lopment through closer economic integration"; and the ASEAN Socio-Cultural Community to "nurture human, cultural and natural resources for sustained development in a harmonious and people-centred ASEAN". The Vientiane Action Programme included Measure 1.1.4.7, which called for the establishment of an ASEAN Commission on the Promotion and Protection of the Rights of Women and Children. Subsequently at the 14th ASEAN Summit in 2009, ASEAN leaders agreed to the "Cha-am Hua Declaration on the Road Map for the ASEAN Community, 2009–2015". This road map reiterated the establishment of the ACWC to promote and protect the rights of women and children to ensure their equitable development in the region. The development of the ACWC will provide an important narrative as its mandate links international commitments with local realities. The regional level of governance is particularly important where the developments of AICHR and ACWC have provided fertile ground for exploring other avenues for better protection of civilians. It is important to highlight the key areas where these different institutions can cooperate in order to avoid duplication and also to encourage cooperation and information-sharing towards more robust and efficient governance in the region for the protection of civilians.

While the establishment of the ACWC is an important step for the region, analysts note that multiple avenues need to be used to promote the protection of civilians. The ACWC was born out of an action plan, which is a part of the ASEAN Socio-Cultural Community. The AICHR emerged out of the ASEAN Political-Security Community and is formally mentioned in the ASEAN Charter. It is important to highlight this key difference between the two bodies, because AICHR will be able to function cross-sectorally, having the mandate to influence and engage with all three ASEAN communities. This contrasts with ACWC which will be operating as part of the socio-cultural pillar through its reporting to the ASEAN Ministers Meeting on Social Welfare and Development (AMMSWD), with copy to the ASEAN Committee on Women (ACW) and other relevant sectoral bodies. In addition, ACWC has a much more defined focus than AICHR, as its mandate calls for a clear emphasis on women's and children's protection concerns in the region. Both of these commissions have the protection of civilians' agenda under their mandates, highlighting that no single policy avenue or community will suffice as a "lone star" for the protection of civilians. Ultimately while it is important to minimize overlap between institutions, it is also important for institutions to keep investigating new and creative ways to interact with one another and to recognize what one another's comparative advantages are.

For instance, in an interview, AICHR Commissioner, Mr Rafendi Djamin[61] highlighted that since AICHR is mandated to provide technical advice on human rights to all ASEAN sectoral bodies, it can help ACWC in mainstreaming important women's and children's issues under both the political-security and economic pillars of ASEAN. ACWC, in turn, can aid AICHR in providing specialized technical expertise on women's and children's protection issues in the region. There are many issues that AICHR and ACWC could work together on. Two key areas of potential collaboration for AICHR and ACWC may include:

- Raising awareness on reservations held by ASEAN member states on substantive articles of the Convention on the Rights of the Child (CRC) and the Convention on the Elimination of all Forms of Discrimination Against Women (CEDAW).[62]
- Violence rooted in economic issues (for example, violence against women due to economic related causes).

During the last AICHR meeting in March 2010, it was decided that the two areas of focus for its five-year work plan would be (1) migration, and (2) business and human rights. Although the AICHR's rules of procedure have not been adopted as yet, its commissioners are scheduled to meet for five days at the end of June, where it is hoped the rules of procedure be formally adopted; AICHR activities from July to December 2010 will be defined (for example, commissioning of studies on specific issues, stock-taking, mobilization of funds and technical advisory activities to ASEAN sectoral bodies); and taskforces for (1) migration, (2) business and human rights, and (3) the procedure for an ASEAN Human Rights Declaration, will be set up.

The Terms of Reference (TOR) for the ACWC were agreed upon by the ASEAN Ministers Responsible for Social Welfare and Development prior to the 15th ASEAN Summit in 2009. The TOR includes promoting the implementation of internationally agreed-to standards such as those included in CRC and CEDAW. Each ASEAN member state has two appointed representatives in ACWC, one for women's rights and another for children's rights. During the selection process, the TOR mandates that potential commissioners possess competence in the fields of women's and children's rights, and that member states exercise integrity and equality when appointing their representatives (Article 6.3). The TOR also outlines that each member state shall conduct, in respect to their respective internal processes, a transparent, open, participatory, and inclusive selection process (Article 6.4). This process allows for more specific accountability than does the selection process of AICHR. AICHR only calls for member states "to consult if required by their respective internal processes, with appropriate stakeholders" (Article 5.4).

The ACWC will meet for the first time in August 2010. There is a chance that member states will change the TOR during this meeting. It should also be noted that the ACWC has not adopted its rules of procedures as yet. Realistically, the first time AICHR and ACWC commissioners will be able to meet will be after both have finalized their respective TORs, adopted rules of procedures and defined activities for the coming months.

Once both bodies meet, they will have to clearly define what each body is responsible for in overlapping issue areas, such as human trafficking. In addition, if there is to be an "alignment" of the two commissions, this needs to be clearly defined in terms of day-to-day practice.

While there are various differences between the AICHR and ACWC mandates, both commissions will ultimately work together to achieve progress in areas of mutual interest if they are to maximize their effectiveness in furthering the protection of civilians' agenda. With this in mind, it is also important to understand the larger role of ACWC, which is not only for it to work alongside and in collaboration with AICHR, but also to assist individual member states in developing their institutional capacity to implement the necessary changes to advance, protect and promote the rights of women and children in the region. It is through the identification of partners at both the national and local levels that implementation of these rights can take place. This can be accomplished through regular interaction with individuals and communities as well as formal state structures. In this vein, civil society will provide an important informal resource to ensure that regional institutions and mechanisms respond to the issues that matter to those whose situations it is mandated to improve.

AICHR and ACWC are able to work with civil society partners in the region; one potentially instrumental partner from the region is the Southeast Asia Women's Caucus on ASEAN. It is coordinated by two regional organizations: the International Women's Action Watch Asia Pacific (IWRAW Asia Pacific) and Asia Pacific Forum on Women, Law and Development (APWLD). It represents a network of women's human rights groups from Myanmar, Cambodia, Indonesia, Lao PDR, the Philippines, Malaysia, Thailand and Vietnam, engaging with key ASEAN structures and in key processes towards ensuring the realization and protection of women's rights on a regional level. The Thai ACWC Commissioner, Dr Saisuree Chutikul agreed in a interview[63] that the Southeast Asia Women's Caucus on ASEAN has consistently done good work on a macro and regional level, but needs to make more of an effort to connect with local partners in ASEAN member states.

The following sections give suggestions for adapting current tools and indicators that would be helpful to the ACWC, in particular, when assessing the situation of women and children in ASEAN member states. Such tools and indicators include the Gender-related Development Index (GDI) developed by the United Nations Development Programme (UNDP), the ASEAN Economic Community Scorecard, and the Key Children and Young Persons Indicators (KCYPI) developed by the United Nations Children's Fund (UNICEF).

Gender-Related Development Index

Since 1995, the UNDP *Human Development Report* has disaggregated its data when compiling the Human Development Index and has produced the GDI, which is the Human Development Index accounting for gender inequality. Table 7.6 shows the results from the UNDP *Human Development Report 2009*. The results illustrate, where available, that there is not a regional norm on gender inequality and it remains quite diverse across the region. This is best represented by the world rankings of ASEAN member states (with data available for analysis) ranging from 15th in the world out of 155 countries down to 104th in the world.

From these collated findings, we are able to rank the member states in the region according to their GDI scores. Using the data collected by the UNDP will assist the ACWC in evaluating the progress that member states have made since the inauguration of the ACWC. Indeed, the table compares the annual levels of gender inequality and human development in ASEAN member states. According to the table, some states score highly on the HDI World Ranking but fare poorly when the data is disaggregated; likewise other

Table 7.6
ASEAN Gender Inequality Rankings

ASEAN GDI Rank	Member State	GDI	GDI World Ranking/155	HDI	HDI World Ranking/182
1	Thailand	0.999	15	0.783	87
2	Vietnam	0.997	31	0.725	116
3	Philippines	0.996	40	0.751	105
4=	Cambodia	0.992	75=	0.593	137
4=	Lao PDR	0.992	75=	0.619	133
6	Malaysia	0.993	76	0.829	66
7	Indonesia	0.989	90	0.734	111
8	Brunei	0.906	104	0.92	30
n/a	Singapore	n/a	n/a	0.944	23
n/a	Myanmar	n/a	n/a	0.586	138

Source: UNDP, *Human Development Report 2009*.

states score poorly on the overall HDI but fare better in the disaggregated GDI. Through the information available, it is evident that while a country's overall HDI score may be high, it does not necessarily impact on individual human development areas such as gender inequality. One observation that remains constant is that development does not necessarily lead to less gender inequality; rather there are other significant factors which need to be accounted for and investigated in the region to better understand the root causes of gender inequality.

Gendered Policy Directions

It would be useful for the ACWC to borrow ideas from another branch of the ASEAN community — the ASEAN Economic Community, which has produced an ASEAN Economic Community Scorecard in March 2010 to track the developments of the association in implementing the road maps towards realizing an integrated ASEAN community. This scorecard approach can be developed based on information provided by supporting institutions and civil society, to track development on the level of implementation of internationally-agreed to standards on women's and children's rights by member states'. This scorecard can highlight the inequalities present in the region and offer some areas for cooperation between member states. This can be achieved through information-sharing to learn how different states develop policies to address these inequalities. Efforts such as this will assist the region to integrate further as envisioned in 1997 under the ASEAN Vision 2020:

> We see vibrant and open ASEAN societies consistent with their respective national identities, where all people enjoy equitable access to opportunities for total human development regardless of gender, race, religion, language, or social and cultural background.

A significant challenge that faces those engaged in the promotion and protection of the rights of women and children is the challenge to turn words into deeds. As the United Nations Development Fund for Women (UNIFEM) has pointed out, the challenge is to "define and enact gender 'mainstreaming', 'women's empowerment', and 'gender equality'" UNIFEM.[64] It further notes that even though legal changes have been made, these changes still fall significantly short of making an impact on the ground. In other words, these efforts "fall short because of poor enforcement, limited capacity, and weak accountability" UNIFEM.[65]

"Key Indicators" on Children and Young Persons

UNICEF documents the status of the provisions and protection of children the world over in an annual report titled *The State of the World's Children 2009*. The findings in this report can assist the ACWC to target the key areas of concern in the region and allow for region-wide data collection and analysis in a further effort to assist member states to realize their ASEAN Vision 2020:

> We envision a socially cohesive and caring ASEAN where hunger, malnutrition, deprivation and poverty are no longer basic problems, where strong families as the basic units of society tend to their members particularly the children, youth ...

Table 7.7 is a snapshot of some of the data available in the UNICEF report that illustrates some of the challenges faced in the region and highlights some areas of concern.

According to data in Table 7.7, it is clear that there remain wide differences in ASEAN over the provisions and protection of children. Indeed, there are significant areas that need to be addressed in order for the ASEAN Vision 2020 of "reducing the social risks faced by children, women, the elderly and persons who are disabled" to be realized. Most notably, there is a large variation in child mortality rates across the region, ranging from countries like Singapore which has the lowest regional child mortality rate of 3 deaths per 1,000 live births and which is placed 188th out of 193 countries in a global ranking of the mortality rate of children under the age of 5, to Myanmar which has the highest regional child mortality rate of 98 deaths per 1,000 live births and a global ranking of 35 out of 193. While statistics only reveal part of the picture, they offer a basis for regional and global comparison that allows for the identification of areas of concern and areas worthy of further investigation as to the causes of these variations within the region and around the world.

Some other areas not illustrated in the table but recognized by UNICEF as challenges in the region are the growing disparities within countries between the rich and the poor; the need to maintain poverty reduction strategies; environmental issues; the escalation of HIV infections and the growing number of AIDS orphans; the limited social protection that allows for the occurrence of violence, abuse and human trafficking; and recurrent natural disasters. These are the issues that can be assessed at the regional level to further investigate why some member states fare better than others

Table 7.7
ASEAN Children and Young Persons Core Benchmark

Member State	Under 5 Mortality Rate Rank/193	GNI Per Capita (US$)	Total Adult Literacy (%) 2003–2008*	Primary School Enrolment/ Attendance (%) 2003–2008 *
Brunei	153	26740	95	93
Cambodia	41	600	76	89
Indonesia	66	2010	91	85s
Laos PDR	54	750	73	84
Malaysia	158	6970	92	100
Myanmar	35	220x	90x	84s
Philippines	81	1890	93	91
Singapore	188	34760	94	–
Thailand	125	2840	94	94
Vietnam	125	9230	90x	93x

Note: – : Data unavailable.

    x : Data refer to years or periods other than those specified in the column heading, differ from the standard definition or refer to only part of a country. Such data are not included in the calculation of regional and global averages.

    s : National household survey data.

    * : Data refer to the year available during the period specified in the column heading.

Source: UNICEF — The State of the World's Children 2009.

in international comparisons and how member states can learn from one another's experiences in this regard. It will be important for the ACWC to facilitate this process and investigate ways and means to realize the ASEAN Vision 2020 of a regional integrated community.

Despite a lack of implementation in regional human rights related instruments, the years 2009 and 2010 have established some positive entry points for the protection of civilians to be improved in the ASEAN region. In 2008, both AICHR and ACWC constituted just a part of discussions surrounding the ASEAN Charter. Now, both exist as official bodies. Just as it takes time for norms to be accepted and institutionalized, it will take time before both bodies become fully functioning, have finalized TORs and adopt rules of procedures, but ASEAN member states are better off with AICHR and ACWC, rather than without them. Both bodies have key comparative advantages, which can only be strengthened and mainstreamed into all ASEAN sectoral bodies, if both work together on a consistent basis.

Ms Wathshlah Naidu, Programme Officer with the International Women's Rights Action Watch Asia Pacific (IWRAW Asia Pacific), emphasized in a written response:

Both bodies should coordinate, complement and ensure the collaboration in areas such as standards setting; producing thematic reports; conducting "exchanges of visits"; building capacity of member states on issue [sic] related to women and children; and ensuring constructive engagement with civil society representatives which includes participation and representation of women and children from all sectors and marginalized groups (May 2010).

It will be vital for AICHR and ACWC commissioners to meet as soon as the ACWC August meeting is over, in order for both bodies to define a working relationship and ensure that there is not an excessive overlap in the issues each body is mandated to address. It is also recommended that both bodies take into consideration the other suggested tools and indicators, such as the GDI and KCYPI, when finalizing the framework of their working relationship to establish policy recommendations for consideration at the ASEAN Summits, where they have access to key decision-makers in the region.

Notes

1   UNHCR, *Global Trends: Refugees, Asylum-seekers, Returnees, Internally Displaced and Stateless Persons Report* (Geneva: UNHCR, 2008), available at <http://www.unhcr.org/4a375c426.html>.

2   David Weissbrodt and Clay Collins, "The Human Rights of Stateless Persons", *Human Rights Quarterly* 28 (2006).

3   David Steinberg, *Burma/Myanmar: What Everyone Needs to Know* (New York: Oxford University Press, 2010).

4   "A Right to Belong", UNESCO film on stateless Thai hill tribe people, 2002. A. Zhou and Thomson E., "The Development of Biofuels in Asia", *Applied Energy* 86 (2009): 11–20.

5   US State Department, *Trafficking in Persons Report*, Washington, D.C., 2009, available at <http://www.state.gov/g/tip/rls/tiprpt/2009/>.

6   Kitty McKinsey, "Vietnam Sets the Pace for Asia with New Law to Prevent Statelessness", UNHCR News Stories, 1 July 2009, available at <http://www.unhcr.org/4a4b809d9.html>.

7   Thawdar, "No Country to Call Their Own", *The Irrawaddy*, vol. 17, no. 5, (August 2009).

8   International Observatory on the Stateless, "South Asia — Nepal", 2008, available at <http://www.nationalityforall.org/nepal>.

9   Sarah Davies, *Legitimising Rejection: International Refugee Law in Southeast Asia* (Leiden, Boston: Martinus Nijhoff, 2008).

10 Brad K. Blitz, "Statelessness, Protection and Equality", Forced Migration Policy Briefing 3, Refugees Studies Centre, September 2009.

11 Shafiq Alam, "Myanmar Rohingyas Swap Suppressier for Squalor", Agence France Press, 11 November 2009, available at <http://www.google.com/hostednews/afp/article/ALeqM5i-C9GrlqIRND-D4IMwP81_Wj_6Dw>.

12 Philip John Eldridge, *The Politics of Human Rights in Southeast Asia* (Abingdon, Oxon: Routledge, 2002).

13 Usa Pichai, "Thai Citizenship to Grant Stateless near Burma Border", Mizzima, 25 August 2009, available at <http://www.mizzima.com/news/regional/2671-thai-citizenship-to-grant-stateless-near-burma-border-.html>.

14 Refugees International, "Citizens of Nowhere: The Stateless Biharis of Bangladesh" (Washington, D.C.: Refugees International, 2006).

15 SAFHR, "Bangladesh State and the Refugee Phenomenon", South Asia Forum for Human Rights, available at <http://www.safhr.org/refugee_watch18_4.htm>.

16 Waliur Rahman, "Vote for 'Stranded Pakistanis'", *BBC News*, 6 May 2003, available at <http://news.bbc.co.uk/2/hi/south_asia/3003949.stm>.

17 "Citizenship for Bihari Refugees", *BBC News*, 19 May 2008, available at <http://news.bbc.co.uk/2/hi/south_asia/7407757.stm>.

18 Nattha Keenapan, "The Stateless Classroom", *Bangkok Post*, 23 June 2009.

19 Chris Lewa, "North Arakan: An Open Prison for the Rohingya in Burma", *Forced Migration Review*, vol. 32 (2009).

20 Chris Lewa, "Asia's New Boat People", *Forced Migration Review*, vol. 30 (April 2008): 40–42.

21 "Perilous Plight: Burma's Rohingyas Take to the Seas", Human Rights Watch, May 2009.

22 "Perilous Plight: Burma's Rohingyas Take to the Seas", Human Rights Watch, May 2009.

23 Ruma Paul, "Bangladesh says Myanmar to Take Back 9,000 Refugees", Reuters India, 29 December 2009, available at <http://in.reuters.com/article/southAsiaNews/idINIndia-45038920091229>.

24 Lawi Weng, "Bangladesh, Burma Agree on Repatriation of Some Rohingya", *The Irrawaddy*, 30 December 2009, available at <http://www.irrawaddy.org/article.php?art_id=17511>.

25 Physicians for Human Rights, *No Status: Migration, Trafficking & Exploitation of Women in Thailand* (Boston, MA: Physicians for Human Rights, 2004), available at <https://s3.amazonaws.com/PHR_Reports/thailand-women-trafficking-2004.pdf>.

26   Vital Voices Global Partnership, *Statelessness and Vulnerable to Human Trafficking in Thailand*, June 2007, available at <http://www.humantrafficking.org/uploads/publications/Vital_Voices_Stateless_and_Vulnerable_to_Human_Trafficking_in_Thailand.pdf>.

27   Human Rights Watch, "Perilous Plight: Burma's Rohingyas Take to the Seas", May 2009, available at <http://www.hrw.org/sites/default/files/reports/burma0509_brochure_web.pdf>.

28   Khin Maung Lay, "Burma Fuels the Rohingya Tragedy", *Far Eastern Economic Review*, 6 March 2009, available at <http://www.feer.com/essays/2009/march/burma-fuels-the-rohingya-tragedy>.

29   UNHCR, "Global Appeal" (Geneva: UNHCR, 2010/2011), available at <http://www.unhcr.org/ga10/index.html>.

30   Interview with Chris Lewa, 2009.

31   Interview with Chris Lewa, 2009.

32   Katherine Perks and Jarlath Clifford, "The Legal Limbo of Detention", *Forced Migration Review* 32 (2009).

33   Eva-Lotta Hedman, "Refuge, Governmentality and Citizenship: Capturing 'Illegal Migrants' in Malaysia and Thailand", *Government and Opposition* 43, no. 2 (2008).

34   Seth Mydans, "A Growing Source of Fear for Migrants in Malaysia", *New York Times*, 10 December 2007.

35   Eva-Lotta Hedman, "Refuge, Governmentality and Citizenship: Capturing 'Illegal Migrants' in Malaysia and Thailand", *Government and Opposition* 43, no. 2 (2008).

36   Seth Mydans, "A Growing Source of Fear for Migrants in Malaysia", *New York Times*, 10 December 2007.

37   Chris Lewa and Amal de Chickera, "Trapped in a Cycle of Flight: Stateless Rohingya in Malaysia", A Report for the Equal Rights Trust, 2010, available at <http://www.equalrightstrust.org/ertdocumentbank/ERTMalaysiaReportFinal.pdf>.

38   Ibid.

39   Ibid.

40   McCartan, Brian, "Fallen Pawns in US's Strategic Game", *Asia Times*, 8 January 2010.

41   Ibid.

42   "Thailand Discloses Official Policy to Deport Rohingya Refugees", Mizzima, 5 February 2009, available at <http://www.mizzima.com/news/regional/1657-thailand-discloses-official-policy-to-deport-rohingya-refugees.html>.

43   UNDP, *Human Development Report 2009*, United Nations Development Programme, October 2009, available at <http://hdr.undp.org/en/reports/global/hdr2009/>.

44   Katherine Perks and Jarlath Clifford, "The Legal Limbo of Detention", *Forced Migration Review* 32 (2009).

45 UN High Commissioner for Refugees, *The World's Stateless People*, Questions & Answers, September 2007, UNHCR/MRPI Q&A A•4/ENG 1, available at <http://www.unhcr.org/refworld/docid/47a707900.html>.

46 Chris Lewa and Amal de Chickera, "Trapped in a Cycle of Flight: Stateless Rohingya in Malaysia", A Report for the Equal Rights Trust, 2010, available at <http://www.equalrightstrust.org/ertdocumentbank/ERTMalaysiaReportFinal.pdf>.

47 K. Sadiq, *Paper Citizens: How Illegal Immigrants Acquire Citizenship in Developing Countries* (US: Oxford University Press, 2008).

48 Maureen Lynch and Melanie Teff, "Childhood Statelessness", *Forced Migration Review* 32 (2009).

49 Chris Lewa and Amal de Chickera, "Trapped in a Cycle of Flight: Stateless Rohingya in Malaysia", A Report for the Equal Rights Trust, 2010, available at <http://www.equalrightstrust.org/ertdocumentbank/ERTMalaysiaReportFinal.pdf>.

50 Ibid.

51 <http://www.admincourt.go.th>.

52 Supatatt Dangkrueng, "1,143 Villagers Made Stateless", *Chiangmai Mail*, 2002.

53 Ibid.

54 Ambika Ahuja, "Stateless Boy Gets Thai Passport for Origami Event", *Taiwan News*, 4 September 2009, available at <http://www.etaiwannews.com/etn/news_content.php?id=1049164&lang=eng_news&cate_img=logo_world&cate_rss=WORLD_eng>.

55 Sarah Davies, *Legitimising Rejection: International Refugee Law in Southeast Asia* (Leiden, Boston: Martinus Nijhoff, 2008).

56 Plan International, "Count Every Child", Report by Plan International, 2009.

57 Ibid.

58 Ruma Paul, "Bangladesh Says Myanmar to Take Back 9,000 Refugees", Reuters India, 29 December 2009, available at <http://in.reuters.com/article/southAsiaNews/idINIndia-45038920091229>.

59 Vitit Muntarbhorn, "Human Rights: Burma's Rohingyas in Flight and the Solutions to Their Plight", *Bangkok Post*, 11 March 2009.

60 Simon Roughneen, "One Step Forward, Two Steps Back", International Relations and Security Network, 29 October 2009, available at <http://www.isn.ethz.ch/isn/Current-Affairs/Security-Watch/Detail/?lng=en&id=108891>.

61 Interview with Rafendi Djarmin, 3 June 2010.

62 For a detailed account of these reservations, see Mely Caballero-Anthony and Priyanka Bhalla, "Reserving the Right Not to Comply: ASEAN Legal Reservations on CEDAW and CRC", NTS Alert (Singapore: RSIS Centre for Non-Traditional Security [NTS] Studies for NTS-Asia, June 2010).

[63]   Interview with Dr Saisuree Chutikul, 13 May 2010.
[64]   UNIFEM, "Southeast Asia Regional Overview", 2010, available at <http://cedaw-seasia.org/regional_overview.html>.
[65]   Ibid.

References

Ahuja, Ambika. "Stateless Boy Gets Thai Passport for Origami Event". *Taiwan News*, 4 September 2009. Available at <http://www.etaiwannews.com/etn/news_content.php?id=1049164&lang=eng_news&cate_img=logo_world&cate_rss=WORLD_eng>.

Alam, Shafiq. "Myanmar Rohingyas Swap Suppressier for Squalor". Agence France Press, 11 November 2009. Available at <http://www.google.com/hostednews/afp/article/ALeqM5i-C9GrlqIRND-D4IMwP81_Wj_6Dw>.

Blitz, Brad K. "Statelessness, Protection and Equality". Forced Migration Policy Briefing 3. Refugees Studies Centre, September 2009.

Caballero-Anthony, Mely and Priyanka Bhalla. "Reserving the Right Not to Comply: ASEAN Legal Reservations on CEDAW and CRC". NTS Alert. Singapore: RSIS Centre for Non-Traditional Security [NTS] Studies for NTS-Asia, June 2010.

"Citizenship for Bihari Refugees". BBC News, 19 May 2008. Available at <http://news.bbc.co.uk/2/hi/south_asia/7407757.stm>.

Dangkrueng, Supatatt. "1,143 Villagers Made Stateless". *Chiangmai Mail*, 2002.

Davies, Sarah. *Legitimising Rejection: International Refugee Law in Southeast Asia*. Leiden, Boston: Martinus Nijhoff, 2008.

Eldridge, Philip John. *The Politics of Human Rights in Southeast Asia*. Abingdon, Oxon: Routledge, 2002.

Hedman, Eva-Lotta. "Refuge, Governmentality and Citizenship: Capturing 'Illegal Migrants' in Malaysia and Thailand". *Government and Opposition* 43, no. 2 (2008).

Human Rights Watch. "Perilous Plight: Burma's Rohingyas Take to the Seas", May 2009. Available at <http://www.hrw.org/sites/default/files/reports/burma0509_brochure_web.pdf>.

International Observatory on the Stateless. "South Asia — Nepal", 2008. Available at <http://www.nationalityforall.org/nepal>.

Keenapan, Nattha. "The Stateless Classroom". *Bangkok Post*, 23 June 2009.

Khin Maung Lay. "Burma Fuels the Rohingya Tragedy". *Far Eastern Economic Review*, 6 March 2009. Available at <http://www.feer.com/essays/2009/march/burma-fuels-the-rohingya-tragedy>.

Lewa, Chris. "Asia's New Boat People". *Forced Migration Review*, vol. 30 (April 2008): 40–42.

————. "North Arakan: An Open Prison for the Rohingya in Burma". *Forced Migration Review*, vol. 32 (2009).

Lewa, Chris and Amal de Chickera. "Trapped in a Cycle of Flight: Stateless Rohingya in Malaysia". A Report for the Equal Rights Trust. Available at <http://www.equalrightstrust.org/ertdocumentbank/ERTMalaysiaReportFinal. pdf>.

Lynch, Maureen and Melanie Teff. "Childhood Statelessness". *Forced Migration Review* 32 (2009).

McCartan, Brian. "Fallen Pawns in US's Strategic Game". *Asia Times*, 8 January 2010.

McKinsey, Kitty. "Vietnam Sets the Pace for Asia with New Law to Prevent Statelessness". UNHCR News Stories, 1 July 2009. Available at <http://www. unhcr.org/4a4b809d9.html>.

Muntarbhorn, Vitit. "Human Rights: Burma's Rohingyas in Flight and the Solutions to Their Plight". *Bangkok Post*, 11 March 2009.

Mydans, Seth. "A Growing Source of Fear for Migrants in Malaysia". *New York Times*, 10 December 2007.

Paul, Ruma. "Bangladesh Says Myanmar to Take Back 9,000 Refugees". Reuters India, 29 December 2009. Available at <http://in.reuters.com/article/southAsiaNews/ idINIndia-45038920091229>.

"Perilous Plight: Burma's Rohingyas Take to the Seas". Human Rights Watch, May 2009.

Perks, Katherine and Jarlath Clifford. "The Legal Limbo of Detention". *Forced Migration Review* 32 (2009).

Physicians for Human Rights. *No Status: Migration, Trafficking & Exploitation of Women in Thailand*. Boston, MA: Physicians for Human Rights, 2004. Available at <https://s3.amazonaws.com/PHR_Reports/thailand-women-trafficking-2004.pdf>.

Pichai, Usa. "Thai Citizenship to Grant Stateless Near Burma Border". Mizzima, 25 August 2009. Available at <http://www.mizzima.com/news/regional/2671-thai-citizenship-to-grant-stateless-near-burma-border-.html>.

Plan International. "Count Every Child". Report by Plan International, 2009.

Rahman, Waliur. "Vote for 'Stranded Pakistanis'". BBC News, 6 May 2003. Available at <http://news.bbc.co.uk/2/hi/south_asia/3003949.stm>.

Refugees International. "Citizens of Nowhere: The Stateless Biharis of Bangladesh". Washington, D.C.: Refugees International, 2006.

Roughneen, Simon. "One Step Forward, Two Steps Back". International Relations and Security Network, 29 October 2009. Available at <http://www.isn.ethz. ch/isn/Current-Affairs/Security-Watch/Detail/?lng=en&id=108891>.

Sadiq, K. *Paper Citizens: How Illegal Immigrants Acquire Citizenship in Developing Countries*. US: Oxford University Press, 2008.

SAFHR. "Bangladesh State and the Refugee Phenomenon". South Asia Forum for Human Rights. Available at <http://www.safhr.org/refugee_watch18_4.htm>.

Steinberg, David. *Burma/Myanmar: What Everyone Needs to Know*. New York: Oxford University Press, 2010.

"Thailand Discloses Official Policy to Deport Rohingya Refugees". Mizzima, 5 February 2009. Available at <http://www.mizzima.com/news/regional/1657-thailand-discloses-official-policy-to-deport-rohingya-refugees.html>.

Thawdar. "No Country to Call Their Own". *The Irrawaddy*, vol. 17, no. 5 (August 2009).

UN High Commissioner for Refugees. *The World's Stateless People*. Questions & Answers, September 2007. UNHCR / MRPI / Q&A A•4 / ENG 1. Available at <http://www.unhcr.org/refworld/docid/47a707900.html>.

UNDP. *Human Development Report 2009*. United Nations Development Programme, October 2009. Available at <http://hdr.undp.org/en/reports/global/hdr2009/>.

UNHCR. "Global Appeal". Geneva: UNHCR, 2010/2011. Available at <http://www.unhcr.org/ga10/index.html>.

———. *2008 Global Trends: Refugees, Asylum-seekers, Returnees, Internally Displaced and Stateless Persons*. Geneva: UNHCR, 16 June 2009. Available at <http://www.unhcr.org/4a375c426.html>.

UNIFEM. "Southeast Asia Regional Overview", 2010. Available: <http://cedaw-seasia.org/regional_overview.html>.

US State Department. *Trafficking in Persons Report*. Washington, D.C., 2009. Available at <http://www.state.gov/g/tip/rls/tiprpt/2009/>.

Vital Voices Global Partnership. *Statelessness and Vulnerable to Human Trafficking in Thailand*, June 2007. Available at <http://www.humantrafficking.org/uploads/publications/Vital_Voices_Stateless_and_Vulnerable_to_Human_Trafficking_in_Thailand.pdf>.

Weissbrodt, David and Clay Collins. "The Human Rights of Stateless Persons". *Human Rights Quarterly* 28 (2006).

Weng, Lawi. "Bangladesh, Burma Agree on Repatriation of Some Rohingya". *The Irrawaddy*, 30 December 2009. Available at <http://www.irrawaddy.org/article.php?art_id=17511>.

Zhou, A. and Thomson E. "The Development of Biofuels in Asia". *Applied Energy* 86 (2009): 11–20.

8

ENERGY

Mely Caballero-Anthony, Kevin Punzalan and Koh Swee Lean Collin

As East Asia rapidly develops, greater demands are being placed on governments to efficiently supply energy to sustain economic growth. Simultaneously, public awareness of environmental issues has placed new imperatives on energy planning. To meet these challenges, the concept of sustainable development must be incorporated into energy security strategies in order to balance the three priorities of energy security, economic growth and environmental protection. Alternative energy forms a cornerstone of such a strategy. From a brief examination of the contemporary developments in alternative energy sources in East Asia, this chapter shows that the use of "nuclear renaissance" for describing the energy future of the region is still premature, given that progress in this field has not been uniform and has largely stagnated. Instead, renewable energy developments show better progress and hold greater promise for East Asia. Instead of a "nuclear renaissance", a "renewables renaissance" may be taking hold in the region.

LURKING UNCERTAINTIES

Continuing debates on energy security have been affected by two important global developments. First, the December 2009 Copenhagen Summit failed to reach a global consensus on a concrete plan to curb carbon emissions. As such, socioeconomically driven national self interests have led many states to focus on national-level carbon emissions reduction and energy efficiency strategies.

Second, as the world economy has begun to recover, it may lead to increasing energy demand. Since this increase follows patterns of population growth and development in Asia, many energy economists point to the long-term upward trend in energy prices. Michael Quah from Singapore's Energy Studies Institute has forecast that rising energy prices will continue despite erratic hydrocarbon prices and an uneven economic recovery.[1]

East Asia at the "3Es" Crossroads

For rapidly-growing East Asia in particular, given the increasing energy demand and continued price volatility of fossil fuels, continual reliance on just hydrocarbons is no longer sustainable for economic development. Moreover, the need to mitigate climate change means that energy has to be harnessed in an environmentally sustainable manner. These interrelated dynamics constitute an energy-economic-environment (also known as the "3Es") nexus which can only be fruitfully resolved through sustainable development, in which energy diversification could play a pivotal role in satisfying rising demands, circumvent supply volatility and mitigate climate change through the employment of cleaner, alternative energy sources.

Setting the Scene

Nuclear energy carries considerable appeal in East Asia. However, whether the much touted "nuclear renaissance" has taken place in the region remains debatable. Problems regarding waste disposal and nuclear proliferation among a range of nuclear concerns continue to be salient. This thus points to an indispensable need to explore possible alternatives. To date, gradual economic recovery has spurred revival of interest in renewable energy (RE) sources.

To explore how far either technology has progressed in terms of acceptance and implementation in East Asia, a comparison between developments in nuclear energy and progress in implementing RE projects will be outlined.

NUCLEAR RENAISSANCE IN EAST ASIA?

Since the late 1990s to early 2000s, it has been widely claimed by some scholars and industrial leaders that East Asia is on the throes of experiencing a "nuclear renaissance". With the race to develop alternative energy now in momentum, prospects for nuclear energy appear bright, as Mr Kenji Uenishi, President of GE Energy Asia Pacific, remarked in mid-February 2010 about the "massive potential for nuclear energy in this region".

According to the World Nuclear Association (WNA), "nuclear renaissance" implies a revival of the nuclear power industry that has been lying dormant or in decline for some time.[2] Various factors are thought to drive this "nuclear renaissance", such as increasing energy demand, climate change, economic considerations and the security of supply. However, a point to note is that, according to WNA, "no revival of nuclear power is possible without the acceptance of communities living next to facilities and the public at large, as well as the politicians they elect".[3] The problem of public acceptance has appeared to be the stumbling block for "nuclear renaissance" in some East Asian nuclear energy aspirants.

Following the east Japan earthquake and tsunami on 11 March 2011, the Fukushima I Nuclear Power Plant experienced a series of equipment failures, nuclear meltdowns and release of radioactive materials, which has led to a debate over the use of nuclear power in the region. The most important outcome of the debate to date is a call "to ensure transparency, build confidence, and meet the high expectations of the public".[4] While repairs at the Fukushima I Nuclear Power Plant continue to progress, the IAEA has updated its projections for nuclear power. The IAEA now expects the number of nuclear power plants in the world to increase by 90 by 2030, in their lowest estimate, or by 350 in their highest — a slower projection than before the Fukushima accident. However, the IAEA still projects that most growth will occur in countries which already host nuclear power plants, particularly in Asia. The IAEA predict that both China and India will remain the powerhouses of expansion in this area, unaffected in their 2030 predictions by the Fukushima accident, save for a temporary period immediately after it occurred. Japan, however, did immediately initiate some nuclear power plant shutdowns pending a policy review.[5] As a result of these IAEA policy prescriptions and predictions, it appears that Asia is still on course to significantly increase its reliance on nuclear power with the longer term constraints noted earlier and in the policy prescriptions. To determine whether these constraints will continue to hamper nuclear energy development in East Asia, some countries in the region are selected for deeper analysis.

NORTHEAST ASIA: THE EXISTING CLUB MEMBERS

The bulk of nuclear development activities taking place in East Asia are dominated by existing primary users — China, Japan (pending current policy review), South Korea and Taiwan. However, the share of nuclear energy in each of their overall power generation capacities saw little change. In fact, there is even a slight decline in the nuclear share registered for all except China.

China's phenomenal economic growth means that its steadily increasing power consumption needs would soon outpace its energy supplies, which are mostly made up of fossil fuels. To ensure energy security whilst addressing climate change, China has decided to raise the use of non-hydrocarbon energy to 15 per cent of the overall energy mix by 2020. In this effort, nuclear energy is expected to play a crucial role, given the nascent state of development of RE sources. Hence, China appears determined to accelerate its nuclear power development, as indicated by the remarks from Wu Yin, Deputy Director of the Chinese National Energy Administration in February 2010. In all, Beijing envisages the installation of 40 gigawatts (GW) operational and another 18GW under construction by 2020. The Fukushima accident led to a review by China of its current nuclear power plant projects and it has also started to formulate a new China National Plan for Nuclear Safety.[6]

In South Korea, the government is keen to expand domestic nuclear usage, which is already significant. Its nuclear power plants currently supply one third of its electricity. In addition, it is also keen to expand its nuclear horizons abroad, as shown in its recent nuclear deal with India in July 2011.[7] Seoul has devoted national effort into driving its nuclear research and development, viewing the industry as its new-generation growth engine. According to the Korean Ministry of Knowledge Economy, South Korea is reportedly aiming to export up to 80 nuclear reactors by 2030.

Southeast Asia: Aspirations Mostly in the Pipeline

Once believed to be the hotspot for "nuclear renaissance", Southeast Asia has produced fairly mixed results over the past years. Notwithstanding the huge amount of optimism about a "nuclear renaissance" in Southeast Asia, nuclear planning has effectively stalled in the regional nuclear aspirant countries, with the exception of Vietnam. So far, the country has planned to increase the share of nuclear power in its total electricity generation capacity to 11 per cent by 2025. In November 2009, Hanoi signed a deal with Russia for the construction of its first 2GW NPP, due to come on line in 2020.

Jakarta remains undecided on nuclear power, and lacks concrete measures for implementing a nuclear programme, as indicated in the exclusion of nuclear power in its Power Distribution General Plan 2009–18, which in turn is based on the National Power Master Plan 2008–25. However, the National Atomic Energy Agency has planned to connect the first NPP to the Java-Bali grid by 2016. Non-governmental organizations such as the World Wide Fund and even Muslim clerics have opposed the plan due to concerns about geologic stability, waste disposal, as well as the possible need for the state to subsidize its operation. As a result, the Yudhoyono Administration had indefinitely postponed the bidding for the construction of its first NPP despite having gained endorsement from the International Atomic Energy Agency to proceed. After the Fukushima accident, Jakarta's government-owned Antara news agency reported that the NPP plan is delayed even though it had previously gained public acceptability.[8]

In the Philippines, the reactivation of the Bataan NPP (BNPP) has been stalled by public debate over a range of issues since 1986. A broad spectrum of actors, including geologists such as Kevin Rodolfo of the University of Illinois-Chicago, civil society organizations such as the Freedom from Debt Coalition, and the officials of the Philippine Catholic Church have expressed concerns about the geologic safety of BNPP as well as the potential debt burden that would be incurred by its rehabilitation cost, estimated by the Korea Electric Power Corporation in January 2010 to be US$1 billion. However, in light of the ongoing opposition, increased by the recent Fukushima accident, the Bataan plant was opened up as a tourist and education facility in 2011.[9]

Philippine Congressman Mark Cojuangco, a strong proponent of nuclear power, also proposed that the local government of Pangasinan province bid for the purchase of two 1GW reactors, costing US$5 billion a piece, from the Korean Peninsula Energy Development Organization. He warned of a serious power shortfall, as supply shortages have already occurred in parts of the Visayas and Mindanao regions. The El Niño phenomenon has been blamed by analysts, cited in reports by Remo and Alcuin in February 2010, for the declining water levels in several major dams, reducing hydroelectric generation capacity.[10]

Previously believed to be the next rising nuclear aspirant in Southeast Asia, Thailand has also seen its nuclear plan bogged down by public opposition. While it still harbours long-term plans for at least two NPPs, Bangkok has lately altered its strategy to emphasize dissemination of nuclear knowledge in an attempt to "sweeten" public perceptions. In 2010, Thailand's National Energy Policy Council commissioned a feasibility study for a nuclear power plant and in its Power Development Plan 2010–30 there is 5,000MW envisaged, with 1,000MW starting in the 2020s. It also identified two sites, subject to cabinet approval, in Ubon Ratchathani, 200 km North of Bangkok.[11]

As far as Malaysia and Singapore are concerned, nuclear power remains deliberated in policy statements but no concrete plans exist yet. The Malaysian Minister of Energy, Green Technology and Water, Datuk Peter Chin was reported to have said during an interview with the Oxford Business Group in late January 2010 that Malaysia's implementation of nuclear energy is inevitable. A proposal by the Singapore Government to embark upon a nuclear power feasibility study could be seen as the clearest indication that the country is now seriously considering its use of small and medium-sized reactors (SMRs) but due to siting issues, cooperation with Malaysia is likely, according to Steve Kidd of Nuclear Engineering International.[12]

From an examination of East Asia, it is premature to conclude that a "nuclear renaissance" is occurring, as nuclear expansion has been taking place in countries that already utilize nuclear power. With the exception of Vietnam, virtually all the rest of the nuclear aspirants in Southeast Asia have largely seen their nuclear developments progress no further beyond rhetoric or feasibility studies due to domestic opposition based on cost and environmental safety.

RENEWABLE ENERGY DEVELOPMENTS IN EAST ASIA: A REGIONAL OVERVIEW

Since a nuclear renaissance in the region remains debatable, it is pertinent to examine the growth of other energy sectors. This section outlines some of the renewable energy developments in East Asia to date.

Hydropower

As one of the most abundant renewable energy resources in East Asia, hydropower has long been in use by several countries. For some countries, such as China and Vietnam, hydropower is not considered an alternative energy but a conventional power source. Indeed, China is a substantial hydropower user, with its major Three Gorges Project taking centre-stage in national hydropower efforts.[13] It has large quantities of rivers, more than 50,000 of which cover a basin area over 100 km, and 3,886 of which have hydropower potential over 10MW. Research and invesetigation on hydro resources have been carried out for about sixty years in China, and plans accelerated rapidly under the People's Republic of China. Southwest China has the most hydropower resources in the four provinces of Sichuan, Yunnan, Tibet, and Guizhou.[14] In all, 26 generators that make up the initial plan of this project were already in place, with current plans to increase that to 32 generators to provide a total capacity of 22.4GW.

Vietnam is another country where hydropower is tipped for an increased share of the national power capacity. Like Thailand, Hanoi also faces environmental resistance to large-scale hydropower projects and has turned to small-scale ones that could contribute to rural electrification. One notable example has been a new programme to build 37 small-scale hydropower plants in the Northern provinces bordering China.

Hydropower projects are among the key renewable energy initiatives in Malaysia. The state government of Sarawak has announced plans to build up to 6,200MW of additional installed power capacity, with hydropower making up approximately 80 per cent by 2020 under the Sarawak Corridor of Renewable Energy with at least five more hydropower plants, according to state public utilities minister Awang Tengah.[15] The key challenge to confront Malaysia will be the implementation of such large-scale projects in an environmentally sustainable way.

Taiwan also has huge hydropower potential which has been under-used. Nonetheless, several of Taiwan's new and ongoing hydropower plants are expected to be operational in the next few years, with a potential for con-stituting up to 3.5 per cent of total generating capacity. Indeed, after fifteen years preparation and construction, the Bihai Hydropower Plant in eastern Taiwan's Hualien County is to open providing 61,200KW of electricity.[16]

The Philippines envisages an increase in hydropower capacity from 3.2 to almost 4GW by 2014 through the development of all viable small and mini-hydro plants. Philippine National Oil Company Renewables has recently entered into a strategic alliance with the Canada-based Constellation Energy Corp (CEC) to develop renewable energy in the Philippines illustrating the interaction between local and international actors.[17]

Indonesia has approximately 75GW of hydropower potential and there are over 100 hydro sources of varying sizes identified by the end of 2010 but less than 8 per cent of capacity is used.[18] While the development of mini- or micro-hydropower projects is encouraged by the government through various incentives such as guaranteed purchase of electricity for projects generating up to 4MW of electricity, there remain bureaucratic and land ownership issues which stymie the development of this sector,[19] ostensibly geared towards rural, community-level electrification.

However, hydropower has relatively limited potential in other East Asian countries such as Japan, and virtually no such potential in Singapore. Hydropower project has a limited scope in South Korea too, where major effort has been devoted towards solely expanding existing works such as the 79.6MW Cheongpyeong hydroelectric project.[20]

Wind Power

A previously unharnessed renewable energy source, wind power is now in vogue in East Asia. China appears determined to become the world leader in this field. It is expanding its offshore wind power to 5GW by 2015 and 30GW by 2020, according to the Chinese Renewable Energy Industries Association (CREIA).[21] Furthermore, the China National Offshore Oil Corporation has announced plans to construct the world's largest offshore wind farm outside Shandong Province in a decade's time. In February 2010, Beijing issued regulations for the development of offshore wind power projects to mitigate possible environmental consequences.

High costs of investment might also potentially deter some East Asian countries, though aid programmes may alleviate costs. For example, Vietnam in early February 2010 announced it would utilize official development aid provided by the Danish Government to fund a wind power project in the Ninh Thuan province. Hanoi is intent on developing its considerable wind energy potential (some 100GW waiting to be tapped) as indicated by the National Renewable Energy Centre's recent move to devise incentives for wind power development projects.

A wind resource analysis and mapping exercise by the U.S. National Renewable Energy Laboratory (US-NREL) in 2000 estimated that the Philippines has potentially 70,000MW.[22] The first large wind farm in the country and in Southeast Asia was constructed in 2005 in Ilocos Norte province, generating over 24.75MW of power at a cost of US$44 million. In September last year, a Filipino corporation, Trans-Asia Oil and Energy Development Corporation, announced plans to invest at least US$1 billion for a 400MW portfolio of wind power projects.

Since wind power requires large areas to be efficiently harnessed, massive construction may be ruled out for smaller countries in East Asia. Nonetheless, Singapore does not foreclose the possibility of utilizing "micro-turbines" installed on top of buildings, despite limited generation capacity.

Solar Power

Solar power is another increasingly popular form of renewable energy. Like wind power, solar power has also become a focal point of industrial competition among some East Asian countries. In December 2009, Taiwan unveiled what was dubbed Asia's largest solar power plant, probably a precursor to major efforts by Taipei to raise the share of solar power in its national mix.

China appears to be hot on Taiwan's heels in solar power developments, with a project to complete a 30MW to 2GW solar power plant in Ordos City, Inner Mongolia, by 2019.[23] China is also developing the use of solar thermal power, a technology that concentrates sunlight at water to generate steam for turbines. However, the ability of China to effectively harness this technology has been cast in doubt due to its geographic constraints.

In Southeast Asia, Malaysia too is keen to develop its solar power industry. In late January 2010, the Minister for International Trade and Industry Datuk Seri Mustapa Mohamed stated the country's intention to develop "solar valleys" to enable small- and medium-sized enterprises especially to support the solar industry. So far, Malaysia has attracted major solar energy industrial players such as First Solar from the U.S. and Q-Cells from Germany to compete in its solar energy industry. Kuala Lumpur was reportedly interested in taking the lead in becoming the solar hub in Southeast Asia.

Thailand too has stated its intention to become a solar power innovator, developing a plan to build one of the world's largest solar farms, capable of generating over 55MW, at Lop Buri by November 2011.[24]

The Philippines also has a nascent solar photovoltaic (PV) panel fabrication industry. SunPower and Solaria, two major PV manufacturers based in the U.S., have established local manufacturing sites and research and development centres to improve PV efficiency and to improve manufacturing processes. The companies already export PV panels to the United States (U.S.).

Solar power projects are decidedly of smaller scale in countries such as Indonesia, which is planning to spend US$84 million on rural solar power projects, including a programme to supply solar power panels to 192,000 rural households.

It is interesting to note that despite its space constraints, solar power constitutes the primary renewable energy programme for Singapore, which envisages the installation of 50,000 square metres of solar thermal systems by 2012.

Strangely, despite its vast solar power potential, in Vietnam there has not yet been any significant programmes to develop the industry both nationally and at the rural and community-levels.

Geothermal Power

In this area, Indonesia and the Philippines are spearheading efforts. Manila in particular has an ambition of becoming a leading producer of geothermal energy as part of its strategy of doubling the amount of power generated from renewable sources from over 4.5 to 9GW, with a target of installing an additional 1.2GW to the existing 1.93GW by 2013. At present, it is the second largest producer of geothermal power in the world,[25] after the U.S. While geothermal power accounted for an estimated 13 per cent of its power generating capacity, the Philippines has experienced a series of power shortages that have been attributed to rapidly growing energy demand as well as reduced hydroelectric generation capacity due to the El Niño phenomenon. A programme of maintenance and servicing for several large fossil fuel power plants, in preparation for the country's May 2010 national elections, has also reduced the total generation capacity of the country.

In December 2009, the Philippine Department of Energy announced its plans to approve nineteen geothermal exploration and development projects. Currently the department of energy has approved 984MW of geothermal projects for the Visayas and 138.48MW of geothermal proects for Mindanao.[26] Worth about US$2.5 billion in all, these projects are envisaged to produce about 620MW additional capacity for the country.

Indonesia is the fourth largest geothermal energy producer in the world, and possesses up to 28GW generating capacity, which is untapped still. However, major geothermal projects conceived back in the 1990s were scrapped during the Asian Financial Crisis in 1997–98.

Geothermal power development originally saw hopes of revival in recent times, but latest news indicated that Jakarta had downsized its geothermal power projects by 18 per cent — trimming from an envisioned 4,733MW to 3,900MW capacity by 2025. Indeed, while it is often cited that Indonesia has great geothermal potential, much of the reserves are in Sumatra, which has significant geographic difficulties and financial costs.[27]

Other Forms of Renewables

Compared to hydropower, wind and solar power especially, other forms of renewable energy sources have received less attention. More often than not, this is attributed to cost and resource availability. Biomass is a prime example in this respect. In the case of Thailand, the two largest biomass resources are bagasse, a byproduct of sugar cane and rice husks, have been stifled by too many rice husk power plants in the same area, which are mostly located in central and northern Thailand.[28]

For Vietnam, biomass utilization is largely hampered by high initial investment costs involved, as well as because of a lack of a policy framework. In contrast, Singapore signed a deal in February 2010 with Japanese trading giant Marubeni Corp. to build one of the world's largest biomass and clean coal co-generation plants for US$220 million.[29] According to a Marubeni official, the plant, which is to be partly fuelled by woodchips and palm kernel shells imported from neighbouring countries, would be the largest of its kind in Southeast Asia.

While biofuels production has encountered barriers such as technological bottlenecks and food security concerns, second generation biofuels (namely cellulosic fuel ethanol) has developed apace. The second generation biofuels industry holds great promise in China in particular. Malaysia has also been developing the use of biomass waste for power generation, according to its Minister of Plantation Industries and Commodities Bernard Dompok in early February 2010.

Manila has also tapped biomass power to satisfy its energy needs.[30] It was reported in January 2010 that a huge programme, envisaging twenty-four biomass power projects, is to be implemented in the Philippines within the next decade. A UK-based company, Global Green Power PLC Corp., is investing US$120 million to construct three 15MW biomass power plants in the islands of Luzon, Panay and Negros.

A previously untapped resource is tidal or ocean power, which utilizes kinetic energy of marine wave movement to power turbines (in contrast, conventional hydropower relies on the potential energy of water stored in a reservoir). While tidal energy technology harnesses an unlimited resource, its deployment has been limited by high costs for initial capital investment. Nonetheless, cost issues have not deterred some countries like South Korea from attempting to utilize it. Seoul unveiled its first tidal power plant in Jindo, on the country's south-western coast. According to the Korean Ministry of Land, Transport and Maritime Affairs, this US$9.9 million plant would provide a 90MW generating capacity by 2013, sufficient for about 46,000 households. Even more ambitiously, South Korea is tipped to build what is acclaimed to be the world's largest tidal power plant in Incheon Bay on its west coast, starting this year and due to be completed in 2017. It has run into opposition however, as local civic groups have been campaigning against the massive project claiming that it could damage the marine ecosystem of the area.

"Renewables Renaissance" in East Asia?

Alternative energy has indeed emerged as one of the cornerstones of East Asian strategy towards sustainable development, and serves as a primary solution to the problem of "3Es". From the survey of alternative energy developments, split along two prongs of analysis — nuclear and renewable energy sources — one can conclude the following:

First, saying that a "nuclear renaissance is occurring in Asia" may be exaggerated, due to the lack of uniformity in nuclear development across the region. More progress has been met in Northeast Asia, though countries in that sub-region are merely expanding their already substantial nuclear energy industry with the exception of Japan that remains in the midst of a policy review following the Fukushima accident.

Southeast Asia, a focal point of the "nuclear renaissance" debate, has had limited progress. With the exception of Vietnam, on the whole Southeast Asia's nuclear energy future remains clouded in uncertainty, due to the prevailing domestic political wrangling over the environment, costs and safety grounds, as well as lack of concrete policy blueprints that set out clear directions for nuclear power development in the remaining Southeast Asian nuclear aspirants. As such, any generalization of progress in nuclear power advancement in the region is untenable.

Second, it could be argued that renewable energy prospects appear to be promising, given the magnitude of investments for this sector. This might not come as a surprise, as most, if not all, RE sources are considered less risky, environmentally and politically, than nuclear power. The key mitigating factors remain technological and financial challenges. Nonetheless, it would seem that East Asian countries are determined to overcome these barriers. As such, a "renewables renaissance" appears to be more applicable to East Asia.

That being said, however, overcoming technical and financial hurdles do not guarantee the success or mainstreaming of RE technologies. Well-conceived policy frameworks are essential for integrating RE technologies in a country's energy security strategy. Policy-makers must optimize existing technologies at their disposal to the most suitable applications.

Going further, the next section will examine policy frameworks adopted by five selected East Asian countries in the field of alternative energy developments. By doing so, the section hopes to examine how policy-makers intend to harness the technologies and resources at their disposal in the context of a debated "nuclear renaissance" in East Asia.

A SURVEY OF RENEWABLE ENERGY POLICIES
IN EAST ASIA

This section conducts a brief survey of renewable energy policy frameworks among five selected East Asian countries — China, Indonesia, the Philippines, Thailand and Vietnam. There appears to be agreement among East Asian countries on the importance of alternative energy as a solution in addressing the energy-economics-environment nexus. National efforts have been undertaken in recent times to tap these underutilized resources, in part due to the possible recognition that other alternative sources, nuclear power especially, are politically and economically riskier. While earlier energy policies in these five nations were plagued by technical and financial barriers, concerted efforts have been undertaken by these governments to overcome them. However, the effectiveness of these policy revisions remains to be seen. Moreover, notwithstanding better policy frameworks, certain renewable energy technologies might be better suited to some countries than others, thus careful national planning is necessary to evaluate the feasibility of every available renewable energy source, prior to exploitation.

In the previous section, progress in the development of alternative energy sources in East Asia was outlined. It was argued that a "nuclear renaissance" does not best describe the state of energy development in the region, given the many socio-political and economic hurdles encountered by some of the nuclear aspirants. In conclusion, a "renewables renaissance" was deemed more fitting for energy development in East Asia, as is evident from the significant progress observed to date in renewable energy programmes in the region.

Despite the great renewable energy potential East Asia possesses, sustainable growth of the sector requires sustainable policy frameworks to ensure that these resources are developed according to the needs and limitations of national contexts. Different RE technologies have varying levels of efficiency, cost, and "density" — a concept highlighted by Michael Quah from Singapore's Energy Studies Institute. Some RE sources require larger material inputs (land, space, etc.) in order to match comparable hydrocarbon sources to satisfy energy demands. National energy policies should therefore recognize the inherent limitations of certain renewable energy sources, and deploy these technologies in the most suitable and cost-effective applications.

As such, this section shall examine the policies adopted by select nations in East Asia, to see how policy-makers are attempting to harness the renewable energy technologies and resources at their disposal. By doing so, the section hopes to identify the direction each country is taking to address its energy security goals.

Renewable Energy Policy Frameworks in East Asia

Five East Asian countries — China, Indonesia, The Philippines, Thailand and Vietnam — are selected as case studies. Their selection is based on the following criteria: (1) each of these countries has outstanding electrical power needs (see Table 8.1); (2) they all have plans to either expand or consider the use of nuclear energy; and lastly (3) they each possess a vast RE potential (see Table 8.2).

China

Poised to experience a steady increase in electricity demands (from 2009, a total of 3,588 terawatt hour (TWh) to a projected 5067TWh by 2014), China has devoted tremendous efforts to ensure energy security, while simultaneously attempting to reduce carbon emissions. Alternative energy sources are sought, yet at present China's power generation is based mainly on coal (77 per cent), with the remainder mostly fulfilled by nuclear and hydropower (which China has relied upon as a traditional and important source of energy).

Table 8.1
Electricity Access in Selected East Asian Countries in 2008

Country	Electrification Rate (%)			Population Without Electricity (millions)
	Total	Urban	Rural	
China	99.4	100	99	8
Indonesia	64.5	94	32	81.1
The Philippines	86	97	65	12.5
Thailand	99.3	100	99	0.4
Vietnam	89	99.6	85	9.5

Source: Data compiled from International Energy Agency, *World Energy Outlook 2009 New Electricity Access Database*, available at <http://www.worldenergyoutlook.org/database_electricity/electricity_access_database.htm>.

Table 8.2
Renewable Energy Potential in Selected East Asian Countries

Country	Wind	Solar	Hydropower	Biomass	Geo-thermal	Marine
			Renewable Energy			
China[a]	1,000GW	3–7.5kWh per square-metre per day	694GW (theoretically exploitable); 542GW (technically exploitable); 402GW (economically exploitable)	500 million tce; some estimates put it at 1 billion tce	6GW	110GW (theoretical tidal reserve); 21.8GW (developable)
Indonesia[b]	10GW	4.8kWh per square-metre per day	75.67GW (plus 0.5GW small-hydro)	49.81GW	13.44GW	0.01–0.035GW per km coastline
The Philippines[c]	76.6GW	5–5.1kWh per square-metre per day	13.097GW (plus 1.784GW small-hydro)	277 MMBFOE	2.6GW	170GW
Thailand[d]	1.6GW	4.7–5.1kWh per square-metre per day	0.7GW (small hydro only)	3.3GW	0.01–0.02GW	Under evaluation

Table 8.2 (Cont"d)

Country	Renewable Energy					
	Wind	Solar	Hydropower	Biomass	Geo-thermal	Marine
Vietnam[e]	513GW (theoretical); 120.5GW (economically exploitable)	2.4–5.9kWh per square-metre per day	18–20GW (large) and 2–4GW (small hydro)	1–1.6GW	1.4GW	Under evaluation

Legend: GW = gigawatt; kWh = kilowatt hour; MMBFOE = million barrels of fuel oil equivalent; tce = ton of coal equivalent

Sources: [a] Data for China compiled from *Recommendations for Improving the Effectiveness of Renewable Energy Policies in China*, Renewable Energy Policy Network for the 21st Century, October 2009 and *Medium and Long-Term Development Plan for Renewable Energy in China*, National Development and Reform Commission, People's Republic of China, September 2007.

[b] Data for Indonesia compiled from *Indonesia's Renewable Energy Potential*, Ministry of Energy and Mineral Resources, Republic of Indonesia, 25 August 2008; and Public State Electricity Corporation, Republic of Indonesia, "Renewable Energy Development Program in Indonesia", presented at the Global Workshop on Grid-Connected Renewable Energy, Washington, D.C., United States of America, 28 August–5 September 2009.

[c] Data for the Philippines compiled from the *DOE Portal*, Department of Energy, Republic of the Philippines, available at <http://www.doe.gov.ph/ER/Renenergy.htm> (accessed 5 March 2010); and from the "Philippine Energy Plan: 2009–2030", DOE Portal, available at <http://www.doe.gov.ph/PEP/PEP%202009-2030.pdf> (retrieved 11 March 2010).

[d] Data for Thailand compiled from Thailand Board of Investment, *Thailand's Energy Policy and Development Plan*, National Energy Policy Council (approved 6 and 21 November 2006); and Dr Pallapa Ruangrong, Energy Regulatory Commission of Thailand, "Thailand's Approach to Promoting Clean Energy in the Electricity Sector", presented at the Forum on Clean Energy, Good Governance and Regulation, Singapore, 16–18 March 2008.

[e] Data for Vietnam compiled from Nhan T. Nguyen and Minh Ha-Duong, "Economic potential of renewable energy in Vietnam's power sector", *Energy Policy* 37 (2009): 1601–13.

According to a three-step strategic renewable energy development road-map outlined by China's National Development and Reform Commission, by 2050 over a third of China's total primary energy consumption will be satisfied by renewable energy sources. At present however, renewable energy sources have yet to make a meaningful contribution to the country's overall energy mix, although Beijing has been taking steps to tap into its vast solar and wind resources.

The Renewable Energy Law (REL) was introduced in 2005, and since then, the use of RE sources has increased steadily, from 7 per cent of the total power generation capacity in 2005 to 9 per cent by 2008. However, policy inconsistencies, weak fiscal incentive systems and inadequate renewable energy investments were some of the problems identified in the REL as preventing renewable energy sources from being able to compete with fossil fuels. In addition, Zhou and Thomson have pointed out that the biofuels industry in China faces problems with regard to domestic sources of feedstocks. According to a study by Zhou and Thomson, published in 2009, traditional sources such as inedible corn are running low, necessitating the use of edible corn and thus leading to an increase in food prices. To supply biofuels demand, efficient alternatives such as cassava would have to be imported from countries such as Thailand and Vietnam, though this has consequences for food prices for cassava as well.[31]

Some of these problems have been addressed by a major revamp of the REL, passed by China's legislature in December 2009. Under this new amendment, power operators are obliged to purchase all the power produced by non-hydrocarbon energy sources, envisaged under the plan to supply up to 15 per cent of China's total power consumption by 2020. The REL Amendments were designed to address the following systemic policy, technological and fiscal barriers, including the chronic lack of assured interconnection of RE projects to the national grid.

In addition, a Renewable Energy Development Fund will be established to encourage grid interconnection and to support other RE development projects. A study published by McElroy et al. in 2009 suggested that wind power alone could potentially satisfy all of China's power demands by 2030. Recognizing this, China has invested US$2.9 billion to build six 100GW wind farms in Inner Mongolia, and is expected to invest US$4.4 billion in grid infrastructure connecting the farms and the coastal provinces of China. However, Li also points out that progress in the wind energy industry has been hampered by limited indigenous research and development, opaque bidding processes for power purchasing agreements that often underestimate costs and favour domestic wind power companies, the variability of wind power output in certain areas, and the engineering challenges of linking wind farms to areas with high electricity demand given the vast distances and poor grid infrastructure.[32] Thus, wastages may occur unless bidding processes and checks and balances are refined.

Even with these limitations, renewable energy continues to grow at a brisk pace in China. While renewable energy sources are projected to constitute an ever-increasing share of the power generation mix, the technical uncertainties of renewable energy development appear to nudge China towards a two-pronged, hedging strategy, which is, to continue investing in nuclear energy and devoting more effort to renewable energy sources. However, whether the latest renewable energy policy developments could allow China to reduce its dependence on hydrocarbons remain to be seen.

Indonesia

Previously a member of the Organisation of Petroleum Exporting Countries, Indonesia became a net oil importer in 2006. This has necessitated a diversification of its energy mix away from fossil fuels. Also, even though approximately 65 per cent of the population has electricity access, over 80 million rural residents remain unconnected to the national power grid. Fortunately, like China, Indonesia is endowed with a significant, yet untapped, renewable energy potential — primarily geothermal and biomass.

In Indonesia, renewable energy development is regulated by the Presidential Decree No. 5/2006 which states that nuclear and renewable energy sources should comprise 17 per cent of the total power generation mix by 2025. Although Jakarta's energy policy champions energy diversification, barriers against renewable energy development exist, such as inadequate policies, incentives, as well as legal and institutional frameworks. With an aim of improving the renewable energy investment climate, the Energy Law No. 30, passed in July 2007, has met with little success. According to statistics published by the Ministry of Energy and Mineral Resources, renewable energy sources account for merely 3.4 per cent of the total power generation mix. Despite the fact that the prices of cooking fuels are rising, the government has not promoted biomass sources as a primary alternative due to the risk that inefficient production of biomass could increase the country's net carbon emissions, especially from deforestation.

The generally small scale of renewable energy development as compared to hydrocarbon-based energy projects means higher relative transaction costs for renewable energy sources. This deters small-scale investors from opting for renewable energy and also discourages Jakarta from supporting such projects. Halting of the construction of seven geothermal plants in the 1990s during the Asian Financial Crisis demonstrated the aversion investors have towards "high-risk" projects. Also, traditional approaches to stimulate greater renewable energy investments, such as feed-in tariffs and capital subsidies, are deemed ineffective since production costs far exceed the tariffs that could be collected in the biofuels sector for instance. Renewable energy growth in Indonesia will be limited unless serious governmental support and investment are forthcoming for renewable energy development.

Small efforts have been undertaken by Jakarta to encourage renewable energy development. A notable instance has been the introduction of a ministerial decree which stipulates the benchmarking of prices of geothermal-generated electricity sold to Perseroan Terbatas Perusahaan Listrik Negara (PT PLN), the state-owned electricity firm. In September 2009 the Indonesian legislature passed a new electricity law that revoked PLN's monopoly over transmission, distribution and retail operations, thus allowing central and regional governments to issue power permits.

This move facilitates the opening up of the Indonesian electricity market to competition and thus might encourage some of the country's more prosperous, resource-rich provinces to embark on new power projects, including RE sources, for local utilization. In February 2010, Indonesian Finance Minister Sri Mulyani Indrawati remarked that the country was lagging behind other nations in power and renewable energy developments. As such, Jakarta has announced plans to offer fiscal incentives, including tax exemption, to bolster the development of geothermal and biomass sources especially. The country has also encouraged micro-hydro schemes to electrify remote villages, as this form of technology is cleaner and cheaper than using diesel generators.

The Philippines

For the archipelagic Philippines, which is experiencing a power shortage due to a combination of a drought and routine power plant maintenance, renewable energy development could play a pivotal role in raising energy self-sufficiency from 55.5 per cent in 2004 to 58.2 per cent by 2013, according to the Philippine Department of Energy (DOE). Grand plans are envisaged by Manila in the field of RE development, such as doubling hydropower capacity, and the installation of 130–250MW of biomass, solar and tidal capacities by 2013.

The country pioneered the use of renewable energy in the region after the 1973 oil crisis. As it was dependent on 95 per cent of its energy needs on oil, the Marcos administration embarked on an energy diversification programme instituted by the executive branch of government that involved the installation of geothermal, hydroelectric, and nuclear facilities. While the nuclear programme did not come to fruition, geothermal and hydroelectric facilities contributed significantly to national energy capacity, and have successfully reduced dependence on foreign oil. At present, 34 per cent of the country's energy is sourced from renewable energy, according to DOE Assistant Secretary Mario Marasigan. The Philippines also declared its aim of becoming the world's largest geothermal power producer, a leading Southeast Asian wind energy producer and a solar power manufacturing export hub.

In September 2009, the Philippine Government established the National Renewable Energy Board (NREB), composed of representatives from the Department of Energy and other executive departments, as well as representatives from NGOs and the private sector. This act catalyses the implementation of mechanisms and incentives essential for putting the December 2008 Renewable Energy Act (REA) of the Philippine Congress (which mandated income and value-added tax holidays, tax credits, and cash incentives for the RE industry) into motion. The NREB helped develop feed-in tariffs that could make planned RE development projects economically more viable.

In January 2010, the Philippine DOE was reported to have contracted eighty-seven renewable energy projects, and is "working to immediately provide fiscal perks to the investors" according to DOE undersecretary Roy Kyamko. On 1 February 2010 alone, it was reported that DOE had signed around 100 renewable energy contracts, spurring huge optimism that approximately US$9–10 billion of renewable energy investments could be generated in the next decade. This development might also see the doubling of RE-generated power capacity from the current 4,500 to 9,000MW.

Even though the Philippine Government has made substantial progress in exploiting its colossal renewable energy potential, some hurdles need to be overcome in order to increase investment in the renewable energy sector. These include restrictions on foreign ownership of RE projects, and the comparative cost disadvantage that RE-generated electricity has *vis-à-vis* traditional sources due to the existing system of power purchase agreements. In addition, the government will need to take into account various external factors, such as droughts in the case of hydropower, which may limit minimum base-loads for the generation of renewable energy. For the current "RE frenzy" in the Philippines to maintain its momentum, the above-mentioned problems faced by the Philippine RE development process will need to be addressed.

Thailand

The Pros and Cons of Nuclear

While nuclear energy carries certain appeal, it is not without its drawbacks. The following benefits and costs of nuclear energy could be briefly summarized to highlight the contemporary debates over its use worldwide, East Asia in particular.

Advantages of Nuclear Energy: compared to most other alternative energy sources, nuclear power is a proven, arguably mature, technology. It emits minimal carbon emissions compared to the use of hydrocarbons, while the world's existing uranium reserves could, in the view of some analysts, last the world for millions of years in providing relatively clean source of power. Compared to highly-polluting coal as a source of energy, said an Australian opposition politician, nuclear is "the lesser of the two evils". The key point of attraction is that nuclear power contributes greatly to slashing electricity costs, taking France for example, where nuclear power accounts for more than 70 per cent of its national energy.

Disadvantages of Nuclear Energy: while modern nuclear technology is deemed by proponents as considerably safer these days, attendant risks still revolve around the potential hazards of radioactive leakage and environmental contamination. A guarantee against the proliferation of nuclear materials among unstable, sometimes hostile, governments, and by terrorists remains far from assured. In addition, a long-term storage solution for radioactive waste has yet to be devised. Modern nuclear projects are marred by cost overruns and have been the source of public controversies among some countries, taking East Asia for instance. Lastly, some other alternative energy sources are cleaner, and hence more sustainable, compared to nuclear.

In a bid to reduce carbon emissions and its reliance on fossil fuels, the present Abhisit administration has showed its commitment to renewable energy development through the establishment of alternative energy policies as part of its national agenda. The Alternative Energy Development Plan (AEDP) 2008–2022 aims to increase the share of renewable energy sources to 20 per cent of the total power generation mix by 2022. Envisaging "proper and fair incentive", it strives to promote renewable energy development through supporting R&D for all renewable energy types. Detailed planning for demand growth for electricity is managed by the Energy Policy Planning Office.

Community-based renewable energy projects, revolving around the use of biomass, are perceived as an essential component of Thailand's present and future renewable energy developments, and as part of the concerted effort to bolster rural electrification. Renewable energy development in Thailand carries a broader strategic goal, too. Some Thai policy-makers have called for Thailand to develop itself as the export hub, learning centre and successful role model for other countries in the field of renewable energy development, if the country is to stand at the forefront as a leading nation in renewable energy usage.

Various incentives and promotional schemes have been applied under the AEDP; most importantly the provision of pricing subsidies/feed-in tariffs through the Small and Very Small Power Producer (SPP & VSPP) programmes using RE, co-generation and micro-hydropower projects for instance. The Board of Investment offers an extensive package of tax and non-tax incentives in a bid to promote renewable energy development.

Despite having a strategic plan in the form of AEDP for renewable energy development, a lack of collaboration between agencies and companies involved has been identified as delaying the implementation of many renewable energy projects. Widespread renewable energy deployment has also been hampered by their cost competitiveness against other energy types, as well as high initial capital costs and environmental costs, as is the case with expanding oil palm plantations for biofuels. Siriwardhana et al. in a study published in 2009 have also noted that oil palms are vulnerable to climate variations, such as droughts, and require heavy investments in irrigation and fertilizers. The growth of oil palm plantations has resulted in the deforestation of virgin forests to clear land for plantations. Prices of palm oil, widely used as cooking oil in Thailand, have also increased as a result of increasing biofuels demand, thus increasing food prices.[33]

Bangkok appears satisfied with the results of the AEDP, at least for now. According to Mr Krairit Nilkuha, Director-General of the Thai Energy Ministry's Department of Alternative Energy Development and Efficiency in December 2009, the plan achieved better than expected results, by raising the RE mix by 8 per cent in the last two years. At present, greater interest has been shown among Thai investors in solar and wind energy instead.

Given the progress made to date by the Thai Government in promoting renewable energy investments, it appears that nuclear development, subject to a policy review due in 2011, will take much longer to gestate than renewable energy. This is notwithstanding some barriers, which still need to be overcome before the full realization of Thailand's ambitious RE goals.

Vietnam

According to one study published in 2009, the use of renewable energy sources could reduce the use of coal in Vietnam's power generation mix, from 44 per cent to 39 per cent, and at the same time negate the necessity for the installation of 4.4GW fossil fuel capacity, decrease hydrocarbon imports, conserve domestic coal supplies and improve energy self-sufficiency. Even as Vietnam pushes onwards with a nuclear power programme, the country possesses great renewable energy potential, which is beginning to be recognized.

One of the earliest attempts by Vietnam to explore renewable energy sources was the Vietnam Renewable Energy Action Plan (REAP), conceived in 1999. It envisaged hydropower and biomass as the foremost potential RE sources which could bolster rural electrification. REAP provided the basis for further creation of more coherent RE-related policies. Under Decision No. 110/2007.QD-TTg passed in July 2007 by the Vietnamese Government, installed renewable energy-generated electricity is envisaged to total 4,051MW within the 2006–25 timeframe. The Master Plan on Renewable Energy Development in Vietnam up to the year 2015, with an outlook for 2025, was completed at the end of 2008.

However, Vietnam still lacks a broad target-oriented sustainable energy strategy. For instance, as Uddin et al. had identified, there is no timeframe for the expansion of the use of renewable energy sources, especially in areas where grid extension is too costly and where the use for such technologies are economically warranted. Practical limitations to renewable energy development in Vietnam include limited financing due to regulation, as well as inadequate information, analysis and assessment of Vietnam's renewable energy potential. These hurdles would have to be removed in order to allow renewable energy investments to proceed smoothly.[34]

Hydropower, in which Vietnam possesses vast potential, does not appear to be the focus of the country's renewable energy development. Authorities in the central province of Quang Nam had decided to cancel eight hydropower projects, in addition to the five cancelled much earlier. This is due to concerns of the impact caused by construction of hydropower dams on the surrounding ecosystems, which could affect the quality of water supply essential to the livelihood of the residents in the affected zones. The socio-economic consequences of resettling affected communities from the hydropower project zones could be considerable. Nonetheless, Vietnam continues to explore other viable sources, so as to reach the target of 5 per cent for RE sources in the power generation mix by 2020.

There is still potential for the growth of certain renewable energy sources, taking wind power especially, given interest expressed by Hanoi in this aspect. Sadly, even though Vietnam does have considerable wind energy potential, investments have been stymied by the lack of a national policy framework, inadequate infrastructure, very low price of power, as well as costs involved in wind turbines. Nonetheless, Hanoi appears determined to tap wind power. A February 2010 report stated that the Vietnam National Renewable Energy Centre is devising incentives for wind power development projects.

CONCLUSION

This brief survey of renewable energy policy frameworks in the five East Asian countries derives some observations. Before summarizing these observations, it is important to note that the five East Asian nations are chosen along the following lines: (1) projected increase in electricity demand; (2) vast indigenous RE potential; and (3) plans for either expanding or instituting nuclear energy, among all alternative energy sources.

Firstly, there appears to be a widespread, tacit agreement among East Asian countries that alternative energy is the way to go to address the energy-economics-environment nexus. RE potential in the region is underutilized and national efforts have been undertaken in times to tap these abundant and more environmentally friendly sources. Part of the reason for this intensified focus on renewable energy sources in Southeast Asia in particular could be attributed to the possible recognition that other alternative sources, especially nuclear power, are both politically and economically risky.

Secondly, while earlier energy policies in these nations were plagued by technical and financial barriers, a concerted effort has been undertaken by these governments to overcome them. However, the effectiveness of these policy revisions, such as the rationalization of incentive structures and legislative amendments, remains to be seen. Even with better policy frameworks, certain renewable energy technologies are better suited to some countries than others, and policy-makers must identify which technologies should be given priority. Governments must take technical, financial, and environmental limitations into account to ensure that money is not wasted on projects with limited potential. For instance, due to environmental and socio-economic concerns, the huge hydropower potential in countries like Thailand and Vietnam cannot be fully exploited.

A final observation may be made about the "renewables craze" in East Asia. While several countries envision themselves becoming leaders in promoting certain renewable energy sources, careful planning is necessary to evaluate the feasibility of every available renewable energy source, prior to exploitation. It may be one thing to have the "inherent potential" but quite another to effectively tap this potential. Without manpower, technical capabilities, support from the private sector, and effective government support, renewable energy will only remain a "potential" resource.

Notes

[1]   Comments made during a panel presentation by Dr Michael Quah at the Workshop on Nuclear Energy and Human Security, organized by the Centre for Non-Traditional Security Studies, S. Rajaratnam School of International Studies, Singapore, 23 April 2010.

[2]   John Ritch, "The Nuclear Renaissance in a Global Context", in *It's All About People: The Future of Nuclear*, Plenary Session, American Nuclear Society Annual Meeting, Boston, 25 June 2007.

[3]   John Ritch, "Nuclear Energy at a Moment of Truth", Remarks given at the British Nuclear Energy Society: 40th Anniversary Celebration, London, 2 July 2002, available at <http://www.world-nuclear.org/reference/default.aspx?id=664&LangType=2057&terms=communities%20acceptance%20nuclear%20renaissance>.

[4]   IAEA Director General, Yukiya Amano, "Introductory Statement to Board of Governors", Vienna, Austria, 12 September 2011, available at <http://www.iaea.org/newscenter/statements/2011/amsp2011n019.html#fukushima>.

[5]   Ibid.

[6]   World Nuclear Association, *Nuclear Power in China*, 22 September 2011, available at <http://www.world-nuclear.org/info/inf63.html>.

[7]   BBC News, "South Korea and India Sign Nuclear Deal", BBC News Website, 26 July 2011, available at <http://www.bbc.co.uk/news/business-14287086>.

[8]   Joao Peixe, "Indonesia's First Nuclear Power Plant Delayed", *Oil Price.Com*, 18 October 2011, available at <http://oilprice.com/Latest-Energy-News/World-News/Indonesia-s-First-Nuclear-Power-Plant-Delayed.html>.

[9]   Kate McGeown, "Philippines Opens Bataan Nuclear Plant to Tourists", BBC News Online, 24 July 2011, available at <http://www.bbc.co.uk/news/world-asia-pacific-14184234>.

[10] Ibid.

[11] Steve Kidd, "Nuclear in Southeast Asia — Where and When?" *Nuclear Engineering International Magazine*, 12 August 2011, available at <http://www.neimagazine.com/story.asp?sectioncode=147&storyCode=2060380>.

[12] Ibid.

[13] XiaoLin Chang, Xinghong Liu, and Wei Zhou, "Hydropower in China at Present and Its Further Development", *Energy* 35 (2010).

[14]   Hailun Huang and Yan Zheng, "Present Situation and Future Prospect of Hydropower in China", *Renewable and Sustainable Energy Reviews* 13, nos. 6–7 (2008).

[15]   Hydro World, "Malaysia's Sarawak Plans to Boost Hydropower Capacity, Other Power by 2020", Hydroworld.com, June 2011, available at <http://www.hydroworld.com/index/display/article-display/0598999523/articles/hrhrw/hydroindustrynews/newdevelopment/2011/06/malaysia_s-sarawak.html>.

[16]   Aaron Hsu, "Hualien Hydropower Plant Ready to Operate in October", *Taiwan Today*, 12 August 2011, available at <http://taiwantoday.tw/ct.asp?xItem=1739 87&CtNode=453>.

[17]   PNOC, "PNOC and Constellation Energy Form Renewable Energy Alliance", available at <http://www.pnoc.com.ph/news/news.php?id=17>.

[18]   GBG, "Opportunities in Energy: Beyond Fossil Fuels", *Global Business Guide*, 2011, available at <http://www.gbgindonesia.com/en/energy/article/2011/opportunities_in_energy_beyond_fossil_fuels.php>.

[19]   Ibid.

[20]   Eco2data, "Korea Hydro & Nuclear Power Co. (KHNP) Cheonpyeong Hydro Power Plant Unit 4 Project", Eco4data, 2011, available at <http://eco2data.com/project/52192>.

[21]   Xinhua, "China to Boost Offshore Wind Power Generation", *China Daily*, 16 May 2011, available at <http://www.chinadaily.com.cn/china/2011-05/16/content_12520766.htm>.

[22]   RERIC, *Renewable Energy Technologies in Asia: A Regional Research and Dissemination Programme*, 2002, available at <http://www.retsasia.ait.ac.th/booklets/Dissemination%20Booklets-Phase%20II/Full%20book-Ph.pdf>.

[23]   "Update 2-First Solar Sees Contract for China Power Supply", Reuters, 23 February 2010, available at <http://www.reuters.com/article/2010/02/23/firstsolar-idUSN2310311420100223?type=marketsNews>.

[24]   Heather Lackey, "Thailand's Lopburi Solar Project to Power 70,000 Homes", *Southeast Asia Global Solar Technology*, 3 March 2011, available at <http://www.globalsolartechnology.com/solar/index.php?option=com_content&view=articl e&id=7188:thailands-lopburi-solar-project-to-power-70000-homes&catid=8:india-news&Itemid=29>.

[25]   Leonora Walet, "Philippines Targets $2.5 Billion Geothermal Development", *Reuters*, 5 November 2009, available at <http://www.reuters.com/article/2009/11/05/us-philippines-renewable-idUSTRE5A43HC20091105>.

[26]   Donnabelle Gatdula, "Department of Energy Set to Review Geothermal Deals", *Philippine Star*, 2 January 2011, available at <http://www.philstar.com/Article.aspx?articleId=644478&publicationSubCategoryId=66>.

[27]   Peter McCawley, "Indonesian Geothermal Talk is Mostly Hot Air", *The Interpreter*, 17 June 2011, available at <http://www.lowyinterpreter.org/post/2011/06/17/Indonesia-Geothermal-talk-is-mostly-hot-air.aspx>.

28 M. Barz and M.K. Delivand, "Agricultural Residues as Promising Biofuels for Biomass Power Generation in Thailand", *Journal of Sustainable Energy & Environment*, Special Issue, 2011.
29 Cogeneration/CHP, "Japan's Marubeni Wins Cogeneration Contract in Singapore", *Cogeneration & On-Site Power Production magazine*, 27 September 2011, available at <http://www.cospp.com/articles/2011/09/japan-marubeni-wins-cogeneration-contract-in-singapore.html>.
30 Donnabelle Gatdula, "Department of Energy Set to Review Geothermal Deals", *Philippine Star*, 2 January 2011, available at <http://www.philstar.com/Article.aspx?articleId=644478&publicationSubCategoryId=66>.
31 Zhou and Thomson, "The Development of Biofuels in Asia", *Applied Energy* 86 (2009).
32 Michael B. McElroy, Xi Lu, Chris P. Nielsen, and Yuxuan Wang, "Potential for Wind-Generated Electricity in China", *Science* 11 (September 2009).
33 P. Abdul Salam, S. Kumar, and Manjula Siriwardhana, "Report on the Status of Biomass Gasification in Thailand and Cambodia", prepared for Energy Environment Partnership (EEP), Mekong Region, October 2010, available at <http://eepmekong.org/_downloads/Biomass_Gasification_report_final-submitted.pdf>.
34 S.N Uddin, Ros Taplin, and Xiaojiang Yu, "Sustainable Energy Future for Vietnam: Evolution and Implementation of Effective Strategies", *International Journal of Environmental Studies* 66, no. 1 (2009).

References

Amano, Yukiya, IAEA Director General. "Introductory Statement to Board of Governors". Vienna, Austria, 12 September 2011. Available at <http://www.iaea.org/newscenter/statements/2011/amsp2011n019.html#fukushima>.

Barz, M. and M.K. Delivand. "Agricultural Residues as Promising Biofuels for Biomass Power Generation in Thailand". *Journal of Sustainable Energy & Environment*, Special Issue, 2011.

BBC News. "South Korea and India Sign Nuclear Deal". BBC News Website, 26 July 2011. Available at <http://www.bbc.co.uk/news/business-14287086>.

Cogeneration/CHP. "Japan's Marubeni Wins Cogeneration Contract in Singapore". *Cogeneration & On-Site Power Production magazine*, 27 September 2011. Available at <http://www.cospp.com/articles/2011/09/japan-marubeni-wins-cogeneration-contract-in-singapore.html>.

Eco2data. "Korea Hydro & Nuclear Power Co. (KHNP) Cheonpyeong Hydro Power Plant Unit 4 Project". Eco4data, 2011. Available at <http://eco2data.com/project/52192>.

Gatdula, Donnabelle. "Department of Energy Set to Review Geothermal Deals". *Philippine Star*, 2 January 2011. Available at <http://www.philstar.com/Article.aspx?articleId=644478&publicationSubCategoryId=66>.

GBG. "Opportunities in Energy: Beyond Fossil Fuels". *Global Business Guide*, 2011. Available at <http://www.gbgindonesia.com/en/energy/article/2011/opportunities_in_energy_beyond_fossil_fuels.php>.

Hailun Huang and Yan Zheng. "Present Situation and Future Prospect of Hydropower in China". *Renewable and Sustainable Energy Reviews* 13, nos. 6–7 (2008).

Hsu, Aaron. "Hualien Hydropower Plant Ready to Operate in October". *Taiwan Today*, 12 August 2011. Available at <http://taiwantoday.tw/ct.asp?xItem=173987&CtNode=453>.

Hydro World. "Malaysia's Sarawak Plans to Boost Hydropower Capacity, Other Power by 2020". Hydroworld.com, June 2011. Available at <http://www.hydroworld.com/index/display/article-display/0598999523/articles/hrhrw/hydroindustrynews/newdevelopment/2011/06/malaysia_s-sarawak.html>.

Kidd, Steve. "Nuclear in Southeast Asia — Where and When?" *Nuclear Engineering International Magazine*, 12 August 2011. Available at <http://www.neimagazine.com/story.asp?sectioncode=147&storyCode=2060380>.

Lackey, Heather. "Thailand's Lopburi Solar Project to Power 70,000 Homes". *Southeast Asia Global Solar Technology*, 3 March 2011. Available at <http://www.globalsolartechnology.com/solar/index.php?option=com_content&view=article&id=7188:thailands-lopburi-solar-project-to-power-70000-homes&catid=8:india-news&Itemid=29>.

McCawley, Peter. "Indonesian Geothermal Talk is Mostly Hot Air". *The Interpreter*, 17 June 2011. Available at <http://www.lowyinterpreter.org/post/2011/06/17/Indonesia-Geothermal-talk-is-mostly-hot-air.aspx>.

McElroy, Michael B., Xi Lu, Chris P. Nielsen, and Yuxuan Wang. "Potential for Wind-Generated Electricity in China". *Science* 11 (September 2009).

McGeown, Kate. "Philippines Opens Bataan Nuclear Plant to Tourists". BBC News Online, 24 July 2011. Available at <http://www.bbc.co.uk/news/world-asia-pacific-14184234>.

Peixe, Joao. "Indonesia's First Nuclear Power Plant Delayed". *Oil Price.Com*, 18 October 2011. Available at <http://oilprice.com/Latest-Energy-News/World-News/Indonesia-s-First-Nuclear-Power-Plant-Delayed.html>.

PNOC. "PNOC and Constellation Energy Form Renewable Energy Alliance". Available at <http://www.pnoc.com.ph/news/news.php?id=17>.

RERIC. *Renewable Energy Technologies in Asia: A Regional Research and Dissemination Programme*, 2002. Available at <http://www.retsasia.ait.ac.th/booklets/Dissemination%20Booklets-Phase%20II/Full%20book-Ph.pdf>.

Ritch, John. "The Nuclear Renaissance in a Global Context". In Plenary Session, "It's All About People: The Future of Nuclear". American Nuclear Society Annual Meeting, Boston, 25 June 2007.

———. "Nuclear Energy at a Moment of Truth". Remarks given at the British Nuclear Energy Society: 40th Anniversary Celebration. London, 2 July 2002. Available at <http://www.world-nuclear.org/reference/default.aspx?id=664&LangType=2057&terms=communities%20acceptance%20nuclear%20renaissance>.

Salam, P. Abdul, S. Kumar, and Manjula Siriwardhana. "Report on the Status of Biomass Gasification in Thailand and Cambodia". Prepared for Energy Environment Partnership (EEP). Mekong Region, October 2010. Available at <http://eepmekong.org/_downloads/Biomass_Gasification_report_final-submitted.pdf>.

Towie, Narelle. "The Pros and Cons of Nuclear Energy". *Sunday Times (Perth)*, 31 January 2010.

Uddin, S. N., Ros Taplin, and Xiaojiang Yu. "Sustainable Energy Future for Vietnam: Evolution and Implementation of Effective Strategies". *International Journal of Environmental Studies* 66, no. 1 (2009).

"Update 2-First Solar Sees Contract for China Power Supply". Reuters, 23 February 2010. Available at <http://www.reuters.com/article/2010/02/23/firstsolar-idUSN2310311420100223?type=marketsNews>.

Walet, Leonora. "Philippines Targets $2.5 billion Geothermal Development". *Reuters*, 5 November 2009. Available at <http://www.reuters.com/article/2009/11/05/us-philippines-renewable-idUSTRE5A43HC20091105>.

World Nuclear Association. *Nuclear Power in China*, 22 September 2011. Available at <http://www.world-nuclear.org/info/inf63.html>.

XiaoLin Chang, Xinghong Liu, and Wei Zhou. "Hydropower in China at Present and Its Further Development". *Energy* 35 (2010).

Xinhua. "China to Boost Offshore Wind Power Generation". *China Daily*, 16 May 2011. Available at <http://www.chinadaily.com.cn/china/2011-05/16/content_12520766.htm>.

A. Zhou and Thomson Elspeth. "The Development of Biofuels in Asia". *Applied Energy* 86 (2009).

9

TRANSNATIONAL CRIME

Mely Caballero-Anthony and
Pau Khan Khup Hangzo

Transnational organized crime is considered one of the major threats to human security, impeding the social, economic, political and cultural development of societies. Much attention has been given to the dynamics of professional criminal groups but little has been given to the existence of the markets in which they operate. This chapter argues that a focus on both of these is needed to address the underlying social, political, and economic factors that allow for transnational organized crime to thrive. In order to address the market dimensions of transnational organized crime, this chapter is framed as a "threat assessment". Drawing data from reliable open-source information, it analyses the size and magnitude of high-priority crimes in Southeast Asia.

TRANSNATIONAL CRIME:
AN OVERVIEW

The term "transnational crime" was coined by the then United Nations (UN) Crime and Criminal Justice Branch in 1974 in order to identify certain criminal phenomena transcending international boundaries. In order to provide more clarity, the UN in 1994 defines organized transnational crime as "offenses whose inception, prevention and/or direct effect or indirect effects involved more than one country".[1] Under this definition, a list of eighteen crimes were identified: money laundering, illicit drug trafficking, corruption and bribery of public officials and of party officials and elected representatives as defined in national legislation, infiltration of legal business, fraudulent bankruptcy, insurance fraud, computer crime, theft of intellectual property, illicit traffic in arms, terrorist activities, aircraft hijacking, sea piracy, hijacking on land, trafficking in persons, trade in human body parts, theft of art and cultural objects, environmental crime, and other offences committed by organized criminal groups.

APPROACHES TO TRANSNATIONAL CRIME

Broadly, transnational crime can be analysed from two perspectives: multi-crime groups of professional criminals, and illicit markets (UNODC, June 2010).[2] To date, most of the attention has been given to the first approach and this is reflected in the United Nations Convention against Transnational Organized Crime adopted on 15 November 2000. The Convention specifically focuses on the "organized criminal group" which is defined as:

> a structured group of three or more persons, existing for a period of time and acting in concert with the aim of committing one or more serious crimes or offences ... in order to obtain, directly or indirectly, a financial or other material benefit.[3]

As the preceding definition shows, existing efforts against organized crime tend to focus on organized groups. This approach is also loosely known as the law enforcement approach because it is the law enforcement agencies — investigators, courts of law, etc. — that take the lead in pursuing and prosecuting organized criminal groups and persons. This approach is no more than a national response strategy against criminals and traffickers within a country's national jurisdiction. For example, most countries in Southeast Asia impose strict policies against drugs, with the death penalty prescribed for drug traffickers. To be sure, this policy acts as a deterrent against criminal groups and traffickers alike. However, despite such draconian measures, most countries in the region are flush with illegal drugs. Disrupting or deterring criminal organizations and traffickers does not solve the problem because the incentives and the drivers remain in place; and as long as they remain unaddressed, the problems will persist.

The second approach on the other hand focuses on the "illegal market", which is defined as:

> a place ... within which there is an exchange of goods and services, the production, selling and consumption of which are forbidden or strictly regulated by the majority of states and/or by international law.[4]

Most transnational organized criminal activities are rooted in market forces of demand and supply, not the plotting of professional criminal groups. While arresting and incarcerating individual perpetrators is important for its general deterrent effect, doing so is not sufficient to counteract illicit trade. So long as there is standing demand, and there remain areas where illicit goods can be sourced and trafficked, the market will adapt to any loss of personnel. The next section analyses the nature of the illicit markets in Southeast Asia.

Illicit Drug Trafficking

According to the World Drug Report 2010 more than 15 million people worldwide consume illicit opiates — opium, morphine and heroin. The global demand for these substances is estimated at 3,700 metric tonnes (mt), which yields a market value of US$65 billion annually. Heroin is by far the most lucrative of all illicit opiates and commands an estimated annual market value of US$55 billion. It is estimated that some 340 mt of the substance is consumed worldwide each year. Afghanistan is the largest producer of heroin at 380 mt in 2008. Of this, 15–20 mt is trafficked into China (which has the world's largest number of heroin users — 2.2 million), and another 35 mt to South and Southeast Asian countries. Myanmar, the world's second largest producer at 40 mt in 2008, is another major source of illicit heroin to China, Southeast Asia and Oceania.[5]

The size of the annual opium market on the other hand is estimated at US$7–10 billion and there are an estimated 4 million consumers world-wide. The opium consumed in Southeast and East Asia originates mainly in Myanmar and to a much lesser extent Lao PDR. Together they produced 75 mt in 2008. It is important to note that there has been a gradual decline in opium cultivation in Southeast Asia. Between 1998 and 2006, opium cultivation in Myanmar, Lao PDR and Thailand decreased from an estimated total of 157,900 hectares (ha) in 1998, to only 24,157 ha in 2006.[6] However, since then, opium poppy cultivation has increased in Myanmar and a mixed pattern of increases and decreases has been observed in Lao PDR and Thailand. The overall trend of declining opium poppy cultivation was largely due to successful eradication efforts undertaken by the governments of Myanmar, Thailand and Lao PDR.

Although Myanmar is still the second largest producer of opium after Afghanistan, its share of opium production fell from 32 per cent in 1998 to just 5 per cent in 2009. Opium poppy is now confined almost entirely to the Shan State with a few pockets of cultivation in other states. The success of opium poppy eradication in Myanmar is due in large part to ceasefire agreements that the government signed with a number of insurgent groups. This paved the way for control of opium poppy growing regions and allowed the implementation of measures to reduce opium poppy cultivation. At the same time, in 1999, the Government of Myanmar and local authorities in areas cultivating opium poppy decided to engage in a fifteen-year plan to eliminate the illicit crop by the year 2014.[7]

As a result of sustained efforts by the respective governments, as well as with the active support of international agencies such as the United Nations Office on Drugs and Crime (UNODC), Thailand and Lao PDR have been able to eradicate a large part of their opium poppy cultivation. Opium eradication programmes such as crop conversion and alternative development have been a part of the narcotics crop control strategy of both governments. As a result they have now reached such low levels of cultivation and production that they no longer produce opium for the international market. Table 9.1 shows the scale and magnitude of opium poppy cultivation in Lao PDR, Thailand and Myanmar over a two-year period. It shows an increase in opium poppy cultivation in both Lao PDR and Myanmar whereas cultivation of the crop declines in Thailand. But when this is analysed in the context of the overall trend in opium poppy cultivation, the increase in Lao PDR and Myanmar is marginal.

Even as the production of illicit opiates declined in Southeast Asia, the production, trafficking and consumption of amphetamine-type stimulants (ATS) have increased substantially. ATS refers to various synthetic substances broadly categorized into amphetamine-group substances (amphetamine, methamphetamine, methcathinone) and ecstasy-group substances. Globally, between 13.7 and 52.9 million people used amphetamine-group substances at least once in the preceding year, with a corresponding annual prevalence range of 0.3 to 1.2 per cent of the population aged 15 to 64.[8] The East and Southeast Asia region, with an estimated 3.4 to 20.7 million users, has by far the largest number of amphetamine-group substance users of any region in the world. The Philippines, Thailand and Lao PDR have the highest annual prevalence of amphetamine-group substance use in the region. See Table 9.2.

Thailand is one of the biggest markets for ATS trafficked primarily from Myanmar. In 2009, Thai police intercepted 1.2 million amphetamine pills trafficked from Myanmar. Already, in the first six months of 2010, 5 million pills had been intercepted. It was estimated that between 300 and 400 million pills will be trafficked by the end of 2010.[9] Table 9.3 presents the annual prevalence of use of four types of drugs as a percentage of the population in Southeast Asia. It shows that use of amphetamine-type stimulants has overtaken other drugs.

Table 9.1

Southeast Asia Opium Survey 2009

	2008	2009	Change From
Opium poppy cultivation of which			
Lao PDR	30,388 ha	33,811 ha	+11%
Thailand	1,600 ha	1,900 ha	+19%
Thailand	288 ha	211 ha	–27%
Myanmar	28,500 ha	31,700 ha	+11%
Potential production of opium of which			
Lao PDR	424 mt	345 mt	–19%
Lao PDR	9.6 mt	11.4 mt	+19%
Thailand	4.5 mt	3.3 mt	–27%
Myanmar	410 mt	330 mt	–20%
Average price of opium			
Lao PDR	US$1,227/kg	US$1,327/kg	+8%
Thailand	US$1,250/kg	n/a	+17%
Myanmar	US$301/kg	US$317/kg	+5%
Total potential value of opium production of which			
Lao PDR	US$140.4 million	>US$119 million	n/a
Thailand	US$ 11.8 million	US$15.1 million	+28%
Thailand	US$5.6 million	n/a	n/a
Myanmar	US$123 million	US$104 million	–15%

Source: UNODC, December 2009, p. 5.

Table 9.2

Estimated Number of People Who used Amphetamine-group Substances at Least Once in the Past Year and Prevalence Among Population Aged 15–64, 2008

Region	Estimated Number of Users Annually (lower)	Estimated Number of Users Annually (upper)	Per Cent of Population Aged 15–64 (lower)	Per Cent of Population Aged 15–64 (upper)
East/Southeast Asia	3,430,000	20,680,000	0.2	1.4
Global	13,710,000	52,900,000	0.3	1.2

Source: "World Drug Report 2010" (UNODC 2010).

Table 9.3
Annual Prevalence of Use as a Percentage of the Population Aged 15–64

Country/Territory	Opiates	Cocaine	Cannabis	Amphetamine-Type Stimulants
Brunei Darussalam	0.01	..	..	0.3
Cambodia	0.01–0.09	..	3.5	0.6
Indonesia	0.16	<0.1	0.7	0.3
Lao PDR	0.37	..	0.7–1.1	1.1–1.7
Malaysia	1.11–1.56	..	1.6	0.6
Myanmar	0.60	..	0.9	0.2
Philippines	0.05	<0.1	0.7–0.9	1.9–2.4
Singapore	<0.01	..	..	–
Thailand	0.20	<0.1	1.2	1.4
Timor Leste	..	..	..	..
Vietnam	0.25–0.28	..	0.3	0.2

Source: "World Drug Report 2009" (UNODC 2009), pp. 235–54.

Human Trafficking

The United Nations' "Protocol to Prevent, Suppress, and Punish Trafficking in Persons" defines trafficking in persons as:

> the recruitment, transportation, transfer, harbouring or receipt of persons, by means of the threat or use of force or other forms of coercion, of abduction, of fraud, of deception, of the abuse of power or of a position of vulnerability or of the giving or receiving of payments or benefits to achieve the consent of a person having control over another person, for the purpose of exploitation.[10]

It is one of the most egregious violations of human rights. The International Labour Organization (ILO) estimates that there are at least 12.3 million people worldwide who are victims of forced labour of which 2.4 million are a result of human trafficking.[11] The prevalence rate of trafficking victims worldwide is estimated at 1.8 per 1,000 inhabitants whereas in Asia and the Pacific region, it is 3 per 1,000 inhabitants.[12]

The International Organization for Migration estimates that at least 200,000 to 225,000 women and children from Southeast Asia are trafficked annually.[13] Victims from East and Southeast Asia were detected in more than twenty countries in regions throughout the world, including Europe, the Americas, the Middle East, Central Asia and Africa.[14] See Table 9.4.

An analysis of the profile of trafficked victims in Table 9.5 shows that female (women and girls) and children constitute the majority of people trafficked for the purpose of both sexual and economic exploitation.

Table 9.4
Regional Distribution of Forced Labour as a Result of Trafficking

Region	Number of People in Forced Labour as a Result of Trafficking
Asia and Pacific	1,360,000
Industrialized countries	270,000
Latin America and Caribbean	250,000
Middle East and North Africa	230,000
Transition countries	200,000
Sub-Saharan Africa	130,000
World	**2,450,000**

Source: ILO (2005).

Table 9.5
Profile of Victims of Trafficking

	UNODC	ILO	U.S. Department of State
Female (women and girls)	13% (Girls) 66% (Women)	56% (forced commercial exploitation) 98% (commercial sexual exploitation)	80%
Children and Minor	–	40–50%	50%
Male (men and boys)	Men (12%) Boys (9%)	44% (forced commercial exploitation)	–

Source: UNODC (February 2009), p. 11; ILO (2005); US Department of State (2008).

Trafficking for the purpose of sexual exploitation and forced labour are the most common forms of human trafficking. A groundbreaking study of prostitution in Southeast Asia by the ILO estimated that between 0.25 and 1.5 per cent of the female population work as prostitutes in Indonesia, Malaysia, the Philippines and Thailand, and the sex sector accounts for between 2 and 14 per cent of the gross domestic product (GDP).[15]

Human trafficking as a business is highly profitable. According to reports, human traffickers and smugglers charge Baht 700,000 (around US$22,000) per person to smuggle Thai workers into Japan, and Baht 800,000 (around US$25,000) per head to get Chinese workers into Canada.[16] At the global level, the total illicit profits produced annually by trafficked forced labourers is estimated to be about US$32 billion. Half of this profit is made in industrialized countries (US$15.5 billion) and close to one-third in Asia (US$9.7 billion). This represents an average of approximately US$13,000 per year or US$1,100 per month for each forced labourer.

Maritime Piracy

Maritime shipping is the lynchpin of the global economy. Ninety per cent of the global trade is carried by sea and the Malacca Strait alone accounts for over 40 per cent of that volume. Thus the Malacca Strait is one of the world's most important waterways: 43,965 vessels passed

Table 9.6
Forms of Human Trafficking

| | Estimates by Various Agencies | |
Forms of Human Trafficking	UNODC	ILO
Commercial sexual exploitation	79%	43%
Forced economic exploitation	18%	32%
Others (mixed or undetermined)	3%	25%

Source: UNODC (February 2009), p. 11; ILO (2005); U.S. Department of State (2008).

Table 9.7
Annual Profits from All Trafficked Forced Labourers

Region	Profits Per Forced Labourer in Commercial Sexual Exploitation (US$)	Profits Per Forced Labourer in Other Economic Exploitation (US$)	Total profits (million US$)
Industrialized economies	67,200	30,154	15,513
Transition economies	23,500	2,353	3,422
Asia and the Pacific	10,000	412	9,704
Latin America	18,200	3,570	1,348
Sub-Saharan Africa	10,000	360	159
Middle East and North Africa	45,000	2,340	1,508
World			31,654

Source: ILO (2005), p. 55.

through the waterway in 1999 and this volume increased to 70,718 in 2007.[17] Singapore, according to the Maritime and Port Authority of Singapore (MPA), is the premier port of not only Southeast Asia, but also the world. Singapore is connected to more than 600 ports in over 120 countries. An estimated 140,000 vessels call at its port annually, making it one of the world's busiest ports. Moreover, the maritime sector contributes about 7 per cent of its GDP. Thus, the potential disruption of maritime trade by piracy is therefore a major concern not only for Southeast Asian countries, but also for those in the wider region that rely on the Malacca Strait for trade.

It was estimated that acts of robbery against ships in the Malacca Strait earned pirates anywhere between US$5,000 to US$20,000. Ransoms demanded for the release of crew members on the other hand ranges from US$100,000 to US$200,000.[18]

Table 9.8
Earnings of Pirates

Southeast Asia	Somalia-Horn of Africa
Harbour and anchorage attacks: US$5,000–10,000	Average ransom payment: US$500,000–2 million (2008)
Attacks against vessels at sea (robbery): US$10,000–20,000	Earnings per pirate (for a US$1 million ransom): US$6,000–10,000
Attacks against vessels at sea (hijacking): NA	Annual earning: US$30 million (2008)
Kidnap-for-ransom: US$100,000–200,000	

Source: Raymond, 2005 (for Southeast Asia); UNODC, June 2010 (for Somalia-Horn of Africa).

Table 9.9
Locations of Pirate Attacks in Southeast Asia since 2003

Locations	2003	2004	2005	2006	2007	2008	2009
Indonesia	121	94	79	50	43	28	15
Malacca Strait	28	38	12	11	7	2	2
Malaysia	5	9	3	10	9	10	16
Myanmar	0	1	0	0	0	1	1
The Philippines	12	4	0	6	6	7	1
Singapore Strait	2	8	7	5	3	6	9
Thailand	2	4	1	1	2	0	1
Southeast Asia total	170	158	102	83	70	54	45
World total	**445**	**329**	**276**	**239**	**263**	**293**	**406**

Source: ICC International Maritime Bureau (January 2008); ICC International Maritime Bureau (January 2010).

Although the money earned by pirates in Southeast Asia is not much when compared to Somali pirates, it is the threat that they pose to freedom of navigation that concerns states. The other major concern is that extremist groups will seek to overcome existing operational constraints in sea-based capabilities by working in conjunction with or subcontracting out missions to maritime crime gangs and syndicates. Finally, there is the danger of an environmental disaster. As pirates become more assertive and sophisticated, they are likely to be more daring in pursuing their objectives, and this increases the risk of, say, their intentionally or unintentionally firing at an oil tanker. Although piracy in Southeast Asia has declined significantly as a result of decisive state actions and improved maritime cooperation among littoral states, the threat still remains. Its elimination, therefore, continues to be one of the highest priorities on the policy agenda of countries in the region.

Financial Crime

Government revenue is critical to development. However, most Southeast Asian countries suffer from a chronic shortage of revenues due to tax evasion. The following section analyses the leakage of revenues as a result of illicit financial flows and trade mispricing.

Illicit Financial Flows

Illicit financial flows refer to "cross-border movement of money that is illegally earned, transferred, or utilized"[19] with the intention of evading taxes. Global Financial Integrity (GFI) estimates the worldwide volumes

Table 9.10

Illicit Financial Flows from Selected Countries of Southeast Asia, 2002–06

Country	Illicit Financial Flows (US$ million)
Malaysia	19,027
Philippines	12,154
Indonesia	10,361
Thailand	6,302
Brunei Darussalam	3,299
Vietnam	876
Myanmar	624
Cambodia	382

Source: Kar and Cartwright-Smith (2008), pp. 65–67.

of illicit financial flows from developing countries for the period 2002–06 at between US$859 billion and US$1.06 trillion. This amounts to over ten times the value of Official Development Aid (ODA) for the same period. Table 9.10 shows the volume of financial flows from Southeast Asia.

Trade Mispricing

Trade mispricing moves more illicit money across borders than any other single phenomenon. It is a major conduit through which profits of companies are shifted from developing countries to banks and tax havens in developed countries. It can occur when the underlying trade involves transactions between related parties, such as trade transactions between international subsidiaries of a large parent corporation. It can also involve transactions between unrelated parties; for example, a local company trading with an independent foreign supplier. As such, trade mispricing presents a channel through which legitimate profits are transferred abroad illegally. GFI's analysis found that the average tax revenue loss to all developing countries was between US$98 billion and US$107 billion annually during the years 2002–06. This figure represents an average loss of about 4.4 per cent of the entire developing world's government revenue.

Table 9.11

Tax Revenue Loss as a Per Cent of Government Revenue, 2002–06

Country	Average Tax Revenue Loss (US$ million)	Average Government Revenue Minus Grants (US$ million)	Loss of Tax Revenue (as a per cent of government revenue)
Brunei Darussalam	0.00	689.00	0.0%
Cambodia	76.39	550.93	13.9%
Indonesia	3,108.40	40,657.30	7.6%
Malaysia	4,947.11	32,130.18	15.4%
Myanmar	0.00	–	–
Philippines	4,253.88	13,859.11	30.7%
Thailand	1,382.01	34,578.05	4.0%

Source: Hollingshead (2010), p. 31.

Environmental Crime

Environmental crime is defined as "illegal acts which directly harm the environment".[20] They include: illegal trade in wildlife; smuggling of ozone-depleting substances (ODS); illicit trade in hazardous waste; illegal, unregulated, and unreported fishing; and illegal logging and the associated trade in stolen timber. This section specifically analyses illegal trade in wildlife, illegal fishing, and illegal logging.

Illegal Trade in Wildlife

Wildlife trade, defined as "any sale or exchange by people of wild animal and plant resources",[21] involves live animals and plants for the pet and horticultural trades, or the trade in a diverse range of wild animal and plant products needed or prized by humans, including skins, medicinal ingredients, tourist curiosities, timber, fish and other food products. Southeast Asia contains 20 per cent of all known plant, animal, and marine species, most of which are found nowhere else in the world. In all, there are 64,800 known species of which 2 per cent are endangered (ASEAN Centre for Biodiversity). At the same time, Southeast Asia also accounted for an estimated 25 per cent of the global value of illicit wildlife trade.[22] A study published in the December 2009 issue of *Biodiversity and Conservation* found that between 1998 and 2007, more than 35 million animals listed in the Convention on International Trade in Endangered Species of Wild Fauna and Flora (CITES) were exported from Southeast Asia.[23] The top animal groups traded were reptiles (17.4 million), seahorses (16 million), birds (1 million), mammals (0.4 million), butterflies (0.3 million) and fish (0.1 million). More than 85 per cent (30 million) of animals were wild-caught, with Malaysia, Vietnam, Indonesia, and China the major exporters of such animals (around 300 species), and the European Union and Japan the most significant importers. One animal species that has attracted the most attention is the tiger. According to the World Wildlife Fund (WWF), the tiger population in the Greater Mekong — Thailand, Vietnam, Cambodia, Lao PDR and Myanmar — dropped from 1,200 in 1998 to 350 in 2010.[24] This is primarily due to the deliberate and large-scale illegal hunting of tigers for their body parts, mostly for use in traditional medicine. Table 9.12 provides the estimated market value of selected wildlife products marketed from Southeast Asia.

Table 9.12
Market Value of Selected Wildlife Products from Africa and Southeast Asia to Asia

Products	Black Market Price	Source
Elephant ivory	US$850 per kilogram Annual value at SEA and Asian markets: US$100 million	Africa
Rhino horn	Asian-rhino horn: US$20,000–30,000 per kilo Annual value at SEA and Asian markets: US$8 million	Africa and India
Tiger	Skin: US$20,000 (China) Raw bones: US$1,200 per kg (China) Bone wine: US$88 per bottle (China–Myanmar border) Annual value at SEA and Asian markets: US$8 million	Southeast Asia
Pangolin	Malaysia: US$15 Indonesia: US$5–10 Guangdong: US$100	Southeast Asia

Source: Compiled from UNODC (June 2010); and Thompson (2010).

Illegal, Unreported and Unregulated Fishing (IUU)

The total value of current illegal and unreported fishing losses worldwide was estimated at between US$10 and US$23.5 billion annually.[25] This represents between 11 and 26 million tonnes or between 10 and 22 per cent of the total fisheries production. Illegal fishing is rampant in the waters of Southeast Asia. Indonesia, for example, has declared itself to be the world's biggest victim of IUU fishing with around 1.6 million tonnes of its fish poached annually resulting in the loss of about US$3 billion every year.[26] An estimated 1,000 foreign vessels conduct IUU fishing in 12 per cent of Indonesia's territorial waters each year.

Illegal Logging and the Associated Trade in Stolen Timber

Illegal logging occurs when timber is harvested, transported, processed, bought, or sold in violation or circumvention of national or sub-national laws.[27] Between 8 and 10 per cent of global wood products stems from illegal logging, with annual global market value of losses estimated at over US$10 billion.[28] Southeast Asia is a major supplier of illicit timber with an estimated annual turnover of US$3.5 billion. As much as 40 per cent of wood-based products imported into the EU in 2008 and half of China's imports in 2007 (worth US$900 million) originated from illegal logging.

Indonesia remains the country most heavily affected by illegal logging. The country possesses 123 million ha of forest (10 per cent of global forest cover) including the third largest tropical rainforest. As much as 80 per cent of timber logged in Indonesia is suspected to be illegally sourced with annual losses in government revenue estimated at US$2 billion.[29] The Indonesian Ministry of Forestry estimates that the country lost between 1.6 and 2.8 million ha of forest annually (between 3 and 5 ha a minute) to illegal logging and land conversion up until 2010.[30]

The threat assessment presented in this section clearly reflects the seriousness of the problem. It points to the reality that the traditional law enforcement approach is no longer sufficient because most trafficking flows are driven more by the market rather than by the groups involved in them. A case in point is Thailand's "war against drugs". Officially launched in February 2003, the initial three-month phase of the campaign alone killed 2,275 people.[31] To be sure, the campaign eliminated many drug lords in Thailand and reduced the volume of illicit drug flow. However, since the demand for drugs still exists in Thailand, the flow of drugs continues. In 2009, Thai police intercepted 1.2 million amphetamine pills trafficked from Myanmar. In the first six months of 2010 alone, 5 million pills have already been intercepted. Law enforcement agencies expect that as many as 300 to 400 million amphetamine pills will be trafficked into Thailand by the end of 2010.[32] Most of these drugs originate from rebel armies in Myanmar, most notably the Wa State Army, who use revenues generated by the drug trade to finance their war against the Myanmar government.

Efforts that target criminal groups are therefore unlikely to be successful on their own. To deal comprehensively with these intractable and interlinked issues, it is necessary to have a good understanding of the socio-political-economic drivers of illicit markets, and most importantly, it requires international cooperation. The next section will look exclusively at the drivers of transnational organized crime and the regional cooperation framework instituted by ASEAN.

RESPONDING TO TRANSNATIONAL ORGANIZED CRIME: CASE STUDY OF HUMAN TRAFFICKING AND DRUG TRAFFICKING

Human trafficking and illicit drug trafficking are arguably the most intractable of all transnational crimes. They are an issue of both domestic and foreign policy concern and a subject of longstanding multilateral policy commitment. This section reviews past and present policies adopted by countries in Southeast Asia in response to human trafficking and illicit drug trafficking. It argues that the approach adopted by countries in the region is still skewed in favour of a traditional law enforcement approach. This approach, which primarily targets organized criminal groups and individuals, is not sufficient as most trafficking flows are driven by the market rather than by the groups involved in them.

Human Trafficking

According to the International Labour Organization (ILO), there are at least 12.3 million people worldwide who are victims of forced labour. Of these, 2.4 million are a result of human trafficking.[33] Approximately 800,000 people are trafficked across national borders each year[34] out of which 200,000 to 225,000 hail from Southeast Asia.[35] Thus, Southeast Asia is a major source of human trafficking with victims from the region detected in more than twenty countries.[36]

In Southeast Asia, trafficking in persons is primarily considered a criminal problem, with high importance attached to the role of the criminal justice system and criminal law in the fight against trafficking. This has necessitated legislative reforms, which often means responding to the call for higher penalties and more stringent laws, training of law enforcement officials, and establishing and strengthening inter-agency, regional and international cooperation in the fight against international organized crime, amongst others. The next section looks at anti-trafficking efforts at the regional as well as national levels.

Regional Framework

At the regional level, the Association of Southeast Asian Nations (ASEAN) provides the key framework for policy development on trafficking in persons in Southeast Asia. ASEAN has addressed the issue of trafficking in persons since the early 1990s. Table 9.13 summarizes the legal instruments

Table 9.13
Key ASEAN Declarations on Human Trafficking

	Key Declarations
ASEAN Vision 2020 (1997)	The ASEAN Vision 2020 sets the broad framework for ASEAN action. Within the framework of this vision, ASEAN member countries work on a range of specific issues, including transnational crime.
ASEAN Declaration on Transnational Crime (1997)	Member countries expressed their commitment to working together to formulate "agreed rules of behaviour and cooperative measures" to deal with "problems that can only be met on a regional scale". They specifically agreed to work together to combat trafficking in women and children.
ASEAN Declaration against Trafficking in Persons, Particularly Women and Children (2004)	This Declaration was adopted on 29 November 2004. It lays the groundwork for a regional approach aimed at preventing and combating trafficking in persons.

outlining the key commitments of ASEAN member countries regarding trafficking.

It is important to note that the ASEAN Declaration against Trafficking in Persons, Particularly Women and Children follows the adoption by the United Nations of the Convention against Transnational Organised Crime and the Protocol to Prevent, Suppress and Punish Trafficking in Persons, Especially Women and Children (also known as the Trafficking Protocol) in 2000. The Trafficking Protocol lays the framework and acts as a guide to preventing and combating trafficking in persons worldwide. Most ASEAN countries are party to not only the Trafficking Protocol, but also other conventions relevant to the issue.

As noted earlier, most ASEAN countries are not only party to various United Nations conventions relevant to human trafficking but they have also ratified them. Upon ratification, States are required to adapt their domestic laws and law enforcement procedures in order to take due account of the broader dimensions of human trafficking as defined in the Trafficking Protocol. The next section will look at the status of domestic legislation in Southeast Asia.

Table 9.14

Selected Conventions Related to Human Rights and Human Trafficking

Country	TOC	TIP	CRC	OP to CRC	CEDAW	ICCPR	MW	ILO 29	ILO 105	ILO 182
Brunei Darussalam	–	–	A	A	A	–	–	–	–	–
Cambodia	R	R	A	R	A	A	S	R	R	R
Indonesia	S	S	R	S	R	A	S	R	R	R
Lao PDR	A	A	A	A	R	S	–	R	–	R
Malaysia	R	–	A	–	A	–	–	R	–	R
Myanmar	A	A	A	–	A	–	–	R	R	–
Philippines	R	R	R	R	R	R	R	R	R	R
Singapore	R	–	A	–	A	–	–	R	–	R
Thailand	S	S	A	A	A	A	–	R	–	R
Vietnam	S	–	R	R	R	A	–	R	–	R

Note: R = ratified; A = acceded; S = signed

TOC	Convention against Transnational Organised Crime, United Nations, 2000.
TIP	Protocol to Prevent, Suppress and Punish Trafficking in Persons, Especially Women and Children, Supplementing the United Nations Convention against Transnational Organized Crime, United Nations, 2000.
CRC	Convention on the Rights of the Child, United Nations, 1989.
OP to CRC	Optional Protocol to the Convention on the Rights of the Child on the Sale of Children, Child Prostitution and Child Pornography, United Nations, 2000.
CEDAW	Convention on the Elimination of All Forms of Discrimination against Women, United Nations, 1979.
ICCPR	International Covenant on Civil and Political Rights, United Nations, 1966.
MW	International Convention on the Protection of the Rights of All Migrant Workers and Members of Their Families, United Nations, 1990.
ILO No. 29	Convention concerning Forced or Compulsory Labour, International Labour Organization, 1932.
ILO No. 105	Convention concerning the Abolition of Forced Labour, International Labour Organization, 1957.
ILO No. 182	Convention concerning the Prohibition and Immediate Action for the Elimination of the Worst Forms of Child Labour, International Labour Organization, 1989.

Source: ASEAN (February 2008); UNDP (October 2009), pp. 163–66.

National Frameworks

At the national level, most ASEAN countries have improved their domestic laws against human trafficking. However, not all states have adopted a single law which encompasses all dimensions of human trafficking, and they have relied on existing domestic laws to make arrests, lay charges, and bring trafficking cases to court. For example, Singapore criminalizes trafficking through its Penal Code, Women's Charter, Children and Young Persons Act, Employment of Foreign Manpower Act, Employment Agencies Act, Employment Agency Rules, and the Conditions of Work Permits. Charges can be filed for deploying foreign workers illegally, for providing false information for the purpose of hiring phantom workers, for not paying salaries on time, etc. Similarly, Vietnam uses a diverse set of domestic laws including the Penal Code, Labour Laws, Decree No. 38 on the Administrative Sanctions against Violations of Labour Legislation, Decree No. 49 on Sanctions against Administrative Violation in the Domain of Security and Order, Law on Marriage and Family, National Action Plan on Combating Trafficking in Women and Children 2004–2010, etc. The absence of a single law on human trafficking can prove problematic because each existing law focuses narrowly on specific offences. Moreover, it could also lead to confusion regarding the types of domestic legislation to use because of the multiple dimensions of human trafficking issues. The absence of a single, all-encompassing anti-trafficking law could thus be proved to be a hindrance to effectively combating human trafficking in all its forms.

However, there are also countries in the region that have enacted a completely new law specifically targeting human trafficking in all its forms. Table 9.15 summarizes the current state of legislation adopted by countries in Southeast Asia.

Despite recent anti-trafficking legislation enacted by countries in Southeast Asia, there are still major deficiencies. For example, most legislation primarily covers trafficking for sexual exploitation and anti-trafficking efforts have mainly been directed at that sector. As such, trafficking in women and children for the purpose of sexual exploitation (and forced labour) receives the most attention whereas trafficking in men and boys for the purpose of forced labour does not attract the attention it deserves.

Drug Trafficking

The illicit production of, demand for, and traffic in narcotic drugs and psychotropic substances pose a serious threat to the health and welfare of

Table 9.15

Summary of Legal Frameworks Instituted by ASEAN Member States

Country	Legislation	Nature of Punishments
Brunei Darussalam	Trafficking and Smuggling of Persons Order 2004	4 to 30 years imprisonment, up to B$1 million fine, whipping
Cambodia	Law on the Suppression of Human Trafficking and Commercial Sexual Exploitation 2008	1 day to life imprisonment, 3,000 to 10,000,000 riels fine
Indonesia	Elimination of Crimes of Human Trafficking 2007	3 to 15 years imprisonment, Rp 120 million to 5 billion fine
Lao PDR	No specific human trafficking law	5 years life imprisonment, fine
Malaysia	Anti-Trafficking in Persons Act 2007	Up to 20 years imprisonment, RM 500,000 fine, whipping
Myanmar	Anti Trafficking in Persons Law 2005	3 years to life imprisonment, fine, death
Philippines	Anti-Trafficking in Persons Act 2003	1 year to life imprisonment, 50,000 to 5 million pesos fine
Singapore	No specific human trafficking law	Imprisonment, fine, caning
Thailand	Anti-Trafficking in Persons Act B.E 2551 (2008)	6 months to 15 years imprisonment, 60,000 to 1 million baht fine.
Vietnam	No specific human trafficking law	Imprisonment, fine

Source: Compiled by the author.

human beings and adversely affect the economic, cultural and political foundations of society. Illicit drug trafficking also generates large financial profits and wealth enabling transnational criminal organizations to penetrate, contaminate and corrupt the structures of government, legitimate commercial and financial businesses, and society at all levels. Illicit possession, cultivation and purchase of drugs are therefore criminal offences and their suppression demands urgent attention. Illicit drug trafficking is thus an issue of both domestic and foreign policy concern and a subject of longstanding multilateral policy commitment.

ASEAN has advocated a collective regional response to drug abuse and illegal drug trafficking almost from the start of its cooperative efforts. The Declaration of ASEAN Concord of 24 February 1976 called for "the intensification of cooperation among member states as well as with the relevant international bodies in the prevention and eradication of the abuse of narcotics and the illegal trafficking of drugs". This Declaration subsequently led to the adoption of the ASEAN Declaration of Principles to Combat the Abuse of Narcotic Drugs in Manila on 26 June 1976, which requires each member country to intensify their preventive and penal measures, organize cooperation in the fields of drug research and education, and institute improvements in national legislation aimed at intensifying the fight against the abuse of drugs and its consequences. The Declaration was followed by the ASEAN Declaration on Transnational Crime signed on 20 December 1997 which, among others, aims to expand the scope of member countries' efforts against transnational crimes including illicit drug trafficking.

The most ambitious of all, however, is the ASEAN Vision 2020 adopted by the ASEAN Heads of State/Government on 15 December 1997 at the Second Informal Summit held in Kuala Lumpur. ASEAN Vision 2020 envisioned a Southeast Asia free of illicit drugs, that is, their production, processing, trafficking and use, well before 2020. To achieve this goal, leaders signed the Joint Declaration for a Drug-Free ASEAN by 2020 at the 31st ASEAN Ministerial Meeting (AMM) on 25 July 1998. At the 33rd AMM in July 2000, governments reiterated their concerns on the threat from the manufacturing, trafficking and abuse of illegal drugs on the security and stability of the ASEAN region and agreed to advance the target year for realizing a Drug-Free ASEAN to 2015.

Supply-Side Measures

The main focus of international and regional drug control efforts traditionally has been on the supply side and aimed at reducing the supply, and therefore availability, of drugs in consumer countries. Countering drug traffickers, who are a major part of the problem on the supply side because they facilitate the availability of drugs, therefore require the implementation of tough laws and penalties including capital punishment for trafficking in significant amounts of the most harmful drugs. Southeast Asia has some of the harshest drug laws in the world. All ASEAN countries, with the exception of the Philippines and Cambodia, currently have legislation allowing for the use of capital punishment in drug cases. Some countries have instituted it solely to punish drug-related offences, and drug offenders make up a significant portion — if not the outright majority — of those executed each year. However, the actual implementation of capital punishment varies. Some states never execute drug offenders despite laws prescribing capital punishment for such offences. In these countries, the laws appear to be symbolic statements of strong national opposition to drug use and trafficking rather than a functioning death penalty policy. Table 9.16 provides an overview of drug policies in Southeast Asia.

Table 9.16
Drug Policies in Southeast Asia

Countries	Law	Principle Punishments
Brunei Darussalam	Misuse of Drugs Act 2001	Imprisonment, fine, death
Cambodia	Law on the Control of Drugs 1997	6 days to life imprisonment, fine
Indonesia	Law no. 5/1997 on Psychotropic Drugs, Law no. 22/1997 on Narcotics	Imprisonment, fine, death
Malaysia	Dangerous Drugs Act 1952	2 years to life imprisonment, whipping, death
Philippines	Republic Act No. 9165 2002	1 day to life imprisonment, fine, death
Singapore	Misuse of Drugs Act (Cap. 185)	6 months to life imprisonment, fine, caning, death
Thailand	Narcotics Act 1979	1 year to life imprisonment, fine, death

Source: Compiled by the authors.

The other measure that has proved successful in drug-producing countries is crop eradication. Crop eradication involves aerial spraying (spraying chemicals over poppy or cocoa plantations); forced crop eradication programmes (destroying standing crops); and alternative development (replacing illicit crops with legal alternatives). Alternative development in its many guises (for example, crop substitution, socioeconomic development, integrated rural development) has been attempted most vigorously in Thailand and Lao PDR. It is more politically acceptable than aerial spraying and forced crop eradication programmes since it promises new income opportunities within a context of socioeconomic development.

Demand-Side Measures

Despite the implementation of strict measures to counteract the supply of drugs, Southeast Asia still has a large number of drug users, the largest of any region in the world. Table 9.17 presents the annual prevalence of the use of drugs as a percentage of population in Southeast Asia. It shows that the demand side was not addressed as robustly compared to the wide range of efforts employed to curb the supply of drugs.

Table 9.17
Annual Prevalence of Use as a Percentage of the Population Aged 15–64

Country/Territory	Opiates	Cocaine	Cannabis	Amphetamine-Type Stimulants
Brunei Darussalam	0.01	–	–	0.3
Cambodia	0.01 – 0.09	–	3.5	0.6
Indonesia	0.16	<0.1	0.7	0.3
Lao PDR	0.37	–	0.7 – 1.1	1.1 – 1.7
Malaysia	1.11 – 1.56	–	1.6	0.6
Myanmar	0.60	–	0.9	0.2
Philippines	0.05	<0.1	0.7 – 0.9	1.9 – 2.4
Singapore	<0.01	–	–	–
Thailand	0.20	<0.1	1.2	1.4
Vietnam	0.25 – 0.28	–	0.3	0.2

Source: UNODC (2009).

Efforts aimed at reducing demand for illicit drugs include both sanctions and incentives. Sanctions focus on law enforcement initiatives meant to apprehend and deter consumers through fines, jail sentences and loss of privileges. Positive incentives have also been developed to offer people reasons to cease, or at least to greatly reduce, illicit drug use. The combination of sanctions and incentives is meant to create a climate wherein non-users are reluctant to take up the habit. Aside from law enforcement initiatives designed to raise risks for consumers, the demand reduction strategies of principal consuming countries include:

Treatment programmes. Drug dependence is a health disorder (a disease) that arises from exposure to drugs in persons with pre-existing psycho-biological vulnerabilities. Such an understanding of drug dependence suggests that punishment is not the appropriate response to persons who are dependent on drugs. Treatment is useful not only for addressing the addiction of individuals, but also for reducing the spread of drug addiction. The Single Convention on Narcotic Drugs, 1961 (Article 36b) stipulates that "abusers shall undergo measures of treatment, education, after-care, rehabilitation and social reintegration" and that one of the most effective methods of treatment for addiction is "treatment in a hospital institution having a drug free atmosphere". The Convention therefore encourages the adoption of a health-oriented approach to illicit drug use and drug dependence rather than relying solely upon a criminal justice sanctions approach. In the case of non-dependent drug users, a health-oriented approach may involve providing education, reliable information, brief motivational and behavioural counselling, and measures to facilitate social reintegration, and reduce isolation and social exclusion. In the case of drug dependent individuals it may also involve more comprehensive social support and specific pharmacological and psychosocial treatment, and aftercare.

Education. Education is one of the primary elements of the positive component of demand reduction strategies. If education within the classroom is to reduce demand, it needs to be coupled with community-wide integrated efforts, including the dissemination of explicit anti-drug values and peer modelling begun at a fairly early age. The mass media in several consuming nations have had some success in targeting certain audiences for such anti-drug campaigns.

Civic action. This involves community support for voluntary anti-drug service, the creation of self-help groups for addicts and an anonymous hotline for residents to report drug-related activities in their neighbourhoods, etc.

Developing an anti-drug ethos. One of the strongest deterrents to the use of illicit drugs is people's conviction that drug use is inappropriate, whether for moral reasons or otherwise. If the fundamental values of a specific group of people change in ways which disfavour drugs, the reduction in consumption will be more lasting. This kind of value change is more likely to be brought about by persuasion than by coercion. Thus, calls are made for the mobilization of community efforts to re-establish eroded social values and to provide substantial social incentives for people to reform their lifestyles.

Case Study: Singapore — Whole-of-Society Approach

Singapore has pursued a comprehensive national strategy to combat drugs, comprising a high-profile public education campaign, treatment and rehabilitation of drug offenders, as well as strict laws and stiff penalties against those involved in the drug trade. Over two decades, the number of drug abusers arrested each year has declined by two-thirds, from over 6,000 in the early 1990s[37] to about 2,000 in 2009.[38] On the supply side, Singapore has instituted strict laws and tough penalties against those involved in the drug trade, including capital punishment. The mandatory death penalty for drugs was introduced in a 1975 Amendment to the Misuse of Drugs Act 1973 and given to those found guilty of importing, exporting or trafficking certain quantities of cannabis, cocaine, heroin, and methamphetamine. See Table 9.18.

On the demand side, the main feature of Singapore's drug policy is the comprehensive and costly compulsory rehabilitation programmes for abusers in specialized centres aimed at preparing them for a drug-free life. Such remedial training imposes on the trainees strict discipline and offers them a choice of highly structured workshops, including university courses, music, construction trades and computer technology. They are given two chances in a drug rehabilitation centre. If they go through counselling, kick their drug habit and return to society with useful skills, they will not have any criminal record. Those who are still addicted go to prison, where they are put on general rehabilitation programmes to help them reintegrate into the community. To raise awareness and engage the wider community, Singapore observes a month-long anti-drug campaign each year. Organized by the National Council against Drug Abuse (NCADA), the campaign kick-off is 26 June each year. On this day, a special green-and-white ribbon is worn to serve as a reminder that the constant vigilance and sustained commitment of every concerned member of the society is the only way to overcome the drug problem. The programmes of the campaign are usually activity-based and entertaining. They are intended to appeal to the target groups of students and out-of-school youths so that the anti-drug message

Table 9.18
Selected Lists of Commonly Abused Drug Types

Commonly Abused Drug Types	Penalties
Heroin	• More than 15 grams – death • Possession and consumption of heroin – up to S$20,000 fine or 10 years imprisonment or both.
Cocaine	• Illegal traffic in cocaine of more than 500 grams – death • Illegal import or export of cocaine of more than 30 grams – death • Possession and consumption of cocaine – up to S$20,000 fine or 10 years imprisonment or both
Methamphetamine	• Illegal traffic, import or export of Yaba of more than 250 grams – death • Possession and consumption of Yaba – up to S$20,000 fine or 10 years imprisonment or both
Cannabis	• Cannabis resin of more than 200 grams – death • Cannabis mixture of more than 1 kilogram – death • Possession and consumption of cannabis – up to S$20,000 fine or 10 years imprisonment or both
Ecstasy	• Illegal traffic of Ecstasy – up to 20 years imprisonment and 15 strokes • Illegal import or export of Ecstasy – up to 30 years imprisonment and 15 strokes • Possession and consumption of Ecstasy – up to S$20,000 fine or 10 years imprisonment or both
Ice	• Illegal traffic, import or export of Ice of more than 250 grams – death • Possession and consumption of Ice – Up to S$20,000 fine or 10 years imprisonment or both
Opium	• Illegal traffic, import or export of opium of more than 1,200 grams and containing more than 30 grams of morphine – death • Possession and consumption of opium – up to S$20,000 fine or 10 years imprisonment or both

Source: National Council against Drug Abuse (NCADA), Singapore.

can be more effectively disseminated. For this purpose, a campaign would usually consist of a concert put up by both local and foreign artistes as well as various exhibitions and seminars organized by the NCADA or community and welfare groups. Selected student leaders such as school prefects and class monitors are invited to participate in these seminars with the aim of grooming them to counsel youths who could be tempted to take drugs. This is because youths can usually relate better to their peers and the student leaders can also double as role models to them.

CONCLUSION

In Southeast Asia, trafficking in persons is primarily considered a criminal problem and as such much of the anti-trafficking efforts have been aimed at criminalizing the phenomenon. This was done by either enacting new anti-trafficking legislation or by changing existing domestic laws. Although these efforts are commendable, states must now move beyond criminalization and should focus on putting legislation into practice. However, this is not an easy task. In most countries, the criminal system cannot be relied upon to combat trafficking due to corruption, lack of expertise on the part of law enforcement officials, lack of resources etc. Thus, for anti-trafficking legislation to be effective, it is important to revamp the entire criminal justice system and improve governance at all levels. In the case of illegal drug trafficking, states have primarily relied on traditional approaches aimed at reducing the flow of drugs (supply side). However, these measures cannot by themselves fully address the challenge. As the Singapore case study has shown, a balanced approach that emphasizes both the supply side as well as the demand side is essential to effectively combat the problems posed by illegal drug trafficking.

Notes

1. United Nations, Organised Transnational Crime, Economic and Social Council Resolution 1994/12.
2. UNODC, *World Drug Report 2010* (Geneva: UNODC, 2010).
3. United Nations, "Convention against Transnational Organized Crime and Its Protocols", 2000, available at <http://www.unodc.org/unodc/en/treaties/CTOC/index.html>.
4. P. Arlacchi, "The Dynamics of Illegal Markets", in *Combating Transnational Crime: Concepts, Activities, and Responses*, edited by P. Williams and Dimitri Vlassis (London: Frank Cass, 2001).

5   UNODC, *World Drug Report 2010* (Geneva: UNODC, 2010).

6   UNODC, *Opium Poppy Cultivation in South-East Asia: Lao PDR, Myanmar*
     (Geneva: UNODC, 2009), available at <http://www.unodc.org/documents/crop-
     monitoring/SEA_Opium_survey_2009.pdf>.

7   Ibid.

8   UNODC, *World Drug Report 2010* (Geneva: UNODC, 2010).

9   Ben Doherty, "Drug Smuggling into Thailand Soars Ahead of Burma Elections",
     guardian.co.uk, 21 June 2010, available at <http://www.guardian.co.uk/world/
     2010/jun/21/drug-smuggling-thailand-burma-elections>.

10   United Nations, "Protocol to Prevent, Suppress, and Punish Trafficking in
     Persons", (Geneva: UN, 2000).

11   ILO, "A Global Alliance against Forced Labor", Global Report under the follow-
     up to the ILO Declaration on Fundamental Principles and Rights at Work
     2005, Report I(B), International Labour Conference, 93rd Session (Geneva:
     International Labour Office, 2005), available at <http://www.ilo.org/public/
     english/standards/relm/ilc/ilc93/pdf/rep-i-b.pdf>.

12   U.S. Department of State, *Trafficking in Persons Report 2010*, June 2010,
     available at <http://www.state.gov/g/tip/rls/tiprpt/2010/>.

13   Annuska Derks, "Combating Trafficking in South East Asia: A Review of Policy
     and Programme Responses", International Organisation for Migration, 2000,
     available at <http://www.unesco.org/most/migration/ctsea.pdf>, p. 16.

14   UNODC, "World Drug Report 2009", United Nations Office on Drugs and
     Crime, 2009, available at <http://www.unodc.org/unodc/en/data-and-analysis/
     WDR-2009.html>.

15   Lim Lin Lean, ed. *The Sex Sector: The Economic and Social Bases of Prostitution
     in Southeast Asia* (Geneva: International Labour Office, 1998).

16   "2 Japanese Men Deported over Smuggling Workers", *The Star*, 27 May
     2010, available <http://www.asiaone.com/News/AsiaOne+News/Crime/Story/
     A1Story20100527-218795.html>.

17   Raman Iyer, "Malaysia Proposes Capping Number of Ships at Malacca Strait",
     Top News, 21 October 2008, available at <http://www.topnews.in/law/malaysia-
     proposes-capping-number-ships-malacca-strait>.

18   Catherine Zara Raymond, "Piracy in Southeast Asia: New Trends, Issues and
     Responses", *Harvard Asia Quarterly*, vol. IX, no. 4 (Fall 2005), available at
     <http://www.asiaquarterly.com/content/view/30/>.

19   Dev Kar and Devon Cartwright-Smith, *Illicit Financial Flows from Developing
     Countries 2002–2006* (Washington, D.C.: Global Financial Integrity, 2008).

20   Environmental Investigation Agency, "Environmental Crime: A Threat to Our
     Future", October 2008, available at <http://www.eia-international.org/files/
     reports171-1.pdf>.

21   Traffic, "What's Driving the Wildlife Trade?", World Bank Discussion Paper,
     October 2008, available at <www.traffic.org/.../traffic_pub_gen24_executive%
     20summary.pdf>.

22 Alison Hoare, "International Environmental Crime, Sustainability and Poverty", Background paper for Session 1, The Growth and Control of International Environmental Crime, Chatham House workshop, 10–11 December 2007 (London: Chatham House, 2007).

23 Vincent Nijman, "An Overview of International Wildlife Trade from Southeast Asia", *Biodiversity and Conservation*, published online 23 December 2009, available at <http://www.springerlink.com/content/h2484mj16755071q/fulltext.pdf>.

24 Christian Thompson, "Tigers on the Brink: Facing Up to the Challenge in the Greater Mekong: Cambodia, Laos, Myanmar, Thailand and Vietnam", (Vientiane: WWF Greater Mekong, 2010), available at <http://assets.panda.org/downloads/tiger_report_pdf_webversion_1.pdf>.

25 David J. Agnew et al., "Estimating the Worldwide Extent of Illegal Fishing", PLoS ONE, 4(2): e4570, 25 February 2009, available at <http://www.plosone.org/article/info:doi/10.1371/journal.pone.0004570>.

26 Dalih Sembiring, "Indonesian Minister Calls for International Effort Against Illegal Fishing", *Jakarta Globe*, 16 August 2009, available at <http://thejakartaglobe.com/home/indonesian-minister-calls-for-international-effort-against-illegal-fishing/324320>.

27 Frank Miller, Rodney Taylor, and George White, "Keep It Legal: Best Practices for Keeping Illegally Harvested Timber Out of Your Supply Chain", WWF's Global Forest & Trade Network, July 2006, available at <http://assets.panda.org/downloads/keep_it_legal_final_no_fsc.pdf>.

28 UNODC, *World Drug Report 2010* (Geneva: UNODC, 2010).

29 HRW, "Perilous Plight: Burma's Rohingyas Take to the Seas", Human Rights Watch, May 2009.

30 UNODC, *World Drug Report 2010* (Geneva: UNODC, 2010).

31 Human Rights Watch, "Not Enough Graves: The War on Drugs, HIV/AIDS, and Violations of Human Rights", Human Rights Watch, vol. 16, no. 8 (C), June 2004, available at <http://www.hrw.org/sites/default/files/reports/thailand0704.pdf>.

32 Ben Doherty, "Drug Smuggling into Thailand Soars Ahead of Burma Elections", guardian.co.uk, 21 June 2010, available at <http://www.guardian.co.uk/world/2010/jun/21/drug-smuggling-thailand-burma-elections>.

33 ILO, "A Global Alliance against Forced Labour", Global Report under the follow-up to the ILO Declaration on Fundamental Principles and Rights at Work 2005, Report I(B), International Labour Conference, 93rd Session (Geneva: International Labour Office 2005), available at <http://www.ilo.org/public/english/standards/relm/ilc/ilc93/pdf/rep-i-b.pdf>.

34 U.S. Department of State, *Trafficking in Persons Report 2008*, June 2008, available at <http://www.state.gov/g/tip/rls/tiprpt/2008/>.

35 Annuska Derks, "Combating Trafficking in South East Asia: A Review of Policy and Programme Responses", International Organisation for Migration, 2000, available at <http://www.unesco.org/most/migration/ctsea.pdf>, p. 16.

[36] UNODC, "World Drug Report 2009", United Nations Office on Drugs and Crime, 2009, available at <http://www.unodc.org/unodc/en/data-and-analysis/WDR-2009.html>.
[37] Central Narcotics Bureau, "Drug Situation Report 2006", available at <http://www.cnb.gov.sg/drugs/drugsituationreport/drugsituationreport2006.aspx>.
[38] Central Narcotics Bureau, "Drug Situation Report 2009", available at <http://www.cnb.gov.sg/drugs/drugsituationreport/drugsituationreport2009.aspx>.

References

"2 Japanese Men Deported over Smuggling Workers". *The Star*, 27 May 2010. Available at <http://www.asiaone.com/News/AsiaOne+News/Crime/Story/A1Story20100527-218795.html>.

Agnew, David J. et al. "Estimating the Worldwide Extent of Illegal Fishing". PLoS ONE, 4(2): e4570, 25 February 2009. Available at <http://www.plosone.org/article/info:doi/10.1371/journal.pone.0004570>.

Arlacchi, P. "The Dynamics of Illegal Markets". In *Combating Transnational Crime: Concepts, Activities, and Responses*, edited by P. Williams and Dimitri Vlassis. London: Frank Cass, 2001.

Central Narcotics Bureau. "Drug Situation Report 2009". Available at <http://www.cnb.gov.sg/drugs/drugsituationreport/drugsituationreport2009.aspx>.

———. "Drug Situation Report 2006". Available at <http://www.cnb.gov.sg/drugs/drugsituationreport/drugsituationreport2006.aspx>.

Derks, Annuska. "Combating Trafficking in South East Asia: A Review of Policy and Programme Responses". International Organisation for Migration, 2000. Available at <http://www.unesco.org/most/migration/ctsea.pdf>.

Doherty, Ben. "Drug Smuggling into Thailand Soars Ahead of Burma Elections". guardian.co.uk, 21 June 2010. Available at <http://www.guardian.co.uk/world/2010/jun/21/drug-smuggling-thailand-burma-elections>.

Environmental Investigation Agency. "Environmental Crime: A Threat to Our Future", October 2008. Available at <http://www.eia-international.org/files/reports171-1.pdf>.

Hoare, Alison. "International Environmental Crime, Sustainability and Poverty". Background paper for Session 1. The Growth and Control of International Environmental Crime, Chatham House workshop, 10–11 December 2007. London: Chatham House, 2007.

HRW. "Perilous Plight: Burma's Rohingyas Take to the Seas". Human Rights Watch, May 2009.

Human Rights Watch. "Not Enough Graves: The War on Drugs, HIV/AIDS, and Violations of Human Rights". Human Rights Watch, vol. 16, no. 8 (C), June 2004. Available at <http://www.hrw.org/sites/default/files/reports/thailand0704.pdf>.

ILO. "A Global Alliance against Forced Labour". Global Report under the follow-up to the ILO Declaration on Fundamental Principles and Rights at Work 2005, Report I(B), International Labour Conference, 93rd Session. Geneva: International Labour Office, 2005. Available: <http://www.ilo.org/public/english/standards/relm/ilc/ilc93/pdf/rep-i-b.pdf>.

Iyer, Raman. "Malaysia Proposes Capping Number of Ships at Malacca Strait". *Top News*, 21 October 2008. Available at <http://www.topnews.in/law/malaysia-proposes-capping-number-ships-malacca-strait>.

Kar, Dev and Devon Cartwright-Smith. *Illicit Financial Flows from Developing Countries 2002–2006*. Washington, D.C.: Global Financial Integrity, 2008.

Lim, Lin Lean, ed. *The Sex Sector: The Economic and Social Bases of Prostitution in Southeast Asia*. Geneva: International Labour Office, 1998.

Miller, Frank, Rodney Taylor, and George White. "Keep It Legal: Best Practices for Keeping Illegally Harvested Timber Out of Your Supply Chain". WWF's Global Forest & Trade Network, July 2006. Available at <http://assets.panda.org/downloads/keep_it_legal_final_no_fsc.pdf>.

Nijman, Vincent. "An Overview of International Wildlife Trade from Southeast Asia". *Biodiversity and Conservation*, published online 23 December 2009. Available at <http://www.springerlink.com/content/h2484mj16755071q/fulltext.pdf>.

Raymond, Catherine Zara. "Piracy in Southeast Asia: New Trends, Issues and Responses". *Harvard Asia Quarterly*, vol. IX, no. 4 (Fall 2005). Available at <http://www.asiaquarterly.com/content/view/30/>.

Sembiring, Dalih. "Indonesian Minister Calls for International Effort Against Illegal Fishing". *Jakarta Globe*, 16 August 2009. Available at <http://thejakartaglobe.com/home/indonesian-minister-calls-for-international-effort-against-illegal-fishing/324320>.

Thompson, Christian. "Tigers on the Brink: Facing Up to the Challenge in the Greater Mekong: Cambodia, Laos, Myanmar, Thailand and Vietnam". Vientiane: WWF Greater Mekong, 2010. Available at <http://assets.panda.org/downloads/tiger_report_pdf_webversion_1.pdf>.

Traffic. "What's Driving the Wildlife Trade?" World Bank Discussion Paper, October 2008. Available at <www.traffic.org/.../traffic_pub_gen24_executive%20summary.pdf>.

United Nations. "Convention against Transnational Organized Crime and Its Protocols", 2000. Available at <http://www.unodc.org/unodc/en/treaties/CTOC/index.html>.

———. "Protocol to Prevent, Suppress, and Punish Trafficking in Persons". Geneva: UN, 2000.

UNODC. *World Drug Report 2010*. Geneva: UNODC, 2010.

———. *Opium Poppy Cultivation in South-East Asia: Lao PDR, Myanmar*. Geneva: UNODC, 2009. Available at <http://www.unodc.org/documents/crop-monitoring/SEA_Opium_survey_2009.pdf>.

————. "World Drug Report 2009". United Nations Office on Drugs and Crime, 2009. Available at <http://www.unodc.org/unodc/en/data-and-analysis/WDR-2009.html>.

US Department of State. *Trafficking in Persons Report 2010*, June 2010. Available at <http://www.state.gov/g/tip/rls/tiprpt/2010/>.

————. *Trafficking in Persons Report 2008*, June 2008. Available at <http://www.state.gov/g/tip/rls/tiprpt/2008/>.

10

CYBER SECURITY

Nur Azha Putra and
Kevin Punzalan

The cyber-attacks on South Korea and the United States, as well as those on Georgia in 2008 and Estonia in 2007 have awakened a certain consciousness in the minds of the international community, particularly that of the security community. As if triggered by a sense of vulnerability, when these cyber-attacks managed to disrupt normal services, states were hard pressed to extend national security policies to the realm of cyberspace especially those with highly developed information and communication technology structures. This chapter traces the securitization of cyberspace and ponders its implications for human security.

The secretary-general of the United Nation's (UN) International Telecommunication Union (ITU), Dr Hamadoun Toure, warned that the next world war could take place in cyberspace. Speaking to stakeholders from across all sectors including heads of state, Dr Toure called for global cooperation across all industries and sectors to provide cyber security which includes the protection of children, businesses and governments. He stressed that cyber security could only be achieved within an international global framework comprising countries who are committed towards protecting their citizens and privacy. "The next world war could happen in cyberspace and that would be a catastrophe. We have to make sure that all countries understand that in that war, there is no such thing as a superpower", said Dr Toure.[1]

Although Dr Toure's remarks seem alarming, he is not alone. The proliferation of cyber wars and cybercrimes have driven multilateral institutions such as the European Union (EU), North Atlantic Treaty Organization

(NATO) and the Association of Southeast Asian Nations (ASEAN) as well as national governments such as the United States (U.S.), the United Kingdom (UK), Australia, Malaysia and Singapore towards securing their cyberspace.

Anti-cybercrime laws empower the national cyber security agencies with the legal mandate to protect the state's critical information and communications technology (ICT) networks and infrastructure, particularly from international cyber criminals and cyber terrorists. The initial phase of delivering ICT infrastructures which drove the transformation from the Industrial Society to the Information Society has now been coupled with efforts to secure cyberspace. ICT, which was initially meant to reduce the spatial dimension and enhance global communication, has now taken the added burden of national security and sovereignty.

GLOBAL ISSUES AND POLICY PATHWAYS IN CYBER SECURITY

The issue of vulnerabilities and threats posed in cyberspace go beyond those which are politically motivated.

Global internet security giant, McAfee in its 2007 virtual criminology report, *Cybercrime: The Next Wave*, identified three emerging global trends in cyberspace — a growing threat to national security from web espionage, an increasing threat to online services and an emergence of a sophisticated market of software vulnerabilities.

In its 2008 report, *Cybercrime versus Cyberlaw*, McAfee highlighted several issues:

- Governments have not given enough priority to cybercrime;
- There is a lack of a transnational law enforcement regime to combat cybercrime which thus impedes international cooperation; and
- Law enforcement at the national and local levels are ill-equipped to cope with increasing cybercrimes especially in digital forensics and evidence collection.[2]

Earlier this year at the World Economic Forum, McAfee projected that companies worldwide have lost more than US$1 trillion in 2008 due to the loss of intellectual property rights and the costs of repairs to damaged data, amongst other things which were revealed in its report titled *Unsecured Economies: Protecting Vital Information*. In particular, the report revealed that cyber mafia gangs are increasingly trying to infiltrate corporations. Using phishing techniques, cyber criminals target top executives in an attempt to steal vital information.

A 2005 global report by Symantec Corporation, a global information security corporation, showed that Denial of Service attacks grew by nearly 700 per cent. These attacks increased by 119 per day to an average of 927 a day. The largest increase occurred in the small business sector and the education industry. The U.S., Germany and the UK are the top three locations where these attacks occurred.

The *Symantec Internet Security Threat Report* observed that amongst the threat activity occurring in the government and infrastructure sectors, malicious activities occured the most in the telecommunications infrastructure sector.[3] China, as a country of origin, accounted for 22 per cent of the total attacks conducted against governments worldwide. This represented an increase of 8 per cent in 2007. The most common form of attack against government sectors was in Denial of Service attacks. Meanwhile, 28 per cent of attacks originated from within the U.S. and targeted the government sectors in Europe, the Middle East and Africa.

Telus Security Solutions, an international internet security firm, pointed out the rising rate of identity theft, increasing vulnerability due to shrinking time between exposure and attacks, increased incidents of spams, the targeting of desktop computers and web-based applications, and risks stemming from mobility of data. Perhaps, more importantly is the "professionalisation" of cybercrime. In recent years and perhaps due to the global economic recession, hacking has transformed from a personal hobby to that of an organized criminal business activity. In fact, Telus has singled out criminals rather than terrorists as the main perpetrators of internet-based attacks.[4]

In addition to the proliferation of cybercrimes and cyber espionage, there have been an increased number of alleged incidents of international cyber wars and cyber terrorism.

International Cyber-Attack Incidents

In 2007, Estonia was in the middle of a diplomatic dispute with Russia over their removal of a Russian public war memorial. As a result, or by coincidence, the Baltic state came under intense cyber warfare attacks. According to several news reports, these attacks resulted in the disabling of several government websites, newspaper organizations, two of the country's largest banks and companies specializing in communications. Estonia was especially vulnerable considering that it is one of the most wired countries in Europe.[5]

Cyberspace and the Military

Although the issue of cyber security is not new, political observers noted that there has been an increase in the militarization of cyberspace especially since 9/11. Deibert for instance, pointed out that, fuelled by the fear of the potential use by terrorists of electronic networks and an "electronic Pearl Harbour", states have been gradually adopting offensive information warfare capabilities. Drawing upon the theory of the Revolution in Military Affairs, Deibert explained that states have increasingly adopted the innovative use of technologies and organization structures as a product of the advances made in the communication and computing technologies. Consequently, cyber war tools such as remote sensing and electronic viruses have led to a major change in the nature of warfare.[6]

According to him, the U.S. is leading the cyber arms race and employs computer hackers, developed advanced computer viruses, worms and Trojan horses and has drawn up guidelines for conducting cyber warfare. The guidelines include establishing the rules and framework within which the U.S. would penetrate and disrupt foreign states' computer systems.[7] Deibert however was unable to cite or refer to any other sources apart from news reports.

Nevertheless, he was quick to point out that many observers are sceptical over the degree of threat involved due to the technological limitation of the ICT architecture, which limits assaults only to the realm of cyberspace and also because of the low pay-off for terrorists whose ultimate aim is premised on physical bodily harm.

Furthermore, Deibert highlighted that there has not been any real evidence of actual acts of cyber terrorism unless one adopts a maximalist perspective and considers any form of hacking and DDoS attacks as attempts towards mass destruction. To Deibert, hacking and DDoS attacks are merely attempts to periodically disrupt internet traffic.[8]

For nearly three weeks, these websites were barraged with Distributed Denial of Service (DDoS) attacks which inevitably paralysed the targeted websites. DDoS is a situation whereby the host computer (or web server), which houses the targeted website, is unable to respond or communicate with legitimate requests from other computers because its resources have been consumed by the barrage of requests from the attackers. Thus a DDoS attack serves to deny service to other legitimate users by consuming the web server's resources with an overwhelming number of requests.

A similar attack occurred in Georgia in August 2008 when the former Soviet state was under "cyber siege". DDoS attacks were carried out against several government websites following a period of armed conflict between Georgia and Russia over the issue of South Ossetia. The affected websites were those of the Georgian presidential office, Ministry of Defense and Ministry of Foreign Affairs. Interestingly, independent security researchers found that the attacks came from internet traffic which originated in Germany but were re-routed to Georgia via Russia.

In July 2009, South Korea and the U.S. were subjected to three waves of DDoS attacks. According to news reports, a leading South Korean national newspaper and its spy agency were hit by an unnaturally high volume of internet traffic. In the U.S., the White House and Pentagon were targeted. Perhaps to coincide with the American Independence Day, the first wave started on 4 July, followed by 7 July and finally on 9 July. However, subsequent statements from the affected government agencies and cyber security experts claimed that these attacks, while malicious, were not detrimental as it did not lead to any major disruptions.

Nearer to home, several Malaysian government websites, universities and private institutions were allegedly penetrated by Indonesian hackers during the Malaysia-Indonesia Ambalat dispute in 2005, according to a report by Malaysia's Centre for Maritime Security and Diplomacy. High-profile websites that were hacked included the Malaysian Communication and Multimedia Commission, the Universiti Sains Malaysia and the Public Works Department. The hackers left behind a political message alluding to the disputed Ambalat issue and Malaysia's Ops Tegas. Ops Tegas was a nationwide law enforcement operation which targeted illegal immigrants.

The report further mentioned that the hacker left the following message on the Public Works Department website:

With respect,

In the name of the law, I order you, Malaysian government, please retreat from Indonesian area. Please don't be too greedy. Indonesia is having bad days recently. The natural disasters, increasing poverty, etc. Your country is much more prosperous than Indonesia. Don't you be ashamed?

FYI. I'm not a hacker.

Re-Rationalizing Cyber-Attacks

This section uses the word "alleged" repeatedly throughout to exercise caution when linking international cyber-attacks to conflicts between states, for several reasons. The main reason is that, while ICT has developed rapidly over the last few decades, most states are still ill-equipped in evidence gathering and digital forensics. While there is the technological capability to trace and therefore locate the physical location of cyber-attacks, it remains difficult to determine the actual perpetrators and their motives unless they are caught and prosecuted. In the minds of traditional security analysts, cyber vandalism could easily be passed off as acts of terrorism while commercial hacking could be misintepreted as cyber espionage.

In all of the international cyber-attacks cited above, news reports, political observers and security specialists were quick to frame and link these cyber-attacks to strained diplomatic and international relations and armed conflicts, particularly in the case of Georgia. Despite the lack of actual evidence and in the absence of any arrests, attempts at rationalizing cyber conflicts remain speculative at best and politicized at worst. As pointed out by political observer, Ronald Deibert,

"In spite of the alarm, there are no empirical examples of cyber-terrorism to date, unless the term is used so broadly as to encompass politically motivated hacks on websites and occasional inconveniences caused by denial of service attacks."[9]

Perhaps more worrying is the potential for such speculation and politicisation to intensify already deteriorating diplomatic relations between affected nations.

POLICY PATHWAYS IN
NATIONAL CYBER SECURITY POLICIES

Following the spate of international cyber-attacks in the 2000s, the issue of cyber security has inevitably received increased attention from the security community. In certain countries, the issue of cyber security has been elevated to the level of high politics and figures prominently in the national security agenda and ICT architecture. Cyber security policies have been formulated with the intent to defend the integrity of states' information systems and communication networks while national cyber security agencies in its different permutations have been created to institutionalize these policies. Most of these cyber security doctrines were articulated within the language of traditional security norms that emphasizes state security and sovereignty.

For instance, at the highest international forum and as mentioned earlier, the Secretary-General of the UN's ITU, Dr Toure warned that the next world war may occur in cyberspace. His warning leaves little to the imagination.[10]

In a U.S. government report titled *Cyberspace Policy Review* released in May 2009, it was mentioned that threats to cyberspace have security implications for the global economic and security challenges of the 21st century. Other news reports quoted the Director of U.S. National Intelligence as saying that the biggest cyber threat facing the U.S. is from other nation-states, particularly Russia and China.[11]

In an interview with the British Broadcasting Corporation, the U.K. prime minister said that terrorists are using the internet in an exploitative way and therefore Britain needs to develop a national security strategy to protect itself from organized crime and terrorist threats from individuals, companies and governments.[12]

Suleyman Anil, a senior official with NATO, was quoted in news reports as saying that "cyber defence is now mentioned at the highest level along with missile defence and energy security". In the same report, Anil suggested that rogue nations would resort to cyber terrorism to shut down formal online communication networks and the websites of official institutions.[13]

In Southeast Asia, Singapore and Malaysia have taken a stand on cyber security albeit with slight variations in conceptual models. Prior to the launching of the Singapore Infocomm Technology Security Authority (SITSA) on 1 October 2009, the Ministry of Home Affairs announced that the SITSA mission is to secure the country's information technology environment against external threats to national security such as cyber terrorism and cyber espionage. Amongst its other area of focus, SITSA is also responsible for the country's planning, preparedness and response against major external cyber-attacks. Its immediate tasks is twofold: first, it plans to strengthen the critical information infrastructure against cyber-attacks and second, to achieve a higher level of national preparedness in response to cyber-attacks.

The Malaysian cyber security agency, CyberSecurity Malaysia, was established in 2007 under the purview of the Ministry of Science, Technology and Innovation, to reduce the nation's vulnerability in ICT systems and networks, amongst other objectives. However, CyberSecurity Malaysia is not a law enforcement agency but instead provides cyber forensics and analysis and also provides expert witnesses in court. The agency operates within a larger national cyber security policy framework designed to support a K-economy (knowledge-based economy). Although there was no mention of specific threats such as cyber terrorism, it frames cyber threats as one which is detrimental towards its use of ICT for socio-economic development.

Securitization of Cyberspace

Judging by the national cyber security policies as highlighted earlier, it appears that cyberspace has effectively been securitized to the extent that states have generally adopted a defensive cyber security posture. Most cyber security policies are framed within the language of national security and in the interests of protecting national economies. States and the business community are increasingly vulnerable to cyber-attacks, cyber espionage and commercial hacking. The security threats posed by cyber terrorists from rogue nations and "hackers" posed significant danger to the social, political and economic survival of nations, as security specialists and policy-makers have argued. In fact, if left undeterred, cyber wars could even lead to a third world war, as Dr Toure has warned.[14] Thus, the survival of states and the global economy is dependent on the institutionalization of a cyber-security agenda, which is primarily targeted at securing the integrity of the national communications and information architecture and the protection of classified data.

Humanizing Cyberspace

However, there is also the element of human security in cyberspace which must be taken into consideration in analysing the security implications of cyberspace. States are not the only referent object as the widespread implementation of ICT has transformed society into one which is dependent on the production and delivery of information. The general consensus is that ICT was responsible for the transformation from the Industrial Society to the Information Society. Access to information has been a key characteristic of the Information Society. In fact, to a certain extent, vulnerabilities in the Information Society is measured by the degree of an individual or society's acessibility to information.

In his speech which appeared on the *Bangkok Post* news website, Professor Vitit Muntarbhorn outlined several issues which test the linkage between human security and the information age. Amongst these issues are "access to information and education, reduction of internet gap, cyberspace law and human capacity building for information security and community-based approach".[15] Professor Vitit opines that human security is dependent on the access to information and education, and are interlinked with access to quality education, which can be delivered on the ICT platform.[16]

Furthermore, a person's potential for development can be increased if there is access to modern communication channels. Thus computer literacy, which is a basic prerequisite for many jobs, is necessary in the employment market in the Information Society. However, he pointed out that there is a wide internet gap between developed and developing societies which further disadvantages developing communities' economies.[17] The internet gap has to be reduced to decrease this disparity.

The liberalization of cyberspace serves as a liberating force for human security because people are free to express themselves and communicate via cyberspace. However, state regulations which attempt to control cyberspace may be met with resistance, although it could serve to protect copyright laws and prevent human rights abuses. Professor Vitit advocates human-capacity building to deter any compromise in information security. Staff who are information-proficient and skilled in computer skills and are of the suitable psychological make-up could respond to the needs of an information security environment better than those who lack these attributes.

Finally, a community-based approach towards the promotion and protection of human security would lead towards the positive use of information. This requires the drawing in of community participation of civil society organizations, community watchdogs as well as the media in generating the right information, which could then be disseminated to the larger society.[18]

The international cyber-attacks incidents in recent years have awoken a certain consciousness on the need to extend national security interests to the realm of cyberspace. As if triggered by the international DDoS attacks which occurred in Georgia and then Estonia, followed by the U.S. and South Korea, states which have a highly developed ICT structure have taken the issue of cyber security to the next level. The institutionalization of cyber security agencies and national cyber security policies marked a turning point in the evolution of international politics, conflicts and warfare.

Amidst these developments, there is also a growing concern amongst non-governmental organizations, global civil society and political observers of the impact of the securitization of cyberspace on human security. This development also raises questions about the impact of national cyber security policies on national governments in terms of governance and bureaucratic procedures. Another issue of concern is how would these national cyber security policies affect international cooperation? Would it lead to greater cooperation or to a widened technological or internet gap that would leave developing economies and societies further behind? These are some of the issues that will be discussed in the next section.

EU Convention on Cybercrime

Opening for Signature	Entry Into Force
Place: Budapest Date: 23/11/2001	Conditions: 5 Ratifications including at least 3 member States of the Council of Europe Date : 1/7/2004

Status as of October 14, 2009.

Presently, transnational cooperation on cyber security is certainly not comprehensive enough. To begin with, international cooperation lacks adequate global participation and thus support. It is not as extensive as the global use of ICT. As of 12 October 2009, despite its limitations, the European Union (EU) Convention on Cyber Security is perhaps the most comprehensive and extensive, although the agreement is only signed by E.U. member states, the U.S. and a handful of others.

Refer to **appendix** for complete list.

Glossary of Key Cyber Security Terms

Cyberspace	An environment in which digitized information is distributed on networks of computers.
Cyber Security	Measures taken to protect computers or critical infrastructure, although some experts suggest that it is about protecting everything of value.
Cyber Warfare	Using computers and the Internet to attack others via their computer systems. Targets may include military computer networks, power grids, banks, and government and media Web sites. Most often the goal is to disrupt the functioning of the target system.
Cybercrime	Criminal activities that make use of computers or networks.
Distributed Denial-of-Service Attacks	Flooding the networks or servers of individuals or organizations with false data requests so they are unable to respond to requests from legitimate users.

Cyber Terrorism	The premeditated, politically motivated attack against information, computer systems, computer programs, and data which result in violence against noncombatant targets by sub-national groups or clandestine agents.
Cyber Espionage/ *Cyber Spying*	The act or practice of obtaining secrets (sensitive, proprietary or classified information) from individuals, competitors, rivals, groups, governments and enemies also for military, political, or economic advantage using illegal exploitation methods on internet, networks, software and or computers. *Source:* wikipedia
Note:	*There is no standard definition of cyber security terms since perception of security threats varies according to context. Therefore, this list is to be treated as a general reference only.*

Source: The U.S Federal Bureau of Investigation
Link: <http://www.america.gov/st/peacesec-english/2009/September/20090917175715sjhtrop0.2718012.html>.

NON-TRADITIONAL APPROACHES
TO CYBER SECURITY

The discourse on Cyber Security, a relatively new field in non-traditional security studies, has been dominated by the need to protect information infrastructure from both state and non-state actors. However, this conception fails to consider alternative definitions of Cyber Security. Alternate conceptions value information, access and integrity as equal to the need to protect the confidentiality of information, and allows non-state actors to act as agents of securitization.

In the previous section, current trends and issues in the securitization of cyberspace were discussed, along with contemporary threats and their potential to disrupt electronic infrastructure. It was pointed out that analysts have begun to consider cyber security as an aspect of national security that must be guaranteed, as illustrated by the cyber-attacks on Estonia and Malaysia.

These attacks, which so far have consisted of Distributed Denial-of-Service (DDoS) attacks aimed at disrupting information systems, belong to a dominant narrative of cyber security. However, a clearer picture forms when the narrative is analysed through the Copenhagen School's securitization model. In deconstructing the narratives, the state as the securitizing actor identified its cyberspace as a national security concern which therefore requires the allocation of the government's resources to mitigate the threats. Hence, in this narrative, the state's national information and communications networks are the primary referent of security and threats emanate from rogue actors via unsecured global networks.

Despite this dominant narrative, other conceptions exist, which utilize different agents and referents in place of the state and its security concerns. This chapter examines the alternative and perhaps contending conceptions of Cyber Security and the corresponding issues.

The Dualistic Model of Technical Computer Security and Cyber Security

Helen Nissenbaum illustrated the contrasting conceptions of computer security and cyber security. While the two conceptions share similar elements, each model embodies different values. While "technical computer security" is defined by its goals of ensuring information availability, integrity, and confidentiality through the protection of computer systems and users, "Cyber Security" is defined by its goals of protecting the state from the use of networked computers for subversive purposes, actual attacks on critical societal infrastructure dependent on computers, and from the threat of network disablement.[19]

Her model of "technical computer security", in essence, makes the protection of information the referent of securitization, and allows a number of actors, including individuals, private institutions such as private internet security companies, the media, and non-government organizations (NGOs) to become agents of securitization. In contrast, her model of "Cyber Security" firmly ensconces the state as the sole and primary agent, and elevates the "national interest" as the referent. The implications of the differences between these two models are profound.[20] While the former model requires that the strength of the various actors affected by breaches of security to strengthen their individual capacities and to reduce their vulnerabilities, the latter model allows the state to justify measures that may curtail the freedom of other actors in the name of national security, including the centralization of control over networks, technical barricades

Table 10.1
Nissenbaum's Conceptions of Security

	Technical Computer Security Model	Cyber Security Model
Securitizing Actors	Individuals, media, NGOs, business, private internet security companies	State, government organs
Referents	Protection of information availability, integrity, and confidentiality	Protection of classified information infrastructure from subversion, disruptive attacks and network disablement
Measures to attain security	Reduction of security vulnerabilities, strengthening of individual security capacity	Centralisation of network control, technical barricades, monitoring and filtering information from users, surveillance

Source: Nissenbaum 2005.

that restrict access to online information, and mechanisms that monitor and filter information flows.

Ironically, the Cyber-Security model may enhance network security, but also marginalizes the ability of cyberspace to adhere to its original role: as a realm of public exchange, as pointed out by Nissenbaum.[21] This in effect increases the security of the state, but may harm the human security of non-state actors who are also end-users of the network infrastructure that the state aims to protect. This point is further developed in the next model to be discussed.

The "Panopticon": Surveillance and Cyber Security

In essence, the creation of a surveillance regime has helped transpose elements of Jeremy Bentham's "Panopticon Model" of maintaining discipline onto society itself. While the Panopticon was intended as a system for efficiently maintaining surveillance over prisoners, it may now be used to characterize a modern "capitalist surveillance regime". Richard Fox has suggested that modern forms of surveillance allow the state to not only ensure compliance with laws, but also to allow it to shape and tailor policies based on the information it has collected on its citizens. While it is true that this form of surveillance has not occurred without the awareness or consent of modern citizenry, its collective effect has been to induce "conformity through deterrence", and to minimize the risks posed by individuals by "excluding potential rule breakers from opportunities".[22] The surveillance regime essentially creates an imbalanced relationship between the state (or private entities) and the monitored individuals, because the latter have little control or knowledge of how information collected on them is used.

In the process of protecting national security in the case of the state, or pursuing commercial competitiveness in the case of business entities, *passive surveillance has the potential to endanger the security of those being monitored in terms of their right to privacy.* In contrast to the state's referent of national security (an existential prerogative), an individual or organization being monitored is inhibited from the exercise of freedom of movement, association, assembly and speech.[23] The prevention of the exercise of these rights impedes human security in both the personal and political dimensions, as outlined by the 1994 United Nations Human Development Report.

However, it is simultaneously impractical and problematic to discount all forms of surveillance as unnecessary, as the state possesses the responsibility to pursue cyber criminals and to monitor genuine and imminent threats to national security. To accommodate both perspectives, better designed controls on the surveillance powers of the state and private organizations are necessary. Progress on this front remains to be seen, however. As late as April of this year, the director of the National Cyber Security Center at the Homeland Security Department of the United States (U.S.), Mr Rod Beckstrom, resigned over concerns that the National Security Agency would acquire surveillance powers over federal employees, even as these were ostensibly targetting foreign cyber security threats.[24] In the same article, the Director of National Intelligence, Dennis Blair, admitted that there had been occasions that the U.S. government had "intercepted the wrong communications", but did not reveal the scale or frequency of these incidents.

Nevertheless, the expansion of electronic surveillance has greatly increased since the advent of the information revolution. The employment of this tool has become routine, especially in securing sensitive physical infrastructure and in preventing and deterring crime. Surveillance on the internet has also been made possible by legislation which allows national authorities to intercept different forms of electronic communication without legal hindrances.

In 1994, the United States enacted federal laws that required telecommunication agencies to ensure that their services are open to interception by law enforcement agencies. In 2000, the United Kingdom enacted legislation that required companies to install decoding equipment that allowed law enforcement agents to monitor emails on their networks. Government databases may now be interlinked, allowing police databases to share information with other government offices, such as with social welfare or child protection services.[25]

> Ironically, the Cyber-Security model may enhance network security, but also marginalises the ability of cyberspace to adhere to its original role: as a realm of public exchange, as pointed out by Nissenbaum.

The International Telecommunications Union (ITU) is in the process of drafting an international protocol on cyber security and cybercrime, which was proposed in November 2008. In 2007, the United States ratified the Council of Europe Convention on Cybercrime, which came into force in January of that year. Singapore, Malaysia and Brunei signed a joint initiative on cybercrime on 23 March 2006. Indonesia passed an Electronic Transaction and Information Law in 2005. In the Philippines, a bill on cybercrime was filed in the Philippine Senate in April of 2009.[26]

In comparison, the previous model held the protection of information networks and users as the primary referents of security while the current model considers the enforcement of laws and the prevention of cybercrimes as its referents. The state remains important, but private corporations, particularly those that have an interest in protecting intellectual property rights (such as media companies) are also considered securitizing actors.

Innovations in communications technology and the outsourcing of government functions to the private sector have allowed the latter to assume powers of surveillance that it did not previously possess. Databases of many large companies collect information on prospective consumers and aim to discern consumer practices. Internet giant Google's AdSense program allows web developers to earn revenue by displaying advertisements tailored to the interests of the visitors of their websites.[27] For example, "Cookies", a text file utilized by internet web browsers to store personalized information about the user's web preferences, is a form of passive surveillance, which is why internet browsers offer users the choice to disable them.[28]

Other examples include the use of credit records, which are stored online and transmitted via credit reference associations, and may be used against individuals with bad credit records from accessing a full array of online services.[29] In 2009, a cyber-spying network was uncovered by the Citizen Lab, a think-tank based at the University of Toronto. The network had compromised thousands of computer around the world, many of which were considered "sensitive targets" such as those located in "foreign ministries, embassies, news organizations, international organizations, and NGOs. They included the offices of the Dalai Lama, the Russian embassy in Beijing, foreign affairs ministries in Iran and Indonesia, the Indian diplomatic service, and the Asian Development Bank".[30]

Although these innovations have contributed to greater efficiency in the apprehension of crime in the public sector and the efficiency of marketing and advertising strategy in the private sector, the increase in reach and capabilities of surveillance regimes could potentially compromise the individual's right to privacy as pointed out by Richard Fox. He warned that routine surveillance "creates an abiding sense of communal unease in which awareness of such scrutiny tends to chill the exercise of accepted civic rights, which include freedom of movement, association, assembly and speech".[31] In the private sector, data gathered as a result of passive surveillance of commercial transactions may lead to discrimination against consumers, as in the case of "dynamic pricing", where prices offered by a retailer differ based on data of customer purchasing habits.

E-Governance: Managing State and Society in Cyberspace

Another aspect of cyber security that merits examination is how e-governance has affected the relationship between the state and society. E-governance is defined as the application of electronic means in the interaction between government and citizens and government and businesses, as well as in internal government operations. E-governance is utilized to simplify and improve democratic, government, and business aspects of governance.[32] An essential function of e-government is the access and exchange of information, which makes interaction between a government and its citizens more efficient, and has the potential to increase the means of political interaction.[33] In addition, information released by government agencies is often viewed by citizens as coming from "objective authoritative sources", and e-government allows wider and faster dissemination of this information.

> E-government, the use of electronic means to facilitate formal and institutional processes that operate at the national level to maintain public order and facilitate collective action,[34] can take the form of:

- direct email connectivity for public servants;
- online forums for espressing opinions and approval on policies;
- online transactions for government services; and
- networking between different government offices for the sharing of information.

E-government also has the potential to expand political discourse across a greater range of the population, but this has mixed effects. In the case of Usenet online forums, the expansion of political participation has also led to greater polarization of views, as the structure of these forums is topic-based, and tends to bring together people with similar views. Their isolation in topic-based forums leads to their isolation from the general public, and thus prevents them from being exposed to critical responses. In the case of the United States, the fact that most people who make use of such online tools come from the American middle class further limits the plurality of the political discourse.[35]

Governments themselves may also use their e-government resources to present particular policies in a positive light, using their advantage of being a trusted information source to advance particular agendas even if dissent or opposition to these policies from different sectors of society exist. A particular example was that documented by Paul Jaeger: the website of the American "No Child Left Behind" Program. While the website of the said programme was intended to inform stakeholders and the general public of the details and potential benefits, the way the site was designed was so that none of the drawbacks and costs the programme would incur were published online. Because of this, critics viewed the website as partisan and biased towards the programme.[36]

With an e-governance framework of securitization, the referent and agents of securitization differ according to the political framework of the state in question. "Closed" or authoritarian systems hold the state as the sole securitizing agent, with national security as the primary referent. Here, information and policies flow in one direction from the state to its citizenry, and the implementation of e-government simply improves the flow of information. In the case of "Open" or democratic systems, both state and citizenry are securitizing agents. The state may identify issues of national importance and disseminate these to the general public using e-governance, while the citizenry may collectively or individually react to these issues and either support or oppose policies, or securitize issues of their own and forward these to the government using the tools of e-government.[37]

However, it must be pointed out that citizen trust in government, an important issue in democratic systems (and even authoritarian ones), is not directly improved by e-governance. While e-governance may improve the efficiency of information flows and allow citizens of "Open" systems more space to interact with governments, a study demonstrated that e-governance only improved citizen trust in polities where citizen trust was already stable. Polities with less citizen trust in government recorded negligible improvements.[38]

E-governance has the potential to improve discourse between the state and its citizens, and to open new avenues for interaction, but this applies mostly to those societies with open systems. In societies that are closed, or where citizens have limited avenues of interaction with the state, the effects of e-governance merely reinforce existing imbalances in political relationships, or may even exacerbate them if the state uses e-government to reinforce policies in a non-transparent environment.

The Future of Cyber Security

Regardless of the security threats posed by the different permutations of cyber terrorism and cybercrimes, cyberspace fulfils the potential for greater cooperation and multilateralism. The international initiatives on combating the influenza pandemic, global disaster alerts and early warning systems on natural disasters are examples of international cooperation in cyberspace.

> Security, regardless of its different permutations, should be achieved for all in line with the notion of human security. After all, in the information age, information is the basic commodity.

In fact, in March 2009, the ITU launched its International Multilateral Partnership Against Cyber Threats (IMPACT) facilities at Kuala Lumpur, Malaysia. The IMPACT facilities host its Global Cybersecurity Agenda (GCA), which is an international framework for cooperation aimed at finding strategic solutions to boost confidence and security in an increasingly networked information society, according to the ITU's press release.

"Cybersecurity is one of the most critical issues of our time ... it is a global issue, demanding a truly global approach and it is therefore gratifying to see and to be part of this growing coalition against cyber-threats worldwide. The collaboration with IMPACT complements our efforts in strengthening cyber security and we look forward to expanding the cooperation between governments, the private sector and educational institutions", said Dr Hamadoun Touré, ITU Secretary-General in the press release.[39]

In a nutshell, Dr Toure's sentiments echo the general security strategy states are adopting in securing their cyberspace. A tripartite partnership is crucial in ensuring that cyber security is achieved for all stakeholders. However, other non-state actors such as civil society organizations, NGOs and individuals are also consumers of information and technology and appear to have been left out of the mainstream cyber security discourse. Security, regardless of its different permutations, should be achieved for all in line with the notion of human security. After all, in the information age, information is the basic commodity. In the public domain, access to information delineates the line between the information-poor and the information-rich. On the extreme end of the continuum of an information society, the information-rich person makes decisions which are better informed while at the opposite end, the information-poor person is further alienated and isolated. The lack of information may prove to be detrimental especially in an information-based knowledge economy.

Therefore, set against the increasing securitization of cyberspace, the unintended consequences of a global coalition against cyber terrorism and cybercrime may leave the information-poor person or society increasingly vulnerable as access to information becomes more of a commercial and security concern rather than basic human rights entitlement.

Thus, it is imperative that the formulation of international or national security frameworks on cyber security should include civil society organizations and NGOs in addition to the private sector and educational institutions. The bigger challenge, following this "expanded" framework, is to strike a balance between national security, commercial interests and human security.

Notes

1.   AFP, "Threat of Next World War may be in Cyberspace: UN", *The Independent*, 11 October 2009, available at <http://www.independent.co.uk/news/media/threat-of-next-world-war-may-be-in-cyberspace-un-1801134.html>.
2.   McAfee, "Virtual Criminology Report: Cybercrime Versus Cyberlaw", 2008, available at <http://www.ifap.ru/pr/2008/n081212b.pdf>.
3.   Symantec, "Global Internet Security Threat Report — Trends for 2008", updated 29 June 2009, available at <http://www.symantec.com/connect/downloads/

symantec-global-internet-security-threat-report-trends-2008>.

4   Richard Reiner, "Cybersecurity Trends and Threats: 2007 and Beyond", Telus, 2007, available at <http://business.telus.com/en_CA/content/pdf/products/Security/Cybersecurity.pdf>.

5   Ian Traynor, "Russia Accused of Unleashing Cyberwar to Disable Estonia", *The Guardian*, 17 May 2007, available at <http://www.guardian.co.uk/world/2007/may/17/topstories3.russia>.

6   Ronald Deibert, "Black Code: Censorship, Surveillance, and the Militarisation of Cyberspace", *Millenium: Journal of International Studies* 32, no. 3 (2003).

7   Ibid.

8   Ibid.

9   Ibid.

10   AFP, "Threat of Next World War may be in Cyberspace: UN", *The Independent*, 11 October 2009, available at <http://www.independent.co.uk/news/media/threat-of-next-world-war-may-be-in-cyberspace-un-1801134.html>.

11   White House, *Cyberspace Policy Review: Assuring a Trusted and Resilient Information and Communications Infrastructure*, U.S. White House, 2009, available at <http://www.whitehouse.gov/assets/documents/Cyberspace_Policy_Review_final.pdf>.

12   "UK has Cyber-Attack Capability", BBC News Website, 2009, available at <http://news.bbc.co.uk/2/hi/uk_news/politics/8118729.stm>.

13   Frank Gardner, "Nato's Cyber Defence Warriors", BBC News Website, 2009, available at <http://news.bbc.co.uk/2/hi/europe/7851292.stm>.

14   AFP, "Threat of Next World War may be in Cyberspace: UN", *The Independent*, 11 October 2009, available at <http://www.independent.co.uk/news/media/threat-of-next-world-war-may-be-in-cyberspace-un-1801134.html>.

15   Vitit Muntarbhorn, "Human Security as a Challenge for Information Age", *Bangkok Post*, 4 September 2009, available at <http://www.bangkokpost.com/opinion/opinion/23217/human-security-as-a-challenge-for-information-age>.

16   Ibid.

17   Ibid.

18   Ibid.

19   Helen Nissenbaum, "Where Computer Security Meets National Security", *Ethics and Information Technology* 7 (2005).

20   Ibid.

21   Ibid.

22   Richard Fox, "Someone to Watch Over Us: Back to the Panopticon?" *Criminology and Criminal Justice* 1, no. 3 (2001).

23   Ibid.

24   James Risen and Eric Lichtblau, "E-mail Surveillance Renews Concerns in Congress", *New York Times*, 16 June 2009, available at <http://www.nytimes.com/2009/06/17/us/17nsa.html?pagewanted=all>.

25   Richard Fox, "Someone to Watch Over Us: Back to the Panopticon?" *Criminology and Criminal Justice* 1, no. 3 (2001).
26   Stein Schjolberg and Solange Ghernaouti-Helie, "A Global Protocol on Cyber-security and Cybercrime: An Initiative for Peace and Security in Cyberspace", Cybercrimedate, 2009, available at <http://www.cybercrimelaw.net/documents/A_Global_Protocol_on_Cybersecurity_and_Cybercrime.pdf>.
27   For more information on AdSense, available at <hww.google.com/adsense>.
28   Colin J. Bennett, "Cookies, Web Bugs, Webcams and Cue Cats: Patterns of Surveillance on the World Wide Web", *Ethics and Information Technology* 3, no. 3 (2001).
29   Richard Fox, "Someone to Watch Over Us: Back to the Panopticon?" *Criminology and Criminal Justice* 1, no. 3 (2001).
30   Kelly Haggart, "Civil Society Must get up to Speed on Cyber Security, Watchdog Warns", IDRC Archive, 2009, available at <http://idrc.org/es/ev-142823-201-1-DO_TOPIC.html>.
31   Richard Fox, "Someone to Watch Over Us: Back to the Panopticon?" *Criminology and Criminal Justice* 1, no. 3 (2001).
32   M. Backus, "E-government and Developing Countries: An Overview", *Research Report* 3 (2001), available at <http://www.iicd.org/files/report3.doc>.
33   Paul T. Jaeger, "Deliberative Democracy and the Conceptual Foundations of Electronic Government", *Government Information Quarterly* 22, no. 4 (2005).
34   Andrew Haywood, *Politics* (Hampshire: Palgrave Macmillan, 2002).
35   "Online Politics Reserved for the Rich", BBC News Website, 2 September 2009, available at <http://news.bbc.co.uk/2/hi/technology/8233908.stm>.
36   Paul T. Jaeger, "Deliberative Democracy and the Conceptual Foundations of Electronic Government", *Government Information Quarterly* 22, no. 4 (2005).
37   Michael Parent, Christine A. Vandebeek, and Andrew C. Gemino, "Building Citizen Trust through E-government", *Government Information Quarterly* (2005).
38   Ibid.
39   AFP, "Threat of Next World War may be in Cyberspace: UN", *The Independent*, 11 October 2009, available at <http://www.independent.co.uk/news/media/threat-of-next-world-war-may-be-in-cyberspace-un-1801134.html>.

References

AFP. "Threat of Next World War may be in Cyberspace: UN". *The Independent*, 11 October 2009. Available at <http://www.independent.co.uk/news/media/threat-of-next-world-war-may-be-in-cyberspace-un-1801134.html>.
Backus, M. "E-government and Developing Countries: An Overview". *Research Report* 3 (2001). Available at <http://www.iicd.org/files/report3.doc>.

Bennett, Colin J. "Cookies, Web Bugs, Webcams and Cue Cats: Patterns of Surveillance on the World Wide Web". *Ethics and Information Technology* 3, no. 3 (2001).

Deibert, Ronald. "Black Code: Censorship, Surveillance, and the Militarisation of Cyberspace". *Millenium: Journal of International Studies* 32, no. 3 (2003).

Fox, Richard. "Someone to Watch Over Us: Back to the Panopticon?" *Criminology and Criminal Justice* 1, no. 3 (2001).

Gardner, Frank. "Nato's Cyber Defence Warriors". BBC News Website, 2009. Available at <http://news.bbc.co.uk/2/hi/europe/7851292.stm>.

Haggart, Kelly. "Civil Society Must Get Up to Speed on Cyber Security, Watchdog Warns". IDRC Archive, 2009. Available at <http://idrc.org/es/ev-142823-201-1-DO_TOPIC.html>.

Jaeger, Paul T. "Deliberative Democracy and the Conceptual Foundations of Electronic Government". *Government Information Quarterly* 22, no. 4 (2005).

McAfee. "Virtual Criminology Report: Cybercrime Versus Cyberlaw", 2008. Available at <http://www.ifap.ru/pr/2008/n081212b.pdf>.

Muntarbhorn, Vitit. "Human Security as a Challenge for Information Age". *Bangkok Post*, 4 September 2009. Available at <http://www.bangkokpost.com/opinion/opinion/23217/human-security-as-a-challenge-for-information-age>.

Nissenbaum, Helen. "Where Computer Security Meets National Security". *Ethics and Information Technology* 7 (2005).

"Online Politics Reserved for the Rich". BBC News Website, 2 September 2009. Available at <http://news.bbc.co.uk/2/hi/technology/8233908.stm>.

Parent, Michael, Christine A. Vandebeek, and Andrew C. Gemino. "Building Citizen Trust through E-government". *Government Information Quarterly*, 2005.

Reiner, Richard. "Cybersecurity Trends and Threats: 2007 and Beyond". Telus, 2007. Available at <http://business.telus.com/en_CA/content/pdf/products/Security/Cybersecurity.pdf>.

Risen, James and Eric Lichtblau. "E-mail Surveillance Renews Concerns in Congress". *New York Times*, 16 June 2009. Available at <http://www.nytimes.com/2009/06/17/us/17nsa.html?pagewanted=all>.

Schjolberg, Stein and Solange Ghernaouti-Helie. "A Global Protocol on Cybersecurity and Cybercrime: An Initiative for Peace and Security in Cyberspace". Cybercrimedate, 2009. Available at <http://www.cybercrimelaw.net/documents/A_Global_Protocol_on_Cybersecurity_and_Cybercrime.pdf>.

Symantec. "Global Internet Security Threat Report – Trends for 2008", updated 29 June 2009. Available at <http://www.symantec.com/connect/downloads/symantec-global-internet-security-threat-report-trends-2008>.

Traynor, Ian. "Russia Accused of Unleashing Cyberwar to Disable Estonia". *The Guardian*, 17 May 2007. Available at <http://www.guardian.co.uk/world/2007/may/17/topstories3.russia>.

"UK has Cyber-Attack Capability". BBC News Website, 2009. Available at <http://news.bbc.co.uk/2/hi/uk_news/politics/8118729.stm>.

White House. *Cyberspace Policy Review: Assuring a Trusted and Resilient Information and Communications Infrastructure.* US White House, 2009. Available at <http://www.whitehouse.gov/assets/documents/Cyberspace_Policy_Review_final.pdf>.

11

CONCLUSION

Mely Caballero-Anthony and Alistair D.B. Cook

Throughout this book, the contributors have systematically engaged with nine non-traditional security (NTS) threats that face Asian states and societies today. These NTS challenges both in new and ongoing scenarios highlight the strengths and weaknesses of international, national and local responses to them. The different crises under investigation that confronted Asia point to a number of key points and lessons learnt which are hopefully utilized by the policy-making community to mitigate the impact of many of these NTS threats in the immediate future, and also provide evidence to inform longer term debates.

As the region continues to grapple with a host of NTS challenges, be it another outbreak of an infectious disease, natural disasters or the outbreak of internal conflicts, there is no longer any excuse for a lack of preparedness. Within the ASEAN and ASEAN Plus Three frameworks, there are already enough initiatives to enhance regional cooperation in pandemic preparedness and disaster relief. It is time to put more effort into implementing many of these plans and critical to this is the political will by governments to put in place systems and resources to translate many of these plans into actionable deeds.

Whether the region faces challenges in health or disaster preparedness, it is evident that working with other partners, governments, NGOs, civil society and other stakeholders is important. Many of these NTS issues do not only have transnational reach but have also become more complex. Thus, conventional responses to address many of these issues are no longer adequate. While inter-agency coordination is indeed important to deal with complex emergencies within a national domain, more often than not, government resources are limited. In dealing with human insecurities brought on by climate change, the proliferation of small arms and light weapons, an economic downturn, natural disasters and disease outbreaks, there is an increasing realization that global and regional institutions should work closely with national and local partners. This is to ensure that decisions are made at the most appropriate level and the necessary human and financial resources are channelled effectively.

Many of the issues raised in this edited collection illustrate that what happens in one area of the world, can have devastating effects in another part of the world. In dealing with NTS issues, the international community needs to re-examine its governance approach particularly in the areas of health, food, water, climate change and natural disasters, internal conflict, forced migration, energy, transnational crime, and cyber security. The picture that has emerged so far is a global community that is mostly reactive, and oftentimes divided in how to deal with NTS challenges. The latter is clearly illustrated in the poor progress in negotiations for a post-Kyoto protocol to deal with climate change.

What these NTS challenges have highlighted is that there are many strands of global governance to address these issues yet they lack a golden thread to weave it together into a coherent and coordinated whole. Against the emergence of NTS challenges which are complex and multifaceted, there should be renewed interest in working across, and between, the different level of governance to produce the most informed and flexible policies in order to adapt to ever-changing circumstances.

Through this book, there is an investigation into nine key Non-Traditional Security threats to states and societies to introduce the reader to practical examples of current and evolving areas of Non-Traditional Security in Asia. In the second chapter an investigation into how the current system of global health governance evolved and how states and societies in the region respond to HIV/AIDS and SARS.

The third and fourth chapters addressed food and water security and investigated the responses to the challenges of access, poverty and displacement of people across Asia when considering food and water security, particularly the impacts that the transnational and geostrategic dynamic surrounding the politics of water can have on states and societies. Through providing nine case studies of non-traditional security challenges this edited collection provided an introduction to the study of non-traditional security but also included the contemporary NTS challenges that face states and societies in Asia, how and why they respond in particular ways.

The fifth chapter undertook an analysis of current government responses to natural disasters, and provided an assessment of the levels of preparedness in dealing with natural disasters in the region. The second half of the chapter investigated the trend towards adaptation strategies as a policy response to the current challenges that exposure to natural disasters gives states and societies in the region. The sixth chapter focused on internal conflicts and the proliferation of small arms and light weapons across the region, as a significant challenge to resolving the region's simmering conflicts. In the final section, this chapter focused on the challenges surrounding Early Warning Systems through applying two models to the current conflicts in Myanmar. Interconnected to these internal conflicts is the issue of forced migration, which is covered in the seventh chapter and in particular investigated the issue of statelessness and how it affects states and societies across Asia.

The seventh chapter covers energy security which continues to play a significant part in the sustainable development of economies, and is increasingly interconnected with other NTS issues such as food and the environment. In order to respond to the energy needs states and societies have there was a focus on not only who has access to energy but in what form energy is provided. The first half focused on the emergence of nuclear fuel and what threats and challenges are associated with this. The second half of the chapter evaluated the energy policies that governments in Asia have adopted to ensure that they continue developing in a secure and sustainable way.

The eighth chapter investigated the challenges that transnational crime presents to states and societies in the region, and provided an overview of the evolution of the phenomena since it was coined as a phrase in 1974 and how states and societies approach and understand it. The final chapter addresses into cyber security and how states and societies respond to the threats of cyber-attacks, for example those in Georgia in 2008 and Estonia in 2007. These attacks demonstrated an area of vulnerability that affects states and societies which needs an appropriate policy response. In the second half of the chapter the issues and responses to the governance deficit come under close examination to better understand the ways and means to manage, mitigate and adapt to a realm that currently falls far short of responding to the threats and challenges in cyberspace. Indeed, many of these chapters focused on a combination of systematic evaluation of current policies and how and why many of these policies were made and for whom to provide a comprehensive analysis and understanding of how states and societies responded to these nine NTS challenges.

FUTURE RESEARCH CONTRIBUTIONS

This edited collection has contributed to a better understanding of the current evolution of policy responses to NTS threats in Asia. It has provided multiple avenues through which to understand the development of cooperation, regionalism and stakeholder involvement in formulating policies to the plethora of non-traditional security issues faced across the region. It provides a comprehensive analysis of stakeholder interaction in selected cases across Asia and it undertook a detailed evaluation of the impact of these NTS threats on local, national, regional and international stakeholders, providing evidence of emerging trends and critical analysis of these policies responses.

The Politics and Policies of Non-Traditional Security Challenges

This edited collection has provided a comprehensive investigation to the prevalent non-traditional security concerns in Asia. However, that said, there remain areas both within each chapter and not included in this collection that merit further investigation. Indeed, as our approach suggests, responding to non-traditional security threats is the least that we can do. It is in all our interests to investigate the multitude of emerging challenges and critically appraise and analyse these responses, as well as recognizing the role of all stakeholders and not privilege some actors unnecessarily. While states remain the most important actor, their bureaucratic involvement in crafting policy responses should not do so at the expense of involving and being accountable to the people they represent. This is the single largest shift that human security has brought to the policy-making discourse — the focus is no longer on the survival of the state but rather on the survival of its people.

Through the nine policy chapters it became evident that the international system continues to exist within local, national, regional and international constraints. While these examples provided many prevalent policy areas today, these need to be constantly re-evaluated and examined and allow for other non-traditional security challenges to be recognized in a changing environment. This edited collection highlighted the roles of different actors within the system and how they interacted in Asia to respond to these current NTS challenges. While the fifth chapter offered a systematic and comprehensive analysis, with greater resources and space, this analysis would allow for the separation of climate change from natural disasters, which while interconnected, there are also cases when the difference between the two needs to be better enunciated. Likewise, each of the chapters with more space could take a more critical approach to the various civil society actors and in greater detail. However, the purpose of this collection was to bring together the major non-traditional security concerns across the region together in an attempt to illustrate the interconnections and the importance of responding to these policy challenges through robust and systematic policy analysis and academic investigations, to build bridges between these two important constituencies. Indeed, there remains much to be studied and learnt from the parallel civil society structures that are emerging in Asia and the ways in which they interact with states and societies across the region. These civil society networks are found across Asia but outside the formal institutional framework of government. These relationships are of significance in regional advocacy coalition network building, and lobbying policy-makers and government officials, and also in understanding the roles and motivations of all stakeholders in policy decision-making.

This avenue for research will become all the more important to explain what the influences were over the creation of various ad hoc and systematic policy responses at the local, national, regional and international levels, how they came to take the forms that they did, and why they succeeded or failed in meeting the needs of people across the region. Returning to the larger international system, the development of regional architecture across Asia is also important. The global system has many regions with different dynamics. Using regionalism to explain the evolution of a particular policy regime is a powerful explanatory variable. This is especially the case in areas where interaction in the international system is limited, and the numbers of those affected are significant, such as in Central Asia and the Caucasus.

The development of policy responses to non-traditional security concerns within local, national, regional and international constraints will further aid our understanding of how to predict their future shape and responses to emerging NTS challenges. While these issues remain systematically untested, the predictability of international norms will remain difficult. It has been the aim of this edited collection to start the process of analysing NTS policy responses across and between the different levels of governance. It focused on understanding how particular policy responses emerged, who was involved in the decision-making process, and what lessons were learnt. It further highlighted the gatekeeper and framing roles that stakeholders play with a particular NTS policy response. Above all, this edited collection has demonstrated that focusing on identifying all stakeholders at the individual, local, national, regional and international levels both through formal and informal roles and interactions is central to building more systematic and appropriate policy responses.

APPENDIX

Member States of the Council of Europe

States	Signature	Ratification	Entry into force	Notes	R.	D.	A.	T.	C.	O.
Albania	23/11/2001	20/6/2002	1/7/2004				X			
Andorra										
Armenia	23/11/2001	12/10/2006	1/2/2007				X			
Austria	23/11/2001									
Azerbaijan	30/6/2008					X	X	X	X	
Belgium	23/11/2001									
Bosnia and Herzegovina	9/2/2005	19/5/2006	1/9/2006				X			
Bulgaria	23/11/2001	7/4/2005	1/8/2005		X	X	X			
Croatia	23/11/2001	17/10/2002	1/7/2004				X			
Cyprus	23/11/2001	19/1/2005	1/5/2005				X			
Czech Republic	9/2/2005									
Denmark	22/4/2003	21/6/2005	1/10/2005		X			X	X	
Estonia	23/11/2001	12/5/2003	1/7/2004				X			
Finland	23/11/2001	24/5/2007	1/9/2007		X	X	X			
France	23/11/2001	10/1/2006	1/5/2006		X	X	X			
Georgia	1/4/2008									
Germany	23/11/2001	9/3/2009	1/7/2009		X	X	X			
Greece	23/11/2001									
Hungary	23/11/2001	4/12/2003	1/7/2004		X	X	X			

States	Signature	Ratification	Entry Into Force	Notes	R.	D.	A.	T.	C.	O.
Iceland	30/11/2001	29/1/2007	1/5/2007		X		X			
Ireland	28/2/2002									
Italy	23/11/2001	5/6/2008	1/10/2008				X			
Latvia	5/5/2004	14/2/2007	1/6/2007		X		X			
Liechtenstein	17/11/2008									
Lithuania	23/6/2003	18/3/2004	1/7/2004		X	X	X			
Luxembourg	28/1/2003									
Malta	17/1/2002									
Moldova	23/11/2001	12/5/2009	1/9/2009			X				X
Monaco										
Montenegro	7/4/2005			55						
Netherlands	23/11/2001	16/11/2006	1/3/2007						X	X
Norway	23/11/2001	30/6/2006	1/10/2006		X	X	X			
Poland	23/11/2001									
Portugal	23/11/2001									
Romania	23/11/2001	12/5/2004	1/9/2004				X			
Russia										
San Marino										
Serbia	7/4/2005	14/4/2009	1/8/2009	55			X			
Slovakia	4/2/2005	8/1/2008	1/5/2008		X	X	X			
Slovenia	24/7/2002	8/9/2004	1/1/2005				X			
Spain	23/11/2001									
Sweden	23/11/2001									
Switzerland	23/11/2001									
the former Yugoslav Republic of Macedonia	23/11/2001	15/9/2004	1/1/2005				X			
Turkey										
Ukraine	23/11/2001	10/3/2006	1/7/2006		X		X			
United Kingdom	23/11/2001									

Non-member States of the Council of Europe

States	Signature	Ratification	Entry Into Force	Notes	R.	D.	A.	T.	C.	O.
Canada	23/11/2001									
Chile										
Costa Rica										
Dominican Republic										
Japan	23/11/2001									
Mexico										
Philippines										
South Africa	23/11/2001									
United States	23/11/2001	29/9/2006	1/1/2007		X	X	X			

Total number of signatures not followed by ratifications:	20
Total number of ratifications/accessions:	26

Notes:
(55) Date of signature by the state union of Serbia and Montenegro.
a: Accession
s: Signature without reservation as to ratification
su: Succession
r: Signature "ad referendum".
R.: Reservations
D.: Declarations
A.: Authorities
T.: Territorial Application
C.: Communication
O.: Objection.
Source: Treaty Office on <http://conventions.coe.int>.

INDEX

www.ingramcontent.com/pod-product-compliance
Lightning Source LLC
Chambersburg PA
CBHW072047020426
42334CB00017B/1413